MW01247023

FOOD SAFETY PREVENTIVE CONTROLS ALLIANCE

Steering Committee (October 2015)

Executive Committee (October 2015)

Editorial Sub-committee (1st Edition)

Hazard Analysis and Preventive Controls for Human Food Training

The Food Safety Preventive Controls Alliance developed this training curriculum in Food Safety Preventive Controls compliant with the FDA's *Current Good Manufacturing Practice, Hazard Analysis, and Risk-based Preventive Controls for Human Food* regulations. For the most current course information, please consult: http://www.iit.edu/ifsh/alliance/

This publication was developed by the Food Safety Preventive Controls Alliance (FSPCA) and was supported, in part, by a grant from the Food and Drug Administration to the Illinois Institute of Technology's Institute for Food Safety and Health. The views expressed herein do not necessarily reflect the views of these organizations. Direct all inquiries to the FSPCA at fspca@iit.edu

FSPCA PREVENTIVE CONTROLS FOR HUMAN FOOD

TRAINING CURRICULUM

First Edition – 2016

(Version 1.2, February 2016)

Disclaimer

Developed by the

FOOD SAFETY PREVENTIVE CONTROLS ALLIANCE

Version 1.2 contains changes to address technical amendments and corrections published by FDA, and editorial corrections identified in earlier versions. An erratum listing for earlier versions is available on the FSPCA website.

Contributors: FSPCA Preventive Controls for Human Food Training Curriculum

These Working Groups and individuals made significant contributions of time and expertise in developing the Food Safety Preventive Controls Alliance training curriculum and supporting documents since its inception in 2012. Affiliations while work was in progress are noted.

FSPCA Preventive Controls Core Curriculum Development
Jeff Barach, Barach Enterprises – *Chair*
Judy Fraser Heaps, Land O' Lakes, Inc. – *Vice Chair*

Food Categories and Representative Processing
Kurt Deibel, Heinz, North America – *Chair*
Alejandro Mazzotta, Chobani, Inc. – *Vice Chair*
Tim Jackson, Nestlé North America

Allergen Management and Controls
Joseph Scimeca, Cargill, Inc. – *Chair*
Sue Estes, PepsiCo, Inc. – *Vice Chair*

Sanitation, Current Good Manufacturing Practices and Environmental Monitoring
John Allan, American Frozen Food Institute – *Chair*
Joe Shebuski, Cargill, Inc. – *Vice Chair*

Supply Chain and Ingredient Management
Steve Mavity, Bumble Bee Foods, Inc. – *Chair*
Faye Feldstein, Deloitte Consulting, LLC – *Vice Chair*

The following people or organizations made significant contributions to the content of specific chapters:

Sanitation Control Plan
American Frozen Food Institute, Cargill Inc., Ecolab Inc., Leprino Foods

Recall
Grocery Manufacturers Association

Class Exercise Activities
Judy Fraser-Heaps, Land O' Lakes, Inc.
Pamela Wilger, Cargill, Inc.
Katherine Simons, Minnesota Department of Agriculture

TABLE OF CONTENTS

Food Safety Preventive Controls Alliance

The Food Safety Preventive Controls Alliance (FSPCA) provides current and cost-effective education and training programs to assist the food industry to achieve compliance with the U.S. Food and Drug Administration (FDA) *Hazard Analysis and Risk-based Preventive Controls for Human Food* regulation, which is referred to as the *Preventive Controls for Human Food* regulation throughout this course. The requirements of this regulation are designed to promote safe food production. The structure and the delivery of the *FSPCA Preventive Controls for Human Food* training course were built on successful examples from two previous alliances – Seafood HACCP and Juice HACCP.

This course developed by FSPCA is the "standardized curriculum" recognized by FDA; successfully completing this course is one way to meet the requirements for a "preventive controls qualified individual." Note: Under the *Preventive Controls for Human Food* regulation, the responsibilities of a "preventive controls qualified individual" include to perform or oversee 1) preparation of the Food Safety Plan, 2) validation of the preventive controls, 3) records review and 4) reanalysis of the Food Safety Plan.

The FSPCA program is based on collaboration among federal and state regulatory officials, academic food safety researchers and educators and U.S. food industry representatives. The program is directed by a voluntary FSPCA Steering Committee, whose members are listed on the inside front cover. The FSPCA Steering Committee directs development of the curriculum, all training materials and the FSPCA Training Protocol for delivering, documenting and updating these materials. Any individual, company, agency or nation can provide input for the FSPCA program through communications with any member of the FSPCA Steering Committee. Participation in sub-committees and working groups is also possible. Visit the FSPCA website for information on active sub-committees and working groups.

The Association of Food and Drug Officials (AFDO) and the International Food Protection Training Institute (IFPTI) administer certificates for all participants that complete a recognized *FSPCA Preventive Controls for Human Food* course. Contact IFPTI for questions on certificates or how to become an FSPCA Lead Instructor.

The *FSPCA Preventive Controls for Human Food* course will be offered in both a formal classroom setting and a self-guided online version that is coupled with a one-day, in person session to develop skills for conducting a hazard analysis and developing a Food Safety Plan. The FSPCA training materials include the standard training manual, slides, explanations of key terms and concepts, an example model Food Safety Plan, abbreviated models for class exercises and reference material. Examples of model Food Safety Plans for processed food products are maintained on the FSPCA website (http://www.iit.edu/ifsh/alliance/). These examples are for reference, and modifications of example plans will be necessary for specific facilities.

The FSPCA training materials are designed to meet the requirements for training under Title 21 *Code of Federal Regulations* Part 117.180(c)(1) for the preventive controls qualified individual who conducts certain Food Safety Plan activities. Attending an FSPCA course is not mandatory, but it does provide assurances that the course content and resulting knowledge is consistent with regulatory expectations.

The FSPCA course material and information on training for FSPCA Lead Instructors can be found on the FSPCA website.

History of the Alliance

The FSPCA was established in 2011 as part of a grant from FDA to the Illinois Institute of Technology's Institute of Food Safety and Health. The purpose of this broad-based alliance is to develop and maintain a cost-effective education and training program to assist the food industry with understanding and achieving compliance with the *Preventive Controls* regulation requirements applicable to their facilities. Both human food and animal food regulations are covered in separate courses. FSPCA's mission is to support safe food production by developing a standardized curriculum and technical educational materials on food safety risk-reduction controls compliant with the *Preventive Controls* regulations, and providing technical assistance outreach to the food industry, particularly small food companies.

FSPCA Preventive Controls for Human Food Course Agenda

The agenda is intended to be covered in a 2.5 day (20 hours) course, including frequent opportunities for review and classroom exercises designed to provide learning opportunities for understanding *Preventive Controls for Human Food* regulation requirements. The time allotted to each section will vary based on the audience, level of familiarity and experience with Good Manufacturing Practices and risk-based food safety principles, as well as the food product and processing under consideration. A typical agenda appears below.

Day One	Chapter 1	Introduction to Course and Preventive Controls
	Chapter 2	Food Safety Plan Overview
		Break
	Chapter 3	Good Manufacturing Practices and Other Prerequisite Programs
	Chapter 4	Biological Food Safety Hazards
		Lunch
	Chapter 5	Chemical, Physical and Economically Motivated Food Safety Hazards
		Break
	Chapter 6	Preliminary Steps in Developing a Food Safety Plan
	Chapter 7	Resources for Preparing Food Safety Plans
Day Two		Review and Questions
	Chapter 8	Hazard Analysis and Preventive Controls Determination
		Break
	Chapter 9	Process Preventive Controls
		Lunch
	Chapter 10	Food Allergen Preventive Controls
		Break
	Chapter 11	Sanitation Preventive Controls
	Chapter 12	Supply-chain Preventive Controls
Day Three		Review and Questions
	Chapter 13	Verification and Validation Procedures
	Chapter 14	Record-keeping Procedures
		Break
	Chapter 15	Recall Plan
	Chapter 16	Regulation Overview – *cGMP, Hazard Analysis, and Risk-Based Preventive Controls for Human Food*
	Wrap Up	

CHAPTER 1.   Introduction to Course and Preventive Controls

Introduction to Course and Preventive Controls
Objectives

In this module, you will develop awareness of:

- The objectives of the course
- Format of the course
- How preventive controls build on established food safety principles
- Components of a Food Safety Plan
- The responsibilities of a preventive controls qualified individual
- Where to find definitions relevant for the course

FSPCA

The *Current Good Manufacturing Practice, Hazard Analysis, and Risk-based Preventive Controls for Human Food* regulation (hereafter referred to as *the Preventive Controls for Human Food* regulation) was published on September 17, 2015 and is intended to ensure safe manufacturing/processing, packing and holding of food products for human consumption in the United States. The regulation requires that certain activities must be completed by a "preventive controls qualified individual" who has "successfully completed training in the development and application of risk-based preventive controls at least equivalent to that received under a standardized curriculum recognized as adequate by FDA or be otherwise qualified through job experience to develop and apply a food safety system" (see Chapter 16: Regulation Overview and Appendix 1).

This course developed by the FSPCA is the "standardized curriculum" recognized by FDA; successfully completing this course is one way to meet the requirements for a "preventive controls qualified individual."

This chapter reviews the format for the course and provides a brief overview of how preventive controls build on established food safety principles. It then explores the responsibilities of a preventive controls qualified individual to help you to understand the tasks that you will be expected either to do or to oversee. At the end of the chapter, you will also see a list of definitions to help you understand the meaning of specific terms used in the course, most of which are from the *Preventive Controls for Human Food* regulation.

Course Format and Agenda

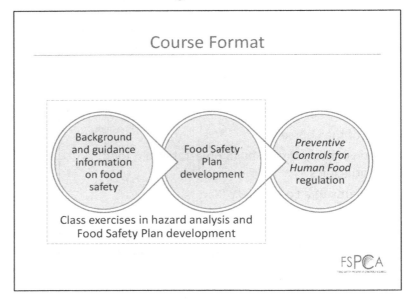

The FSPCA course is divided into three parts:

1. The first part defines the contents of the Food Safety Plan, reviews foundational programs such as GMPs, provides information about specific food hazards and discusses the underlying principles used in food safety preventive controls systems. Learning how to apply these practices and principles will give a better understanding of how a systematic approach can help to assure the safety of food. As each principle is discussed, the class will progressively develop a Food Safety Plan for a model product produced by a fictional company. This example will help you understand how to put together each section of a Food Safety Plan and how these sections relate to a complete preventive controls program and safe food processing.

2. The second part includes practical exercises that introduce the participants to the process of developing a Food Safety Plan, including identification of tools and implementation tasks. During this part, the class will be divided into teams to write a simplified Food Safety Plan for a selected food product.

3. The third part explains the requirements of the *Preventive Controls for Human Food* regulation.

Risk-based Preventive Controls

Risk-based Preventive Controls

- Focus on what matters most for food safety
- Preventive, not reactive
- Work in conjunction with and supported by other programs like Good Manufacturing Practices
- Designed to minimize the risk of food safety hazards

A proactive and systematic approach to food safety emphasizing the preventive controls approach has been universally accepted and adopted throughout the world because it helps to focus attention on the most important areas to prevent food safety issues rather than reacting to problems as they arise. Preventive control programs are structured to work in conjunction with and be supported by other relevant programs such as Good Manufacturing Practices (GMPs), good agricultural practices and good transportation practices as the basis for food safety management. Successful application of preventive controls approaches not only helps to ensure regulatory compliance, but also minimizes the risk of producing products that can harm consumers!

Other Risk-based Food Safety Programs

US Space program   Low-acid canned food regs   FDA Seafood HACCP regs   FDA Juice HACCP regs

USDA HACCP regs   Codex HACCP Annex   NCIMS Dairy HACCP

Image source: Microsoft clip art

Risk-based approaches to managing food safety were pioneered during development of food for the U.S. space program in the 1960s. At that time, end-product testing was the focus of quality control programs. It became evident that the end-product testing necessary to provide assurance that the food was safe would be so extensive that little food would be available for space flights. The focus shifted to preventing hazards through product formulation and process control in a risk-based manner. The concept was called Hazard Analysis and Critical Control Point (HACCP). HACCP implementation expanded voluntarily in the food industry with the understanding that food safety is best assured if each producer and processor understands the significant hazards in their product and operation, and uses scientifically sound preventive controls to significantly minimize or eliminate the hazards.

In the 1970s, FDA used HACCP principles in the development of low-acid canned food regulations. The U.S. National Advisory Committee on Microbiological Criteria for Foods (NACMCF) and the Codex Alimentarius Commission (Codex) published HACCP principles in the 1990s. FDA has HACCP regulations for seafood and juice products; USDA has HACCP regulations for meat and poultry products; and HACCP is endorsed by many countries, including Australia, Canada, New Zealand and European Union countries.

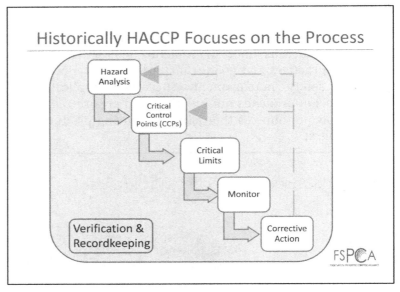

HACCP principles are illustrated in the slide above. A quick review of these principles is useful to understand how the *Preventive Controls for Human Food* regulation complements the risk-based HACCP approach.

In a HACCP system, hazard analysis identifies process-related hazards that, in the absence of control, present a food safety risk. When these hazards are identified, Critical Control Points (CCPs) that are essential to control the process to prevent the hazard from causing illness or injury are identified. When these CCP process controls are identified, the critical limits define the operating conditions in the process that must be met to effectively manage the hazard. Monitoring of the process is done to provide data to demonstrate that critical limits are met, and corrective actions are predefined to enable swift action when things go wrong, thus preventing expansion of a food safety issue. All of the above is recorded and verified to ensure the system is operating as intended and to provide data to others (e.g., inspectors, auditors, management, new employees) to show that this is the case. More information on each of these principles is discussed in this curriculum, recognizing that a HACCP Plan essentially addresses most of the requirements for *process* preventive controls.

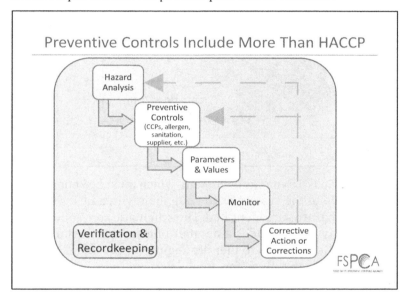

However, the preventive controls process incorporates controls beyond those managed as process-related CCPs in the HACCP framework. These preventive controls address not only CCPs, but also controls for hazards related to food allergens, sanitation, suppliers and others requiring a preventive control. The preventive controls approach also recognizes that critical limits, defined by NACMCF as: "A maximum and/or minimum value to which a biological, chemical or physical parameter must be controlled at a CCP to prevent, eliminate or reduce to an acceptable level the occurrence of a food-safety hazard" may not be required for some preventive controls. The broader term, *parameters and values*, supports identification of a frequency or other metric to assess compliance, rather than setting a precise minimum or maximum value to which a parameter must be controlled. Further, immediate corrections (like re-cleaning a line before start up) may be more appropriate than formal corrective action involving product risk evaluations for some preventive controls. Finally, the extent of validation activities (or demonstrating the controls actually work) may be less rigorous for some preventive controls than others. Each of these concepts is discussed in greater detail in subsequent chapters.

Contents of a Food Safety Plan

GMPs are required because they form the foundation for your Food Safety Plan. Developing a Food Safety Plan helps you to focus most of your activities on what matters most for food safety.

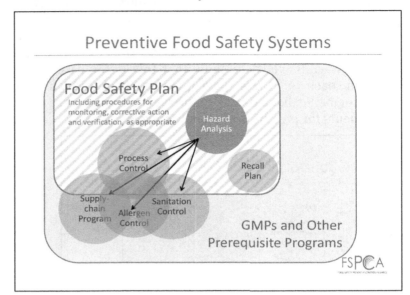

The Food Safety Plan is a dynamic document, which must be kept current if changes are made to the system or to equipment when new products are added, or new hazards are identified. The schematic above illustrates that the Food Safety Plan includes a number of elements. It starts with hazard analysis, which is used to identify required preventive controls for the process, for sanitation, for food allergens and supply-chain programs, where these are needed to address the hazards requiring a preventive control. These elements, along with a recall plan make up the Food Safety Plan. Many GMPs and other prerequisite programs are managed outside of the Food Safety Plan. While these are separate programs and may not require the same level of documentation as the elements of the Food Safety Plan, they are important. They are generally managed using standard operating procedures with documents and records kept as appropriate. Keep in mind that elements of GMPs that are not covered in the Food Safety Plan are still required by regulations.

Preventive Controls Qualified Individual

Preventive Controls Qualified Individual Definition

- A qualified individual who has successfully completed training in the development and application of risk-based preventive controls at least equivalent to that received under a standardized curriculum recognized as adequate by FDA or is otherwise qualified through job experience to develop and apply a food safety system.
  - 21 CFR 117.3 Definitions

See the 21 CFR 117.3 definitions for "qualified individual" and "preventive controls qualified individual," as well as the 21 CFR 117.180 requirements applicable to a preventive controls qualified individual in Appendix 1.

Under the regulation, certain tasks must be performed (or overseen) by a "preventive controls qualified individual." This course developed by FSPCA is the "standardized curriculum" recognized by FDA; successfully completing this course is one way to meet the requirements for a "preventive controls qualified individual." Under the *Preventive Controls for Human Food* regulation, the responsibilities of a "preventive controls qualified individual" include to perform or oversee 1) preparation of the Food Safety Plan, 2) validation of the preventive controls, 3) records review and 4) reanalysis of the Food Safety Plan.

The preventive controls qualified individual may be an employee of the facility but you can also use outside assistance in developing your plan. In some situations, more than one preventive controls qualified individual may be needed to effectively develop and implement a Food Safety Plan. More detail on the different parts of the Food Safety Plan is provided in this course.

What is Expected of the Participant?

Prevention-based food safety management can be integrated into any operation; however, the process can seem complicated until the basic concepts are understood. Asking questions and contributing first-hand experiences during the discussions can help you and other participants to better understand and apply the concepts. This course includes class participation and exercises. The more you contribute to these exercises, the less complicated the system will seem and the easier it will be to develop and implement an effective Food Safety Plan.

How to Use This Training Manual

This manual is yours. Become familiar with it and use it as a reference. It contains forms that can help you develop a Food Safety Plan and resources to locate other basic information. Make as many notes and marks in the manual as needed to assist you in creating and understanding a Food Safety Plan. This manual does not have a copyright. Make as many copies of the forms as necessary or copy the whole manual to share with others in your company.

As you learn more about developing a Food Safety Plan, there are many definitions that you need to understand. To assist you, the definitions of many commonly used terms are listed at the end of the chapter. Refer to these pages as needed. You may also want to add other terms that you may need in developing and implementing your own Food Safety Plan.

Introduction Summary

Introduction Summary

- Successful completion of this course is one way to meet the requirements for a "preventive controls qualified individual" to manage a food safety preventive controls program
- FDA's *Preventive Controls for Human Food* rule builds on existing food safety principles
- Preventive controls reduce risk for the business and for the public
- Definitions used in the course are at the end of this chapter
- Participation is vital to successfully completing this course

By successfully completing this course, you will meet the training requirements for a "preventive controls qualified individual" who can oversee a food safety preventive controls program. You may need assistance from technical experts for certain elements of your food safety program, which will be discussed in chapters later in the course.

Through this course you will learn how to develop a risk-based Food Safety Plan and implement preventive controls to help mitigate and control hazards specific for your product and process. This reduces potential food safety issues for the public and for your business as well.

Participation is vital for understanding the material and your experience and questions can help others in the course as well. Please participate to get as much out of this course as you possibly can.

Definitions and Acronyms

Acid foods or **acidified foods**[3]: Foods that have an equilibrium pH of 4.6 or below. (NOTE: acid foods have a natural pH of 4.6 or below; acidified foods have acid added to reduce the pH.)

Adequate[3]: That which is needed to accomplish the intended purpose in keeping with good public health practice.

Allergen cross-contact[3]: The unintentional incorporation of a food allergen into a food.

Audit[3]: means the systematic, independent, and documented examination (through observation, investigation, records review, discussions with employees of the audited entity, and, as appropriate, sampling and laboratory analysis) to assess an entity's food safety processes and procedures.

a$_w$: Water activity (see below)

CCP: Critical Control Point (see below)

cGMPs: Current Good Manufacturing Practices (see "GMPs" and Chapter 3)

Cleaning[2]: The removal of soil, food residue, dirt, grease or other objectionable matter.

Correction[3]: means an action to identify and correct a problem that occurred during the production of food, without other actions associated with a corrective action procedure (such as actions to reduce the likelihood that the problem will recur, evaluate all affected food for safety, and prevent affected food from entering commerce).

Corrective action[5]: Procedures that must be taken if preventive controls are not properly implemented.

Critical Control Point (CCP)[3]: A point, step, or procedure in a food process at which control can be applied and is essential to prevent or eliminate a food safety hazard or reduce such hazard to an acceptable level.

Critical limit[4]: The maximum or minimum value, or combination of values, to which any biological, chemical or physical parameter must be controlled to significantly minimize or prevent a hazard requiring a process preventive control.

Cross-contact: see allergen cross-contact

Cross-contamination: The unintentional transfer of a foodborne pathogen from a food (where it may occur naturally) or insanitary object to another food (where it may present a hazard).

Defect action level[3]: means a level of a non-hazardous, naturally occurring, unavoidable defect at which FDA may regard a food product "adulterated" and subject to enforcement action under section 402(a)(3) of the Federal Food, Drug, and Cosmetic Act.

Deviation[2, 9]: Failure to meet a critical limit.

e.g.: For example, (Latin *exempli gratia*)

Environmental pathogen[3]: A pathogen capable of surviving and persisting within the manufacturing, processing, packing or holding environment such that food may be contaminated and may result in foodborne illness if that food is consumed without treatment to significantly minimize the environmental pathogen. Examples of environmental pathogens for the purposes of this part include *Listeria monocytogenes* and *Salmonella* spp. but do not include the spores of pathogenic sporeforming bacteria.

Facility[3]: A domestic facility or foreign facility that is required to register under section 415 of the Federal Food, Drug, and Cosmetic Act, in accordance with the requirements of 21 CFR part 1, subpart H.

FDA: Food and Drug Administration

Food[6]: Includes (1) articles used for food or drink for man or other animals, (2) chewing gum, and (3) articles used for components of any such article. Examples of food include fruits, vegetables, fish, dairy products, eggs, raw agricultural commodities used for food or as components of food, animal feed (including pet food), food and feed ingredients, food and feed additives, dietary supplements and dietary ingredients, infant formula, beverages (including alcoholic beverages and bottled water), live food animals, bakery goods, snack foods, candy, and canned foods. Does not include pesticides or food contact substances not intended to have any technical effect in the food.

Food allergen[7]: Any of the following: (1) Milk, egg, fish (e.g., bass, flounder or cod), Crustacean shellfish (e.g., crab, lobster or shrimp), tree nuts (e.g., almonds, pecans or walnuts), wheat, peanuts and soybeans. (2) A food ingredient that contains protein derived from a food specified in paragraph (1), except any highly refined oil derived from a food specified in paragraph (1) and any ingredient derived from such highly refined oil.

Food-contact surface[3]: Those surfaces that contact human food and those surfaces from which drainage, or other transfer, onto the food or onto surfaces that contact the food ordinarily occurs during the normal course of operation. "Food contact surfaces" includes utensils and food-contact surfaces of equipment.

Food Safety Plan: A set of written documents that is based on food safety principles; incorporates hazard analysis, preventive controls, supply-chain programs and a recall plan; and delineates the procedures to be followed for monitoring, corrective actions and verification.

Food safety system: The outcome of implementing the Food Safety Plan and its supporting elements.

GMPs (Good Manufacturing Practices): The regulation (117 Subpart B) that outlines the conditions and practices the regulated food industry must follow for processing safe food under sanitary conditions, including personnel, plant and grounds, sanitary operations, sanitary facilities and controls, equipment and utensils, processes and controls, warehousing and distribution, and defect action levels considerations.

HACCP: Hazard Analysis and Critical Control Point (see below)

Hazard [3]: Any biological, chemical (including radiological), or physical agent that has the potential to cause illness or injury.

Hazard analysis: The process of collecting and evaluating information on hazards and conditions leading to their presence to decide which are significant for food safety and therefore must be addressed in the HACCP or Food Safety Plan.

Hazard Analysis and Critical Control Point[2]: A system which identifies, evaluates, and controls hazards which are significant for food safety.

Hazard requiring a preventive control[3]: means a known or reasonably foreseeable hazard for which a person knowledgeable about the safe manufacturing, processing, packing, or holding of food would, based on the outcome of a hazard analysis (which includes an assessment of the severity of the illness or injury if the hazard were to occur and the probability that the hazard will occur in the absence of preventive controls), establish one or more preventive controls to significantly minimize or prevent the hazard in a food and components to manage those controls (such as monitoring, corrections or corrective actions, verification, and records) as appropriate to the food, the facility, and the nature of the preventive control and its role in the facility's food safety system.

Known or reasonably foreseeable hazard[3]: A biological, chemical (including radiological), or physical hazard that is known to be, or has the potential to be, associated with the facility or the food.

Lot[3]: The food produced during a period of time and identified by an establishment's specific code.

Microorganisms[3]: Yeast, molds, bacteria, viruses, protozoa and microscopic parasites and includes species that are pathogens. The term "undesirable microorganisms" includes those microorganisms that are pathogens, that subject food to decomposition, that indicate that food is contaminated with filth, or that otherwise may cause food to be adulterated.

Monitor[3]: To conduct a planned sequence of observations or measurements to assess whether control measures are operating as intended.

NACMCF (National Advisory Committee on Microbiological Criteria for Foods)[10]: Chartered under USDA to provide impartial, scientific advice to U.S. Federal food safety agencies for use in the development of an integrated national food safety systems approach from farm to final consumption to assure the safety of domestic, imported, and exported foods.

Non-food-contact surface: Those surfaces that *do not* contact human food and from which drainage, or other transfer, onto the food or onto surfaces that contact the food ordinarily *does not* occur during the normal course of operation.

Operating limits[9]: Criteria that are more stringent than critical limits and that are used by an operator to reduce the risk of a deviation.

Parameter: a characteristic, feature or measurable factor that can help in defining a particular system.

Pathogen[3]: A microorganism of public health significance.

Pest[3]: Any objectionable animals or insects including birds, rodents, flies, and larvae.

Potable water: Water that meets the standards for drinking purposes of the State or local authority having jurisdiction, or water that meets the standards prescribed by the U.S. Environmental Protection Agency's National Primary Drinking Water Regulations (40 CFR 141).

Prerequisite programs: Procedures, including Good Manufacturing Practices (GMPs), that provide the basic environmental and operating conditions necessary to support the Food Safety Plan.

Preventive controls[3]: Those risk-based, reasonably appropriate procedures, practices and processes that a person knowledgeable about the safe manufacturing, processing, packing or holding of food would employ to significantly minimize or prevent the hazards identified under the hazard analysis that are consistent with the current scientific understanding of safe food manufacturing, processing, packaging or holding at the time of the analysis.

Preventive controls qualified individual[3]: A qualified individual who has successfully completed training in the development and application of risk-based preventive controls at least equivalent to that received under a standardized curriculum recognized as adequate by FDA or is otherwise qualified through job experience to develop and apply a food safety system.

Qualified auditor[3]: A person who is a qualified individual as defined below and has technical expertise obtained through education, training or experience (or combination thereof) necessary to perform the auditing function as required by 117.180(c)(2). Examples of potential qualified auditors include:
> (1) A government employee, including a foreign government employee; and
> (2) An audit agent of a certification body that is accredited in accordance with regulations in part 1, subpart M of this chapter.

Qualified individual[3]: a person who has the education, training, or experience (or a combination thereof) necessary to manufacture, process, pack, or hold clean and safe food as appropriate to the individual's assigned duties. A qualified individual may be, but is not required to be, an employee of the establishment.

RTE (Ready-to-eat) food[3]: Any food that is normally eaten in its raw state or any other food, including a processed food, for which it is reasonably foreseeable that the food will be eaten without further processing that would significantly minimize biological hazards.

Reanalysis: A verification procedure to assure that the Food Safety Plan remains valid and the food safety system is operating according to the plan (see Section 117.170).

Receiving facility[3]: A facility that is subject to subpart C [*Hazard Analysis and Risk-based Preventive Controls*] and subpart G [*Supply-Chain Program*] of this part and that manufactures/processes a raw material or ingredient that it receives from a supplier.

Rework[3]: Clean, unadulterated food that has been removed from processing for reasons other than insanitary conditions or that has been successfully reconditioned by reprocessing and that is suitable for use as food.

Risk[1]: A function of the probability of an adverse health effect and the severity of that effect, consequential to a hazard(s) in food.

Safe-moisture level[3]: A level of moisture low enough to prevent the growth of undesirable microorganisms in the finished product under the intended conditions of manufacturing, processing, packing, and holding. The safe moisture level for a food is related to its water activity (a_w). An a_w will be considered safe for a food if adequate data are available that demonstrate that the food at or below the given a_w will not support the growth of undesirable microorganisms.

Sanitize[3]: To adequately treat cleaned surfaces by a process that is effective in destroying vegetative cells of pathogens, and in substantially reducing numbers of other undesirable microorganisms, but without adversely affecting the product or its safety for the consumer.

Sanitary conditions: The result of a combination of cleaning and sanitizing, as appropriate for the environment, that prevents the adulteration of food.

Severity[8]: The seriousness of the effects of a hazard.

Significantly minimize[3]: To reduce to an acceptable level, including to eliminate.

Small business[3]: A business (including any subsidiaries and affiliates) employing fewer than 500 full-time equivalent employees.

SOP: Standard Operating Procedure

Supplier[3]: The establishment that manufactures/processes the food, raises the animal, or grows the food that is provided to a receiving facility without further manufacturing/processing by another establishment, except for further manufacturing/processing that consists solely of the addition of labeling or similar activity of a *de minimis* nature.

Supply-chain-applied control[3]: A preventive control for a hazard in a raw material or other ingredient when the hazard in the raw material or other ingredient is controlled before its receipt.

Unexposed packaged food[3]: Packaged food that is not exposed to the environment.

Validation[3]: Obtaining and evaluating scientific and technical evidence that a control measure, combination of control measures, or the food safety plan as a whole, when properly implemented, is capable of effectively controlling the identified hazards.

Verification[3]: The application of methods, procedures, tests and other evaluations, in addition to monitoring, to determine whether a control measure or combination of control measures is or has been operating as intended and to establish the validity of the food safety plan.

Very small business[3]: A business (including any subsidiaries and affiliates) averaging less than $1,000,000, adjusted for inflation, per year, during the 3-year period preceding the applicable calendar year in sales of human food plus the market value of human food manufactured, processed, packed, or held without sale (e.g., held for a fee).

Water activity[3] **(a_W):** A measure of the free moisture in a food and is the quotient of the water vapor pressure of the substance divided by the vapor pressure of pure water at the same temperature.

Written procedures for receiving raw materials and other ingredients[3]: Written procedures to ensure that raw materials and other ingredients are received only from suppliers approved by the receiving facility (or, when necessary and appropriate, on a temporary basis from unapproved suppliers whose raw materials or other ingredients are subjected to adequate verification activities before acceptance for use).

Source of definitions:

[1] Food and Agriculture Organization/World Health Organization (FAO/WHO). 2014. Section IV. Risk Analysis, *Codex Alimentarius Procedural Manual*, 22nd Edition.

[2] FAO/WHO. 2003. *General Principles on Food Hygiene*. CAC/RCP 1-1969, Rev. 4-2003

[3] Food and Drug Administration (FDA). 21 CFR 117.3 Definitions

[4] FDA. Derived from 21 CFR 117.135(c)(1)(ii)

[5] FDA. Derived from 21 CFR 117.150(a)(1)

[6] FDA. Section 201(f) of the Federal Food, Drug and Cosmetic Act

[7] FDA. Section 201(qq) – Based on requirements in that section

[8] National Advisory Committee on Microbiological Criteria for Foods. 1998. Hazard Analysis and Critical Control Point Principles and Application Guidelines. *Journal of Food Protection* 61(9):1246-1259.

[9] National Seafood HACCP Alliance. 2011. *Hazard Analysis and Critical Control Point Training Curriculum*. 5th ed.

[10] United States Department of Agriculture, 2014. Advisory Committee Reports.

NOTES:

CHAPTER 2.   Food Safety Plan Overview

> ## Food Safety Plan Overview Objectives
>
> In this module you will learn:
> - The benefits of using a Food Safety Plan
> - The principles applied to build a Food Safety Plan
> - A roadmap for building a Food Safety Plan
>
>

The Food Safety Plan is the primary document that guides your preventive controls food safety system. The Food Safety Plan is developed using a systematic approach to identify those hazards that require preventive controls to prevent foodborne illness or injury. This chapter provides an overview of the components of a Food Safety Plan that are needed to comply with the *Preventive Controls for Human Food* regulation.

This module also provides a few examples of outbreaks and recalls that occurred when preventive controls that should be included in a Food Safety Plan were lacking. Learning from past outbreaks and recalls can help protect consumers and your business from similar unfortunate incidents.

As discussed in Chapter 1, the requirements in the *Preventive Controls for Human Food* regulation are based on well-established food safety principles. This chapter also provides a brief discussion of the systematic process involved in building a Food Safety Plan.

While this chapter provides an overview to help you visualize how you might structure a Food Safety Plan specific to your operation, the details are covered in chapters later in the course.

> **Definitions:**
>
> *Food Safety Plan*: A set of written documents that is based on food safety principles; incorporates hazard analysis, preventive controls, supply-chain programs and a recall plan; and delineates the procedures to be followed for monitoring, corrective actions and verification.
>
> *Food safety system*: The outcome of implementing the Food Safety Plan and its supporting elements.

Contents of a Food Safety Plan

Required
- Hazard analysis
- Preventive controls*
  - Process, food allergen, sanitation, supply-chain and other
  - Recall plan*
- Procedures for monitoring, corrective action and verification*

Useful
- Facility overview and Food Safety Team
- Product description
- Flow diagram
- Process description

* Required when a hazard requiring a preventive control is identified

A written hazard analysis is the first required element in a Food Safety Plan. When the hazard analysis process identifies hazards requiring a preventive control, the written preventive controls portion of the plan must address relevant process preventive controls, food allergen preventive controls, sanitation preventive controls, supply-chain or other preventive controls. These are the preventive controls needed to control the hazards identified in the hazard analysis as requiring a preventive control. Monitoring, corrective action and verification procedures for each of the preventive controls identified must also be included in your plan as appropriate to ensure the effectiveness of the controls. A recall plan is also a required element of a Food Safety Plan when a hazard requiring a preventive control is identified. You are also required to maintain implementation records to document that you have implemented your Food Safety Plan.

Because your Food Safety Plan will be used or reviewed by regulators, employees, auditors, customers and potentially consultants, it may also be useful to include a brief description of your facility or company along with a list of your Food Safety Team members, a product description, a process flow diagram and a process description to help people understand the structure of the plan. This course includes these optional elements in the Food Safety Plan example to help class participants visualize the hypothetical operation and resulting documentation examples. The remainder of the course goes into more detail on the elements of an effective Food Safety Plan.

Examples of Outbreaks and Recalls

Don't Let This Happen to You!

Examples of Outbreaks and Recalls

Outbreak and/or Recall	Preventive Controls Lacking

Salmonella in peanut products for commercial use 2008-09 U.S.
• ~3900 products recalled by 200+ companies
• 714 ill, 9 dead in 46 states
	Primary Processor –
	  Process -- Roaster validation
	  Sanitation – cross-contamination prevention and environmental pathogen control
	Customers – Supply-chain program

Botulism from hazelnut yogurt 1989 England • 27 cases, 1 death	*Primary Processor* – Process – validation or refrigeration of hazelnut conserve *Customers* – Supply-chain program
Allergen recalls • Undeclared allergens account for over 1/3 of FDA food recalls • Most common root cause – wrong package or label	Allergen controls – accurate labeling and prevention of allergen cross-contact

FSPCA

You may wonder "What's in it for me?" when you consider what it will take to develop your Food Safety Plan. There are numerous outbreak and recall examples that illustrate the need for controls to prevent illness, as well as the benefit of having an effective and operational plan to avoid being involved in an outbreak or recall. Here are a few examples.

Peanut butter is typically a safe product because effective roasting of peanuts can destroy potential pathogens, such as *Salmonella*. However, an extensive outbreak in the U.S. associated with commercially-used peanut products illustrates the importance of process validation, sanitation controls and supplier controls. The outbreak investigation found that the peanut roasting process had not been validated so it was not known how effective this control measure was. Further, *Salmonella* was found in the processing environment, which suggests the environment was a potential source of product recontamination and that sanitation controls were not adequate. The incident involved hundreds of companies that had used the peanut ingredients in their products without an additional kill step. A supply-chain program, including determining that any pathogen kill step has been validated and that the supplier has controls to prevent recontamination, is another important preventive control to include in a robust food safety system. Together, these preventive controls could have prevented or minimized the size of this incident and associated recalls.

Another example involves a botulism outbreak that occurred in England in 1989. The manufacturer of the hazelnut conserve ingredient for the yogurt used a process that was similar to that used for fruit products. Because fruits have a lower pH than hazelnuts, the process was not adequate to kill *C. botulinum* spores and the formula was not adequate to control growth of *C. botulinum* when the ingredient was held at room temperature. Process validation or storage of the ingredient at refrigeration temperatures may have prevented the issue. Understanding supplier capabilities is another important lesson from this outbreak – the hazelnut conserve manufacturer did not understand that their new product required more stringent controls. An appropriate supply-chain program could have identified this shortcoming and addressed the issue before the yogurt manufacturer used the hazelnut conserve that had been inadequately processed.

Avoiding or minimizing the potential for a recall is another benefit of having a robust Food Safety Plan. Allergen recalls are responsible for at least a third of food safety recalls for FDA regulated food products (See Additional Reading at the end of the chapter). The root cause for most of these recalls is not declaring the presence of the food allergen on the label. Chapter 10: Food Allergen Preventive Controls provides more information on how to control this food safety hazard.

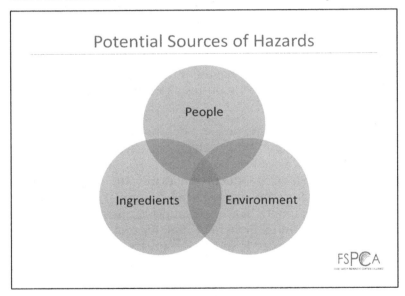

Contamination of food products typically comes from one of three different sources – 1) ingredients, 2) the processing environment, including equipment or 3) people. This is discussed further in Chapter 4: Biological Food Safety Hazards and Chapter 5: Chemical, Physical and Economically Motivated Hazards.

Principles Applied to Build a Food Safety Plan

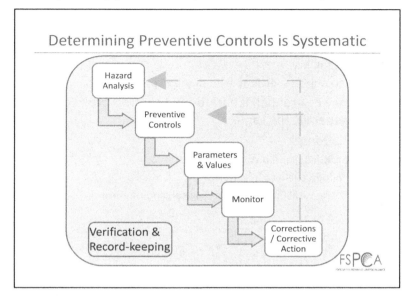

If you currently have a HACCP plan, it likely will be the part of your Food Safety Plan that addresses hazard analysis and process preventive controls (see Chapters 8 and 9). The hazard analysis may need adjustments to identify allergen, sanitation, supply-chain and potentially other preventive controls in addition to those addressed in a traditional HACCP plan.

Developing a Food Safety Plan, including determining where preventive controls are needed, involves a systematic process based on science to help ensure the safety of the product. It starts with hazard analysis (covered in Chapter 8), which is intended to identify hazards requiring a preventive control – in other words, the ones that matter most for food safety. When these hazards are known, preventive controls that are essential to prevent the hazard from causing illness or injury are identified. As previously discussed, preventive controls may include process preventive controls, allergen preventive controls, sanitation preventive controls, supply-chain preventive controls or other preventive controls that you determine are essential for your product. Once preventive controls are identified, you need to determine relevant parameters that define the conditions that must be met to effectively manage the hazard. Monitoring provides documentation that demonstrates these conditions are met. Corrective actions or corrections are predefined to enable swift action when things go wrong, thus preventing expansion of a food safety issue. When things go wrong, you also have to ask if it was because a hazard was overlooked (in which case you must adjust the hazard analysis), or if a preventive control was not properly identified or implemented. All of the above is recorded and verified to ensure the system is operating as intended and to provide a record for others (e.g., inspectors, auditors, management) to show that this is the case.

Some elements of a preventive controls system also require validation to demonstrate that the controls actually work. This activity may be less rigorous for some preventive controls than others. These differences will become more apparent as we go through the course.

Scope of the Food Safety Plan

Scope of the Food Safety Plan

- Specific to a facility
  - Preventive controls specific to a product and process
- Products may be grouped if hazards and controls are managed generally the same
- Define and address:
  - Specific product(s) and process(es)
  - Part of the food chain to be studied
  - Biological, chemical (including radiological) and physical hazards

FSPCA

Food Safety Plans are specific to a facility, with preventive controls specific to a food product and process. It is possible to group products that have the same hazards and controls in one Food Safety Plan provided and differences are clearly identified. Some operations choose to organize Food Safety Plans around unit operations in production (e.g., making a blend that is used in several products) to reduce overlap or avoid inconsistency. The organization of your Food Safety Plan is up to you.

In defining the scope of the Food Safety Plan, you should:
- determine the specific product(s) and process(es) that the Food Safety Plan will address, define the part of the food chain to be considered (e.g., products sold to retail may have different considerations than those sold to foodservice, to manufacturers or directly to the consumer), and
- address biological, chemical (including radiological) and physical hazards associated with the above.

The scope of the Food Safety Plan may be influenced by regulatory requirements or specific requirements instituted by a customer.

Food Safety Plan Example

The specific format of a Food Safety Plan is not defined. Each facility can organize the required information in a manner that suits their systems, the needs of their employees, the needs of their customers and the requirements of the regulation. The important thing is to have a plan that is easy to understand, implement and manage; that it is kept up to date; and that it is organized and accessible for inspection. The following is an example of how a Food Safety Plan might be set up, using a notebook. Note that there is no requirement that all components of a Food Safety Plan even be in a notebook – we are just using this as a model.

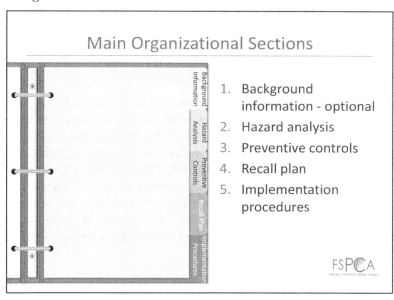

2-7

This course is organized around building a Food Safety Plan. In our example, we use the five main sections or tabs for the Food Safety Plan, including background information, hazard analysis, preventive controls, recall plan and implementation records.

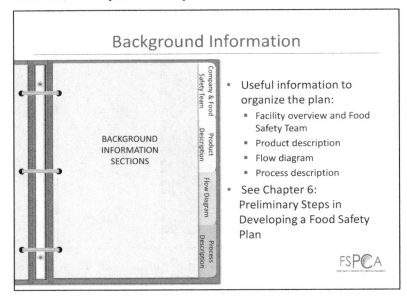

The information behind the Background Information tab is covered in Chapter 6: Preliminary Steps in Developing a Food Safety Plan. Background information is not required by regulations, but provides a useful framework for organizing the Food Safety Plan and for explaining the plan to others. Anything included as part of the plan may be subject to regulatory access and review. A brief description of the facility or company may be included.

Listing members of the food safety team, along with required records on training, could be included in this section. Two types of training are required by the regulation: 1) food hygiene and food safety training, as appropriate to an individual's duties and 2) training, if applicable, for a preventive controls qualified individual.

The product description section helps people understand important elements of the product that may impact food safety. An accurate flow diagram is useful to ensure that all steps of the process are evaluated to identify food safety hazards and it serves as a useful organization format for the required written Food Safety Plan. Finally, the process description could provide information needed to fully understand how the product is made. This can be helpful to those who are looking at the plan to understand, for example, the types of preventive controls applied. A facility can use other documents to meet these goals, if that works for their system.

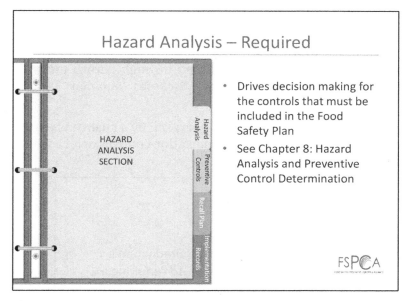

The hazard analysis drives decision making on which hazards requiring a preventive control. Thus, the hazard analysis forms the basis for other required elements in the plan. Careful analysis of the hazards that may be relevant for your product will help you to focus the controls on what matters most. See Chapter 8: Hazard Analysis and Preventive Control Determination.

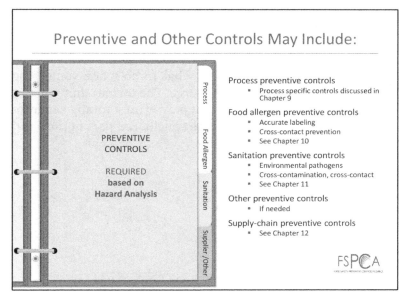

The Preventive Controls section describes the essential controls that ensure safe product is produced. The required preventive controls for a specific product are determined through the hazard analysis process, which considers the nature of the preventive control and its role in your facility's food safety system. Process preventive controls are discussed in Chapter 9. Food allergen preventive controls are covered in Chapter 10, and sanitation preventive controls are

2-9

discussed in Chapter 11. Supply-chain preventive controls include supplier approval and verification activities for ingredients and raw materials that have hazards for which the control is applied by the supplier. These ingredients are identified through hazard analysis. Chapter 12: Supply-chain Program discusses supplier related activities.

In some cases there may be other controls used by a facility as part of their food safety system, such as transportation controls, which would also be included here.

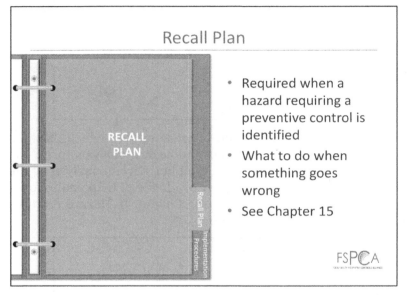

A recall plan describes, ahead of time, what to do when something goes wrong and the product is in commerce. The format that you use can vary considerably. For example, you may want a totally separate recall plan notebook but it would still be considered part of the Food Safety Plan.

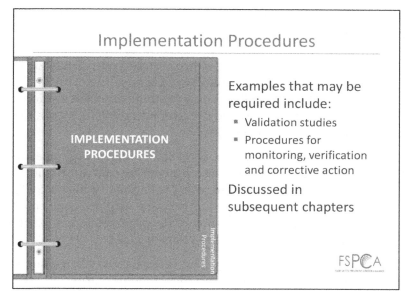

The Implementation Procedures tab includes other information required to support your plan. This may include validation studies that demonstrate that the preventive controls you selected are actually effective in controlling the identified hazards. Procedures for and records of monitoring, corrective actions or corrections, and verification activities may also be required to demonstrate that the food safety system was operated as planned on an ongoing basis. Example forms could also be included in a Food Safety Plan notebook. The actual required records could be in a separate notebook, a file cabinet, a computer or whatever format works for your organization.

Food Safety Plan Overview Summary

- A written Food Safety Plan, specific to the facility, is required to include a hazard analysis
- When hazards requiring a preventive control are identified, the following are required, as appropriate:
  - Preventive controls
    - Process, food allergen, sanitation, supply-chain and others determined through the hazard analysis process
    - A recall plan
  - Implementation procedures
    - E.g., validation studies and monitoring, corrective actions and verification procedures
- The format is flexible

In summary, the Food Safety Plan is a written document that is specific to the facility. It must contain a hazard analysis and separate plans or programs that address process preventive controls, allergen preventive controls, sanitation preventive controls, supply-chain programs, and other preventive controls determined to be necessary through the hazard analysis process. It must also contain a recall plan for food where a hazard requiring a preventive control has been identified. There is no required format for these documents or for the Food Safety Plan itself. Some facilities may combine different sections; some may separate them. There is no requirement that all parts of the Food Safety Plan be located in one place.

The important point is that the whole Food Safety Plan is organized in a way that identifies hazards requiring a preventive control so that 1) the hazards are effectively managed and 2) the facility has records that demonstrate these preventive controls are in place and being implemented. These documents should be organized and easily retrievable when needed, e.g., for inspections or audits.

Each of the elements of a Food Safety Plan is discussed in subsequent chapters, using examples from a hypothetical food operation.

Additional Reading

Centers for Disease Control and Prevention (CDC). 2010. Multistate outbreak of *Salmonella* Typhimurium infections linked to peanut butter, 2008-2009 (Final Update).

Food and Drug Administration (FDA). 2009. Peanut products recall.

Gendel, S.M., J. Zhu, N. Nolan, and K. Gombas. 2014. Learning from FDA food allergen recalls and reportable foods. *Food Safety Magazine* April/May 2014.

O'Mahony, M., E. Mitchell, R.J. Gilbert, et al. 1990. An outbreak of foodborne botulism associated with contaminated hazelnut yoghurt. *Epidemiol. Infect.* 104:389-395.

CHAPTER 3. Good Manufacturing Practices and Other Prerequisite Programs

---

GMPs & Other Prerequisite Programs Objectives

In this module, you will learn:
- The definition of prerequisite programs and their importance in a food safety system
- Basic requirements of Good Manufacturing Practices (GMPs) for human food
- Where to find more information on GMPs

The Food Safety Plan is not a stand-alone program, but rather part of a larger food safety system. The foundational programs that are part of the food safety system are frequently termed *prerequisite programs*. The term was coined to indicate that they should be in place before HACCP-based systems are implemented in order to effectively manage risk from foodborne hazards. The *Current Good Manufacturing Practice* (GMP) regulations address requirements for many prerequisite programs. There are other programs that are likely to apply to most facilities, such as supplier and manufacturing specifications.

In this chapter you will learn the definition of prerequisite programs and their importance in a food safety system. An overview of GMP requirements is provided; however, <u>further reading or training is important to ensure that you understand these foundational programs and the regulatory requirements</u>! You will also learn about other prerequisite programs that may be important for your facility.

Prerequisite programs provide the basic environmental and operating conditions that are necessary to support the Food Safety Plan and in some cases these programs will be part of the Food Safety Plan. Many of these programs are required by regulation (e.g., GMPs). The specific prerequisite programs required may vary depending on the type of food produced and the facility where it is processed or held. Some people use the terms prerequisite program, GMP, cGMP ("c" stands for current), "good hygienic practice" and "sanitation standard operating procedures" interchangeably. The important thing to remember is that these are foundational programs included in an overall food safety system. Without these programs, the Food Safety Plan may not successfully prevent food safety issues. Remember that the Food Safety Plan focuses on what matters most to ensure the safety of the food being produced.

Good Manufacturing Practices

> This is not a comprehensive discussion of GMP requirements. Certain regulatory requirements are addressed in Chapter 16: Regulation Overview – *cGMP and Hazard Analysis and Risk-based Preventive Controls for Human Food*. Regulations are provided in 21 CFR 117 Subpart B in Appendix 1.

Components of Good Manufacturing Practices (GMPs)

- The regulation (21 CFR 117 Subpart B) lists these components that establish the conditions and practices the food industry must follow for processing safe food under sanitary conditions:
  - Personnel
  - Plant and grounds
  - Sanitary operations*
  - Sanitary facilities and controls
  - Equipment and utensils
  - Processes and controls*
  - Warehousing and distribution
  - Holding and distribution of human food by-products for use as animal food, and
  - Defect action levels

*Some components may be preventive controls based on hazard analysis

---

GMPs are federal regulations that apply to all facilities that manufacture, process, pack or hold FDA-regulated food. GMPs are the basis for determining whether food products have been processed under sanitary conditions. They outline the minimum sanitary standards that a food processing facility must meet, including personnel, plant and grounds, sanitary operations, sanitary facilities and controls, equipment and utensils, processes and controls, and warehousing and distribution. They also provide for defect action levels for natural or unavoidable defects that at low levels are not hazardous to health. There may be some instances where a specific GMP task is so important to the safety of the product that it is designated as a preventive control in a Food Safety Plan. This is determined during hazard analysis and most likely would occur if there are cross-contamination (in a ready-to-eat food) or allergen cross-contact issues that need to be addressed in written sanitation or allergen preventive controls. Chapter 8: Hazard Analysis and Preventive Control Determination covers this selection process. This chapter focuses on basic GMP requirements.

The GMP regulations do not require written procedures, monitoring or record-keeping (except for training records); however, they are recommended as part of a facility's Standard Operating Procedures (SOPs) to manage the GMPs and document the results of these important programs. This can be very helpful to limit the amount of product that may be subject to corrective actions or recalls when an incident occurs. For example, product made from cleanup to cleanup, as reflected in records, defines impacted product for some recalls. Written SOPs are also helpful for employee training. The rest of this module highlights GMPs that are basic to making sure that products are processed under sanitary conditions.

Training

- Individuals must be qualified by education, training, or experience to manufacture, process, pack or hold food
- Individuals must receive food hygiene and food safety training
- Supervisors responsible for ensuring compliance must have appropriate knowledge, training or experience

 FSP©A

Employee education and training is an important prerequisite program. Employee training must cover cleanliness, health requirements, how to perform their job and how their work can impact the safety of product. This employee training must be documented. Supervision and setting a good example is also an important part of the system.

Personnel

Personnel

- Restricting persons with illness or open wounds
- Proper handwashing and sanitizing
- Adequate personal cleanliness
- Suitable gloves maintained in satisfactory condition

- Suitable outer garments
- Jewelry removed
- Hair restraint
- Personal items stored away from production areas
- No eating, drinking or tobacco use in production area

Selected GMPs related to personnel practices are listed on the slide above. While we will not go into detail on each of these, a few comments regarding personnel are warranted.

Food handlers with vomiting, diarrhea, jaundice, sore throat with fever, wounds or open lesions could be a source of microbiological contamination that could lead to foodborne illness. Your procedures and practices must make sure that sick people are not around food, and employees must receive training on this.

People can also carry potential contaminants into the processing environment. Clothing must be clean. Uniforms, smocks, dedicated footwear, color coding and other clothing options should be considered depending upon the needs of the operation.

Proper hand washing (and hand sanitizing when handling ready-to-eat foods) is essential to prevent direct contamination, cross-contamination and allergen cross-contact. This should be done each time employees are away from the work station.

Direct contamination – transfer of human pathogens, e.g. after using the restroom
Cross-contamination – Unintentional transfer of a pathogen from a food or surface to another food or surface.
Allergen cross-contact – Unintentional incorporation of a food allergen into a food.

Plant and Grounds

Plant and Grounds

- Removal of debris, unused equipment and uncut vegetation
- Proper drainage of grounds
- Proper waste disposal
- Adequate space for operations and cleaning
- Proper separation of operations to prevent cross-contamination and allergen cross-contact

- Cleanable walls, floors and ceilings kept in good repair
- Prevent drip or condensate from contaminating the product
- Adequate lighting
- Guard against glass breakage
- Adequate ventilation that does not contaminate the product
- Screened openings to the outside

GMPs listed above for the plant and grounds help to ensure that the buildings and structures are suitable for food-production purposes, and to reduce the potential for pathogen recontamination. For example, make sure that the grounds outside the food facility are clean, that there is no standing water and that waste is collected and disposed of frequently. Inside the facility provide adequate space and proper separation for operations (e.g., between cooked and raw product and between food with different allergen profiles, if applicable). Also, make sure that walls, floors and ceilings are in good repair. It is also important to ensure that condensate does not drip onto in-process product, that there is adequate light for operations, and that any glass is guarded against breakage.

Sanitary Operations

Sanitary Operations

- Plant maintained in good state of repair
- Cleaning operations not a source of contamination
- Cleaning and sanitizing compounds safe and free from contamination
- Unnecessary toxic chemicals not stored
- **Toxic chemicals properly identified, stored and used**

- **Pest control safe and effective**
- **Food-contact surfaces cleaned and sanitized before use and after interruptions**
- Non-food-contact surfaces cleaned as necessary
- Single service articles protected from contamination
- Recontamination of portable equipment and utensils prevented

Bold items discussed in text

These GMPs cover specific operations needed to keep a plant in good sanitary condition. Making sure that the food facility is in good condition and that any cleaning or storage of chemicals do not contribute to product contamination are important for all food facilities. As pests can be vectors for contamination, they should be prevented from entering the facility. Food-contact surfaces need to be cleaned and sanitized as often as necessary to ensure they are not a source of contamination. A brief discussion of the **bold** provisions on the slide for sanitary operations follows.

Toxic Chemical Storage

Certain potentially toxic chemicals are essential for effective plant operations. Only cleaning and sanitizing chemicals, laboratory testing chemicals, and chemicals needed for plant and equipment maintenance (e.g., lubricants) may be used or stored in a plant where food is processed or exposed. These chemicals must be properly labeled, used and stored in a manner that protects food, food-contact surfaces and packaging material from contamination. Store toxic chemicals in a secured area with limited access, and separated from food processing areas and areas where food and packaging materials are stored. Follow the label instructions for these chemicals to ensure safe application.

Precautions are necessary for application of insecticides and rodenticides. This frequently requires application by a licensed operator. These toxic compounds are generally used only outside of the processing facility unless special precautions are taken. For example, thorough cleaning of all food-contact surfaces after application would be necessary if insecticides were used to treat an internal infestation.

Pest Control

Pests, such as rodents, birds, insects, amphibians, reptiles, and feral or domestic animals must be excluded or controlled in all areas of a food processing or food storage facility. The presence of pests can impact overall sanitation of a facility so it is important ensure the effectiveness of pest control. Even if pest control is contracted to an outside company, the facility must assure that there are no pests in the facility. Take measures to exclude pests (e.g., eliminate holes that allow entry), and remove vegetation or structures that attract or provide a harborage for pests. Proper waste removal reduces the availability of a food source or harborage that can attract pests.

Sanitation of Food-contact Surfaces

Sanitary Operations

Condition and Cleanliness of Food-contact Surfaces

- Food-contact surfaces must be:
  - Smooth and easy to clean
  - Cleaned and sanitized as necessary to protect against allergen cross-contact and cross-contamination of food
- Potentially hazardous situations that may require Food Safety Plan documentation include:
  - Allergen cross-contact
  - Environmental pathogen harborage sites
  - Sanitation frequency to prevent pathogen growth

The *Preventive Controls for Human Food* regulation requires documentation of sanitation controls for hazards requiring a preventive control in the Food Safety Plan. Only those sanitation procedures that address hazards requiring a preventive control (e.g., sanitation to address environmental pathogens if relevant) must be documented in a Food Safety Plan. This is discussed further in Chapter 11: Sanitation Preventive Controls. Adequate cleaning and sanitizing procedures and frequencies must be established for all food-contact surfaces, including equipment, utensils and food containers. Gloves and uniforms that contact food may also be included in this category. Suggested frequencies for cleaning and sanitizing include before use, after processing interruptions and as necessary to prevent pathogen growth.

Different methods of cleaning may be relevant in different plant environments. Allergen removal requires cleaning but not use of sanitizers – sanitizing is not intended to have an impact on allergens. Use of water in dry processing areas is discouraged because it can infiltrate cracks, crevices and difficult to clean areas, establishing potential harborage sites for environmental pathogens. Wet processing environments typically use detergent and potable water at a suitable temperature for cleaning, followed by sanitizing with a sanitizer that is registered for food-contact surface applications, such as chlorine-, quaternary ammonium- or iodine-based compounds. Follow manufacturer's use instructions to ensure efficacy and regulatory compliance.

Sanitation of Non-food-contact Surfaces
As discussed above, sanitation of non-food-contact surfaces is needed in most facilities to eliminate potential food sources for pests. For facilities that make ready-to-eat products that are exposed to the environment prior to packaging, cleaning and sanitizing of certain non-food-contact surfaces may be included as a sanitation preventive control in a Food Safety Plan to minimize the potential for finished product contamination with environmental pathogens. This is discussed further in Chapter 11: Sanitation Preventive Controls. Additional information on general cleaning and sanitation is discussed in Appendix 5: Sanitation Basics, including information on potential spread of contamination by inappropriate use of high pressure hoses through creation of aerosols.

Sanitary Facilities and Controls

Sanitary Facilities and Controls

- **Adequate potable water supply**
- **Proper plumbing**
- Adequate floor drainage
- Proper sewage disposal
- **Adequate, accessible, sanitary toilet facilities**
- **Convenient hand-washing and sanitizing facilities**
- Proper trash and waste disposal

Bold items discussed further

Sanitary facilities and controls include the water supply, plumbing, sewage disposal, toilet facilities, hand-washing facilities, and trash and waste disposal. A brief discussion of the water supply and plumbing, as well as toilet and hand-washing facilities, follows.

Water Supply and Plumbing

Sanitary Facilities and Controls
Water Supply and Plumbing

- Potentially hazardous situations include:
  - Non-potable water contacting food
  - Cross-connections/backflow between potable and non-potable sources
  - Regional hazards
    - Radiological hazards
    - Biological and chemical hazards
- Safe source and treatment, including ice
- Suitable temperature and pressure

Water and ice that contacts food, food-contact surfaces and food-packaging material must be of safe and adequate sanitary quality.

- The source of water and the plumbing system that conveys it to the building must provide a safe supply. In many regions, the water treatment authority is responsible for ascertaining the safety of the water source and conveyance to the building. In these situations, a company's documentation should include annual water quality tests from the water authority. Facilities using private water systems (e.g., wells) are directly responsible for adequate monitoring and documentation of the safety of the water source. Municipalities in many regions can provide guidance.

- Ice must be made with potable water and protected from contamination with the same care used for food when ice contacts food (or food-contact surfaces).

- The temperature and pressure of water must be suitable for the facility's use. For example, hot water may be needed for effective cleaning and sanitizing.

- To ensure water is safe, cross-connections between potable and non-potable water lines must be prevented. There must be no cross-connection or backflow potential between the water supply and piping for wastewater or sewage.

Developed regions typically have mature water safety programs, while developing regions may not have uniform delivery of safe drinking water. Potential hazards and controls must be considered for those regions.

> **Definition**
>
> *Potable water*: Water that meets the standards for drinking purposes of the State or local authority having jurisdiction, or water that meets the standards prescribed by the U.S. Environmental Protection Agency's National Primary Drinking Water Regulations (40 CFR 141).

Hand Washing, Hand Sanitizing and Toilet Facilities

Sanitary Facilities and Controls
Hand Washing, Hand Sanitizing and Toilet Facilities

- Potentially hazardous situations include:
  - Apparently-healthy humans can carry and shed pathogens
  - Cross-contamination or allergen cross-contact via employee hands to food, food-contact surfaces or packaging
- Must be adequate and readily accessible
- Must be kept clean to prevent creation of contamination source
- Must maintain an adequate sewage disposal system
- Hand washing signs are useful reminders

Employees, even those who are healthy, can carry and shed human pathogens that can be transmitted through food, thus hand washing and sanitary toilet facilities are essential for food safety. Each establishment must provide hand-washing facilities designed to ensure that an employee's hands are not a source of contamination of food, food-contact surfaces or food-packaging materials, by providing facilities that are adequate, convenient, and furnish running water at a suitable temperature.

Hand washing and, where appropriate, hand sanitizing facilities should be at each location where good sanitary practice requires their use. Effective hand hygiene training should be accompanied by available hand washing supplies that remove food soils from hands; e.g., soap, running water. Hand washing signs are useful reminders. Water at a comfortable temperature must be available and single-use towels or suitable drying devices should be provided to prevent recontamination. Wet hands are more prone to spread contamination than are dry hands.

An adequate sewage disposal system is required. Readily accessible toilet facilities must be maintained in sanitary condition and not be a source of contamination. Toilet facilities should have self-closing doors that do not open into processing areas. Additionally, toilet facilities should be in good repair (e.g., not leaking) and should be properly supplied with personal hygiene products, including hand washing supplies.

Equipment and Utensils

Equipment and Utensils

- Cleanable and maintained food-contact and non-food-contact areas
- Preclude adulteration
- Corrosion resistant and nontoxic food-contact surfaces
- Compressed gases properly filtered
- Freezers and coolers have temperature indicating devices and automatic temperature control or alarm
- Properly maintain accurate process control instruments

Equipment, including utensils, must be designed to be adequately cleaned and maintained in a sanitary condition. For example, food-contact surfaces must be made of corrosion resistant and nontoxic materials to prevent adulteration. Seams should have smooth welds to ensure cleanability. Also, compressed air introduced into food must be treated so that it does not contain adulterants and be properly filtered to prevent particles from getting into food.

Cooling equipment, such as freezers and coolers must be equipped with temperature indicating devices, such as thermometers or chart recorders. Automatic temperature control or an alarm system helps to ensure that the proper temperatures are maintained. Thermometers and similar equipment must be accurate (close to the correct measure), precise (appropriately narrow ± range) and maintained.

Processes and Controls

Processes and Controls

- General
    - Appropriate quality control procedures employed
    - Overall sanitation under the supervision of competent individuals
    - Adulterated foods must not enter commerce
- Raw materials and ingredients
- Manufacturing operations

Processes and controls used for food must ensure that the food remains suitable for human consumption. This provision covers general and more specific requirements for raw materials, ingredients, and manufacturing operations. Take adequate precautions to ensure that procedures do not contribute to allergen cross-contact or contamination from any source, and minimize the potential for microbial growth. When food is adulterated, it usually must be rejected. FDA may allow the food to be treated or processed to eliminate contamination (see 21 CFR 117.80(a)(6)). Appropriate quality control procedures are required to assure success. Some tasks may require special attention. For example, overall sanitation of the facility must be supervised by qualified individuals who understand what it takes to maintain appropriate sanitary conditions in a food facility.

Raw Materials and Ingredients

> Processes and Controls
> ## Raw Materials and Ingredients
>
> * Comply with FDA requirements for pests, extraneous material or undesirable microorganisms, as assured by testing, supplier certification or heat treatment
> * Inspect for suitability
> * Store and handle to prevent contamination and deterioration
> * Properly identify rework and prevent contamination, allergen cross-contact and deterioration
>
> FSPCA

Raw materials must be free from pests, extraneous material (e.g., string, plastic, metal, etc.), and undesirable microorganisms. You are responsible for assuring this using whatever techniques are appropriate for the material and your source of supply. Raw materials must be inspected for suitability. They must be stored and handled to prevent contamination (e.g., properly packaged) and deterioration (e.g., appropriate time, temperature and humidity conditions). This also applies to thawing. If you use rework, ensure that it is properly identified, stored and handled to prevent contamination, allergen cross-contact and deterioration.

Manufacturing Operations

> Processes and Controls
> ## Manufacturing Operations
>
> * Prevent microbial growth through:
>   * Cooking, time/temperature control, water activity control, pH etc.
> * Use clean and sanitized equipment, utensils and finished product containers
> * Manufacture ice from potable water in a sanitary manner
> * Prevent cross-contamination and allergen cross-contact
>
> FSPCA

All manufacturing operations must be conducted to minimize microbial growth. Pasteurizing, freezing and refrigerating are food processing methods that may be used to prevent spoilage and ensure safety of certain food products. The extent to which these are used depends on the particular product and its distribution. When used, these processes must be done in a manner that ensures the conditions are adequate to maintain product safety and prevent deterioration, including use of time and temperature combinations that kill pathogens of concern (for pasteurization) and that prevent the growth of microorganisms during cooling in refrigeration and freezing processes. Rapid cooling or further processing without delay of blanched foods is necessary to prevent microbial growth. Certain bacteria, called thermophiles (thermo=heat, phile= loving), can grow at hot temperatures. Minimize thermophilic growth through proper temperature and timely cleaning. Certain moist foods such as batters, breading, sauces, gravies, and stuffing can support rapid growth of microorganisms. Protect these from contamination through good quality ingredients, heat treatment, time/temperature controls, and physical protection such as covers. Conversely, dry foods that depend on reduced water activity to control microbial growth (discussed in Chapter 4: Biological Food Safety Hazards) must have parameters (e.g., soluble solids/water ratio or water activity) monitored to assure that growth is controlled, and must be protected from moisture pickup. Factors that influence microbial growth are discussed in Chapter 4: Biological Food Safety Hazards.

Clean and sanitize equipment, utensils and finished product containers as necessary to ensure sanitary conditions. This may require disassembly of equipment to facilitate cleaning. Ice is a common ingredient for many operations. If made in-house, use potable water and produce it in a sanitary manner. Ice machines, like other food processing equipment, must be cleaned and sanitized periodically.

Finished or in-process food must be protected from contamination by raw materials or refuse. This includes exposed food on conveyors in the ambient environment, as well as in freezers and coolers. Use of sieves, traps, magnets and metal detectors can be useful to prevent inclusion of metal and extraneous material, or to detect metal if such contamination does occur. Destruction and reconditioning operations should not serve as sources of contamination and methods used should be shown to be effective.

Warehousing and Distribution

Warehousing and Distribution

Storage and transportation of food must be under conditions that protect against:

* Microbial growth
* Allergen cross-contact
* Contamination of the food with hazards
* Deterioration of the food and the container

Sanitary conditions apply not only to manufacturing areas, but also to warehousing and distribution. Microbial growth must be prevented. Allergen cross-contact must be prevented. GMPs require that food is protected from biological, chemical (including radiological) and physical hazards, as well as from deterioration during warehousing and distribution.

Human Food or By-products sent to Animal Food

GMPs for By-Products Sent to Animal Food

* Human food by-products sent to animal food use must comply with GMPs during holding and distribution; e.g.
    * Must be held under conditions that will protect against contamination
        * Ensure the safety of containers
        * Avoid contamination from trash or garbage
        * Identify the material through labeling
* Companies that further process food or by-products for use as animal food must comply with preventive controls for animal food (21 CFR Part 507)

Food companies often send unusable food or by-product materials to the animal food supply chain. Food may be unsalable to humans for quality or safety reasons, but could be safe (or made safe) for animals to consume. By-products might be sent to animal feed converters, manufacturers or wholesalers; or directly to animal producers that may feed it directly to animals or, if necessary, process the food to mitigate any hazards.

Human food and by-products held and sent to the animal food supply chain in general are not subject to the requirements for hazard analysis and risk-based preventive controls for animals, but must comply with specific holding and distribution GMPs to keep the by-product safe (21 CFR 117.95 and 21 CFR 507.28). For example, containers used to hold animal food before distribution need to be constructed of appropriate material, cleaned and maintained to prevent them from contaminating the by-products.

By-products must also be held in a way that prevents contamination from trash and garbage (e.g.; employee lunches, maintenance department debris). Use of color-coded containers to designate the contents (e.g., for trash versus for human food by-products going to the animal food supply chain) may be useful. Additionally, by-products must be labeled on the container or shipping documents with the common or usual name, such as "cereal food fines" for particles of breakfast cereals obtained as a by-product of their processing (See AAFCO in Additional Reading).

Note that if a human food manufacturer also processes the by-product materials (e.g., drying, pelleting, grinding), they must comply with the *Preventive Controls for Animal Food* regulation in 21 CFR Part 507. These companies should consider participating in the FSPCA course for animal food.

Defect Action Levels

Definition

Defect action level: A level of a non-hazardous, naturally occurring, unavoidable defect at which FDA may regard a food product "adulterated" and subject to enforcement action under section 402(a)(3) of the Federal Food, Drug, and Cosmetic Act.

- 21 CFR 117.3

Defect Action Levels

- Maximum levels established for natural or unavoidable defects in food that present no health hazard
- However, quality control operations must be used to reduce these defects to the lowest level currently feasible.

FSPCA

Even when produced under GMPs, some foods contain natural or unavoidable defects that do not present a hazard to health. The FDA set these action levels because it is economically impractical to grow, harvest or process raw products that are totally free of non-hazardous, naturally occurring, unavoidable defects. FDA establishes maximum levels for these defects and will use these levels when deciding whether to recommend regulatory action. The manufacturer is still responsible for managing these defects, and trying to keep them to the lowest level currently feasible. For example, a few pit fragments in pitted dates, olives and prunes may be considered unavoidable even under GMPs. Mixing of food containing defects above the defect action level with another lot of food with low levels is not permitted – the entire batch would be considered adulterated regardless of the level present.

Other Prerequisite Programs

Other Prerequisite Programs

- Hygienic zoning in ready-to-eat facilities
- Supplier and product specifications
- Preventive maintenance
- Signage or color coded equipment
- Others specific to plant

In addition to GMPs, other common prerequisite programs include hygienic zoning, supplier and product specifications, preventive maintenance, special signage (e.g., allergen icons) or color coded equipment (e.g., a special color for waste material containers) and other programs specific to the operation.

Hygienic Zoning

Hygienic zoning is useful to reduce the potential spread of pathogens in facilities that manufacture ready-to-eat (RTE) products. For example, areas of the facility that handle the raw ingredient (e.g., raw peanuts) may have less stringent expectations for hygiene than those handling the RTE product (e.g., roasted peanuts). Zoning typically involves separation of, for example, cooked product from raw product, and may include different uniforms for "cooked side" and "raw side" employees, dedicated equipment (e.g., carts or fork lifts) for different zones, traffic flow and air flow considerations, etc. Hygienic zoning is discussed further in Appendix 6: Hygienic Zoning and Environmental Monitoring Supplemental Information. Some elements of hygienic zoning may be a preventive control as determined through the hazard analysis process.

Purchasing and Manufacturing Specifications

Written specifications for the products you produce and the processes you use to make them, as well as ingredient and packaging materials, are common in business transactions. Well written specifications help to ensure that expectations are understood by both the customer and the supplier.

This is particularly important for ingredients that have a history of association with foodborne hazards. Efforts should be made to know your suppliers, such as learning about their facilities and practices, and the safety and quality of their products. Buying ingredients on the open market without knowledge of the supplier's food safety practices or program can add risk to your operation.

Written ingredient and packaging material specifications should be developed for all suppliers, and verification of compliance with those specifications is recommended for ingredient classes that have a history of contamination. Adherence to the specification is commonly confirmed through the use of a letter of continuing guarantee or a certificate of analysis (COA) that verifies the ingredient or product meets specifications. Chapter 4: Biological Food Safety Hazards and Chapter 5: Chemical, Physical and Economically Motivated Food Safety Hazards review some ingredients that have a history of outbreaks associated with specific foodborne hazards.

Periodic reviews of the supplier's product against ingredient specification requirements should be an element of supply-chain programs. Use of a third-party auditing firm that reviews the supplier's food safety program is one way to verify that controls are in place at the supplier. The extent to which controls are used should be risk-based and consistent with regulatory requirements. Chapter 12: Supply-chain Programs provides more detail on requirements when hazards requiring a preventive control are addressed by a supplier.

Others Specific to the Operation

Some organizations develop detailed procedures that may also be considered prerequisite programs. These may include receiving, storage and shipping procedures, labeling and label review, ingredient handling practices, glass control, visitor control, etc. The impact of these programs on food safety can be considered during the hazard analysis process. For example, labeling foods that contain food allergens is a preventive control that must be included in the Food Safety Plan, but label review for other information may be a prerequisite program. Similarly, glass control programs may be a prerequisite program for facilities that do not pack in glass containers; however, preventive controls would be required if glass containers are used in a facility.

Other Regulatory Requirements

Other Regulatory Considerations

The following are examples of regulations that are outside of the scope of the *Preventive Controls for Human Food* regulation and may or may not be related to food safety concerns:

Other Regulations
- Local regulations
- Food defense and biosecurity requirements
- Nutritional labeling
- Procedures to guard against economic fraud

Other Food Safety Regulations
- Seafood HACCP
- Juice HACCP
- USDA Pathogen Reduction Regulation
- International HACCP regulations
- Preventive Controls for Animal Food
- Produce Safety regulations
- Sanitary Food Transport regulation

This is not a comprehensive list of other regulations that are outside of the scope of the *Preventive Controls for Human Food* regulation.

Finally, there are a number of requirements that are outside of the scope of the *Preventive Controls for Human Food* regulation and may not be related to these regulations. These, however, are regulatory requirements under other programs and processors should be aware of these requirements as they may need to be included in their overall food safety program. For example, seafood products are not subject to the *Preventive Controls for Human Food* regulation but are subject to GMPs and the seafood HACCP regulation.

GMPs and Other Prerequisite Programs Summary

GMP and Prerequisite Programs Summary

- GMPs and other prerequisite programs provide the foundation necessary for production of safe and wholesome food
- GMPs are required and most are managed as prerequisite programs outside the Food Safety Plan
- Training is needed to understand and effectively implement GMPs

Good Manufacturing Practices and other prerequisite programs must be in place to provide a solid foundation for your Food Safety Plan.

These programs establish the foundation for effectively implementing your food safety system. GMPs are required by regulations, and most elements are managed as prerequisite programs outside of your Food Safety Plan. GMPs are operationalized by workers, frequently through written SOPs. The course provided a brief overview of GMPs. Because all GMPs are required, additional training or in-depth reading of the GMP regulations is important to ensure that the specific requirements are addressed.

This course cannot discuss all prerequisite programs in detail. Depending on the product or business, there may be additional programs to consider and implement.

Additional Reading

Links to GMP training and some of the additional references are available on the FSPCA website http://www.iit.edu/ifsh/alliance/resources/

American Meat Institute. 2003. Sanitary Equipment Design.
AAFCO (Association of American Feed Control Officials) 2015 Official Publication.
Cramer, M.M. 2006. *Food Plant Sanitation: Design, Maintenance, and Good Manufacturing Practices.* Taylor & Francis.
FDA. 21 CFR 117, Subpart B – Current Good Manufacturing Practice
Graham DJ. 2006. Snapshots in Sanitary Equipment: Developing an Eye for Hygiene. *Food Safety Magazine.*
Grocery Manufacturers Association. Equipment Design Checklist for Low Moisture Foods.
Imholte, T.J. and Imholte-Tauscher, T.K. 1999. *Engineering for Food Safety and Sanitation.* 2nd ed. Technical Institute of Food Safety.
Innovation Center for US Dairy. 2012. Pathogen Control Program Tools.
Marriott, N.G. and Gravani, R.B. 2010. *Principles of Food Sanitation.* 2010. 5th ed. Aspen Publications.
NACMCF (National Advisory Committee on Microbiological Criteria for Foods) 1998. J Food Prot. 61(9):1246-1259.
National Conference on Interstate Milk Shipments. 2013. NCIMS dairy HACCP Questions and Answers – Prerequisite Programs.
National Seafood HACCP Alliance. 2000. *Sanitation Control Procedures for Processing Fish and Fishery Products*, First Edition (Available in English and Spanish).
Pehanich, M. 2005. Designing food safety into your plant. Food Processing March 7, 2005.
United Fresh Produce Association. 2003. Sanitary Equipment Design Buying Guide & Checklist.

CHAPTER 4. Biological Food Safety Hazards

Biological Food Safety Hazards Objectives

In this module you will develop awareness of:

- The definition of the term "hazard"
- Biological hazards
- Potential controls for these hazards

In developing or modifying a Food Safety Plan, it is important to be aware of the potential hazards that are associated with the food products and processes under consideration. When hazards are understood, preventive measures can be implemented to control those hazards, thus preventing illness or injury. This chapter introduces the definition of the term "hazard," discusses biological hazards that are commonly of concern in food processing plants and facilities holding food products, and reviews potential controls for biological hazards.

Definition: Hazard

- Any biological, chemical (including radiological), or physical agent that has the potential to cause illness or injury.
  - 21 CFR 117.3

The *Preventive Controls for Human Food* regulation defines *hazard* as "any biological, chemical (including radiological), or physical agent that is reasonably likely to cause illness or injury." Biological hazards include pathogenic bacteria, viruses and parasites. Chapter 5: Chemical, Physical and Economically Motivated Hazards covers chemical (including radiological) and physical hazards mentioned in the definition. Information from this chapter on biological hazards and Chapter 5 is useful for conducting a hazard analysis for a food, which identifies the hazards that require a preventive control. The hazard analysis process is discussed in Chapter 8: Hazard Analysis and Preventive Controls Determination.

"Hazard" Does Not Necessarily Refer To:

- Violations of regulatory standards not directly related to food safety, e.g.:
  - Economic fraud*
  - Many standards of identity
- Undesirable conditions that generally are not hazards requiring a preventive controls, e.g.:
  - Spoilage*
  - Insect fragments
  - Hair
  - Filth
- The above may be subject to other regulatory requirements

* Unless associated with a specific safety issue

It is important to understand that, for the purposes of food safety, the term "hazard" refers only to the conditions or contaminants in food that has the potential to cause illness or injury to people. Many conditions are highly undesirable in food, such as the presence of insects, hair, filth or spoilage. Economic fraud and violations of regulatory food standards are equally undesirable. All of these defects should be controlled in food processing; however, many times they are not directly related to the safety of the product. Unless these conditions directly affect food safety, they are not included in a Food Safety Plan. The *Preventive Controls for Human Food* regulation considers decomposition to be a food safety hazard when biogenic amines or other toxic substances are produced.

How a hazard is addressed in a Food Safety Plan depends on both the likelihood of its occurrence in the absence of its control and the severity of the illness or injury that would result if the food is consumed. The difference between a known or reasonably foreseeable hazard and a hazard requiring a preventive control is explained in Chapter 8: Hazard Analysis and Preventive Controls

Determination. The current chapter provides a general discussion of biological hazards in food products.

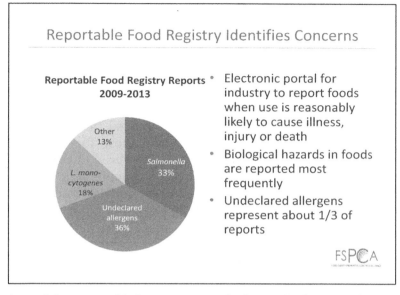

A useful source of information on the hazards that may be present in different foods is FDA's Reportable Food Registry (see Additional Reading). This registry collects information from the food industry and from public health authorities on foods or feed that are likely to cause serious adverse health consequences or death to humans or animals if they are used. Biological hazards represent the primary category of hazards reported through the registry. However, undeclared allergens in food represent about one third of the reports. These are discussed in Chapter 5: Chemical, Physical and Economically Motivated Hazards.

Biological Agents Cause More Outbreaks

Reported Foodborne Illness Outbreaks 2009–2013

Hazard Type	Outbreaks	Illnesses	Hospitalizations	Deaths
Biological	2,545	52,750	3,552	99
Chemical	163	663	67	5
Physical	Not collected			
Unknown	1,204	13,770	286	3

Adapted from: CDC Surveillance for Foodborne Disease Outbreaks, United States Annual Reports, 2009-10, 2011, 2012, 2013

FSPCA

CDC surveillance data include confirmed and suspected foodborne illnesses that are reported by states. These numbers are just the tip of the iceberg and do not include adjustment factors for under reporting.

The CDC estimates that one in six (or 48 million) people get sick from eating food every year in the U.S. and 3000 die.

The Centers for Disease Control and Prevention (CDC) surveillance data on foodborne disease outbreaks (i.e., two or more people become ill from consuming the same food item) are illustrated above. The number of illnesses reported is just the "tip of the iceberg" because many foodborne illnesses are not reported to CDC; however, the data are useful to understand the types of hazards that are likely to cause illness.

Biological hazards, including bacteria, viruses and parasites, are the most frequently reported hazard group associated with foodborne illness in the U.S. Chemical agents are also reported, but as you can see, reported numbers are much lower than those for biological hazards. Food allergen reactions may not be captured in these CDC data because an "outbreak" requires 2 or more people to be ill from the same food – allergenic reactions are sporadic and likely involving one person at a time. CDC surveillance systems do not report physical hazard outbreaks.

Definition

Pathogen: A microorganism of public health significance.
- 21 CFR 117.3 Definitions

In this course, the term is generally used to refer to microorganisms that cause illness through consumption of food.

Potential Biological Hazards

- Microorganisms in foods may include:
  - Bacteria
  - Viruses
  - Protozoa
  - Yeasts
  - Molds
- Prions
- Some are pathogens, many are not!

Most biological hazards belong to a group of living life forms that are too small to see with the naked eye, called *microorganisms*. Microorganisms are present in air, dirt, water, skin, hair, animal fur, plants and numerous other sources like saliva and air expelled with coughs and sneezes. Microorganisms are classified into various groups including bacteria, viruses, protozoa, yeasts and molds.

Prions are the agent responsible for "mad cow disease" (or in technical terms, bovine spongiform encephalopathy or BSE) and similar diseases in other animals including certain types of game. Prions are not covered in this course, but see FDA's *Bad Bug Book* listed in "Additional Reading" for more information if you process game.

Many microorganisms are beneficial. Certain kinds of yeasts, molds and bacteria help make cheese, sour cream, yogurt, sausage, pickles, sauerkraut and other fermented products. Particular strains of yeasts are used in making bread, beer, wine and other fermented products. These microorganisms are intentionally added to foods and they cause no harm. People come into contact with thousands of kinds of yeasts, molds, bacteria, viruses and protozoa daily without ill effect. In fact, bacteria live naturally on our skin, in our noses, mouths and digestive tract. They play an important role in digesting our food and are part of a healthy human system.

| Bacteria, parasites and viruses are different kinds of biological hazards. Control strategies are discussed later. |

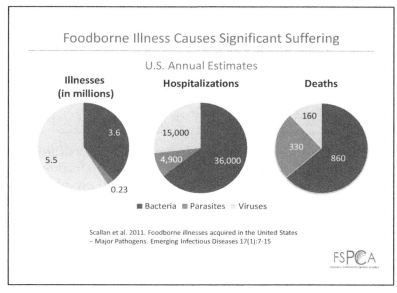

Foodborne pathogens, however, may be hazardous to humans under certain conditions. Viruses and bacteria are the most common foodborne pathogens. Many different types of bacteria can cause foodborne illness. Most foodborne virus outbreaks are caused by norovirus (typically in foodservice settings), but others, such as hepatitis, are also known. Some molds produce hazardous toxins called mycotoxins, which are considered chemical hazards in this course (See Chapter 5: Chemical, Physical and Economically Motivated Food Safety Hazards).

Remember that biological hazards can be introduced into a food product from ingredients and other raw materials, from food processing equipment and environments used to make the final product, and from people handling the product during harvesting or processing. Understanding how biological hazards can behave when they are introduced into a food can help you to determine how best to control them.

Infections and Intoxications

Infections and Intoxications

Foodborne infection
- Pathogen invades the body after consumption of contaminated food
- Growth in the food may not be necessary to cause illness
- Examples
  - Pathogenic *E. coli*
  - *Salmonella*
  - *Listeria monocytogenes*
  - All viruses and parasites

Foodborne intoxication
- Pathogen growth in the food produces a toxin that causes illness when consumed
- No growth in food = No toxin = No illness
- Examples
  - *Staphylococcus aureus*
  - *Clostridium botulinum*
  - *Bacillus cereus*

Foodborne pathogens may cause illness in humans by either infection or intoxication after the food is eaten. Foodborne infections are caused by consuming live pathogens that grow in the body, usually in the intestinal tract, and cause illness. Because growth in the body is required for an infection, considerable time can pass before symptoms occur – typically more than 12 hours and sometimes days or even weeks. In other instances, the high numbers of some pathogens release toxins in the intestinal tract; e.g., *Clostridium perfringens* and certain strains of *Bacillus cereus*. The specific infection symptoms depend on the pathogen and the susceptibility of the person eating the food, and can include nausea, vomiting, diarrhea, and sometimes fever. Illness can sometimes lead to hospitalization and even death. Viruses, parasites and many bacteria of concern in food cause infections. While viruses and parasites cannot grow in food, prevention of bacterial growth is important because the greater then number of pathogens present in a food the more likely it is that someone will become ill. More information on growth is discussed later in this chapter and in Appendix 4: Foodborne Pathogen Supplementary Information.

Foodborne intoxication is caused by consuming toxins produced by high numbers of certain bacteria (e.g., *Staphylococcus aureus* and certain strains *B. cereus*) after they have grown in the food. Symptoms from foodborne intoxication usually occur more rapidly than those from a foodborne infection, and illness can occur a few hours after consumption. Prevention of pathogen growth in food prevents foodborne intoxications. Some toxins are not destroyed by heat, so reheating food that was temperature abused does not necessarily make it safe.

Many infectious bacteria, such as *Salmonella*, can present a potential hazard simply due to presence in the food when consumed, whereas other bacterial pathogens require growth to a level that can make people sick. Some knowledge of bacterial pathogens and what it takes to create a hazardous condition in food is important for selecting preventive controls. Because of the diversity of the food supply, it is reasonable to assume that some potentially hazardous bacteria will be present in ingredients and food processing environments. See Appendix 4: Foodborne Pathogen Supplementary Information for information on different foodborne pathogens, including symptoms, and parameters that can control growth.

Foodborne Bacterial Hazard Prevention

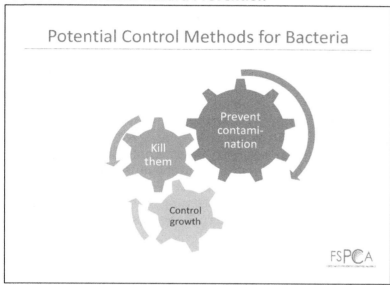

Three basic strategies can be used to control bacterial pathogens in food – prevent contamination, kill them and control growth.

Prevent Contamination
Keeping pathogens out of the food can be accomplished through practice of good personal hygiene by food workers, prevention of cross-contamination through effective sanitation practices, and use of a safe supply of ingredients and other raw materials to minimize the introduction of pathogens into the facility and the food. Much of this is managed through GMPs discussed earlier, like personnel practices as well as sanitation. Good Agricultural Practices and Good Husbandry Practices on farms are also important to minimize contamination of ingredients coming from the farm.

Recontamination of products after cooking or other antimicrobial treatments has also caused outbreaks. Because of this, selection of appropriate preventive controls should consider the potential for bacterial survival and reintroduction after cooking or other inactivation processes.

Kill Them

Appendix 4: Foodborne Pathogen Supplementary Information provides time and temperature guidance for controlling pathogen growth and toxin formation as well as inactivation of *L. monocytogenes*.

FDA's model *Food Code* provides safe cooking time and temperature combinations for a variety of foods (see Additional Reading).

FDA's Dairy Hazards Guide also provides safe cooking temperatures for certain products (see Additional Reading).

Other validated time and temperature combinations may also be appropriate for certain foods.

Kill Them

- Many techniques, including:
  - Heat, acid, antimicrobial chemicals, irradiation, ultrasound, pulsed light, high pressure
- Conditions influence rate of kill
  - Time, temperature, food composition
- Models can predict inactivation
- Appendix 4 has information on inactivating *Listeria monocytogenes*

Inactivation, killing and elimination are all terms that refer to reducing pathogens to a level that is unlikely to cause illness. Cooking is frequently used to destroy pathogens; however, other techniques such as irradiation, high pressure treatments, antimicrobial chemicals (e.g., sanitizers), acidification, ultrasound and pulsed light may also be applied to food or to food contact surfaces. These techniques must be validated to the specific food and processing conditions to ensure that they control the pathogens of concern in the specific food.

For example, for cooking to be successful, the food must reach an adequate temperature for a long enough time to kill the microorganisms of concern. Higher temperatures kill faster than lower temperatures. The required temperature depends on the food, the pathogen of concern and the time involved. Safe cooking temperatures may be established for certain foods (see side bar). Other validated time/temperature combinations may also be appropriate.

Spores are Harder to Kill than Vegetative Cells

Vegetative bacteria
- *Brucella* spp.
- *Campylobacter* spp.
- Pathogenic *E. coli*
- *Listeria monocytogenes*
- *Mycobacterium bovis*
- *Salmonella* spp.
- *Shigella* spp.
- *Staphylococcus aureus*
- *Streptococcus* group A
- *Vibrio* spp.
- *Yersinia enterocolitica*

Sporeformers
- *Bacillus cereus*
- *Clostridium botulinum*
- *Clostridium perfringens*

Note: Sporeformers grow as vegetative cells!

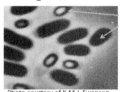 Spores and vegetative cells of *B. cereus*

Photo courtesy of K.M.J. Swanson

Definitions

Spore: A dormant, resistant form of certain bacteria

Vegetative cell: the growing form of bacteria

Bacterial hazards can be classified as sporeformers and non-sporeformers. Bacterial sporeformers are notable for their ability to produce spores that can survive harsh conditions that destroy other pathogens. In the photo above, the bright ovals are heat resistant *Bacillus cereus* spores and the larger, dark rod shaped bacteria are *B. cereus* in its vegetative state. Spores are not hazardous as long as they remain in the spore state. Unfortunately, spores are very resistant to heat, chemicals and other treatments that would normally kill vegetative forms of both sporeformers and non-sporeformers. When spores survive a processing step designed to kill vegetative bacteria, they may become a hazard in the food if they are exposed to favorable conditions that allow germination and growth as vegetative cells. This can be particularly serious when a processing step has removed most of their competition. The process steps used to kill spores are often much more severe than those necessary to kill vegetative cells because spores are more resistant.

Some vegetative cells are more resistant than others to inactivation methods; thus, it is important to understand the potential pathogens of concern in a specific food and to demonstrate, through validation (discussed in Chapter 13: Verification and Validation Procedures), that the controls that you apply actually control these hazards. It is also important to understand if destroying one type of hazard provides an opportunity for other hazards to emerge because competition is eliminated.

Prevent Growth

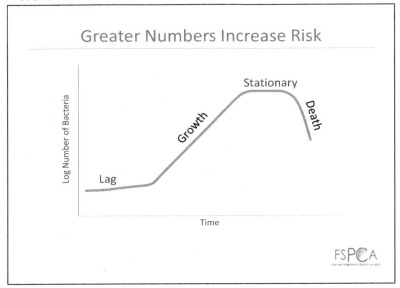

Keeping microorganisms from growing can be an important control when the process does not kill potential pathogens (e.g., spores) or when products may become recontaminated after a lethal process (e.g., ready-to-eat products that are exposed to the environment after cooking). Preventing growth also may reduce the risk of foodborne disease because some pathogens must grow to a sufficiently high number to present a hazardous situation, such as when toxin production or a high infectious dose is needed to cause illness. Time, temperature, the level of acidity (pH), available water (water activity – a_W), the right level of oxygen (atmosphere), the presence of competition by other bacteria and preservative use can all influence growth of potentially harmful bacteria.

It can sometimes take bacteria a bit of time to start growing (lag phase), but then under favorable conditions they take off and grow rapidly with one bacterium dividing into two, two into four, four into eight, eight into sixteen and so on (growth phase). Under ideal conditions, some bacteria double every 20 minutes; thus one bacterium can multiply to more than 30,000 in 5 hours and over 16 million in eight hours. If relevant, toxin formation usually occurs during exponential growth. Growth continues until they run out of what they need to keep multiplying (stationary phase), and then they can start dying off (death phase). Ideally, growth will be prevented due to the nature of the food itself or through application of preventive controls.

Factors that Influence Bacterial Growth

Factors that Influence Bacterial Growth

- Food – a nutrient source
- Temperature and time
- pH – acidity or alkalinity measure
- Water
- Proper atmosphere
  - Atmospheric oxygen, reduced oxygen, no oxygen
- Microbial competition
- Preservatives

Reducing growth reduces risk but may not eliminate it!

The USDA-ARS Pathogen Modeling Program, available at:

http://pmp.errc.ars.usda.gov/PMPOnline.aspx , and similar models exist to evaluate potential for growth.

Bacteria have certain requirements to live and grow, including food with their required nutrients, the appropriate temperature, water available in the food, a suitable pH, the right atmosphere and other factors. If conditions are not favorable for growth, some bacteria die while others persist until their growth requirements are met, such as water being added to a dry environment.

Improper holding temperatures for food may allow foodborne bacteria to multiply. Very rapid growth of foodborne pathogens can occurring between 77° to 104°F (25° to 40°C). The range of temperature that supports pathogen growth varies considerably depending on the specific bacterium (see Appendix 4) and characteristics of the food. Guidelines have been developed for how long food can be held at potential growth temperatures. For example, cooling models have been developed for *C. perfringens* because of the potential for its rapid growth when cooling soups and sauces. The temperature of the food itself is of primary importance. For example, even if a refrigerator or cooler is at the proper temperature, food placed in it may not cool down rapidly if large containers or insulating layers exist. See Table A4.2 in Appendix 4: Foodborne Pathogen Supplementary Information for guidelines on the maximum, cumulative time and food temperature combinations for controlling growth and toxin formations for foodborne pathogenic bacteria.

In general, holding food at temperatures between the proper refrigeration temperature for your product and 135°F (57°C) should be avoided. This is the "danger zone" at which bacterial pathogens can grow.

pH of Selected Foods

NOTE: Lower pH restricts bacterial growth

Food	pH*	Food	pH*
Milk	6.3-8.5	Bread	5.3-5.8
Eggs, whole	7.1-7.9	Carrots	4.9-5.2
Corn	6.0-7.5	Tomatoes	4.2-4.9
Cantaloupe	6.2-7.1	Grapes	3.4-4.5
Yellow cake	6.7-7.1	Mayonnaise	4.2-4.5
Chicken	6.5-6.7	Oranges	3.1-4.1
Rice	6.0-6.7	Apples	3.3-3.9
Flour	6.0-6.3	Dill pickles	3.2-3.5
Beef, ground	5.1-6.2	Vinegar	2.0-3.4
Lettuce	5.8-6.0	Lemons	2.2-2.4

*General values may vary by formulation, season and other factors

FSPCA

Adapted from: FDA 2012 Bad Bug Book 2nd Edition

The pH of a food is a measure of its acidity or alkalinity. Foods with a pH less than 7.0 are acidic. The pH of a food can be measured using a pH meter or pH paper. Foods with a lower pH, like vinegar and lemon juice, is more acidic than those that have higher pH, like milk and eggs. A pH below 4.6 prevents the growth of many bacterial pathogens, such as *Clostridium botulinum*, which is a deadly pathogen. However, some pathogens can grow below 4.6, depending on the food, temperature, and other factors (see Appendix 4: Foodborne Pathogen Supplementary Information). For example, *Salmonella*, the most common bacterial hazard associated with foodborne illness, has been reported to grow in environments with pH as low as 3.7 under otherwise optimum conditions.

While a low pH may prevent bacterial growth, some pathogens can survive! Do not assume that a low pH will necessarily kill a pathogen.

The pH is a measure of acidity. Notice that some foods (e.g., lemons and vinegar) have very low pH values where pathogen growth will not occur. Others (e.g., milk and eggs) have natural pH values where growth is likely if other conditions are favorable.

If the safety of your product depends on pH, you must use a reliable method. FDA methods for measuring pH of acidified foods are found in 21 CFR 114.90 – Methodology.

NOTE: Sometimes addition of other ingredients can change the pH or water activity of a food. Pay attention to this if you use these factors to control growth.

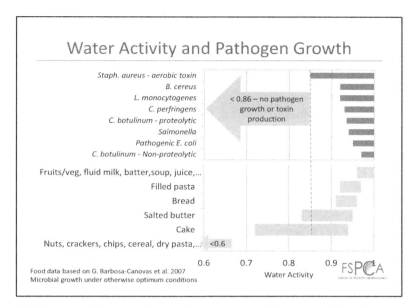

Water Activity and Pathogen Growth

Food data based on G. Barbosa-Canovas et al. 2007
Microbial growth under otherwise optimum conditions

All forms of life require water to grow. Water activity (aw) is a term used to describe the availability of water (free moisture) in a food. Pure water has a water activity of 1.0. Adding substances such as salt, sugar and other food ingredients can reduce the availability of water for microbial growth. Think about sea water – different species thrive in the ocean, than in a freshwater lake. The same is true for microorganisms.

Many fresh foods have aw values above 0.96, which supports the growth of pathogens. There are also many dry foods with aw values below 0.6, which inhibits pathogen growth, although some bacteria, such as *Salmonella*, can survive for long periods of time. In between, there is a range of foods that may have aw values that support growth of some pathogens. Growth of pathogenic bacteria stops when the aw is < 0.86. *Staphylococcus aureus* is the only foodborne pathogen that grows below 0.92. Details on aw limits for specific pathogens are provided in Appendix 4: Foodborne Pathogen Supplementary Information.

It is important to recognize that the range of aw values for some food categories can be quite broad. Specific measurements are needed for these types of products if aw is used as a growth control strategy. For foods that have different components (such as a donut with a cream filling) the pH and aw may be quite different in the components. In the donut example, the filling may be acidic and have a high aw, while the doughnut part may have a near neutral pH and a lower aw. The interface between the filling and the donut may be "just right" for microbial growth, which may be an issue if contamination of the interface is reasonably likely to occur.

Definition

Water activity (aw): A measure of the free moisture in a food and is the quotient of the water vapor pressure of the substance divided by the vapor pressure of pure water at the same temperature.

- 21 CFR 117.3

The report *Evaluation and Definition of Potentially Hazardous Foods* provides information on pH and aw combinations that prevent foodborne pathogen growth. See Additional Reading.

Also see Chapter 13: Verification and Validation Procedures.

4-13

Other Factors Influencing Bacterial Growth

- Atmosphere
  - Anaerobes cannot grow in the presence of oxygen
  - Facultative microbes grow with or without oxygen
  - Strict aerobes require oxygen to grow
  - Implications for modified atmosphere packaging
- Competition
  - Some pathogens grow poorly in the presence of other bacteria
- Preservatives
  - Nitrites, sorbate, benzoate, propionate may inhibit microbes

FSPCA

Note:

Combinations of the factors that inhibit microbial growth can increase effectiveness and in some cases may even provide a level of inactivation. Data are needed to demonstrate that this occurs.

Some pathogens prefer to grow at the concentrations of oxygen present in the air we breathe; others prefer or even require little or no oxygen before they can grow. Of particular concern for food safety are anaerobic conditions (very low or no oxygen) that favor the pathogen *C. botulinum.* Changing the packaging to control oxygen levels may change the hazards of concern for a food. For example, creation of anaerobic conditions through packaging can inhibit spoilage organisms, and extend shelf life. However, this anaerobic environment and longer shelf life may provide an opportunity for unanticipated hazards, such as growth of *C. botulinum.* Such changes should be carefully considered and studies to validate product safety may be necessary.

When there is little competition for nutrients, bacteria can reproduce rapidly. Conversely, the presence of other bacteria can inhibit the growth of certain pathogens. For example, production of toxin by *Staphylococcus aureus* may be suppressed when competitive bacteria are present. Fermented products like yogurt, which have high levels of active cultures, inhibit the growth of pathogens when fermentation proceeds at the normal rate.

Preservatives, like nitrite, sorbate, proprionate and benzoate, may slow or prevent the growth of pathogens as well as spoilage microorganisms. The effectiveness of these preservatives depends on many factors; thus, when relying on preservatives to control pathogen growth, validation (See Chapter 13: Verification and Validation Procedures) is essential to ensure efficacy. If not used at approved concentrations, some preservatives may be chemical hazards.

For many foods, bacterial growth is often controlled using one or more of the factors described above to make the food unsuitable for pathogen growth. Some preservation methods remove water, making this essential component unavailable to bacteria. For example, baking bread or crackers removes water from the food. Acidification is also a common method of preservation (for example, pickles), as is refrigeration (which slows growth), or freezing (which prevents pathogen growth entirely). Combinations of factors such as pH and a_W may inhibit organisms at levels where the individual factor alone would not. Some people refer to this as the hurdle approach. Use of a combination of factors frequently requires expert knowledge to develop a stable combination.

Example: Salmonella as a Bacterial Foodborne Pathogen

Salmonella spp.   Example

- Infection causes nausea, vomiting, diarrhea, fever, headache
- Primary sources: Intestinal tract of people and animals
- Transmitted by meat, poultry, eggs, raw milk, unpasteurized juice, many other foods (nuts, spices, produce, chocolate, flour)
- Contributing factors: cross-contamination, undercooked food, poor agricultural practices

Growth parameters	Minimum	Optimum	Maximum
Temperature	41°F (5.2°C)	95-109°F (35-43°C)	115°F (46.2°C)
pH	3.7	7-7.5	9.5
a_W	0.94	0.99	>0.99
Other	Non-sporeformer		
Atmosphere	Facultative - grows with or without oxygen		

Sources: ICMSF 1995 and Bad Bug Book 2nd edition

FSPCA

Note:

See Appendix 4: Foodborne Pathogen Supplementary Information for similar information for other bacterial pathogens. Understanding the characteristics of the pathogens of concern for the foods that you produce is important to select appropriate preventive controls.

Salmonella is one of the most common foodborne pathogens. The slide above illustrates information that is available in Appendix 4: Foodborne Pathogen Supplementary Information.

Salmonella is among the most common causes of bacterial foodborne illness and can be an environmental pathogen. The infection causes diarrhea, fever, abdominal cramps and vomiting. Occasionally, *Salmonella* may cause bloodstream infections and death. Severe cases may also result in reactive arthritis. Foodborne illness symptoms generally appear 12 to 72 hours after eating contaminated food. The intestinal tract of animals is the primary source of *Salmonella*, thus raw animal products (meat, poultry, eggs, milk products) are frequently associated with outbreaks. Because *Salmonella* survives well in many environments, many foods have been associated with outbreaks, such as yeast, coconut, sauces, cake mixes, cream-filled desserts, gelatin, peanut products, chocolate and cocoa, and soy ingredients. Fresh fruits, vegetables and nuts can be contaminated during growing if Good Agricultural Practices are not applied.

Salmonella is easily killed at traditional cooking temperatures in high moisture environments, grows with or without air, grows best at human body temperature, grows very poorly at refrigeration temperatures and does not grow above 115°F (46°C). Unlike most other pathogens, some strains of *Salmonella* can grow at a pH as low as 3.7 under otherwise optimum conditions. It survives well in frozen and dry foods, as well as in dry processing environments (it can be very heat resistant in a dry state). Attempts to wet-clean dry processing environments have been shown to spread contamination and increase the risk of product contamination because of growth in environmental niches like cracks and crevices that cannot be reached by sanitizers. It is best to keep dry environments dry when *Salmonella* is a potential concern since moisture can allow it to grow.

Foodborne Viral Hazards

Foodborne Viruses

- Do not grow in food
- Do not spoil food
- Foodborne pathogenic viruses survive freezing
- Transmitted by people, contaminated food and contaminated water and environmental surfaces
- Cause illness by infection

Like other microorganisms, viruses are common in the environment. They are very small particles that cannot be seen with a light microscope and cannot reproduce by themselves. Viruses can persist in foods without growing, because they need no food, water or air to survive. Those associated with foodborne illness can survive freezing and do not cause spoilage.

Viruses cause illness by infecting living cells and reproducing inside the host. Viruses grow only in a suitable host and only certain viruses infect humans. Infected people are the primary source of foodborne viruses. Foodborne viruses of concern can survive in human intestines, contaminated water, frozen foods and environmental surfaces for weeks or months.

Primary Viral Foodborne Hazards

- Norovirus
  - #1 cause of foodborne illness
  - Nausea, vomiting, diarrhea, headache and low-grade fever may occur
- Hepatitis A virus
  - Causes fever and abdominal discomfort, followed by jaundice
- Others may emerge as significant foodborne issues

The most common foodborne viral hazards are norovirus (the leading cause of foodborne illness in the U.S.) and hepatitis A virus. Other viruses, such as rotavirus, may occasionally be associated with foodborne illness, and more may be identified in the future. While the vast majority of viral outbreaks occur in foodservice settings, outbreaks have been associated with processed foods. For example, a large norovirus outbreak occurred in Germany that was associated with frozen strawberries imported from China.

Methods to Prevent Viral Transmission

- Proper practices
  - Good personal hygiene practices by food handlers
  - Exclusion of ill food handlers
  - Proper disposal of human feces
  - Elimination of insufficiently treated sewage to fertilize crops
  - Proper treatment of sewage
  - Cleaning and disinfection of restroom facilities
- Cooking

Viruses can infect consumers through contact with infected people or contaminated food or water. People who are ill from a viral illness can shed viruses in very high numbers in vomit or feces. Even when they recover from the illness and no longer show outward signs of illness, people can still shed the virus in saliva and feces. Transmission of

Norovirus is resistant to sanitizer concentrations used for food contact surfaces. An EPA registered disinfectant with claims against norovirus should be used. A general list of these products is available through EPA and the term "norovirus" or "Norwalk-virus" will appear on an EPA-registered disinfectant label. Carefully follow manufacturer's label instructions for use. If used on a food contact surface, rinse the surface after treating and follow with a sanitizer at the appropriate concentration before using the equipment.

4-17

viruses to foods is usually related to poor employee hygienic practices such as improper hand washing or working while actively shedding viruses. Therefore, prohibiting people with viral illnesses from coming into direct contact with food reduces the chance for foodborne transmission of viruses. Person-to-person transmission is very common for the viruses associated with foodborne illness outbreaks, which is another reason for requiring ill individuals to stay home from work – it prevents other workers from contracting the disease and spreading it to food. Outbreaks have been traced to foods exposed to inappropriately treated water. This may be rare in developed countries, but may be a concern in certain regions of the world.

Thorough cooking is also an effective control mechanism and most foods associated with viral foodborne outbreaks are ready to eat. There is some evidence that high pressure processing may also be effective in reducing the risk of transmitting foodborne viruses, and exploration of validated processes for specific foods is necessary for this control strategy.

Foodborne Parasites

Foodborne Parasitic Protozoa

- Do not grow in food
- Major foodborne parasites in the U.S. include:
  - *Cryptosporidium parvum*
  - *Cyclospora cayetanensis*
  - *Giardia intestinalis (lamblia)*
  - *Toxoplasma gondii*
  - *Trichinella* spp.

Like viruses, foodborne parasites do not grow in food. While foodborne parasite outbreaks are reported much less frequently in the U.S. than viral or bacterial agents, it is important to recognize potential issues and sources and control for these agents. Parasitic foodborne and water associated disease are more common in countries with poor sanitation. Appendix 4 provides brief descriptions of the foodborne parasites listed above.

Methods to Prevent Parasite Transmission

- Proper practices
  - Good personal hygiene practices by food handlers
  - Proper disposal of human feces
  - Elimination of insufficiently treated sewage to fertilize crops
  - Proper water and sewage treatment
- Avoiding contact with infected wildlife
- Freezing / freeze-thaw cycling
- Cooking

Some parasites may be transmitted through food or water that is contaminated by fecal material shed by infected hosts or by consuming infected animal tissue. Methods of preventing transmission of parasites to foods by fecal contamination include: good personal hygiene practices by food handlers, elimination of insufficiently treated animal waste to fertilize crops, proper sewage and water treatment. Consumer exposure to parasites depends on food selection, cultural habits and preparation methods. Parasitic infections are normally associated with raw or undercooked foods because cooking procedures that destroy pathogenic vegetative bacteria also kill foodborne parasites. In specific instances, freezing can be used to destroy parasites in food. Freeze/thaw cycles can prevent infectivity of *Giardia, Cryptosporidium, Cyclospora, Trichinella* spp. and seafood-related parasites (which are not covered in this training).

Foods Associated with Foodborne Pathogens

Most *E. coli* are harmless, but enterohemorrhagic *E. coli* (EHEC) can cause serious illness, including bloody diarrhea, blood-clotting problems, and kidney failure and death.

More information on these biological hazards is available in Appendix 4.

Biological Hazards of Concern in Selected Ingredients

Ingredient Source	Potential Biological Hazards
Raw milk and raw milk products	*Campylobacter, Salmonella, Brucella, Mycobacterium* spp., *Strep* group A
Soft cheese	*L. monocytogenes*
Eggs	*Salmonella*
Meat and poultry	*Salmonella*, EHEC*, *C. perfringens*, *Campylobacter* (poultry), *L. monocytogenes*, *Y. enterocolitica* (pork)
Grains and cereal products	*Salmonella*, EHEC, *B. cereus* (rice)
Fruits - fresh	*Salmonella*, EHEC, *L. monocytogenes*, viruses, parasites
Tree nuts/peanuts	*Salmonella*, EHEC
Vegetables - fresh	*Salmonella*, EHEC, *L. monocytogenes*, viruses, *C. botulinum*, parasites
Refrigerated RTE	*L. monocytogenes*
Spices	*Salmonella*, EHEC, *C. perfringens*
Non-potable water/ice	*Salmonella*, EHEC, viruses, parasites

*EHEC = Enterohemorrhagic *E. coli*

Certain pathogenic bacteria, viruses and parasites are closely associated with particular foods. Control of these pathogens should be considered when processing these foods and foods that contain them as an ingredient. If you process food products, it is important to have a basic understanding of the most common foodborne pathogens, including where they come from (source), how they contribute to foodborne illness, when they are a concern and what preventive controls can minimize the risk they present.

The table above is not a complete list of pathogens that may be associated with various foods. It does list some of the pathogens that should be considered when performing a hazard analysis for these particular foods. The hazard analysis process is covered in Chapter 8. Although it is not necessary to list all possible pathogens that could be associated with a specific food, you should take into account those pathogens that are known or reasonably foreseeable, either because of their frequency of occurrence or because of the potentially severe consequences of their presence.

Consideration of the different pathogens allows you to design a food safety system that will control all of the different pathogens. This is usually done by designing the control procedure to be effective against the pathogen that is most resistant to the procedure. For example, if you decide to use cooking or pasteurization to destroy pathogens, setting the cook time and temperature to kill the pathogen that survives at higher temperatures for longer times than the other pathogens would also kill the other pathogens (although sporeforming pathogens may require different controls such as refrigeration). Another reason for considering individual pathogens is that if a new pathogen is identified as a concern (and this happens from time to time), you will know if your plan has considered it.

In addition to pathogens normally associated with particular foods, there are pathogens associated with certain practices. For example, the sporeformer *C. botulinum* grows only under anaerobic (low oxygen) conditions. While the vegetative (growing) form of this pathogen is sensitive to heat, the spores are highly resistant and survive most cooking processes. A process that employs vacuum packaging generates anaerobic conditions that favor growth and toxin production by *C. botulinum* when temperature and other conditions are suitable.

Biological Hazard Sources and Potential Controls

Biological Hazard Sources & Potential Controls

Source of Hazard	Potential Controls
Ingredients	• Supply-chain programs • Process controls, e.g., cooking, chilling
Environment	• Sanitation controls, e.g., cleaning, sanitizing, sanitary design, zoning • Process controls, e.g., cooking in package
People	• Process controls, e.g., cooking in package • Sanitation controls, e.g., zoning • GMPs, e.g., training, personal hygiene, disease exclusion

FSPCA

As previously discussed, biological contamination of food products typically comes from one of three different sources – 1) ingredients, 2) the processing environment, including equipment or 3) people. Controls are needed to manage the hazards introduced from these sources. For example, sometimes ingredient hazards can be reduced to a safe level by using process controls such as a cooking procedure or maintained at a safe level using temperature control. However, not all products receive a cooking step or temperature control, and cooking may not be effective against some pathogens. In many cases the preventive control for the hazard is done by the supplier. In these cases, if an ingredient has a history of being a potential source of a particular hazard, a supply-chain program may be required. This is determined through Hazard Analysis (See Chapter 8: Hazard Analysis and Preventive Controls Determination).

The processing environment, which includes equipment, is a potential source of environmental pathogens and cross-contamination. Cross-contamination occurs when pathogens are transferred from raw products to processed or ready-to-eat (RTE) products. Direct contamination can occur when raw product is stored in a cooler with condensate dripping on processed product. Indirect cross-

4-21

contamination occurs when a surface is used for both a raw product and RTE product, such as putting cooked product back into the raw product container. Cutting boards, work tables, tools and utensils, particularly those with hard to clean surfaces, are other common sources of cross-contamination. Cooking a product in-package can prevent recontamination, but cooking in-package is not possible for many products. Effective sanitation controls, including cleaning, sanitizing and zoning, are useful to reduce the likelihood of post-process and cross-contamination. An environmental monitoring program could also be used to verify the effectiveness of these controls. These types of controls are discussed in Chapter 11: Sanitation Preventive Controls.

People with an illness or infection may potentially contaminate product. Transmission of pathogens by ill employees can typically be controlled when addressed by GMPs and training, which is discussed in Chapter 3: Good Manufacturing Practices and Other Prerequisite Programs. People can also serve as a vector for transmission of pathogens from a raw product to a ready-to-eat product. Effective hand washing procedures are needed to prevent such transfer and again, this is typically managed by GMPs. Effective training is required to make food handlers aware of these situations so they can prevent these occurrences.

Biological Hazards Summary

> Determining which biological hazards require a preventive control for a specific food is covered in Chapter 8: Hazard Analysis and Preventive Controls Determination.

Biological Hazards Summary – 1

- Biological hazards, including pathogenic bacteria, viruses and parasites, may occur in foods
- Hazards, if not prevented and controlled, may seriously affect food safety
- Preventive controls for biological hazards requiring such a control must be documented in the Food Safety Plan

FSPCA

In summary, biological hazards can present a food safety risk if not controlled. The severity of the risk depends on a number of factors, including the consequence of exposure and frequency that the hazard is observed with or without controls in place. Preventive controls must be designed, documented and implemented for all biological hazards requiring a preventive control. Because there are many potential hazards that could be considered in the production of food, it is important to identify those that are of such importance that they must be managed using a preventive approach. This will enable you to focus resources on the most important hazards. The hazard analysis process is an important step to identify those hazards requiring a preventive control. This is addressed in Chapter 8: Hazard Analysis and Preventive Control Determination.

Biological Hazards Summary – 2

Potential controls for biological hazards include:

- Prevent contamination
  - Ingredients, people, and then environment are potential sources of contamination
- Kill them
  - Spores are harder to kill than vegetative bacteria, viruses and parasites
- Control growth (bacteria only)
  - When you can't prevent contamination or kill bacteria, you must control growth
  - Time, temperature, pH, water activity, atmosphere, competition, preservatives and combinations can help

FSPCA

Remember the three main strategies to control biological hazards – prevent contamination, kill them, and control grow. Strategies to prevent contamination must address ingredients, people and the environment, as relevant to the product being produced. Complete assurance that you can prevent contamination may not be possible. When killing pathogens is considered, remember that spores are harder to kill than vegetative bacteria, frequently requiring heating under pressure to achieve effective temperatures. This is not feasible for many foods! Finally, preventing growth using time, temperature, pH, water activity, atmosphere, competition, preservatives or combination of these is important for many foods when contamination cannot be guaranteed.

Additional Reading

Appendix 4: Foodborne Pathogen Supplementary Information

FSPCA website has links to many of the following references used to develop this chapter.

Barbosa-Canovas, G. et al. 2007. *Water Activity in Foods: Fundamentals and Applications*, Blackwell Publishing and the Institute of Food Technologists.
Centers for Disease Control and Prevention. 2012. Food Safety website
FDA. 2004. *Guidance for Industry: Juice HACCP Hazards and Controls Guidance* 1st Edition; Final Guidance.
FDA. 2011. *Fish and Fishery Products Hazards and Controls Guidance* – 4th Edition.
FDA.2013. *Bad Bug Book: Foodborne Pathogenic Microorganisms and Natural Toxins Handbook* – 2nd Edition).

FDA. 2013. *Food Code 2013.*

FDA. 2014. *Dairy Grade A Voluntary HACCP.*

FDA. 2014. *Foodborne Illness-Causing Organisms in the U.S. What You Need to Know.*

FDA. 2014. Reportable Foods Registry.

International Commission on Microbiological Specifications for Foods (ICMSF). 1996. *Microorganisms in Foods 5: Microbiological Specifications of Food Pathogens.* Blackie Academic and Professional, New York

ICMSF. 2005. Microorganisms in Foods 6: Microbial Ecology of Food Commodities. Kluwer Academic/Plenum Publishers, New York

CHAPTER 5.   Chemical, Physical and Economically Motivated Food Safety Hazards

---

> ### Chemical, Physical and Economically Motivated Food Safety Hazards Objectives
>
> In this module you will develop awareness of:
> - Chemical (including radiological) food safety hazards
> - Physical food safety hazards
> - Economically motivated food safety hazards
> - Potential controls for these hazards
>
>

As with biological hazards, in developing or modifying a Food Safety Plan, it is important to be aware of the potential chemical, physical and economically motivated hazards that are associated with the food products and processes under consideration. When these hazards are understood, preventive measures can be implemented to control them, thus preventing illness or injury. This section builds on the overview information presented in Chapter 4: Biological Food Safety Hazards and discusses chemical hazards that are commonly of concern in food processing facilities and those holding food products. Radiological hazards, which are encountered less frequently, are discussed under chemical hazards. This chapter also addresses physical hazards and economically motivated hazards that may be associated with specific types of food or food production practices.

As with biological hazards, information from this chapter is useful for conducting a hazard analysis for a food. The hazard analysis process is discussed in Chapter 8: Hazard Analysis and Preventive Controls Determination.

Recall that the *Preventive Controls for Human Food* regulation defines *hazard* as "any biological, chemical (including radiological), or physical agent that has the potential to cause illness or injury." Chemical hazards include food allergens, mycotoxins, toxic chemicals, radiological agents, etc.; and physical hazards include metal, glass and other objects that can cause injury.

"Hazard" Does Not Necessarily Refer To:

- Violations of regulatory standards not directly related to food safety, e.g.:
  - Economic fraud*
  - Standards of identity
- Undesirable conditions that generally are not hazards requiring a preventive control, e.g.:
  - Spoilage*
  - Insect fragments
  - Hair
  - Filth
- The above may be subject to other regulatory requirements

  * Unless associated with a specific safety issue

You may remember this slide from the previous chapter that identifies many conditions that are highly undesirable in food, such as the presence of insects, hair, filth or spoilage, but that are not necessarily food safety hazards. Economic fraud and violations of regulatory food standards are equally undesirable. All of the defects on this slide should be controlled in food processing or through GMPs; however, many times they are not directly related to the safety of the product. Unless these conditions directly affect food safety, they are not included in a Food Safety Plan. For example, decomposition can be a food safety hazard when biogenic amines or other toxic substances are produced.

Chemical Hazards

Chemical Hazards – General

- Chemicals occurring naturally
- Chemicals used in formulation
- Chemicals unintentionally or incidentally present

Contamination from chemical hazards can happen at any stage in food sourcing, production, processing and distribution. Some "naturally occurring" chemical hazards are a natural component of a food, such as food allergens, or are produced in the natural environment unrelated to human activity, such as seafood toxins or mycotoxins. Other chemical substances may be hazardous due to errors in product formulation, such as sulfites or other food additives. Still others may be unintentionally present in the food, such as heavy metals, industrial chemicals, pesticides or drug residues.

Chemical Hazards Health Effects

- Depend on the chemical and level in food
- Some may cause immediate or near-term illness, e.g.,
  - Undeclared food allergens → allergic reaction
  - Caustic cleaning compounds → tissue injury
- Some may cause long-term effects, e.g.,
  - Lead in candy → impaired cognitive development in children
  - Chronic aflatoxin exposure → liver cancer
- FDA evaluates long-term and short-term exposure risks to establish specific food chemical use policy

---

The presence of a chemical residue in a food is not always a hazard and may be unavoidable. The amount and type of the chemical substance determines whether it is a hazard or not. Some chemical

Action Levels for Poisonous or Deleterious Substances in Human and Animal Feed contains information on levels of chemicals that are prohibited in certain foods. These levels are based on FDA's assessment of long term and short term effects of consuming the specific chemical.

hazards can cause immediate or near-term illness or injury, such as food allergens (discussed below) or high concentrations of certain chemicals. Other chemical hazards require exposure over a prolonged period to have a toxic effect in humans, such as lead contamination of candy resulting in impaired cognitive development in children and cancers caused by certain toxins in food.

The safety of chemicals used in food and food processing must be evaluated on a use-by-use basis. Regulatory limits are set for many chemical contaminants. These limits consider long term and short term exposure consequences, quantity, toxic potency, potential benefits like antimicrobial activity, and similar properties. FDA action levels for specific hazardous chemicals in specific commodities are published in the booklet *Action Levels for Poisonous or Deleterious Substances in Human Food and Animal Feed*. If there is no tolerance, action level or other regulatory limit for a specific hazardous chemical in a specific food product, concentrations must be below the limit of current standards for analytical testing.

Chemical Hazards Examples

- Naturally occurring
  - Food allergens, mycotoxins, decomposition by-products
- Used in formulation
  - Food additives, color additives, preservatives
- Unintentionally or incidentally present
  - Cleaning and sanitizing chemicals, pesticides, industrial chemicals, heavy metals, drug residues, radiological hazards

Chemical hazards of particular concern are listed above and the unique concerns for these hazards are discussed below.

Naturally Occurring Chemicals

As previously mentioned, naturally occurring chemical hazards include those present in a food or produced in the natural environment unrelated to human activity. For example, some cheeses and other food may contain histamine as a result of microbial fermentation converting histidine to histamine. Some people are sensitive to low levels; others require exposure to high levels produced in very ripe products of fermentation (Stratton et al. 1991). Extended fermentation can result in decomposition of the food. Other naturally occurring chemicals include food allergens and mycotoxins, each of which is discussed below.

Food Allergens

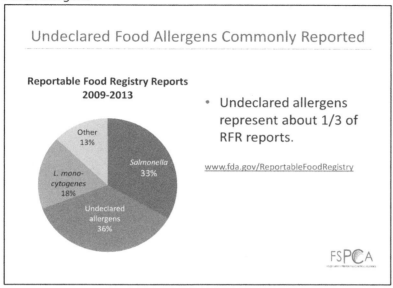

We will start with food allergens as an example of a naturally occurring chemical hazard. As previously mentioned, undeclared allergens in foods represent about one third of the reports in FDA's Reportable Food Registry.

Food allergens are naturally present in certain foods and these foods are examples of ingredients normally used in food that do not present a chemical hazard for most people. However, they can be a life threatening for those with a food allergy. It is estimated that food allergies affect four to six percent of children and two to three percent of adults in the U.S. The presence of undeclared allergens in food is a major cause of product recalls. A food allergen reaction is a body's immunological response to proteins in the food that the body sees as foreign. These reactions are fast-acting and should not be confused with food intolerance, such as lactose intolerance.

Food Allergy Symptoms

- Mouth: swelling and tingling of lips, mouth or tongue
- GI: cramping, vomiting, diarrhea
- Skin: hives, eczema
- Airway: wheezing, coughing, swelling of throat
- Cardiovascular: loss of blood pressure
- Anaphylaxis: most dangerous, life threatening

People with food allergies can experience a variety of symptoms that can be mild to severe and can affect different systems in the body. The severity of the response depends on the amount of the allergen consumed and individual sensitivity. Mild allergic responses can be treated with antihistamine, but serious reactions like anaphylaxis are treated with epinephrine. Anaphylaxis is a generalized reaction, which can include multiple organ failure, any of the other symptoms listed above, severe loss of blood pressure and cardiac arrhythmia. This reaction can be fatal. Tens of thousands of emergency room visits and 150-200 deaths per year can be attributed to anaphylactic reactions.

Reactions usually occur 1 – 30 minutes after exposure, but may take up to 2 hours. Food allergy sufferers may experience multiple severe reactions in their lifetime. Children with asthma and multiple food allergies are at increased risk for anaphylaxis. Milk, soy and egg allergies may be outgrown; but peanut, tree nut and shellfish allergies often persist throughout life.

Major Food Allergens (The Big 8)

- Milk
- Egg
- Peanut
- Tree nuts

- Fish
- Crustacean Shellfish
- Wheat
- Soy

 90% of food allergic reactions are caused by these allergens

FSPCA

Photo Sources: Microsoft Clip Art and KMJ Swanson (soybeans)

Many foods can cause an allergic reaction in people, but eight foods are responsible for over 90% of the allergic reactions in the U.S. These are milk, egg, peanut, tree nut, fish, crustacean shellfish, wheat and soy. The U.S. Food Allergen Labeling and Consumer Protection Act (FALCPA) mandates labeling of these allergens, which cause most of the food allergy reactions. For product groups like tree nuts, fish and crustacean shellfish, the specific type of tree nut or fish must also be labeled.

Avoidance is the Primary Treatment

- Complete avoidance of the allergen is the primary treatment for food allergies
- This requires:
  - Individual responsibility to avoid and prepare for accidental exposure
  - Those supplying or preparing food to provide accurate information and safe food

FSPCA

The FDA has responses to frequently asked questions related to food allergens on their website. See Additional Reading or search the FDA website.

Food allergy sufferers must practice complete avoidance of the food allergen in order to avoid allergic reactions. The ability to practice avoidance depends on factors outside the control of the individual sufferer. Proper labeling of food products along with strict monitoring of labels is required for avoiding specific allergens. Food processors must have accurate information about their ingredients and understand their processing conditions related to allergen cross-contact opportunities in order to fully assess their own products. Accurate allergen labeling is required to be addressed in the Food Safety Plan.

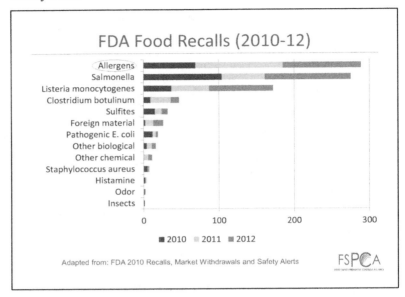

The number of recalls associated with undeclared allergens illustrates that this is a real issue in the market place. More FDA regulated food recalls were associated with undeclared allergens than any other issue for the years 2010, 2011 and 2012 combined. Implementing a comprehensive food allergen management program is not only the right thing to do from a food safety perspective, but also is important to protect a business from recalls.

Known Causes of Allergen Recalls

Most Common		Other	
	Number		Number
Wrong label or package	137	Knowledge	28
Terminology not correct	85	Ingredient mislabeled	26
No carry-through of info from ingredient	70	Not updated after formula change	22
Cross-contact	52	Computer error	21
Wrong ingredient	31	In process	19
Rework	9	Other	14
		No declaration	12

Adapted from Gendel and Zhu 2013

FSPCA

Allergen labeling must be addressed in the Food Safety Plan, which is consistent with the observation that most allergen recalls are related to labeling issues, such as use of the wrong label or package for a product. Specific labeling terminology may be incorrect, such as not labeling butter with the term "milk," which is required by labeling regulations. Sometimes a processor may overlook a minor ingredient in one of their ingredients and not include it on the label. Food allergens in processing aids should also be considered and may need to be included in an allergen labeling declaration. Labeling errors may also involve using the wrong ingredient by mistake or on purpose (e.g., intentionally substituting different nuts, due to shortage or cost saving, without changing the label) or using rework with a different allergen profile in a formulation.

Allergen cross-contact with other foods through inadequately cleaned equipment or food workers handling both an allergen-containing food and a non-allergen containing food is also an issue that can present a risk to allergic consumers. The potential for allergens crossing into non-allergen processing streams must be considered in a Food Safety Plan.

Many of the other causes listed on the slide are related to lack of knowledge of the issue or inadequate management of change. Ensuring that all relevant people are aware of potential allergen issues can minimize the potential for harming a person with a food allergy and can help avoid a recall.

Understanding how undeclared allergens get into products is the starting point for developing an effective allergen management program. Chapter 10: Food Allergen Preventive Controls discusses required food allergen preventive controls, specifically accurate labeling and allergen cross-contact prevention, and approaches to help manage these issues.

> Jackson et al. (2008) review of *Cleaning and Other Control and Validation Strategies to Prevent Allergen Cross-contact in Food-processing Operations* outlines components of a comprehensive allergen control plan, which meets or exceeds the requirements for Preventive Controls compliance.
>
> See Additional Reading.

Allergens in Product Design

- Understand existing allergen profile of the line or facility
- Minimize introduction of unique allergens in product formulation
- Work with ingredient suppliers to remove unnecessary allergens
- Avoid use of allergenic minor ingredients

While not required by the *Preventive Controls for Human Food* regulation, product design can play an important role in minimizing food allergen controls in production. For example, some products require a protein source as a firming agent, and egg, soy or milk protein can potentially have the same functionality. If a developer knows the allergen profile for a production line, they may be able to choose ingredients with the same allergens, thus reducing allergen cross-contact concerns.

Consider only adding new allergens to products when they make an important difference in the taste or functionality of the product. If an allergen-containing ingredient is required, consider different formats to reduce allergen cross-contact issues. For example, it is difficult to make walnut brownies without introducing walnuts, but if you are making a mix, a separate packet containing walnuts could be used instead of loose walnuts in the mix to minimize the exposure of equipment to tiny pieces of walnuts that make cleaning difficult.

Before a new allergen is added to an existing product or line, consider the potential costs to manage the new allergen in the project plan. This can help you to determine if the change is really beneficial. If you decide to add a new allergen to an existing formula, including a label element such as "New formula" is useful to alert allergic consumers that a new allergen is in a product. Many food allergic consumers are very brand loyal.

Mycotoxins

Mycotoxins are chemical hazards produced by certain types of molds when extensive growth occurs on commodities of concern. Aflatoxins are a type of mycotoxin that is produced by certain molds that grow on corn, peanuts and other commodities in the field or during storage. Other mycotoxins, such as ochratoxin A, fumonisins, deoxynivalenol

(DON or vomitoxin) and zearalenone can present a hazard in crops such as grains, fruits and tree nuts. Patulin is a potential issue on fruits. The molds that produce mycotoxins typically become established in commodities of concern under stressful growing conditions. The molds can grow during storage of grains when the grain contains moisture above a certain level, which can vary by crop and mold type. In years and locations with good growing and harvest conditions, mycotoxins are not usually a hazard requiring a preventive control. However, when stressful growth conditions for crops or particularly wet harvest seasons for some crops occur, mycotoxin preventive controls may be warranted. This may include preventive controls for feed used for milk-producing animals, because aflatoxin present in moldy grain can be changed to aflatoxin M by the cow and passed on through milk.

A variety of controls throughout the supply chain can be applied to reduce the potential presence of mycotoxins. Conditions such as insect damage and drought stress can promote mycotoxin formation. After harvest, rapid drying can prevent mycotoxin formation (or maintain the mycotoxin level that came in from the field), while slow drying increases them. Similarly, proper dry storage maintains mycotoxins at incoming concentrations, while in poor storage conditions (e.g., allowing condensation) concentrations can increase again. During processing, color sorting and testing at various stages to reject material with unacceptable concentrations can reduce levels. The effect of processing on mycotoxins has demonstrated that while some reduction may occur, complete elimination does not (Milani and Maleki 2014).

Chemical Substances Used in Formulation

Chemicals Used In Formulation

- Food additives
- Color additives
- Preservatives
- Nutritional additives
- Antimicrobials

Some chemical substances are added during formulation. They include food additives, color additives, preservatives such as sulfites, and nutritional additives. Other chemicals may be used in processing, e.g., antimicrobials used in wash water for fresh-cut produce. These substances are intended to be used at safe levels, but could present a hazard if those levels are exceeded.

FDA sets the concentration, manner of use and maximum allowable residues for certain chemical substances in food (see *Action Levels for Poisonous or Deleterious Substances in Human Food and Animal Feed*). Keeping within these limits is important for safety as well as regulatory compliance. These chemical substances are not hazardous if properly applied and controlled. Potential risks to consumers increase when these substances are not properly controlled, such as exceeding the recommended usage rates or accidentally introduced in the wrong place or food.

Chemicals Unintentional or Incidentally Present

Unintentionally or Incidentally Added Chemicals

- Cleaning chemicals
- Pesticides
- Industrial chemicals
- Heavy metals
- Drug residues
- Radiological hazards

Chemicals can become part of a food without being intentionally added. These incidental chemicals might already be in a food ingredient when it is received. For example, fruits or vegetables may contain small but legal residues of approved pesticides. Packaging materials that are in direct contact with ingredients or the product can be a source of incidental chemicals, such a as inks. Cleaning and sanitizing chemicals are necessary to maintain a sanitary environment for the production of food products, and small amounts of sanitizers may remain on equipment surfaces. It is important to follow label instructions to ensure their safe use.

Most incidental chemicals have no effect on food safety and others are only a concern if they are present in excessive amounts. Incidental chemicals also include accidental additions of prohibited substances. A brief discussion of pesticides, industrial chemicals, heavy metals, drug residues and radiological hazards follows.

Pesticides

Pesticides

- Must be registered with appropriate authority
  - EPA in U.S.
- Must be used according to label instructions
- Regulatory programs may address
  - Applicator licensure
  - Usage instructions
  - Official monitoring for residues
- Compliance
  - High compliance for U.S. operations
  - Imported product compliance rates vary

Certain pesticides can be applied directly to food or crops to control weeds, insects or microbial contamination. Other pesticides cannot be applied directly to food; e.g., for rodents control. Pesticides can be used legally only if they are registered with the appropriate authority (see below) and used according to conditions described on the label. Numerous U.S. regulatory programs address aspects of pesticide usage, like applicator licensure, usage instructions on the label, official monitoring of pesticide residues in foods and enforcement actions against violators. Experience in the U.S. has demonstrated that U.S. grown fruits and vegetables have a high level of compliance with U.S. pesticide tolerance regulations and that the occurrence of unlawful pesticide residues in food is likely to be infrequent and unlikely to have a significant public health impact. Because of this, pesticide use in the U.S. is frequently managed through application of GMPs.

The U.S. Environmental Protection Agency (EPA) registers pesticides for use in the U.S., establishes label instructions for use, and sets tolerances for residues of pesticides in food based on safety and conditions of use. FDA tests food for pesticide residues for compliance with U.S. tolerances. If a U.S. tolerance has not been established for a particular pesticide in a commodity, then any amount measured may be considered violative. Therefore, check to see if pesticides used in foods you import are in compliance with U.S. pesticide laws. While pesticide compliance experience for imported fruits and vegetables is generally comparable to that for U.S. produce, you should ensure that government controls in the country that supplies your imported produce result in a high rate of compliance with U.S. pesticide tolerance regulations. If you cannot achieve this assurance you should evaluate carefully whether pesticide residues pose a hazard requiring a preventive control in your Food Safety Plan.

Industrial Chemicals

The FDA provides information on chemical contaminants on its website. See Additional Reading or search the FDA website to get the latest information.

Industrial Chemicals

- Examples
  - Dioxins
  - Polychlorinated biphenyls
- Break down slowly in the environment and can be concentrated in the food chain

Food crops can be harvested from areas that are contaminated by varying amounts of industrial chemicals including dioxins and polychlorinated biphenyls (PCBs). "Dioxins" is a collective term for a group of environmental contaminants that includes certain dioxin, furan and dioxin-like PCB compounds that are found throughout the world. They are released into the air from combustion processes, such as commercial or municipal waste incineration and from burning fuels, such as wood, coal or oil. Burning of household trash and forest fires can also result in the release of dioxins and furans into the environment. Accidental or intentional release of transformer fluids has resulted in the presence of PCBs in the environment.

Because dioxins break down very slowly, dioxins released in the past from both man-made and natural sources still exist in the environment and cannot be quickly reduced. Dioxins can be deposited on plants that are then eaten by animals. Thus, they may be concentrated in the food chain so that livestock, fish and shellfish can have higher concentrations than the plants, water, soil or sediments around them. An evaluation of the potential for contamination of crops by dioxin and related materials may be worth considering.

Heavy Metals

Heavy Metals

- Examples
  - Arsenic
  - Lead
  - Mercury
- May accumulate in plants or fish

FSPCA

Heavy metals such as arsenic, lead, and mercury may accumulate in fish or plants if the growing environment has high concentrations of these chemical hazards. Examples include arsenic accumulation in rice, mercury accumulation in large fish and lead accumulation in carrots grown in fields that previously were orchards treated with lead-based pesticides. Assessment of the growing region prior to use can help to avoid these hazards.

Heavy metals may also leach from equipment if suitable materials are not used, especially for food contact equipment. GMPs require that food contact surfaces be made of suitable, non-toxic material.

Drug Residues

Drug Residues

- Drugs are important for animal health but require management for safety and effectiveness
- Premarket approval is required and limited to specific uses
- Compliance with U.S. regulatory requirements is high but evaluation should consider potential occurrence in relevant products such as milk

FSPCA

Drugs are an important part of animal health, welfare and management, but may present a chemical hazard when not managed appropriately. The presence of inappropriate drug residues in food may cause short term effects on consumers, allergic reactions or chronic toxic effects.

Animal drugs require premarket approval before they may be legally used. Drug residues (e.g., antibiotics administered to dairy cows) present in food derived from an animal (such as milk) can be a hazard if a tolerance has not been established for the food, or if such a tolerance is exceeded. If drug residues are identified as a hazard requiring a preventive control in the hazard analysis, the application of a supply-chain program would be considered as a preventive control.

Radiological Hazards

Radiological Hazards

- A type of chemical hazard
- Potential sources:
  - Contaminated soil, water or air
  - Ingredients with radionuclides
  - Packaging materials
- Examples include strontium-96, iodine-131 and cesium-137

FSPCA

Frequently a certificate can be obtained from a municipal water supplier that demonstrates compliance of water to EPA standards for radionuclides.

Radiological hazards are rarely encountered in food; however, when they do occur, radiological hazards can present a risk. According to the World Health Organization, radiological hazards in food would have to be consumed over a period of time to present a risk (see additional reading). Examples of radiological hazards include radionuclides such as radium-226, radium-228, uranium-235, uranium-238, plutonium-239, strontium-96, iodine-131 and cesium-137. The most common way these radionuclides are incorporated into foods is through use of water that contains a radionuclide during food production or manufacture. For example, in certain locations in the U.S. high concentrations of radium-226, radium-228 and uranium have been detected in private wells. This should be considered in the hazard analysis in these regions but would not be applicable in most regions.

Radiological hazards also may result from accidental contamination, such as contamination arising from accidental release from a nuclear facility or damage to a nuclear facility from a natural disaster. In 2011, radioactivity was detected in milk, vegetables and seafood produced in areas neighboring a nuclear power plant damaged during an earthquake and tsunami in Japan.

Potential Controls for Chemical Hazards

Chemical Hazards Potential Controls

*   Supply-chain controls
    *   Relevant to almost all chemical hazards
*   Sanitation controls
    *   Relevant to allergens
*   Allergen controls
    *   Relevant to allergens
*   Process controls
    *   Relevant to chemicals used in formulation

FSPCA
FOOD SAFETY PREVENTIVE CONTROLS ALLIANCE

Many chemical hazards can be effectively managed through GMPs and other prerequisite programs. The hazard analysis process determines the chemical hazards requiring a preventive control. Understanding where your ingredients come from and assuring that your supplier has appropriate controls in place to manage chemical hazards is the first step in managing such hazards. This may require a supply-chain program as a preventive control. FDA guidance is available for known chemical hazards in the market place. Your suppliers must comply with regulatory limits. Sanitation preventive controls can be an important preventive control for allergens if you produce products with different allergen profiles. Allergen labeling, of course, is an important and required allergen control if any of your ingredients or raw materials contain food allergens (see Chapter 10: Allergen Preventive Controls). Process preventive controls may be relevant to certain potential chemical hazards depending on the nature of your product.

Chemical Hazards Summary

> ## Chemical Hazards Summary
>
> - Chemical hazards may include those that:
>   - Occur naturally
>   - Are used in formulation
>   - Are unintentionally or incidentally present
> - FDA approval considers specific use and long-term and short-term effects
> - Supply-chain, sanitation, allergen and process preventive controls may be required to control hazards identified through hazard analysis
>
>

Chemical hazards can enter food as naturally occurring substances, as ingredients or raw materials that are used in the formulation, and as unintentionally or incidentally present substances. The allowable levels, if any, are established by FDA (or EPA for pesticides), which also provides guidance on potential controls for many chemical substances. A supply-chain program may play a key role in managing chemical hazard risks. Sanitation, allergen and process preventive controls may also be important controls, depending on your product and process and results of your hazard analysis.

Physical Hazards

> ## Physical Hazards
>
> - Foreign objects
>   - Glass and brittle plastic
>   - Cuts, choking; may require surgery
>   - Metal
>   - Cuts, broken teeth; may require surgery
>   - Wood and stones
> - Choking hazards for young children
>
>

Foreign Objects

Physical hazards include any potentially harmful extraneous matter not normally found in food. Depending on the size and shape of the object, it may cause choking, injury in the mouth or other adverse health effects. FDA's Health Hazard Evaluation Board has supported regulatory action against products with hard, sharp and pointed fragments of 0.3 inches (7 mm) to 1.0 inches (25 mm) in length (see FDA 2005 in Additional Reading). Keep in mind that not all foreign objects found in food during food processing or holding present a true food safety risk. Objects like string and paper, for example, may occur but are unlikely to present a threat to health in most situations. The Food Safety Team should address in their Food Safety Plan only those hazards that are reasonably likely to cause injury.

Glass Hazards

Glass fragments can cause injury to the consumer. Glass inclusion can occur whenever processing involves the use of glass containers. Normal handling and packaging methods, especially mechanized methods, can result in breakage. Glass fragments originating from other sources must be addressed, e.g., through GMPs, and many facilities that do not pack in glass prohibit the presence of glass in the production environment to reduce the risk of glass getting into the product.

Plastic

Plastic is frequently used as a substitute for glass or wood in food handling areas. In selecting the plastic material, use of less brittle material will reduce the need to consider plastic as a true risk to human health. Loose plastic may also be a potential choking hazard.

Metal Hazards

Metal-to-metal contact in equipment can introduce metal fragments into products. Examples include mechanical cutting and blending operations and equipment that has parts that can break or fall off, such as wire-mesh belts or screens. Fine metal shavings may not present a hazard but hard and sharp fragments of the size noted above are a hazard to consumers. This hazard can be controlled by subjecting the product to metal detection devices or by regular inspection of at-risk equipment for signs of damage.

Stones

Certain ingredients, especially those of plant origin, may occasionally have stones present in the raw material. Depending on the size and shape of the stones, they may present a hazard for dental injury or choking. Stones are frequently heavier than the ingredient material, thus washing steps, flotation, riffle tanks and similar steps can remove stones from a process. The Food Safety Team should assess the frequency of observation of stones from their source of supply to determine if they present a hazard requiring a preventive control.

> FDA has taken action against physical hazards that are hard, sharp and pointed and 0.3 inches (7 mm) to 1.0 inches (25 mm) in length.

Wood

Like other potential physical hazards, wood can present a potential choking hazard and less commonly a potential hazard for cuts in the mouth in certain situations. The hazard of cuts depends on sharpness of the edges of the wood, which may not be an issue in a moist food product. Many facilities avoid the need to consider wood as a hazard by limiting or prohibiting the presence of wood in areas where food is exposed. Others may consider history of complaints to determine if a true health hazard exists.

Choking Hazards for Young Children

The American Academy of Pediatrics article on "Prevention of Choking Among Children" provides background information on reducing this hazard for food products. See Additional Reading.

Choking Hazards for Young Children

- Small windpipe, underdeveloped swallowing and chewing increase choking risk
- Cylindrical and compressible foods present greatest risk
- No standards for foods but "small-parts test fixture" used for toys

Image from National Cancer Institute

Section A-A
Image from Consumer Products Safety Commission

FSPCA

Choking occurs when a person cannot breathe because an object blocks the airway (windpipe, esophagus). The potential for a choking hazard is a consideration for foods that are specifically targeted to young children because of their smaller windpipe, and because of their swallowing mechanism and ability to chew are less developed than that of an adult. Foods that are frequently associated with choking in children include those that have a cylindrical shape and can be compressed, which allows them to wedge in a child's throat. Foods that present a high risk for a child's choking hazard include hotdogs and similar sausages, round candy, whole grapes, nuts/peanuts/seeds, raw carrots, apples, popcorn, chunks of peanut butter, marshmallows and chewing gum.

While standards related to choking hazards for foods intended for children do not exist, the Consumer Products Safety Commission has standards for children's toys, including a small-parts test fixture (SPTF) that is used to assess whether a piece size presents a potential choking hazard for young children. This device, pictured in the figure above, may potentially be useful to evaluate foods. If the product fits into the cylinder, it may be a choking hazard for young children.

Manufacturers designing food *specifically* for young children may wish to consider this to evaluate whether the food represents a risk and redesign the product if this is the case.

Economically Motivated Hazards

Economically Motivated Hazards

- Limited to hazards with a pattern of economically motivated adulteration in the past
- Include only those agents that can cause illness or injury
- When a preventive control is needed, a supply-chain program is typical

While it is a rare occurrence, hazards may be introduced into food for the purposes of economic gain. Economically motivated adulteration that affects product integrity or quality, but not food safety, should not be addressed in a Food Safety Plan. The *Preventive Controls for Human Food* regulation only requires consideration of hazards in ingredients with a pattern of economically motivated adulteration in the past. A Congressional Research Service (2013) report provides information on economically motivated adulteration of food and food ingredients. Everstine et al. (2014) identified 137 unique incidents in 11 food categories (See Additional Reading).

An example of a widespread incident of economically motivated adulteration occurred in China, where melamine, a nitrogen-rich industrial by-product, was added to diluted dairy products by some milk firms to increase the apparent protein content. This resulted in more than 290,000 ill infants and 6 deaths in that country. In light of this incident, the potential for melamine to be an economically motivated adulterant in milk products from a country where melamine adulteration has occurred is prudent. Conversely, since none of this adulterated milk was exported to the U.S. and no U.S. suppliers have been a source of food safety problems due to milk products adulterated for economic gain, FDA does not expect a facility to consider the potential for melamine to be an economically motivated hazard when using domestic milk products, or milk products from other countries with no history of melamine adulteration.

Another example of economically motivated adulteration is addition of dyes containing lead to ingredients such as spices or candy to enhance color. Lead can accumulate in the body over time and cause health problems such as impaired cognitive development in children. Lead chromate, a chemical with a vibrant yellow color, has been an adulterant in turmeric to change the color (FDA 2013). Lead oxide, a red chemical, was an adulterant in paprika to enhance its color; resulting in dozens of illnesses and several deaths in Hungary (Anon. 1995). Sudan I, an orange-red powder, used to be added to chili powder as a coloring agent, but is now banned in many countries because it is classified as a category 3 carcinogen (see IARC 2014). Contamination of an ingredient prepared using chili powder containing Sudan I led to a massive recall of food products in the United Kingdom (UK Food Standards Agency 2005).

Economically motivated hazards are typically managed through the facility's supply-chain program. Remember, you only need to focus on economic adulteration that has a history of resulting in a hazard in food.

Summary of Hazards

Chemical, Physical and Economically Motivated Hazards Summary

- Chemical (including radiological) and physical hazards may occur in foods
- Hazards, if not prevented and controlled, may seriously affect food safety
- Companies must know about hazards that may be in their products
- Preventive controls for hazards requiring them must be documented in the Food Safety Plan

Chemical (including radiological) and physical hazards can present a food safety risk if not controlled. The severity of the risk can depend on a number of factors, including the consequence of exposure and frequency that the hazard is. Preventive controls must be designed, documented and implemented for all food safety hazards requiring a preventive control. Because there are many potential hazards that could be considered in the production of food, it is important to identify those that are of such importance that they must be managed using preventive controls to ensure that you will be able to focus resources on these hazards every time. The hazard analysis process is an important step to identify those hazards requiring a preventive control. This is addressed in Chapter 8: Hazard Analysis and Preventive Control Determination.

Additional Reading

The preamble to the final regulation, as well as the proposed and supplemental regulation may provide additional information on economically motivated hazards in human food. Additional reading on other topics is below, and links for many of these articles are available on the FSPCA website.

American Academy of Pediatrics. 2010. Policy Statement – Prevention of Choking Among Children. Pediatrics 125(3):601-607.

Anon. 1995. Adulteration of paprika in Hungary. LEAD Action News 3(3).

Congressional Research Service. 2014. "Food fraud and "economically motivated adulteration" of food and food ingredients, January 10, 2014

Everstine, K., J. Spink, S. Kennedy. 2013. Economically motivated adulteration (EMA) of food: common characteristics of EMA Incidents, J Food Protection 76:723-735.

FDA. 2000. Guidance for Industry: Action Levels for Poisonous or Deleterious Substances in Human Food and Animal Feed.

FDA. 2004. Guidance for Industry: Juice HACCP Hazards and Controls Guidance 1st Edition; Final Guidance.

FDA. 2005. Foods - Adulteration Involving Hard or Sharp Foreign Objects. Compliance Policy Guidelines 555.425.

FDA. 2006a Guidance for Industry: Questions and Answers Regarding Food Allergens, including the Food Allergen Labeling and Consumer Protection Act of 2004 (Edition 4); Final Guidance

FDA. 2006b. Supporting document for recommended maximum level for lead in candy likely to be consumed frequently by small children, November, 2006.

FDA. 2013. Best Value, Inc., Recalls PRAN Brand turmeric powder due to elevated levels of lead. October 16, 2013.

FDA. 2014. Chemical Contaminants

FDA. 2014. Dairy Grade A Voluntary HACCP.

FDA. 2014. Reportable Foods Registry.

Gendel, S.M. and J. Zhu. 2013. Analysis of U.S. Food and Drug Administration food allergen recalls after implementation of the Food Allergen Labeling and Consumer Protection Act. J Food Protection 76(11):1933-1938.

IARC (International Agency for Research on Cancer). 2014. Agents classified by the IARC Monographs, Volumes 1-109," January 14, 2014.

Milani, J. and G. Maleki. 2014. Effects of processing on mycotoxin stability in cereals. J. Sci. Food Agr. 94:2372-2375.

Stratton J.E., RW Hutkins SL. Taylor 1991. Biogenic amines in cheese and other fermented foods: a review. J. Food Protection 54(6):460-470.

U.K. Food Standards Agency. 2005. Sudan I timeline, February 24, 2005.

World Health Organization. 2011. FAQs: Japan nuclear concerns.

NOTES:

CHAPTER 6.   Preliminary Steps in Developing a Food Safety Plan

Before building a Food Safety Plan, organizing information is important. These preliminary steps involve gathering information about the products, processes and facility operations to build a complete picture of the facility. This information is needed to identify potential hazards and preventive control measures when developing a Food Safety Plan.

These preliminary steps are not required by the *Preventive Controls for Human Food* regulation, but the information is needed to provide a sound basis for applying preventive controls principles in developing a Food Safety Plan. They are also consistent with U.S. and internationally recognized principles for developing prevention-based food safety controls. A discussion of each of the five preliminary steps follows, with examples to illustrate the process.

1. Assemble the Food Safety Team

Preliminary Task #1:

Assemble the Food Safety Team

- Management commitment to resources
  - Supports realistic and executable plan
- Team approach:
  - Reduces risk of missing key food safety considerations
  - Encourages ownership of the plan
- Individuals with different specialties and experiences
  - Provides knowledge of daily operations
  - QA, production, sanitation, maintenance, etc. as applicable
- "Preventive controls qualified individual" required
  - Someone within the firm and/or an outside expert
  - Successfully completed training or otherwise qualified

Definition:

Preventive controls qualified individual: A qualified individual who has successfully completed training in the development and application of risk-based preventive controls at least equivalent to that received under a standardized curriculum recognized as adequate by FDA or is otherwise qualified through job experience to develop and apply a food safety system.

Assembling a food safety team is an important step in building a Food Safety Plan. Management commitment is extremely important to ensure that resources dedicated to this effort are appropriate. Effective food safety management not only protects the food; it also protects the business from the risk of a food safety incident or a regulatory non-compliance issue. To develop and implement an effective Food Safety Plan, a budget, resources, and support for change management, potential changes in equipment, new procedures etc. may be required. Without firm management commitment at all levels, it may be difficult to implement an effective Food Safety Plan. Top management commitment to food safety sends a strong message to all personnel that the food safety system is vitally important to the company.

Although one person may be able to analyze hazards and develop a Food Safety Plan successfully, many companies find it helpful to build a food safety team. When only one person develops the Food Safety Plan, some key points can be missed or misunderstood in the process. The team approach minimizes the risk of missing key points or misunderstanding aspects of the operation. It also encourages ownership of the plan, builds company involvement and brings in different areas of expertise. At least one member of the food safety team should be a *preventive controls qualified individual*, who has successfully completed this FDA recognized food safety training curriculum or is otherwise qualified through job experience to develop a Food Safety Plan. The preventive controls qualified individual does not have to be an employee of the facility, but it is beneficial for a facility to have at least one preventive controls qualified individual on staff.

The team should consist of individuals with different specialties and experience with the facility's processes and procedures. The food safety team should include members who are directly involved with the plant's daily operations, and may include personnel from maintenance, production (including equipment experts), sanitation, quality assurance, engineering, purchasing and laboratory, if applicable. These individuals develop the Food Safety Plan under the oversight of a preventive controls qualified individual, and verify ongoing implementation of the food safety system. The team members should be knowledgeable about food safety hazards and food safety principles. When issues arise that cannot be resolved internally, it may be necessary to enlist outside expertise. In small companies, the responsibility for writing the Food Safety Plan may fall to one person. If it is possible to build a food safety team in a small company, employees knowledgeable of various functions, including owners, should be members of the food safety team. Universities, cooperative extension, consulting groups and trade associations can provide additional assistance through model plans, published guidance and, in some cases, personal assistance.

In addition to writing and developing the Food Safety Plan, the food safety team provides oversight of the implementation of the plan in the daily operations of the facility. This includes ensuring that appropriate people are trained to handle their required duties.

6-3

Example

This is from the Food Safety Plan on page A3-3.

E.G. Food Company Example

E.G. Food Company is a fictitious enterprise used as an example throughout this course.

Company Overview
E.G. Food Company's ~150 employees produce egg-based products, including plain omelets, cheese omelets and cheese omelet biscuits. Product is made 5 days a week in one 8 hour production shift, followed by 4 hours for sanitation. Cleaning and sanitizing of all processing equipment is conducted per a master sanitation schedule, which also includes cleaning and sanitizing between different products if needed for allergen control. Municipal water, which is treated and tested per EPA requirements by the city, is used throughout the facility. The company practices hygienic zoning to prevent cooked product exposure to environmental pathogens and employees working in the high hygiene areas wear color coded smocks and dedicated footwear. These employees are instructed on proper hand washing procedures, glove use, and importance of zoning.

Throughout the class a fictional frozen omelet manufacturer, the E.G. Food Company, is used to provide an example. The above is a description of this fictitious company, with some information about how the organization operates. This description helps you visualize the operation.

E.G. Food Company Example

Food Safety Team

Name	Position	Applicable Training (Records are in personnel file)
I.N. Charge	Plant Manager	In plant training
F.S. Leader*	QA Manager	FSPCA class
E.F. Ency	Production Supervisor	In plant training
I.M. Clean	Sanitation Supervisor	In plant training
P.H. Books*	Consultant, PH Books Consulting Service	M.S. & Ph.D. in Food Science and FSPCA lead instructor

*Preventive controls qualified individual

E.G. Food Company's food safety team consists of four employees – the plant manager, the quality assurance manager, the production supervisor and the sanitation supervisor. All have undergone food safety training and use references such as FDA guidance documents. Additionally, they use an external food safety consultant to assist with development of the Food Safety Plan, annual review and, as needed, for changes. They also use recommendations from their chemical supplier on appropriate cleaning and sanitation compounds and procedures for their sanitation controls. A description of their food safety team in their Food Safety Plan is above. This is optional. Appendix 3: Food Safety Plan Example contains the full Food Safety Plan, which will be used for examples throughout the course.

2. Describe the Product and Its Distribution

Preliminary Task #2:
Describe the Product and Its Distribution

- The Product Description should include:
  - The product names(s)
  - Important food safety characteristics of the product, if any (e.g., pH, a_w, preservatives)
  - Ingredients
  - Packaging type
  - Shelf life
  - Storage and distribution

FSPCA

Understanding basic information about a product and how it is distributed is needed to determine if specific controls are important to ensure the safety of the product throughout the distribution cycle. The food safety team should describe the product(s), the type of packaging, shelf life expectations, and the method of storage and distribution. Information on factors that can influence growth of pathogens (e.g., pH, water activity, preservatives, if any) is useful for products that have intrinsic properties that control potential growth of bacteria. It is important to understand these elements to identify the potential food safety hazards that need to be addressed by preventive controls.

A Product Description form has been developed to help record this information and is located in Appendix 2 for your review and use. Other formats may be used, rows may be deleted and a simple paragraph format is also acceptable. The *Preventive Controls for Human Food* regulation does not mandate capturing this information or the format; however, the information contained in this form can be useful to provide an overview of the product to an independent auditor (e.g., when an audit is required by a customer) or a food safety consultant who is helping you to develop a Food Safety Plan. The information may also be useful in the event that a recall is needed. FDA guidance on recall submission recommends providing product information such as the product name (and number) and description such as the form, intended use, expected shelf life (if perishable) and

Elements of the product description and distribution, as well as the information on consumers and intended use (discussed in the next section) are listed in a table on page 6-8.

the type of packaging (See Chapter 15: Recall Plan for more information).

3. Describe the Intended Use and Consumers of the Food

Preliminary Task #3:
Describe the Intended Use and Consumers

- This may be combined with product description information and should include:
  - Intended use and reasonably foreseeable unintended use
  - Intended consumers (e.g., general public, infants, elderly)
  - Labeling instructions relevant to food safety

Intended use of the product refers to its anticipated use by end-users (e.g., other food processors, consumers etc.). Most foods are likely to be intended for the general public. The food safety team should consider these questions.

1) What is the intended use of the product? (e.g., retail, food service, further processing)
2) What is the potential for mishandling and unintended use?
3) What handling and preparation procedures are required of the end users? For example, is the product ready-to-eat, or does it require further preparation such as reheating, cooking etc.?
4) Who are the intended consumers of the product?
5) Is the product intended specifically for use by immune-compromised individuals or other susceptible groups?

Answering these questions provides valuable information for the food safety team as they proceed to the hazard analysis (see Chapter 8: Hazard Analysis and Preventive Controls Determination).

At-risk Populations

- These groups are more susceptible to foodborne illness:
  - Infants and young children
  - Elderly persons
  - Pregnant women
  - Immune-suppressed persons
- Additional controls may be necessary if your product is designed specifically for these populations, e.g.,
  - Infant formula
  - Special diets for medical settings
  - Foods prepared for nursing homes
  - Foods targeted toward young children

The intended consumers may be the general public or a particular segment of the population that is more sensitive to certain hazards. These at-risk groups include:

- *Infants and young children* – Infants and young children do not have a fully developed immune system and are more likely to develop certain types of foodborne illnesses such as infections by bacterial pathogens. Choking hazards from the food itself or packaging material (e.g., small caps) may also be a concern for this group.

- *Elderly persons* – As people age, their immune systems naturally weaken. Elderly persons tend to be more susceptible to infections by foodborne bacterial pathogens than the general population, and illnesses may also be more severe.

- *Pregnant women* – Some pathogens, such as *Listeria monocytogenes* and *Toxoplasma gondii*, are particularly harmful to the developing fetus. Foods targeted specifically toward pregnant women should control potential sources of these pathogens.

- *Immune-suppressed persons* – Other factors can weaken the immune system. For example, persons who are HIV positive, have had organ transplants, are undergoing cancer chemotherapy or have taken other immunosuppressive drug therapies are particularly susceptible to developing illnesses caused by foodborne pathogens. As modern medical treatments improve, it is important to consider that a relatively large percentage of the population fits in this category.

While food targeted to the general population may be consumed by these vulnerable groups, food specifically designed for susceptible

A downloadable Product Description template is available on the FSPCA website.

populations (e.g., for hospitals, nursing homes) may require more stringent controls because most of these food will be consumed by an at-risk population.

The Product Description, Distribution, Consumers and Intended Use form described below and located in Appendix 2 can be used to record this information. This information is important to assure an accurate hazard analysis, but is not required in the rule.

Elements of a Complete Product Description and Intended Use Form

Product name(s)	May include more than one product with similar processing and hazard profile
Product description, including important food safety characteristics	A general description of the product and processing method, assembly, and family of products included in the category. If it is relevant to product safety, intrinsic properties like preservatives, water activity and pH should be listed here.
Ingredients	A simple listing of ingredients, which may be grouped or transferred from the product label, if this is convenient. This could also be an attachment (a list or a recipe) or reference ingredient specification numbers, which would provide more detailed information.
Packaging used	A general description of the packaging, including modified atmosphere or vacuum packaging, if used. This may impact the hazards of concern.
Intended use	Describe the normal expected use of the food (e.g., ready-to-eat, ready-to-cook, raw), and if useful, where it is sold (e.g., retail, foodservice, schools, long term care facilities etc.). May describe a complex distribution system if desired; e.g., frozen distribution with refrigerated or ambient display; use for further processing, etc. If unintended use or abuse is likely to occur (e.g., eating raw cookie dough) this should be identified.
Shelf life	List intended shelf life, if relevant to potential microbial growth.
Labeling instructions	Include label instructions relevant to food safety. This may include refrigeration, cooking instructions etc., if relevant.
Storage and distribution	List the method of distribution, e.g., refrigerated, frozen, ambient.

Product Description Example

PRODUCT(S) Omelet – Plain, Cheese and Cheese Biscuit			PAGE X of Y
PLANT NAME: E.G. Food Company		ISSUE DATE	09/20/2015
ADDRESS: 360 Culinary Circle, Mytown, USA		SUPERSEDES	08/06/2015
Product Description, Distribution, Consumers and Intended Use			
Product Name(s)	**Omelet – Plain, Cheese and Cheese Biscuit**		
Product Description, including Important Food Safety Characteristics	Frozen, cooked egg omelet, with or without cheese filling and a wheat biscuit bun pH 7.1 - 7.9, water activity >0.98, no preservatives		
Ingredients	Plain: Eggs, milk, pan release oil, salt Cheese: Eggs, milk, cheese, pan release oil, salt Cheese Biscuit: Eggs, milk, cheese, biscuit, pan release oil, salt		
Packaging Used	Paperboard trays wrapped with plastic wrap and inserted in a corrugated case.		
Intended Use	The product is considered ready-to-eat, but is typically heated to hot holding temperatures (135°F (57°C)) or above for palatability. Heating is typically conducted using microwaves, convection oven, or induction. End user may thaw at refrigeration temperatures overnight to reduce cooking time. End users may also add toppings or fillings. *Potential abuse: Some establishments may hold thawed product for longer than the recommended 24 hours.*		
Intended Consumers	General public		
Shelf Life	1 year frozen		
Labeling Instructions	Keep frozen or thaw under refrigeration (<41°F (5°C)) for <24 hours before cooking.		
Storage and Distribution	Frozen		
Approved: Signature: F.S. Leader Print name: F.S. Leader	Date: April 11, 2015	**E.G. Food Company Example**	FSPCA

See example in Appendix 3, page 4

Above is an example of a product description that will be used to illustrate the progressive development of a Food Safety Plan for omelet products produced by the fictitious E.G. Food Company. Note that in this example, the potential for abuse is identified in the "Intended Use" section.

4. Develop a Flow Diagram and Describe the Process

Preliminary Task #4:
Develop a Flow Diagram and Describe the Process

- Flow diagram is an important tool to describe the process
- Include all the process steps within the facility's control
- Include reworked product, by-product and diverted product, if applicable
- Develop a written description for each step in the flow diagram

FSPCA

A flow diagram provides an important visual tool that the food safety team can use to describe the process. When developing a process flow diagram, it is important to include all the process steps within the facility's control, from receiving through final product storage, including rework and diverted by-product, if applicable. Each process step should be considered in detail and the information expanded to include all relevant process information. Information may include:

- All ingredients and packaging used
- Where raw materials, ingredients and intermediate products enter the flow
- The sequence and interaction of all steps in the operation
- Where product reworking and recycling take place in the process
- Where product is diverted to waste, if applicable.

The flow diagram for the E.G. Food Company Omelet example appears below.

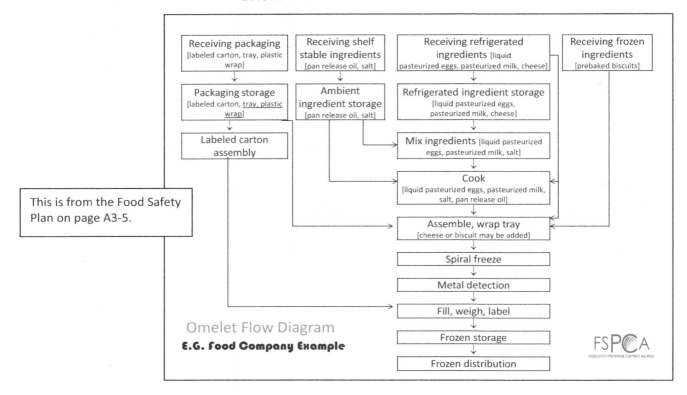

This is from the Food Safety Plan on page A3-5.

Omelet Flow Diagram
E.G. Food Company Example

E.G. Food Company Example

Process Description – Plain, Cheese and Cheese Biscuit Omelet

Receiving Ingredients and Packaging:
Ingredients and raw materials are purchased from reputable suppliers that comply with internationally recognized food safety and quality systems. For each ingredient, the same brand is used consistently to minimize variation. Ingredients are stored according to manufacturers' recommendations when specified.

Receiving packaging: Corrugated shippers, paperboard trays and plastic wrap are received in bulk. Specifications require food grade material for trays and plastic wrap that is compatible with frozen storage of food products.

Receiving shelf stable ingredients:
Salt: Received in 10-pound bags from our distributor. Specifications require food grade salt.
Pan release oil: The pan release oil contains soybean oil, soy lecithin and natural flavor. It is received from our distributor in 10-gallon jugs.

See Appendix 3: Food Safety Plan for full information

A written process description is also useful to explain what happens at each of the process steps and can contain more detail than the flow diagram. This description can be used as a working reference for the development of the Food Safety Plan. You may already have other documents that contain similar information, such as product specifications, recipes or work instructions that can be used in place of the description illustrated in this chapter.

It is important to know what occurs at each process step. For example, information such as the maximum length of time that the product could be exposed to unrefrigerated temperatures, the maximum room air temperature or the internal product temperature after a process may impact food safety, thus it is important to know for an accurate hazard analysis.

The beginning of the process description from the E.G. Food Company example appears above. See Appendix 3: Food Safety Plan for the full process description.

5. Verify the Flow Diagram

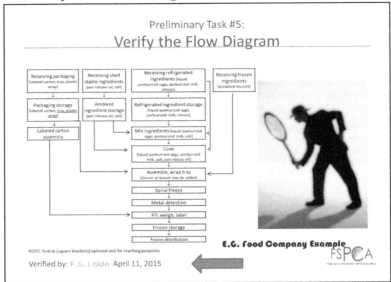

The steps in the flow diagram are used to organize the hazard analysis, which is discussed in Chapter 8: Hazard Analysis and Preventive Controls Determination. Since the accuracy of the process flow is critical to conduct a hazard analysis, the steps outlined in the chart must be verified at the plant. If a step is missed, a food safety hazard requiring a preventive control may be missed. Include every handling, processing and holding step for the product, as well as ingredients and packaging. The food safety team should walk through the facility and make any changes required in the flow diagram. At the same time, the team should make observations related to sanitation, potential for cross-contamination or allergen cross-contact, and potential harborages or introduction points for environmental pathogens. The walk-through allows each team member to gain an overall picture of how the product is made. It may be helpful to invite additional plant personnel to review the diagram during the walk-through. Many times operators can identify issues that may be overlooked by management or the food safety team. The complete, verified flow diagram should be retained and periodically evaluated as a food safety record and part of the Food Safety Plan. A signature is usually used to indicate that the flow diagram has been verified.

Food Safety Plans are dynamic and must be updated to reflect any changes in process or food safety considerations. Therefore, any significant changes to the process must be accurately reflected in the product flow diagram, and the Food Safety Team must evaluate if these changes have an impact on the hazard analysis and preventive controls in place.

Preliminary Steps Summary

Preliminary Steps Summary

Activity	Outcome
1. Assemble the food safety team	Management commitment for resources and training
2. Describe the product and its distribution	Information for hazard analysis
3. Describe the intended use and consumers of the food	
4. Develop a flow diagram and describe the process	Organizing framework for hazard analysis
5. Verify the flow diagram	Essential to assure accuracy

FSPCA
FOOD SAFETY PREVENTIVE CONTROLS ALLIANCE

It is important to have the right people in place, and information available on the ingredients, packaging and processes used before applying preventive controls principles to develop a Food Safety Plan. Preliminary steps include:

1) assembling the food safety team and ensuring that they have management commitment and adequate training to perform an accurate assessment of the food safety hazards that exist for the products being produced,

2) preparing an accurate description of the product and its distribution to understand the characteristics of the product and ensure that potential hazards are not overlooked,

3) identifying the intended use and consumers to ensure that preventive controls used will protect the safety of consumers during intended use and acknowledge potential misuse of the product,

4) creating a process flow diagram that provides the organizational framework for conducting the hazard analysis, which identifies preventive controls to prevent food safety risks for the consuming public, and

5) Verifying the flow diagram and operational conditions to avoid overlooking sources of potential hazards.

If a facility produces more than one product and several Food Safety Plans are needed, it is recommended that the food safety team keep its task simple by only attempting to develop one plan at a time. The team could have the first plan reviewed by a third party before addressing additional plans. This can help to ensure they correctly identify the hazards requiring preventive controls.

Additional Reading

FAO/WHO. 2003. Hazard Analysis and Critical Control Point (HACCP) System and Guidelines for Its Application Annex to CAC/RCP 1-1969, Rev. 4 - 2003

FDA. 2014. Dairy Grade A Voluntary HACCP

National Advisory Committee on Microbiological Criteria for Foods. 1998. Hazard Analysis and Critical Control Point Principles and Application Guidelines. *Journal of Food Protection* 61(9):1246-1259.

CHAPTER 7.   Resources for Preparing Food Safety Plans

Resources for Preparing Food Safety Plans
Objective

In this module, you will learn:

- Information sources to help identify food safety hazards and establish preventive controls
- FDA guidance for hazard analysis and preventive controls

A successful Food Safety Plan identifies hazards requiring a preventive controls and procedures to control them to ensure that the food produced is safe to eat. The first part of this chapter introduces numerous resources that can assist in developing and modifying a Food Safety Plan. The second part provides information on FDA guidance to help you to conduct your hazard analysis and develop a Food Safety Plan.

The FSPCA website maintains a current list of resource material. Please consult this website for the latest information.

Sources of Information

- Personnel
- Publications
- Reliable internet sites
- FDA guidance documents

Before implementing a food safety system, you need to perform a hazard analysis to determine which hazards require a preventive control for your products. To conduct a hazard analysis and develop a Food Safety Plan, gather information from a variety of credible sources and use the information that best applies to your situation. Some of the most useful sources of information are described in this chapter. Sources of information include people, publications, reliable internet sites, miscellaneous agencies and the FDA.

Personnel

Sources of Information - Personnel

- Your employees
- Consultants and auditors
- Process authorities and subject matter experts
- University specialists
- Government agencies
- Trade associations
- Suppliers, buyers and laboratory analysts

FSPCA

Your Employees

You and your employees know your operation better than anyone. Experience is an excellent source of information. You may already have knowledge about hazards that can affect your product, and you may already have preventive controls implemented to control those hazards.

In addition to being a source of information, your employees are essential for implementing the plan. This includes everyone, including senior management (who must demonstrate commitment to effective development, implementation and ongoing maintenance of the Food Safety Plan).

Consultants and Auditors

Food safety consultants, firms and auditors with expertise in the *Preventive Controls for Human Food* regulation can be a useful resource. Consultants may be helpful in developing and reviewing your Food Safety Plan, particularly if you are just starting a new company or need expertise beyond your company's abilities in complying with the regulation, sanitation, sampling, etc. Auditors that you hire may identify deficiencies or include recommendations for improvement in the report they provide.

Process Authorities and Technical Experts

Some food safety professionals have in-depth expertise related to specific types of foods or processes. These are sometimes called processing authorities. They use scientific methods to determine the proper parameters (e.g., time, temperature, atmosphere, flow rate, a_w, oxygen level, pH etc.) to prevent, eliminate or reduce pathogens to acceptable levels. They are a key source for validating the adequacy of a process to ensure that identified controls will actually work to control a hazard. They can also provide technical advice for developing a Food Safety Plan and implementing appropriate corrective action procedures. The FSPCA Technical Assistance Network is discussed in the upcoming section on Reliable Internet Sites.

University Specialists

Many, but not all, Land Grant universities have specialists in Cooperative Extension programs. These programs provide outreach, education and technical assistance to industry. Food safety extension specialists and agents can assist in identifying potential hazards and control measures, but their availability may be limited in some areas of the country. University research groups that conduct company-specific research projects also exist.

Government Agencies

Federal, state and local agencies may be able to assist you in understanding and meeting regulatory requirements. Some states have a food safety task force that provides training opportunities periodically. Websites and call-in Q&A phone lines that provide useful information from government agencies may also be available. See the discussion in Reliable Internet Sites.

Trade Associations

Trade associations can also provide useful information. Some trade organizations provide services such as consulting, educational programs and publications that can help identify hazards and control measures. While some trade association information is available only to members, others provide technical guidance and resources for sale or in an open format (see Internet Resources section).

Suppliers, Buyers and Laboratory Analysts

Suppliers of ingredients, cleaning materials, processing equipment and packaging materials; and analytical laboratories can provide information on potential hazards and control measures. A buyer's specification may point to a hazard in one of your products. For example, a buyer may require *Salmonella*-free product. It is important to note; however, that not all buyers' specifications relate to safety. Analysts at laboratories familiar with food samples are a good source of information in developing validation studies and sampling programs. In seeking recommendations from laboratories, it is important that the laboratory have experience with food because techniques used in food analysis may differ substantially from those used for clinical or environmental analyses.

Publications

Sources of Information – Publications

- *Hazard Analysis and Preventive Controls for Human Food* training curriculum
- FDA publications
- Peer reviewed literature
- Trade association publications
- References used to develop this curriculum

Publications are one type of information source that you may use in developing your Food Safety Plan. It is important that you use credible publications for this purpose. The slide above lists general sources of credible information, and each type is described below.

FSPCA Basic Course

One of the best and most accessible food safety resources available to develop and modify a preventive-controls-compliant Food Safety Plan is this book provided in the Food Safety Preventive Controls Alliance basic course – the *Hazard Analysis and Preventive Controls for Human Food* training curriculum. This training curriculum covers steps for developing a Food Safety Plan using a model food designed to be consumed by the general public. The chapters cover prerequisite programs; biological, chemical (including radiological) and physical hazards encountered in foods and basic information on how these hazards can be controlled; elements of process, food allergen, sanitation and supply-chain program preventive controls; and the *Preventive Controls for Human Food* regulation.

FDA Publications

FDA's *Bad Bug Book* (see link on the FSPCA website) provides technical information on foodborne pathogens in everyday language. FDA hazards guides for seafood and juice products are available, and a comprehensive *Food Safety Preventive Controls for Human Foods Hazards and Controls Guidance* (*Food Hazards Guide*) is under development. The *Food Hazards Guide* will contain information to 1) help identify potential hazards and determine if they require a preventive control, and 2) select approaches to control the hazards. A discussion FDA's hazard guides is included later in this chapter.

Peer Reviewed Literature

Peer reviewed, scientific literature is another useful source of information for developing a Food Safety Plan. As previously mentioned, appropriate expertise is needed to properly apply information to a specific operation. The search tool Google Scholar may be useful to identify peer reviewed literature.

> Google Scholar is a useful tool to search peer reviewed literature.

Trade Association Publications

Trade associations may be a useful source of information, including model recall plans, generic Food Safety Plans and other information. Trade journals often provide general information on potential hazards and controls. Articles on specific processes or products also can be useful. These trade journals are usually made available to industry at no charge, and many are accessible online. While generic Food Safety Plans may be available for products related to your operations, use these with caution, as your plan should be specific for your particular product and how it is made in your facility.

References Used in Development of Chapters

Many references were used in the development of the material in this training curriculum. Refer to the "Additional Reading" section of chapters for references that may be relevant to your operation.

Reliable Internet Sites

Sources of Information – Internet

- FSPCA website
- FDA website
- Other U.S. agency resources
  - Centers for Disease Control and Prevention
  - FoodSafety.gov
  - U.S. Department of Agriculture
- International agency resources, e.g.,
  - Canadian Food Inspection Agency
  - Codex Alimentarius Commission
  - European Food Safety Authority
- Trade association websites

FSPCA

Information on key food safety hazards and controls is available for free online. **WARNING**: Be sure to use peer reviewed and other credible sources when seeking information on the web to avoid use of inaccurate information! A few websites recommended by FSPCA are discussed below. Because web addresses change and information may be removed if it becomes out of date, check the FSPCA website for updated information and links.

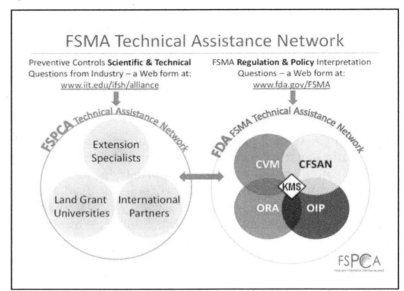

Food Safety Preventive Controls Alliance (FSPCA) Website

FSPCA maintains links to internet resources on its website and provides periodic updates with new sources of information when they are identified. Access to the FSPCA Technical Assistance Network is available through the FSPCA website. The website also provides updates on FSPCA activities and training courses that are available.

Food and Drug Administration (FDA) Website

The FDA website (www.fda.gov) provides quick access to industry guidance, bulletins for health professionals, consumer education materials and other documents and data from FDA's centers and offices. Key FDA web resources include:

- FDA's FSMA Technical Assistance Network, which provides answers to policy interpretation questions
- FDA Guidance for Foods
- FDA Outbreak Investigations
- FDA Recalls, Market Withdrawals and Safety Alerts
- FDA Reportable Food Registry

FDA's FSMA Technical Assistance Network, which provides answers to policy interpretation questions

US Agency Resources

- The **Centers for Disease Control and Prevention** is responsible for characterizing risk factors and prevention strategies for diseases that impact public health. The CDC also assists local health agencies in epidemiological investigations of foodborne illness outbreaks. Certain diseases are reported to the CDC by state epidemiologists. CDC information can provide insight into the outbreaks associated with specific food types. Examples of useful CDC websites for Food Safety Plan development include:

  - Multistate Foodborne Outbreak Investigations – Reports investigations of multistate outbreaks involving food and other sources

  - Foodborne Outbreak Online Database (FOOD) – Searchable database for U.S. outbreaks

  - Attribution of Foodborne Illness – Reports on foods associated with illness

- **FoodSafety.gov** is a gateway to government food safety information, including links to foodborne pathogens, industry assistance and government agencies.

- The **U.S. Department of Agriculture** (USDA) Food Safety Inspection Service (FSIS) provides food safety information and may be a source of information on process controls, studies and prevalence of pathogens in USDA-regulated products. USDA FSIS also has information on recalls that may be on interest for certain product categories.

International Agency Resources

Many agencies around the world provide science-based information on food safety and potential hazards. A few examples are listed below for easy reference. Keep in mind that specific requirements may be different from one country to another, thus information used from these sites may require adjustments to comply with FDA regulations.

- The **Canadian Food Inspection Agency** provides information on food safety for a variety of food categories, including generic HACCP models for several products.

- The **Codex Alimentarius Commission** is sponsored by the Food and Agriculture Organization and the World Health Organization of the United Nations. Its purpose is to facilitate international trade by establishing uniform standards. The commission has developed many standards and guidelines, including recommended international codes of practice for a wide variety of food products.

- The **European Food Safety Authority** (EFSA) provides European food safety information similar to that for the US agencies described above. Look for EFSA foodborne disease monitoring and analysis reports.

Trade Association Websites

- **American Frozen Food Institute** provides food safety information related to frozen products.

- **Grocery Manufacturers Association** provides food safety technical guidance on specific topics on their website to share industry model practices. Some information is available for a fee; other information is available at no charge. Look for resources, research tools and technical guidance and tools information.

- The **Innovation Center for U.S. Dairy** provides science and research information for dairy products.

- The **United Fresh Produce Association** provides food safety information specific to produce.

FDA Hazards and Controls Guidance

FDA Hazards and Controls Guidance

- Currently available
  - *Seafood HACCP Hazards and Controls Guidance*
  - *Juice HACCP Hazards and Controls Guidance*
- In development
  - *Food Safety Preventive Controls for Human Food Hazards and Controls Guidance*

FDA has published hazards and controls guidance for seafood and juice products. These documents represent FDA's current understanding on hazards and controls for these products. FDA is developing *Food Safety Preventive Controls for Human Food Hazards and Controls Guidance (Food Hazards Guide)* for food subject to the preventive controls regulation.

Although the *Food Hazards Guide* was not available when the 1st edition of the FSPCA training launched, select information in the FDA's other hazards guides may be applicable to other food products. For example, chapters from the *Seafood Hazards Guide* that may be useful include:

Chapter 12: Pathogenic bacteria growth and toxin formation (other than *Clostridium botulinum*)

Chapter 13: *Clostridium botulinum* toxin formation

Chapter 14: Pathogenic bacteria growth and toxin formation as a result of inadequate drying

Chapter 15: *Staphylococcus aureus* toxin formation in hydrated batter mixes

Chapter 16: Pathogenic bacteria survival through cooking or pasteurization

Chapter 18: Introduction of Pathogenic Bacteria after Pasteurization and Specialized Cooking Processes

Chapter 19: Undeclared Major Food Allergens and Certain Food Intolerance Causing Substances and Prohibited Food and Color Additives

Chapter 20: Metal Inclusion

Chapter 21: Glass Inclusion

Sections of the *Juice Hazards Guide* may be useful for processors that make fruit or vegetable products, or pack in metal or glass containers. For example, this guide includes discussion of pathogens that may occur in acidic juices (pH ≤4.6) versus those in low-acid juices (pH >4.6), allergens and food intolerance substances added to juice as ingredients, pesticide residues, lead and tin hazards, glass fragments, metal fragments, hazards related to facility sanitation and controls for allergens arising from food contact surfaces.

Keep in mind that the terminology used in both the *Seafood Hazards Guide* and the *Juice Hazards Guide* differs from that used for preventive controls regulation. Because the scientific basis for conducting hazard analysis and determining effective controls for those hazards involves the same process, the information provided can be useful. The recommendations included in FDA Hazards Guides are not, for the most part, binding FDA requirements. Use of the hazards guides in developing Food Safety Plans is not mandatory. Processors and importers are free to choose other control measures that provide an equivalent level of safety assurance than those listed in the guides. There may also be circumstances where a hazard identified in a guide may not apply to a product because of conditions specific to the processor.

Subsequent chapters illustrate how information in the Hazards Guides can be used to make decisions and develop a Food Safety Plan.

Additional Reading
See the FSPCA Website for links to many of the referenced listed in this chapter.

NOTES:

CHAPTER 8. Hazard Analysis and Preventive Controls Determination

<table>
<tr><td>

Hazard Analysis and Preventives Controls
Determination Objectives

In this module, you will learn:
- The definitions of different types of hazards
- Why a hazard analysis is important
- The steps to:
  - Conduct a hazard analysis
  - Identify hazards requiring a preventive control
  - Identify the types of preventive controls that can be used for hazards requiring a preventive control

</td></tr>
</table>

Following the preliminary steps, the next step in developing a Food Safety Plan is to identify the food safety hazards requiring a preventive control. This depends on the food, the ingredients, the equipment, the facility layout and other elements of the facility's food safety system. Once the hazards requiring a preventive control are known, preventive controls can be identified to help ensure the safety of the product. Keep in mind that while many different types of controls may be applied when processing a food, "preventive controls" are risk-based and focus on the hazards that present the greatest risk to food safety. It is important to identify these hazards first to allow resources to focus on the preventive controls that are essential to reduce food safety risks.

The *Preventive Controls for Human Food* regulation includes definitions for several types of hazards. These include:

- *Hazard:* Any biological, chemical (including radiological), or physical agent that has the potential to cause illness or injury.

- *Known or reasonably foreseeable hazard*: A biological, chemical (including radiological), or physical hazard that is known to be, or has the potential to be, associated with the facility or the food.

- *Hazard requiring a preventive control*: A known or reasonably foreseeable hazard for which a person knowledgeable about the safe manufacturing, processing, packing, or holding of food would, based on the outcome of a hazard analysis (which includes an assessment of the severity of the illness or injury if the hazard were to occur and the probability that the hazard will occur in the absence of preventive controls), establish one or more preventive controls to significantly minimize or prevent the hazard in a food and components to manage those controls (such as monitoring, corrections or corrective actions, verification, and records) as appropriate to the food, the facility, and the nature of the preventive control and its role in the facility's food safety system.

The regulation also defines "preventive controls" as follows:

- *Preventive controls:* Those risk-based, reasonably appropriate procedures, practices and processes that a person knowledgeable about the safe manufacturing, processing, packing or holding of food would employ to significantly minimize or prevent the hazards identified under the **hazard analysis** that are consistent with the current scientific understanding of safe food manufacturing, processing, packaging or holding at the time of the analysis.

Importance of a Thorough Hazard Analysis

- Crucial to the success of the overall food safety program
- A proper hazard analysis can:
  - Identify hazards requiring a preventive control
  - Focus resources on essential preventive controls
  - Identify operations that require improvement
- An improper hazard analysis can result in:
  - An ineffective Food Safety Plan
  - An unmanageable Food Safety Plan
  - Potential regulatory action

Conducting a complete and accurate hazard analysis is one of the most difficult but important steps in developing an effective, risk-based Food Safety Plan. Systematic and thorough analysis of potential hazards and their consequences helps to ensure that all hazards requiring a preventive control are identified.

Occasionally a thorough hazard analysis may identify a situation where a newly identified hazard exists and is not being adequately controlled. For example, several years ago scientists demonstrated that *E. coli* O157:H7 tolerated higher levels of acid than other pathogens. Reviewing the hazard analysis for some fermented products suggested that formula or process adjustments were required to ensure that *E. coli* O157:H7 was destroyed.

A proper hazard analysis can also focus limited resources on the most important controls. Improper hazard analysis can result in an ineffective Food Safety Plan if a hazard that must be controlled is overlooked. Conversely, an improper hazard analysis may identify too many controls for hazards that are not reasonably likely to cause illness or injury, which results in a system that cannot be effectively managed by available resources.

Hazard Analysis Definition

- The process of collecting and evaluating information on hazards and conditions leading to their presence to decide which are significant for food safety and therefore must be addressed in the HACCP* or Food Safety Plan.

*a HACCP Plan may be part of Food Safety Plan

FSPCA

For this course, hazard analysis is defined as indicated above. The purpose of the hazard analysis is to develop a list of potential food safety hazards and then determine the hazards requiring a preventive control because they are reasonably likely to cause injury or illness in the absence of control. Once these hazards are identified, then preventive controls that are essential to prevent illness or injury can be determined. Only those hazards that pose a risk to the health of consumers should be included in the Food Safety Plan. Not all potential hazards require a preventive control in an individual operation.

How to Conduct a Hazard Analysis

Process to Identify Hazards and Controls

1. List process steps and ingredients
2. Identify **known or reasonably foreseeable** (i.e., potential) **food safety hazards**
3. Determine if the hazard **requires a preventive control**
   - Severity and probability in the absence of control
4. Justify the decision
5. Identify preventive controls for significant hazards

FSPCA
FOOD SAFETY PREVENTIVE CONTROLS ALLIANCE

A sequence of steps is followed to complete a hazard analysis, and each of the items listed above is discussed in this chapter. The hazard analysis process is based on the information organized in the preliminary steps discussed in Chapter 6: Preliminary Steps in Developing a Food Safety Plan, such as the ingredients and raw materials; activities at each process step; product storage and distribution; and final preparation and use by the consumer. Essentially the information provided through the preliminary steps is a roadmap for conducting the hazard analysis.

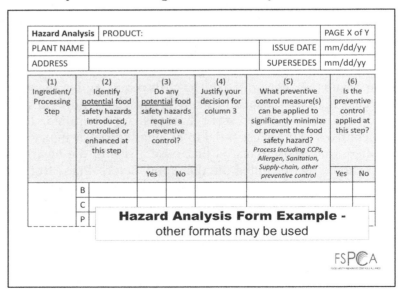

Hazard Analysis		PRODUCT:				PAGE X of Y	
PLANT NAME					ISSUE DATE	mm/dd/yy	
ADDRESS					SUPERSEDES	mm/dd/yy	
(1) Ingredient/ Processing Step	(2) Identify potential food safety hazards introduced, controlled or enhanced at this step	(3) Do any potential food safety hazards require a preventive control?		(4) Justify your decision for column 3	(5) What preventive control measure(s) can be applied to significantly minimize or prevent the food safety hazard? *Process including CCPs, Allergen, Sanitation, Supply-chain, other preventive control*	(6) Is the preventive control applied at this step?	
		Yes	No			Yes	No
	B						
	C						
	P						

Hazard Analysis Form Example - other formats may be used

FSPCA
FOOD SAFETY PREVENTIVE CONTROLS ALLIANCE

A Hazard Analysis Form can be used to ensure that all steps are analyzed and the results are documented. The form also lists the hazards requiring a preventive control and identifies the type of control to be applied. Other formats, including formats that are not form-based (e.g., a written narrative) may be used as long as the hazard analysis is documented and contains the elements of hazard identification, hazard evaluation and preventive controls selection. A justification for decisions should be provided so others can understand the basis for the decisions. In this course:

- Column 1 is used to list each of the process steps from the flow diagram; including the receiving of each raw material or ingredient used in the process (some may be grouped).
- Column 2 (hazard identification) is used to list all raw material-, ingredient-, process-, and environment-related hazards identified for each step. The hazards to consider are discussed below.
- Column 3 is a simple "Yes or No" that states whether the hazard requires a preventive control.
- Column 4 (hazard evaluation) is used to justify your answers in Column 3 (and sometimes in Column 2 if no hazard was identified but the team had a lot of discussion about it).
- Column 5 is used only when there is a "Yes" in Column 3 to identify the preventive controls that significantly minimize or prevent the hazard; e.g., process, allergen, sanitation, supply-chain or other preventive controls.
- Column 6 is used to document if the preventive control will be managed at that step.

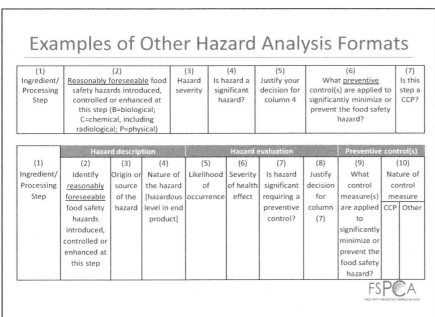

Keep in mind that other formats may be used. The slide above represents two additional formats and others may be used as well. Model plans posted on the FSPCA website illustrate additional formats. Make sure that the format that you use is understood by your

8-5

team in your facility and that it addresses allergen, sanitation, supply-chain and other preventive controls as applicable to the facility and food.

Set Up the Hazard Analysis Form

Column 1 – List Process Steps and Incoming Ingredients and Materials

E.G. Food Company Example

Hazard Analysis	PRODUCT: Omelet – Plain, Cheese and Cheese Biscuit		PAGE X of Y
PLANT NAME	E.G. Food Company	ISSUE DATE	mm/dd/yy
ADDRESS	360 Culinary Circle, Mytown, USA	SUPERSEDES	mm/dd/yy

(1) Ingredient/ Processing Step		(2) Identify potential food safety hazards introduced, controlled or enhanced at this step	(3) Do any potential food safety hazards require a preventive control?		(4) Justify your decision for column 3	(5) What preventive control measure(s) can be applied to significantly minimize or prevent the food safety hazard? *Process including CCPs, Allergen, Sanitation, Supply-chain, other preventive control*	(6) Is the preventive control applied at this step?	
			Yes	No			Yes	No
Other steps above								
Receiving refrigerated ingredients – liquid pasteurized egg	B							
	C							
	P							
Other steps below								

We will use the E.G. Food Company omelet example to illustrate the hazard analysis process and complete a hazard analysis form. Set up the hazard analysis form by entering the firm's name and address, the name of the product or product number(s), the date the analysis is completed and if it is a revision of a previous analysis, the previous date to keep records organized. A separate worksheet may be needed for each product type, but grouping products may be done if the hazards and controls are the same or if any differences are clearly delineated. We have grouped all of E.G. Food Company's omelets in this hazard analysis.

A process flow chart was developed as part of the preliminary steps (Chapter 6). List each of the process steps in Column 1 of the hazard analysis worksheet. This is the framework that guides development of this hazard analysis. One of the first steps from the flow diagram is illustrated in the slide above. The full Hazard Analysis is in Appendix 3: Food Safety Plan Example.

Column 2 – Hazard Identification

E.G. Food Company Example

Hazard Analysis	PRODUCT: Omelet – Plain, Cheese and Cheese Biscuit		PAGE X of Y
PLANT NAME	E.G. Food Company	ISSUE DATE	mm/dd/yyyy
ADDRESS	360 Culinary Circle, Mytown, USA	SUPERSEDES	mm/dd/yyyy

(1) Ingredient/ Processing Step		(2) Identify potential food safety hazards introduced, controlled or enhanced at this step	(3) Do any potential food safety hazards require a preventive control?		(4) Justify your decision for column 3	(5) What preventive control measure(s) can be applied to significantly minimize or prevent the food safety hazard? *Process including CCPs, Allergen, Sanitation, Supply-chain, other preventive control*	(6) Is the preventive control applied at this step?	
			Yes	No			Yes	No
Receiving refrigerated ingredients – liquid pasteurized egg	B	Vegetative pathogens such as *Salmonella*						
	C	Allergen – egg						
	P	None						

The hazard identification is basically a brainstorming exercise where the team generates a list of **potential** ("known or reasonably foreseeable") biological, chemical (including radiological) and physical food safety hazards that may be introduced, increased or controlled at each step described on the product flow diagram developed in Chapter 6: Preliminary Steps in Developing a Food Safety Plan. The process of hazard identification should consider:

- The preliminary information collected while developing the product description.
- Experience within the facility on the likelihood of hazards being present in finished products based on product testing results, consumer complaints or other means. The team may also rely on its knowledge of the facility, including layout, receiving and other processes that can be used to determine where the product is vulnerable to contamination.
- External information, including scientific papers, epidemiological studies and other historical data for similar products, if available.
- Information from the food supply chain on food safety hazards that may be relevant for the end products, intermediate products and the food at the moment of consumption.
- Information from applicable government or industry food safety guidance documents.

Hazard identification considers those potential hazards that may be present in the food because they occur naturally, or hazards that may be unintentionally introduced, or in rare circumstances hazards that may be intentionally introduced for purposes of economic gain.

The U.S. National Advisory Committee on Microbiological Criteria for Foods (NACMCF) report on "Hazard Analysis and Critical Control Point Principles and Application Guidelines" contains a useful set of questions to consider when conducting hazard identification. See Additional Reading.

You may wish to include lines on your form to ensure that each of the three types of potential hazards is considered in the analysis:

- Biological (B) hazards, including bacteria, viruses, parasites, and environmental pathogens
- Chemical (C) hazards, including radiological hazards, food allergens, substances such as pesticides and drug residues, natural toxins, decomposition, and unapproved food or color additives
- Physical (P) hazards, including potentially harmful extraneous matter that may cause choking, injury or other adverse health effects.

These hazard types were discussed in Chapters 4: Biological Food Safety Hazards and 5: Chemical, Physical and Economically Motivated Food Safety Hazards. Assessing the product with respect to each of the hazards in Chapters 4 and 5, as appropriate to the food and your facility, can be one approach to identifying which of them are reasonably foreseeable and thus appropriate for further evaluation to determine if they require a preventive control. The FDA *Hazards Guides* include "potential process-related hazards" tables that list potential hazards that are associated with a variety of finished product forms and package types. When using this table, it is important to review all of the entries to look for the best fit for the product being considered. Note that your product may fit in more than one category.

The *Food Hazards Guide* does not identify all hazards for all processes and is not an exhaustive list. Thus it is recommended that you also perform an on-site assessment and look for information that is not identified in the *Food Hazards Guide* tables. This can help you to avoid overlooking a hazard that could negatively impact product safety.

Columns 3 and 4 – Hazard Evaluation

Hazard Analysis	PRODUCT: Omelet – Plain, Cheese and Cheese Biscuit				PAGE X of Y		
PLANT NAME	E.G. Food Company			ISSUE DATE	mm/dd/yy		
ADDRESS	360 Culinary Circle, Mytown, USA			SUPERSEDES	mm/dd/yy		

E.G. Food Company Example

(1) Ingredient/ Processing Step	(2) Identify potential food safety hazards introduced, controlled or enhanced at this step	(3) Do any potential food safety hazards require a preventive control?		(4) Justify your decision for column 3	(5) What preventive control measure(s) can be applied to significantly minimize or prevent the food safety hazard? *Process including CCPs, Allergen, Sanitation, Supply-chain, other preventive control*	(6) Is the preventive control applied at this step?	
		Yes	No			Yes	No
Receiving refrigerated ingredients – liquid pasteurized egg	B Vegetative pathogens such as *Salmonella*	?	?	?			
	C Allergen – egg	?	?	?			
	P None			?			

Following identification of hazards, the food safety team decides which of the potential hazards identified present a risk to consumers such that it requires preventive controls. This includes consideration of the:

- Severity of the illness or injury and
- Likelihood of occurrence.

Columns 3 and 4 are considered at the same time on this form. Some organizations may add additional columns to capture separate discussion on severity and likelihood.

Hazard Evaluation Considerations

- Formulation of the food
- Condition, function and design of facility and equipment
- Raw materials and ingredients
- Transportation practices
- Processing procedures, including rework
- Packaging and labeling activities
- Storage and distribution
- Intended or reasonably foreseeable use
- Sanitation including employee hygiene
- Others relevant factors

Many factors should be considered when hazards are identified. For example:

- Formulation of the food may result in pH, water activity or other conditions that favor growth of certain pathogens and prevent growth of others (discussed in detail in Chapter 4).
- The condition, function and design of the facility and equipment may enhance the potential for contaminants to be introduced. Some types of equipment may be more difficult to clean than others or more prone to wear or damage (e.g., metal fragments), which could result in an increased risk of hazards being introduced into the product.
- Ingredients and raw materials from your suppliers may introduce hazards, such as food allergens or pathogens known to be associated with specific types of foods. Water and ice as ingredients, and compressed air used in the food (e.g., for overrun in ice cream), could be considered here or could be considered at the process steps in which they are used.
- Transportation practices may influence the potential presence of pathogens. Bulk transportation may be more prone to potential contamination than packaged product transport. Ingredients that are transported under refrigeration may be subject to temperature abuse that could increase the risk of growth of certain hazards. Frozen transport may reduce risk.
- Processing procedures like cooking may reduce some hazards (e.g., vegetative pathogens). Other processing procedures may increase the potential for some hazards, (e.g., metal chopper blades contacting hard materials may break and potentially contribute metal hazards).
- Packaging and labeling can influence hazards of concern. Labeling of allergens or the need for special storage conditions (e.g., keep refrigerated) may help to reduce the risk to consumers. Also, reduced oxygen packaging may increase shelf life but may also create an environment that supports the growth of *C. botulinum* or *L. monocytogenes* for some food. The potential for these hazards must be considered for reduced oxygen packaging. Storage and distribution conditions may suggest preventive controls are needed if pathogen growth is a potential problem. However, this may not be a food safety concern if products are shelf stable. Consideration should also be given to the potential for the food to be contaminated in shipment; e.g., bulk cargoes.
- Some products are intended to be cooked or further treated prior to consumption, which may reduce risk for the consumer. However, it is prudent to consider how the end user may use the products in other ways (i.e., foreseeable use). For example, raw cookie dough is intended to be cooked prior to consumption; however, products such as cookie dough ice

cream have been marketed as a ready-to-eat product. The formulation and processes for ready-to-eat dough must be carefully considered to avoid potential food safety issues because traditional cookie dough may use raw eggs, uncooked flour and other ingredients that may contain pathogens. In addition, it is well-known that some consumers eat raw cookie dough.

- The sanitary conditions of the equipment, environment and employee hygiene are also a consideration for recontamination of certain products. Do the same employees handle both raw and cooked product? Do ready-to-eat product lines come in close proximity to raw product lines? How often do surfaces need to be cleaned to avoid growth in the system? All of these questions and more may influence the risk of creating hazards for certain products.

- Other relevant factors may include ingredient categories that have been implicated in food safety issues related to intentional product adulteration for economic gain (e.g., addition of lead-containing dyes to certain spices to enhance color) See the section on economically motivated hazards in Chapter 5: Chemical, Physical and Economically Motivated Hazards.

Evaluating the Severity

Evaluating Severity of Food Safety Hazards

- Requires consideration of various factors that may include:
  - the magnitude and duration of the illness or injury,
  - the possible impact of secondary problems (chronic sequelae) and
  - the susceptibility of intended customers to foodborne illness (e.g., children versus adults).

Appendix 4: Foodborne Pathogen Supplementary Information provides information on severity of common foodborne pathogens. Consider external assistance if you do not have the technical expertise to evaluate the severity of food safety hazards.

The severity of a food safety hazard depends on a number of factors that may include how long an individual is sick, whether symptoms are mild or severe (e.g., whether hospitalization or death is common), whether there is full recovery or health issues persist for long periods of time, and whether the food's targeted consumer is a member of a vulnerable population such as infants, children, the elderly or the immunocompromised as discussed in Chapter 6: Preliminary Steps in

Developing a Food Safety Plan. The severity of different hazards is discussed in Chapter 4: Biological Food Safety Hazards, Chapter 5: Chemical, Physical and Economically Motivated Food Safety Hazards, and in more detail in Appendix 4: Foodborne Pathogen Supplementary Information. Some facilities may have the expertise necessary to make such evaluations. Others may need to seek outside assistance to complete this step. The bottom line is that when the hazard, if present, is reasonably likely to render the food injurious to health, it should be included.

Evaluating the Likelihood of Occurrence

> Consider outbreaks in similar products and product recall lists to see if similar products are on the list.

Evaluating Likelihood of Occurrence

- Requires consideration of factors including:
  - Data from past foodborne illness outbreaks
  - Recall data from similar products
  - Information in the scientific literature
  - Historical information in the establishment
  - Regulatory guidance
  - Trade association information
  - University extension documents

The other factor the food safety team must evaluate is the likelihood of occurrence of the foodborne hazard. It is important to know how frequently the potential hazard may occur to determine if a preventive control is needed. In addition to food safety reference books, sources of data and information to consider include past outbreaks, recalls, the scientific literature and establishment experience. Regulatory guidance, trade association information, and university extension documents also provide useful information on the likely occurrence of hazards in particular foods. Chapter 7: Resources for Food Safety Plans discussed many sources of information for identifying and evaluating food safety hazards.

Past outbreaks present a tremendous source of information regarding the hazards that are likely to occur in certain food products. The Food Safety Team should take into account lessons learned from these prior events in similar products. The notion that "it has never happened to us" should not be a reason for excluding a hazard if similar products have had an issue with a specific hazard. FDA provides information for the foods that FDA regulates on their findings related to outbreaks, frequently discussing the factors that contributed to the outbreak at a processing or production facility. The CDC has a wealth of information on outbreaks that occurred not only from processed foods, but also foods prepared in restaurants, retail establishments and other locations. The CDC information covers not only FDA-regulated products, but also products regulated by USDA (e.g., meat and poultry) and those regulated by state and local agencies. Outbreaks that occur in other countries may also be relevant to consider, especially for imported foods.

Food recalls are a useful source of information on the potential presence of hazards in specific food products. It is important to note that not all recalls are associated with foodborne illness outbreaks.

- Class I recalls involve products that are likely to cause serious adverse health consequences or death;
- Class II recalls involve products that may cause illness or injury but the probability of serious health consequences is remote; and
- Class III recalls involve products that are not likely to cause illness or injury.

Federal and state government websites post information on food recalls. It may be useful to investigate information on these websites to see if the product you are making has been involved in recalls.

A standard reference book can provide basic information on food safety hazards. Peer-reviewed scientific journal articles and other sources of technical literature contain a wealth of information on foodborne hazards, their occurrence, potential growth in foods (in the case of biological hazards) and their control. A useful search tool is Google Scholar, which may be used to find the specific papers of interest. Microbial modeling programs such as the USDA Pathogen Modeling Program or ComBase are available on-line and can be used to explore the potential for growth under a variety of conditions. Keep in mind that these models may not reflect exactly what will occur in a particular food, but they can indicate relative risk of different handling scenarios.

The Codex Alimentarius Commission maintains internationally recognized codes of practice that are based on scientific literature and available in several languages. Trade associations also provide recommendations targeted to specific types of foods and industry needs.

Establishment's Historical Information

- Laboratory test results
  - Ingredients
  - Finished products
  - In-process materials
  - Environmental monitoring
- Consumer complaint records
  - Especially for physical hazards

The establishment may have information on the likelihood of occurrence of hazards in their food products. This information can be gleaned from previous laboratory tests on finished products, ingredients, in-process materials or environmental monitoring samples. Consumer complaint records can be a useful source of information, particularly for physical hazards.

Factors Affecting Likely Occurrence

- Facility operational programs
- Ingredients used
- Preparation method
- Transportation conditions
- Storage conditions
- Preparation steps

Likelihood may vary among facilities

Various factors can influence the likely presence of food safety hazards, including:

- Effectiveness of plant operational programs such as receiving, storage and personal hygiene
- Frequency of association of the potential hazard with the food or ingredient

- Method of preparation
- Conditions during transportation
- Expected storage conditions
- Likely preparation steps before consumption

Hazards requiring a preventive control in one operation or facility may not require one in another producing the same or a similar product. For example, the probability of metal contamination may be high in one facility but not in another due to differences in equipment. The effectiveness of a preventive maintenance program can also be relevant in determining the likelihood that a metal hazard may be present.

For example, Facility A may have a comprehensive preventive maintenance program that routinely inspects and tightens equipment nuts and bolts to prevent them from falling into product. They may couple this program with a review process for equipment design to avoid installation of equipment with abrasive metal-on-metal contact. They may be able to determine that their prerequisite preventive maintenance program effectively manages the hazard of metal in the product because of their history of not finding missing bolts and lack of observing worn metal in equipment. Conversely, Facility B may not have such programs. It may occasionally find missing nuts that could have fallen into the product stream and metal-on-metal contact may occur on some equipment. They may include metal detection in their Food Safety Plan to investigate findings when "kick outs" occur. Both approaches are reasonable.

Another example may be a facility that does not pack in glass containers; prohibits glass in the facility including instrument gauges with glass faces and watches (even for visitors) in the production area; and uses shields on light fixtures to prevent breakage. They may determine that glass does not require a preventive control. Conversely, a facility that does not have the resources to manage such a program or that packs in glass may conclude that the hazard presented by glass requires implementation of preventive controls.

E.G. Food Company Example

Hazard Analysis	PRODUCT: Omelet – Plain, Cheese and Cheese Biscuit					PAGE X of Y	
PLANT NAME	E.G. Food Company				ISSUE DATE	mm/dd/yy	
ADDRESS	360 Culinary Circle, Mytown, USA				SUPERSEDES	mm/dd/yy	
(1) Ingredient / Processing Step	(2) Identify potential food safety hazards introduced, controlled or enhanced at this step	(3) Do any potential food safety hazards require a preventive control?		(4) Justify your decision for column 3	(5) What preventive control measure(s) can be applied to significantly minimize or prevent the food safety hazard? *Process including CCPs, Allergen, Sanitation, Supply-chain, other preventive control*	(6) Is the preventive control applied at this step?	
		Yes	No			Yes	No
Receiving refrigerated ingredients – liquid pasteurized egg	B Vegetative pathogens such as *Salmonella*	X		While pasteurization minimizes the likelihood of *Salmonella* USDA recommends the product be used in cooked foods. Experience has shown *Salmonella* occasionally occurs in this ingredient.			
	C Allergen – egg	X		Egg is an allergen that must be labeled to inform consumers. Cross-contact is not an issue – all products contain egg.			
	P None						

FSPCA
FOOD SAFETY PREVENTIVE CONTROLS ALLIANCE

In the example above, "vegetative pathogens such as *Salmonella*" is identified as a potential hazard in egg ingredients because of the history of outbreaks associated with egg products. Egg is also identified as a potential allergen hazard because egg can cause an allergic reaction in some consumers. Column 3 is marked "Yes" indicating that a preventive control is required and Column 4 provides a justification of the decision. No additional information is needed for physical hazards because no potential hazards were identified. The facility could enter information in the justification field if desired, such as a comment that they switched from metal containers to bag-in-box to remove metal concerns.

Columns 5 and 6 – Preventive Controls

Preventive Controls Definition

- "Those risk-based, reasonably appropriate procedures, practices, and processes that a person knowledgeable about the safe manufacturing, processing, packing, or holding of food would employ to significantly minimize or prevent the hazards identified under the hazard analysis that are consistent with the current scientific understand of safe food manufacturing, processing, packaging, or holding at the time of the analysis."
  - 21 CFR 117.3 Definitions

FSPCA

Hazards requiring a preventive control based on a hazard analysis for their severity and likelihood of occurrence must be addressed in the Food Safety Plan. The term *"preventive controls"* is defined in the *Preventive Controls for Human Food* regulation as indicated above. Note that the determination of a preventive control is "risk-based," must be "reasonably appropriate" and "consistent with the current scientific understanding." Keep in mind that the specific preventive control management components (e.g., monitoring, corrective actions and verification) required takes into account the nature of the preventive control and its role in the facility's food safety system.

E.G. Food Company Example

Hazard Analysis	PRODUCT: Omelet – Plain, Cheese and Cheese Biscuit				PAGE X of Y		
PLANT NAME	E.G. Food Company				ISSUE DATE	mm/dd/yy	
ADDRESS	360 Culinary Circle, Mytown, USA				SUPERSEDES	mm/dd/yy	
(1) Ingredient/ Processing Step	(2) Identify potential food safety hazards introduced, controlled or enhanced at this step	(3) Do any potential food safety hazards require a preventive control? Yes / No		(4) Justify your decision for column 3	(5) What preventive control measure(s) can be applied to significantly minimize or prevent the food safety hazard? *Process including CCPs, Allergen, Sanitation, Supply-chain, other preventive control*	(6) Is the preventive control applied at this step? Yes / No	
Receiving refrigerated ingredients – liquid pasteurized egg	B Vegetative pathogens such as *Salmonella*	X		While pasteurization minimizes the likelihood of *Salmonella* USDA recommends the product be used in cooked foods. Experience has shown *Salmonella* occasionally occurs in this ingredient.	?	?	?
	C Allergen – egg	X		Egg is an allergen that must be labeled to inform consumers. Cross-contact is not an issue – all products contain egg.	?	?	?
	P None						

FSPCA

For each "Yes" in Column 3, preventive controls that significantly minimize or prevent the hazard **must** be described. If no known or reasonably foreseeable hazard is identified (Column 2 for physical hazards above) or if Column 3 is answered "No," then Columns 5 and 6 are left blank. Factors to consider in your decision making process are described below.

Preventive Controls May Include:

- Process preventive controls
- Food allergen preventive controls
- Sanitation preventive controls } Described in later chapters
- Supply-chain program
- Recall plan
- Other preventive controls

FSPCA

Depending on the hazards identified, preventive controls may include some or all of the preventive controls listed on this slide. Specific types of preventive controls are discussed in chapters later in the course, but a brief description follows. Preventive controls identified at specific processing steps are process preventive controls, such as critical control points (CCPs, see Chapter 9: Process Preventive Controls). Allergen preventive controls (see Chapter 10: Food Allergen Preventive Controls) include the essential allergen management procedures identified in the hazard analysis. Similarly, sanitation preventive controls are those specific sanitation procedures used to control the hazards identified as requiring sanitation preventive controls in the hazard analysis, and may include preventing contamination of ready-to-eat foods that do not receive a final "kill step" or preventing allergen cross-contact (see Chapter 11: Sanitation Preventive Controls). Supply-chain program preventive controls (see Chapter 12: Supply-chain Program) may be necessary when a manufacturer relies on the supplier to control a hazard requiring a preventive control in an ingredient because the receiving facility does not have a step to control the hazard. While a recall plan is not used to manage hazards requiring a preventive control, it can reduce the number of illnesses if contaminated product is recalled quickly. Other preventive controls may be needed, such as hygiene training in sensitive operations.

Potential Preventive Control Examples

Biological hazards
- Process controls that kill
  - E.g., cooking
- Process controls that prevent growth; e.g.,
  - Time/temperature controls
  - Checking formulation
- Supply-chain programs for sensitive ingredients used without a kill step
- Sanitation controls that prevent recontamination

Chemical hazards
- Supply-chain programs
- Allergen labeling
- Sanitation controls to prevent allergen cross-contact

Physical hazards
- Process controls such as
  - Filtering, metal detection, X-ray devices

The term "sensitive ingredient" refers to an ingredient with a history of association with a pathogen when controls are not in place.

A partial list of potential preventive control measures for biological, chemical (including radiological) and physical food safety hazards are listed in the slide above. For biological hazards, common control measures include those that either directly kill the pathogen (e.g., different types of thermal processing, irradiation, high pressure processing) or prevent the germination of spores and/or growth of microbial vegetative cells (e.g., formulation parameters such as acidification, fermentation, drying, and a variety of time and temperature controls such as cooling, refrigeration and limiting time at temperatures that support growth). Supply-chain programs may be relevant, especially if ingredients are used in ready-to-eat applications. Sanitation preventive controls may also be relevant for ready-to-eat products that are exposed to the environment.

Preventive controls for chemical hazards include supply-chain programs such as testing and rejection of ingredients that contain excess concentrations of natural or artificial chemical hazards. Allergen labeling is another allergen preventive control. Prevention of allergen cross-contact through sanitation may be considered an allergen or sanitation preventive control, or both.

Physical hazards can be controlled by methods such as using equipment for straining or aspirating, mechanical separation, metal detection, or x-ray or other detection methods. These may be process preventive controls.

Preventive controls for hazards introduced because of economically motivated adulteration may require a supply-chain program or some of the methods above, depending on the specific hazard.

Other Preventive Control Considerations

- Does it actually control the identified hazard?
- Can you monitor the control?
- Does it have an effect on other preventive controls?
- How much process variability exists where the control is applied?
- How severe are the consequences if the control fails?
- Is the control specifically applied to eliminate or reduce the level of a hazard?
- Does the control enhance other controls?

The food safety team must consider many factors when identifying preventive controls for the food safety hazards requiring them. Selection of preventive controls should also include assessments with regard to:

- its effect on identified food safety hazards,
- its feasibility for monitoring,
- its place in the system relative to other control measures,
- significant processing variability or the likelihood of failure of a control measure,
- the severity of consequences in case of a failure,
- whether the control measure is specifically established and applied to eliminate or significantly reduce the level of hazards, and
- synergistic effects between control measures.

				E.G. Food Company Example	
Hazard Analysis	PRODUCT: Omelet – Plain, Cheese and Cheese Biscuit				PAGE X of Y
PLANT NAME	E.G. Food Company			ISSUE DATE	mm/dd/yy
ADDRESS	360 Culinary Circle, Mytown, USA			SUPERSEDES	mm/dd/yy

(1) Ingredient/ Processing Step	(2) Identify potential food safety hazards introduced, controlled or enhanced at this step	(3) Do any potential food safety hazards require a preventive control? Yes / No	(4) Justify your decision for column 3	(5) What preventive control measure(s) can be applied to significantly minimize or prevent the food safety hazard? *Process including CCPs, Allergen, Sanitation, Supply-chain, other preventive control*	(6) Is the preventive control applied at this step? Yes / No
Receiving refrigerated ingredients – liquid pasteurized egg	B Vegetative pathogens such as *Salmonella*	X	While pasteurization minimizes the likelihood of *Salmonella* USDA recommends the product be used in cooked foods. Experience has shown *Salmonella* occasionally occurs in this ingredient.	Process Control - subsequent cook step	X (No)
	C Allergen – egg	X	Egg is an allergen that must be labeled to inform consumers. Cross-contact is not an issue – all products contain egg.	Allergen Control – allergen labeling at other steps	X (No)
	P None				

FSPCA
FOOD SAFETY PREVENTIVE CONTROLS ALLIANCE

The example above illustrates the hazard analysis decisions for one step in the E.G. Food Company's Food Safety Plan. Process control at a subsequent step (cooking) was identified as the preventive control for *Salmonella* in eggs. Since the eggs are pasteurized, the company could have chosen a supply-chain program instead; however, they may have concluded that it was easier for them to manage the cook step than a supply-chain program. The decision is theirs in this situation. An allergen preventive control to ensure appropriate labeling was also identified as a preventive control. Preventive controls for both of these hazards (*Salmonella* and egg-allergen) are applied later in the production process in this example.

The food safety team, with the assistance of outside experts if necessary, must determine the specific preventive controls needed to control the hazards requiring them. As previously mentioned, other formats for the hazard analysis may be used as long as the essential controls for hazards requiring a preventive control are documented and implemented. More than one hazard requiring a preventive control may be addressed by a specific preventive control measure, e.g., a cook step may address both *Salmonella* and *E. coli* O157:H7 hazards.

For those familiar with HACCP food safety systems, keep in mind that not all preventive controls are CCPs. The actions that are taken for other preventive controls may be different from those required for CCPs. This is discussed in Chapters 9-12 on specific preventive controls.

8-21

Summarize the Hazard Analysis

E.G. Food Company Example

Hazard Analysis	PRODUCT: Omelet – Plain, Cheese and Cheese Biscuit		PAGE X of Y
PLANT NAME	E.G. Food Company	ISSUE DATE	mm/dd/yy
ADDRESS	360 Culinary Circle, Mytown, USA	SUPERSEDES	mm/dd/yy

(1) Ingredient/ Processing Step	(2) Identify potential food safety hazards introduced, controlled or enhanced at this step		(3) Do any potential food safety hazards require a preventive control?		(4) Justify your decision for column 3	(5) What preventive control measure(s) can be applied to significantly minimize or prevent the food safety hazard? *Process including CCPs, Allergen, Sanitation, Supply-chain, other preventive control*	(6) Is the preventive control applied at this step?	
			Yes	No			Yes	No
From flow diagram	B C P	Identify potential hazards that **may be** introduced or increase at this step	Decide if the hazards require a preventive control.		Provide a reason for "yes" or "no" in column 3 when a potential hazard is identified. Optional to justify a "None" in column 2.	For hazards requiring a preventive control ("Yes" in column 3), identify preventive controls (**process, food allergen, sanitation, supplier or other**) that are applied at this step or later	Indicate if the preventive control is applied at this step or later in the process	

FSPCA
FOOD SAFETY PREVENTIVE CONTROLS ALLIANCE

At the completion of the hazard analysis, the food safety team documents the results of the hazard analysis process. A review of what is documented in the different columns for the model form used in this course is presented above. Other formats may be used, as long as they clearly identify the potential hazards, evaluate the likelihood and severity of the risk, and identify preventive control measure(s) that are used for all hazards that are reasonably likely to cause illness or injury in the absence of a preventive control.

Hazards requiring a preventive control must be managed through use of process preventive controls, allergen preventive controls, sanitation preventive controls, supply-chain programs or other preventive controls as appropriate for the food and facility. Operations or equipment in a facility may need to be modified based on the findings of a thorough hazard analysis. If the hazard analysis determines that a known or reasonably foreseeable (i.e., potential) hazard is likely to be present without a preventive control measure, then the product formulation, processing steps, other plant operations or supply-chain programs must be modified to ensure control of the hazard. Alternatively, there is provision for the preventive control to be applied later in the distribution of product. This is discussed in preventive controls chapters.

PRODUCT(S) Omelet – Plain, Cheese and Cheese Biscuit				PAGE **9** of 36		
PLANT NAME: E.G. Food Company				ISSUE DATE	2/13/2016	
ADDRESS: 360 Culinary Circle, Mytown, USA				SUPERSEDES	09/20/2015	

(1) Ingredient/ Processing Step	(2) Identify potential food safety hazards introduced, controlled or enhanced at this step	(3) Do any potential food safety hazards require a preventive control? Yes / No	(4) Justify your decision for column 3	(5) What preventive control measure(s) can be applied to significantly minimize or prevent the food safety hazard? *Process including CCPs, Allergen, Sanitation, Supply-chain, other preventive control*	(6) Is the preventive control applied at this step? Yes / No
Receiving packaging	B None				
	C Undeclared allergens – egg, milk, soy (wheat in biscuit only)	X	Labeled cartons must declare allergens present in the product and print errors have occurred	Allergen Control – label review for allergen information	X
	P None				
Receiving shelf stable ingredients – salt	B None				
	C None				
	P None				
Receiving shelf stable ingredients – pan release oil	B None				
	C Allergen – soy	X	Soy lecithin may contain soy allergen that must be labeled to inform consumers. Cross-contact is not an issue – all products contain soy.	Allergen Control – allergen labeling at subsequent step	X
	P None				

The E.G. Food Company's Plain Omelet Hazard Analysis in Appendix 3 is an example of how a hazard analysis could be documented. In our example form, the step from the flow diagram is recorded in column 1. In column 2, potential hazards that may be introduced or increase at this step are identified. It is possible that a potential hazard is not a hazard requiring a preventive control – the decision is recorded in column 3. Recording the rationale for the decisions made regarding hazards and preventive controls is useful to explain to others how the decision was reached – this is done in column 4. For hazards requiring a preventive control (a "Yes" in column 3), the preventive control that needs to be implemented is identified in column 5. Column 6 identifies if the preventive control occurs at this step. It may occur later in the process and that step would be marked as a preventive control.

The full hazard analysis for the fictitious E.G. Food Company's omelets is in Appendix 3: Food Safety Plan Example. This appendix also includes a description of the process at each step to help visualize how this operation functions.

Hazard Analysis for Several Products

Hazard Analysis for Several Products

- Similar products may be grouped
- Must ensure that the food safety impact of different product characteristics are considered
  - E.g., water activity, pH, allergen profiles

A common hazard analysis may be used for a group of products that are similar in formulation, have similar processing steps, and are otherwise prepared and packaged in a similar manner. For example, the hazard analysis and Food Safety Plan for the E.G. Food Company groups three different omelets into one hazard analysis and one Food Safety Plan. It is important to note, however, that different formulations can have a dramatic impact on product characteristics (e.g., pH, different allergens), and these factors must be carefully considered in the hazard analysis. While the E.G. Food Company groups the omelets in the same hazard analysis, other companies may wish to address the cheese omelet biscuit in a separate plan because of the wheat allergen in the biscuit and the extra assembly step. The Food Safety Team must organize the information in a meaningful way to communicate the significant risks to the staff at the facility.

For reasons discussed previously, the hazard analysis and Food Safety Plan will likely be different for the same product produced in different facilities. The food safety team must take into account the unique characteristics, equipment and procedures used at their establishment when preparing the Food Safety Plan specific for their firm. However, it is perfectly reasonable for the team to refer to generic HACCP or preventive control models, hazards and control guides, and decision trees to help them with their deliberations. Generic Food Safety Plans, however, will rarely consider all of the specific aspects in an actual facility, thus they are for teaching or guidance purposes only. Sources of generic HACCP plans (which could serve as a starting point for a Food Safety Plan) and resources are listed in Additional Reading at the end of the chapter. Other hazard analysis models and decision trees may be available from other reputable sources. As a word of caution, these resources may not consider hazards associated with sanitation, allergens and supply-chain programs to the extent required for Food Safety Plans under the *Preventive Controls for Human Food* regulation.

Pulling It All Together

Pulling It All Together

- Hazard analysis process identifies hazards requiring a preventive control
  - Process preventive controls
  - Food allergen preventive controls
  - Sanitation preventive controls
  - Supply-chain program
  - Other preventive controls

FSPCA

The hazard analysis process identifies those hazards requiring a preventive control because they are known or reasonably likely to cause illness or injury in the absence of a preventive control. The preventive controls needed to manage these hazards may be specific controls in the process and, frequently managed as CCPs. They may be specific sanitation preventive controls to manage environmental pathogens or allergen cross-contact. Allergen preventive controls may also include production run sequencing and product labeling, which is discussed in Chapter 10: Food Allergen Preventive Controls. Some hazards requiring a preventive control need supply-chain programs to verify control of the hazard by the supplier. Finally, the need for other preventive controls may be identified through hazard analysis, such as temperature control during transportation.

The hazards requiring a preventive control in the E.G. Food Company example are summarized below.

E.G. Food Company Example

Omelet – Process Preventive Controls

(1) Ingredient/ Processing Step		(2) Identify potential food safety hazards introduced, controlled or enhanced at this step	(3) Do any potential food safety hazards require a preventive control?		(4) Justify your decision for column 3	(5) What preventive control measure(s) can be applied to significantly minimize or prevent the food safety hazard? Process including CCPs, Allergen, Sanitation, Supply-chain, other preventive control	(6) Is the preventive control applied at this step?	
			Yes	No			Yes	No
Cook [eggs, milk, salt, pan release oil]	B	Survival of vegetative pathogens such as Salmonella	X		Thorough cooking is required to kill vegetative pathogens	Process Control – Cooking to achieve a lethal temperature	X	
Metal detection	P	Metal	X		Metal-on-metal contact on the line may introduce metal fragments	Process Control – metal detection	X	

FSPCA

In the hypothetical omelet example, two process preventive controls were identified: cooking the omelet to inactivate vegetative pathogens and metal detection to prevent metal contamination of the product.

E.G. Food Company Example

Omelet – Allergen Preventive Controls

(1) Ingredient/ Processing Step		(2) Identify potential food safety hazards introduced, controlled or enhanced at this step	(3) Do any potential food safety hazards require a preventive control?		(4) Justify your decision for column 3	(5) What preventive control measure(s) can be applied to significantly minimize or prevent the food safety hazard? Process including CCPs, Allergen, Sanitation, Supply-chain, other preventive control	(6) Is the preventive control applied at this step?	
			Yes	No			Yes	No
Receiving packaging	C	Undeclared allergens – egg, milk, soy (wheat in biscuit only)	X		Labeled cartons must declare allergens present in the product and print errors have occurred	Allergen Control – label review for allergen information	X	
Assemble, wrap	C	Allergen cross-contact from other products handled at this step; e.g., Cheese Omelet Biscuit	X		Biscuits could introduce wheat allergen to other products without control	Sanitation and Allergen Control – prevent cross-contact	X	
Fill, weigh, label	C	Undeclared allergens – egg, milk, soy (wheat in biscuit only)	X		All products contain egg, milk and soy allergens. The cheese biscuit also contains wheat.	Allergen Control – correct labeled carton for product	X	

FSPCA

Some companies may have only one preventive control for allergen labeling – when the label is placed on the package. Others may use two:

1. to check for errors on incoming batches of labels by an individual knowledgeable in label requirements and

2. to check that the correct label is place on the product. Each facility determines the best approach for their situation.

The example illustrates three allergen preventive controls identified:

1. ensuring that labels received from the printer accurately declare the allergens in the product

2. controlling the potential for allergen cross-contact at the Assemble, Wrap step; and

3. ensuring that the correct product labeling with relevant allergens is put on the product.

Some companies may consider the labeling step as a process control if, for example, they use a bar code scanner to monitor proper label application or manually compare a label and formulation each time new labels are added to the line. This is up to the specific operation.

E.G. Food Company Example

Omelet – Sanitation Preventive Controls

(1) Ingredient/ Processing Step	(2) Identify potential food safety hazards introduced, controlled or enhanced at this step	(3) Do any potential food safety hazards require a preventive control?		(4) Justify your decision for column 3	(5) What preventive control measure(s) can be applied to significantly minimize or prevent the food safety hazard? *Process including CCPs, Allergen, Sanitation, Supply-chain, other preventive control*	(6) Is the preventive control applied at this step?	
		Yes	No			Yes	No
Assemble, wrap	B Introduction of environmental pathogens such as *L. monocytogenes*	X		Recontamination may occur if sanitation control is not in place	Sanitation Controls – prevent recontamination	X	
	C Allergen cross-contact from other products handled at this step; e.g., Cheese Omelet Biscuit	X		Biscuits could introduce wheat allergen to other products without control	Sanitation and Allergen Control – prevent cross-contact	X	

FSPCA
FOOD SAFETY PREVENTIVE CONTROLS ALLIANCE

Two sanitation preventive controls were identified:

1. prevent the potential introduction of environmental pathogens at the Assemble, Wrap step, and

2. prevent allergen cross-contact at the same step.

Sanitation of the Assemble, Wrap table would be the appropriate procedure to prevent allergen cross-contact. Hygienic zoning and sanitation procedures in the Assemble, Wrap environment would likely include more than just cleaning and sanitizing the assembly table. This is discussed in more detail in Chapter 11: Sanitation Preventive Controls.

Omelet – Supply-chain Controls

(1) Ingredient/ Processing Step	(2) Identify <u>potential</u> food safety hazards introduced, controlled or enhanced at this step	(3) Do any <u>potential</u> food safety hazards require a preventive control?		(4) Justify your decision for column 3	(5) What preventive control measure(s) can be applied to significantly minimize or prevent the food safety hazard? *Process including CCPs, Allergen, Sanitation, Supply-chain, other preventive control*	(6) Is the preventive control applied at this step?	
		Yes	No			Yes	No
Receiving refrigerated ingredients – pasteurized process cheese	B Vegetative and sporeforming pathogens such as *Salmonella*, pathogenic *E. coli*, *L. monocytogenes* and *C. botulinum*	X		Pathogens listed were identified as significant by ICMSF (2005) in process cheese. These hazards should have been controlled when the cheese was made.	Supply-chain Control - approved supplier and 3rd party supplier audit by a qualified auditor.	X	

FSPCA
FOOD SAFETY PREVENTIVE CONTROLS ALLIANCE

In the hypothetical omelet example, one preventive control for their supply-chain program was identified, i.e., for the pasteurized process cheese used in the omelets. E.G. Food Company does not have any process that would control the identified hazards, thus they rely on the supplier to control the pasteurization process to destroy vegetative pathogens and formulation to control *C. botulinum*. They manage this through their supply-chain program by requiring a third party audit. The details on how they obtain information from a 3rd party audit are discussed in Chapter 12: Supply-chain Program.

Together, process, allergen, sanitation and other preventive controls including supply-chain programs greatly minimize the potential for the E.G. Food Company omelets to cause an illness or injury for the consuming public.

Hazard Analysis and Preventive Controls Determination Summary

> **Hazard Analysis and Preventive Controls Determination Summary**
>
> - There are many types of food safety hazards
> - The hazard analysis process:
>   - Identifies known and reasonably foreseeable hazards (potential hazards)
>   - Evaluates the likelihood and severity of potential hazards to identify those requiring a preventive control
>   - Identifies process, allergen, sanitation, supply-chain or other preventive controls for potential hazards
> - An effective hazard analysis reduces risk and focuses efforts
> - A **written** hazard analysis is required for all products
>
> FSPCA

Hazards are biological, chemical or physical agents that have the potential to cause illness or injury. The hazard analysis process identifies known or foreseeable hazards that are known to be or have the potential to be associated with the facility or food it makes. These potential hazards are then evaluated to assess likelihood and severity to determine, based on risk, those hazards that require a preventive control.

Through this process, an effective hazard analysis reduces risk and focuses implementation efforts on the preventive controls and associated procedures that are the most important controls for food safety. A poorly executed hazard analysis may overlook hazards requiring a preventive control, or may identify too many controls that really are less important for safety, thus making the Food Safety Plan unmanageable.

A written hazard analysis is required. Engaging technical experts may be useful for the hazard analysis to ensure that the hazards requiring a preventive control and appropriate preventive controls are identified.

Additional Reading
FDA. 2014. *Dairy Grade A Voluntary HACCP.*
FDA. 2016. *Food Safety Preventive Controls for Human Food Hazards and Controls Guidance*
National Advisory Committee on Microbiological Criteria for Foods. 1998. Hazard Analysis and Critical Control Point Principles and Application Guidelines. *Journal of Food Protection* 61(9):1246-1259.
Seafood Information Resource Center. 2014.

NOTES:

CHAPTER 9.   Process Preventive Controls

Process preventive controls make up the part of your Food Safety Plan that focuses on controls required at process steps that are critical for the safety of the food. Process preventive controls require documentation of parameters and minimum or maximum values (e.g., critical limits) associated with the control, monitoring procedures, corrective action procedures and validation that the process controls the hazard. The requirements for process preventive controls depend on the role of the process control in the food safety system. This chapter provides information on establishing values for processing parameters (e.g., critical limits), how to monitor process preventive controls, and components of corrective actions to be taken for process preventive controls when deviations occur.

Link to Hazard Analysis

Process preventive controls include parameters and usually limits (maximum or minimum values) associated with the control of a hazard. These science-based values are quite specific and are commonly called critical limits. They are applied at processing steps that are frequently called Critical Control Points (CCPs). A CCP is "a point, step, or procedure in a food process at which control can be applied *and is essential* to prevent or eliminate a food safety hazard or reduce such hazard to an acceptable level." Once a process preventive control, such as a CCP, is identified for a specific hazard, parameters and values that can be used to control the hazard must be established.

> **Definition:**
>
> *Critical Control Point (CCP)*: A point, step, or procedure in a food process at which control can be applied and is essential to prevent or eliminate a food safety hazard or reduce such hazard to an acceptable level.
> - 21 CFR 117.3

Keep in mind that the requirements for process preventive controls depend on the role of the process control in the food safety system.

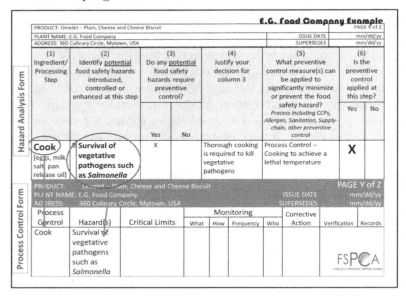

A variety of formats can be used to document this information. This course uses the format above, which includes information that must be documented in the Food Safety Plan. Details on information required on Food Safety Plan records are discussed in Chapter 14: Record-keeping Procedures.

As illustrated above, the steps identified as requiring a process preventive control, including CCPs, along with the hazards requiring a preventive control are transferred by the food safety team from the Hazard Analysis Form to the first and second columns of the Process Control Form. This form may be referred to as a HACCP Chart if desired. The food safety team then lists parameters and critical limits (the minimum or maximum values associated with the parameters) for the controls for each hazard, all elements of monitoring, corrective actions to be taken when deviations from the critical limit occur, verification procedures and records in subsequent columns. This chapter discusses critical limits, monitoring and corrective action elements of the Process Control Form. Elements of verification and record-keeping requirements are addressed in separate chapters.

Parameters and Values such as Critical Limits

Critical Limits – A Food Safety Principle

- Key discussion points
  - Definition of critical limit
  - How to determine critical limits for a CCP
  - The relationship between critical limits and operating limits
  - Use of the Process Control Form

For simplicity, the term "critical limit" is used in the rest of this chapter instead of "minimum or maximum values associated with the parameters to control the hazard." Critical limits play an important role in a preventive control program. If a hazard exists, it is important to understand values for the parameters that must be met to control that hazard. This chapter focuses on how to establish science-based critical limits that help to assure process control. Sources of information on limits are readily available, and these will be discussed later in the chapter. The chapter also discusses different options used to establish a critical limit, as well as the advantages and disadvantages of these approaches. More conservative "operating limits" (e.g., higher or lower temperatures than needed for safety) may be useful during production to minimize failure to meet a critical limit and may be set for meeting quality standards. Finally, the chapter shows how to begin to complete a Process Control Form.

Critical Limit Definition

- The maximum or minimum value, or combination of values, to which any biological, chemical or physical parameter must be controlled to significantly minimize or prevent a hazard requiring a process control.
  - Derived from 21 CFR 117.135(c)(1)(ii)

FSPCA

For most process-related preventive controls, measurable parameters can be identified and the values established for these parameters are called *critical limits*, defined by the slide above. The critical limit must be met at the process control (or CCP) to significantly minimize or prevent the hazard requiring a preventive control. If a critical limit is not met, the step is out of control (i.e., a deviation has occurred) and the potential for producing a product that presents a consumer-health risk exists.

Examples of parameters that may have critical limits identified include time, temperature, flow rate, line speed, product bed depth, weight, viscosity, moisture level, water activity, salt concentration, pH, and others, depending upon the process.

> The FSPCA Website has a list of resources and links that may be useful for a company to determine critical limits appropriate for their product.
>
> Appendix 4 of this manual also has some information that could be used for critical limits for biological hazards.

Sources of Information on Critical Limits

Information Source	Examples
FDA	Hazard Guides; guidelines, tolerances and action levels; Food Code; Pasteurized Milk Ordinance (PMO); Acidified Foods regulations
Other regulatory guidelines	State and local regulations, tolerances and action levels; USDA regulations, tolerances and action levels
Experts (internal and external)	Process authorities, university food scientists/ microbiologists, consultants, equipment manufacturers, sanitarians, trade associations
Scientific studies	In-house experiments, 3rd party challenge studies (universities or contract labs)
Scientific literature	Peer reviewed journals, food science texts, microbiology texts, Food Safety Preventive Controls Alliance information

FSPCA

A number of sources of scientific and technical information can be useful in establishing critical limits, as discussed in Chapter7: Resources for Food Safety Plans. FDA and other government agencies may provide information through technical staff, regulations, guidelines, directives, performance standards, tolerances and action levels. Trade associations, process authorities, industry scientists, university and extension scientists, and consultants can provide expertise and guidelines. Scientific studies for specific products can be conducted in-house, at a contract laboratory or at a university.

Information can also be obtained from peer reviewed scientific literature. Use care when applying information from these sources to critical limits for a specific product and process. There may be important differences between the methods used in a published study and those used for the product and process under consideration. The critical limits may need to be adjusted to account for those differences. For example, higher fat levels may have a protective effect in the microbial lethality of a heat treatment, which may require a higher temperature or a longer time to achieve the same level of kill compared to a lower fat product.

Critical Limit Considerations

- If a critical limit is not met, a hazard is not necessarily controlled and the safety of the product is in question
- Critical limits must be achievable
- Often a variety of options exist for controlling a particular hazard
- The selection of the best control option and critical limit is often driven by practicality and experience

---

Because of the potential safety implications, meeting critical limits at a CCP is essential for the safety of the product. Because of this, it is important that the critical limit *can* be achieved by the process. A critical limit is generally expressed as a parameter equal to or above (or below) a critical value and not at the specific value itself. For example, processing equipment could not easily maintain the exact value of 160°F (71°C) so the critical limit would be set at ≥160°F (71°C). This allows the CCP to be achieved and gives the option of exceeding it, say for being more conservative or to operate at a higher processing limit. Many times, different options can be applied as critical limits to control a specific hazard. The food safety team decides the best option for the particular CCP, taking into account practical considerations such as the process capabilities in question, how measurements can be made, staff capabilities and other appropriate factors.

Critical Limit Examples

Product	Hazard	Critical Control Point	Critical Limit Example*
Battered product	*Staphylococcus aureus* growth and toxin formation	Batter application	Hydrated batter does not exceed 50°F (10°C) for more than 12 hr OR 70°F (21°C) for more than 3 hr, cumulative
Chopped product	Metal inclusion	Metal detector	No detectable metal fragments in finished product OR Knife blades are intact after each run
High a$_w$ ready-to-eat foods	Pathogen growth	Cooler storage	Cooler temperature ≤41°F (5°C)

* Specific critical limits are product dependent

FSPCA

There are many different types of critical limits. They must be specific for the CCP and the hazard that is being controlled. Different critical limits may be needed for ingredient-related hazards and process-related hazards. Each CCP must have one (or more) critical limit for each food safety hazard, as illustrated in the examples above. An effective critical limit defines what can be measured or observed to demonstrate that the hazard is being controlled at that CCP. For example, both time and temperature measurements may be elements of a critical limit to eliminate food safety hazards such as pathogens at a cook step.

Critical Limits Examples w/ Several Parameters*

Product	Hazard	Critical Control Point	Critical Limit Example
Ready-to-eat cooked and refrigerated product	*Listeria monocytogenes* survival	Cooking	≥160°F (71°C) internal product temperature for ≥1.5 min
Dried product	Pathogen growth	Drying oven	Drying schedule – Oven temperature ≥200°F (93.3°C) Time ≥120 minutes Air flow rate ≥2 ft³/min Product thickness ≤0.5 inches (to achieve a_w ≤0.85)
Acidified product	*Clostridium botulinum* in pickled foods	Acidification	Batch schedule – Product weight < 100 lb Soak time ≥8 hr Acetic acid concentration ≥3.5%, volume ≥50 gal (to achieve maximum pH of 4.6)

* Other critical limits may be needed for other pathogens in the same product

FSPCA

Facilities may have different options for controlling a particular hazard. The selection of the best control option and the best critical limit(s) is often driven by practicality and experience. As illustrated in the slide above, critical limits may involve a number of parameters such as time, temperature, air flow, product weight or thickness, and the like, depending on the nature of the product and the process. Some facilities may choose to use a higher air flow and a reduced thickness in the dried product example to achieve the end point more quickly. These parameters must be determined on a product- by-product basis, and consider the role of the control in the food safety system.

Critical Limit Options

Example Critical Limit – Batch Process

Product:	Frozen omelet
Hazard:	Vegetative pathogens such as *Salmonella*
CCP:	Cooking
Critical limit:	Minimum product temperature of ≥158°F (70°C)*
Applicability:	Individual cook, batch process

*Based on 2013 Food Code instantaneous temperature for cooking products containing raw eggs

FSPCA

A variety of approaches could be applied to set critical limits for a cooking CCP intended to eliminate the hazard of vegetative pathogens in a frozen omelet. In the example above the product temperature achieved during cooking is set as the critical limit. However, the product temperature may not be easy to monitor for each individual product cooked. Heat transfer rates during cooking could also vary for several reasons. For a sauce, measuring the product temperature may be practical because the liquid could be mixed. For a product like an omelet, a procedure would need to be developed for measuring the temperature of an omelet. If it is a batch process (e.g., baked in a set of pans), this may be workable. However, if each omelet is individually made, it may be less practical to measure temperature and record temperature because the time for doneness may vary from one omelet to the next. One would need more assurance that the critical limit is met for each individual product.

Example Critical Limit – Continuous Process

Product:	Frozen omelet
Hazard:	Vegetative pathogens such as *Salmonella*
CCP:	Cooking
Critical limits:	• Oven temperature X °F (Y°C) • Belt speed X feet/minute • Batter volume in standard pan size
Applicability:	Belt fed oven

FSPCA

Except in limited circumstances (e.g., the product is a liquid such as milk in a pipe or a continuously stirred liquid product), it seldom is practical to continually monitor the temperature of each individual food product on a processing line to ensure conformance with a critical limit. As an alternative, the example above establishes conditions necessary to ensure that the cooking process achieves the minimum product temperature and time. In this approach, the oven temperature, the belt speed going through the oven, and the volume of batter placed into standard pans are all factors that affect the final temperature. These parameters are easy to monitor and measurements are obtained quickly to determine that critical limits have been met. A scientific study (validation, discussed below and in Chapter 13: Verification and Validation Procedures) must be performed to ensure that controlling these factors at the specified critical limits will always result in an internal product temperature that will destroy pathogens of concern. Typically, this option provides better assurance and may be easier to perform than the previous option, even though more parameters must be monitored at this step.

Critical Limit Example

The E.G. Food Company's hazard analysis described in the previous chapter identified two CCPs, including 1) the Cook step and 2) Metal detection.

Cook: This is a CCP for inactivation of vegetative pathogens such as *Salmonella*. In this operation, each omelet is individually cooked by an operator. Based on validation studies (see Chapter 13: Verification and Validation Procedures) the Food Safety Team determined the critical limit for this CCP: **Omelet temperature is ≥158°F (70°C) instantaneous before transfer to assembly table.**

This critical limit is entered in the Process Control Form.

Metal detection: This step is a CCP for metal that may have been introduced earlier in the process. The food safety team identified metal detection as a CCP, with the critical limits: **1) Metal detector present and operating** and **2) no metal fragments that would cause injury or choking are in the product passing through the metal detector.**

This critical limit is entered in the Process Control Form.

It is essential that the critical limit selected actually controls the identified hazard! This requires application of science to validate that the control is effective. The process of validation is discussed further in Chapter 13: Verification and Validation Procedures, which includes an example of a validation study conducted for the E.G. Food Company.

Monitoring

Monitoring – A Food Safety Principle

- Key discussion points:
  - Definition of monitoring
  - Purpose of monitoring
  - Design of a monitoring system
  - Methods and equipment for monitoring critical limits

This section covers the definition of monitoring, as well as explaining why it is important. Considerations for designing a monitoring system are discussed, as well as different methods that can be used. Monitoring is a preventive controls management component that applies not only to process preventive controls, but also to allergen and sanitation preventive controls, as appropriate to the control and its role in the facility's food safety system.

Monitor Definition

- "To conduct a planned sequence of observations or measurements to assess whether control measures are operating as intended."
  - 21 CFR 117.3 Definitions

Monitoring involves the selection of appropriate measurements or observations at a specified frequency to provide information to assess whether a control measure is operating as intended.

Purpose of Monitoring Process Controls

- To track the operation of the process and enable the identification of trends toward a critical limit that may trigger process adjustments

- To identify when there is a loss of control or when a "deviation" from a critical limit occurs

- To provide written documentation that can be used to verify that the process is under control

The purpose of monitoring is to document that the minimum or maximum values, such as a critical limit, for a parameter have been met, thus ensuring the food safety hazard has been controlled. Monitoring also provides data to document that products were produced in accordance with the Food Safety Plan. It is important that monitoring procedures are specific for the parameter identified in the Food Safety Plan. When monitoring shows that the minimum or maximum values, such as a critical limit, for a parameter are not met, a corrective action is needed, which is discussed later in the chapter.

Elements of Monitoring

1. What to monitor
2. How to monitor
3. Frequency to monitor
4. Who will monitor

Monitoring requires four elements: 1) what measurements or observations will be used to monitor, 2) how to conduct the monitoring, 3) what frequency will be used for monitoring, and 4) who will do the monitoring.

What Might Be Monitored?

Depends on process, examples include:

- Temperature
- Time
- Volume / weight
- Line speed
- Flow rate
- Bed depth

- Acid addition
- pH
- Water activity
- Chemical concentration
- Appearance
- Process performance
- Many others

Monitoring process preventive controls depends on the nature of the control and its role in the facility's food safety system. It may involve measuring a characteristic of the product or process to determine if a critical limit is met. Examples of monitoring measurements could include:

- Cold-storage temperature when the refrigeration unit temperature is the parameter for which a critical limit has been established.

- Line speed and cooker temperature when cook time and temperature are parameters for which critical limits have been established.

- The pH resulting from adding an acidifying ingredient when pH is a parameter for which a critical limit has been established.

- Process parameters such as line speed, flow rate, bed depth or similar elements if these have been established during validation as critical to control the hazard.

- Observing that the metal detector is on when metal is a hazard of concern.

- Checking that the sizing bar that controls thickness by rejecting oversize units is in place if thickness is a parameter important for heat penetration.

How is Monitoring Conducted?

Depends on the nature of the control. Examples include:

- Calibrated thermometer
- Calibrated pH meter
- Calibrated chart recorder
- In-line analyzer
- "Real time" laboratory analysis
- Visual checks

The concept of "real time" laboratory methods is evolving. Ideally it provides immediate results. Sometimes there is a delay of seconds to minutes. It could also include a longer time if the product remains in process or on hold until results are in in for decision making.

Tests that take longer can still play a role in preventive controls through verification procedures. See Chapter 13: Verification and Validation Procedures.

Different methods can be used to monitor critical limits, depending on the nature of the control. These methods need to be real-time and accurate. They should also consider if there are "worst case" locations, like cold spots, that must be monitored. If you are using monitoring instruments in the wrong way or in the wrong location, then the objective of monitoring is likely not being met.

Using calibrated instruments to measure a critical limit parameter is an effective way to conduct monitoring. Examples of monitoring instruments could include thermometers, pH meters, water activity meters, data loggers, etc. A discussion of calibration occurs in Chapter 13: Verification and Validation Procedures.

Monitoring methods can also involve visually checking what you are monitoring. When using visual observation, it must be clear whether or not a critical limit has been violated. In our omelet example, a production employee observes that the metal detector is on and that the reject device is working. The employee records these observations at the beginning, middle and end of the shift.

Monitoring should be designed to provide rapid, real-time results. Some laboratory methods are relatively quick and can be used for decision making. For example, pH measurements are useful to monitor fermentation processes. Viscosity measurements may be useful for processes that require specific flow characteristics for an effective heat treatment. Brix measurements, moisture content, water activity, antimicrobial concentration measurements and other types of tests may have application in a Food Safety Plan. However, lengthy analytical tests (such as many microbiological tests) are not useful for routine monitoring because critical limit failures must be detected quickly and an appropriate corrective action instituted before product is shipped.

9-13

The term "continuous monitoring" may be interpreted differently by some. In this course, continuous monitoring can be performed by a device itself as long as a visual check of the data and/or functionality, as appropriate, is also performed to ensure that the device is functioning properly. Charts run out of ink, pens get stuck, and probes can malfunction; which is why human involvement must occur periodically.

Continuous Monitoring Considerations

- Continuous monitoring is preferred
- Continuous monitoring examples
  - Temperature recording chart
  - Metal detector
  - Dud detector
  - In-line pH probe
  - Bar code scanner
  - Vision system for foreign material

When possible, continuous monitoring procedures should be used. Continuous monitoring is generally performed by an instrument that produces a continuous record. These records can be either affirmative records demonstrating temperature is controlled or "exception records" demonstrating loss of temperature control (See discussion below on exception records). The record needs to be checked by an individual periodically to ensure that the critical limit is being met. The length of time between checks directly affects the amount of rework or product loss that may occur when a critical limit deviation is found. Examples of continuous monitoring could include:

- The time and temperature data for a batch pasteurization process may be continuously monitored and recorded on a temperature-recording chart.
- The temperature of a storage cooler may be "continuously" monitored and recorded by an instrument at a predetermined time interval.
- A functioning metal detector automatically monitors all product that passes through it.
- Oxidation/reduction potential (ORP) is recorded continuously by a calibrated automated probe in a vegetable flume.

The proper functioning and automated records generated, if any, for each of these types of systems must be monitored or verified, as appropriate (see below on "exception records"), by an individual on a periodic basis to document that the system is performing as specified in the Food Safety Plan. For example, the ORP readings may be read twice a shift by a line operator in addition to the continuous record.

Non-continuous Monitoring Considerations

- Used when continuous systems are not feasible
- Frequency of non-continuous monitoring
  - How much does the process normally vary?
  - How close are normal values to the critical limit?
  - How much product is at risk if the critical limit is not met?
- Non-continuous monitoring examples
  - Temperature checks at specified intervals
  - Batch process water activity checks
  - Antimicrobial chemical levels in produce wash water

In many situations, continuous monitoring systems are not feasible because the technology does not exist, the cost is prohibitive or other reasons. It is still necessary to establish a monitoring interval that ensures critical limits are met. The frequency of non-continuous (periodic) monitoring could be influenced by historical knowledge of the product and process. Questions that could help determine the frequency include:

- How much does the process normally vary (e.g., how consistent are the data)? If the monitoring data show a great deal of variation, the time between monitoring checks should be short.
- How close are the normal operating values to the critical limit? If the normal values are close to the critical limit, the time between monitoring checks should be short.
- How much product is at risk if the critical limit is exceeded? If a large amount of product is at risk and cannot be reworked, for example, more frequent monitoring may be prudent.

Examples of non-continuous monitoring include:
- Temperature checks of batter on a breading line at specified intervals if a continuous monitoring system is not feasible.
- Water activity measurements for batch process operations
- Antimicrobial chemical levels in a vegetable flume when automated monitoring systems are not available.

Exception Records

Exception Records

- Exception records are generated only when a limit is not met; e.g.,
  - Cooler records when temperature goes above a set limit
  - X-ray that responds only to foreign material
- Often an alarm alerts the operator of a problem
- Exception record systems must be validated

FSPCA

Exception reporting involves automated systems that are designed to alert operators and management only when a deviation (in other words an exception) from the requirement is observed. Automated exception reporting may be more efficient than that performed by operators, allowing increased sampling frequency (often continuous) and reduction of human error. For example, refrigeration temperature control can notify on exception (e.g., high temperature alarm) and may only record temperatures that exceed the specified temperature. Such systems must be validated and periodically verified to ensure they are working properly. With such systems, monitoring records may not always be necessary, when validation and periodic verification are conducted to ensure that the system is working properly. Therefore, records of refrigeration temperature during storage of food that requires time/temperature control to significantly minimize or prevent the growth of, or toxin production by, pathogens may be affirmative records demonstrating temperature is controlled (e.g., a chart recorder) or exception records demonstrating loss of temperature control (e.g., an alarm system that records when a deviation occurs). If a facility uses "exception records," the facility must have evidence that the system is working as intended, such as a record that the system has been challenged by increasing the temperature to a point at which an "exception record" is generated. Exception records may also be adequate in circumstances other than monitoring of refrigeration temperature, such as monitoring for foreign material with x-rays, which results in a record only when the system detects foreign material. Validation is required.

Who Will Monitor?

- Trained, designated employee
- Not necessarily quality assurance
- Best if it is a different person than the one who verifies records

FSPCA

Individuals assigned to preventive controls monitoring activities must receive training appropriate for the task. They can be:

- Line personnel
- Equipment operators
- Supervisors
- Maintenance personnel
- Quality assurance personnel

Monitoring by line personnel and equipment operators can be advantageous since they are actively watching the product or equipment. Including production workers in food safety activities helps build a broad base of understanding and commitment to the preventive controls program.

The monitor's duties should require that all deviations from critical limits be responded to immediately and reported as necessary to ensure that process adjustments and corrective actions are made in a timely manner. Rapid response when operating limits are not met can prevent critical limit deviations. All records and documents associated with preventive control (including CCP) monitoring, including corrective actions, must be signed or initialed by the person doing the activity and the date, and, where appropriate, the time of the activity recorded.

Monitoring personnel (qualified individuals) are not required to be "preventive controls qualified individuals" but must receive the food safety training required by regulation and be trained to perform their assigned task.

Qualifications for Monitoring Individuals

- Trained in monitoring techniques through on-the-job training or similar approaches
- Fully understand the importance of monitoring
- Accurately report each monitoring activity
- Understand actions to take when deviation occurs
  - Immediate corrective actions related to the process
  - Timely report deviation for other actions

Properly trained ("qualified") personnel must perform monitoring required by the plan. Process Control Forms must specify "who" (i.e., the position) performs monitoring. While this may be assigned to a supervisor, make sure this is realistic for the facility. For example, supervisors are sometimes called away for other activities, such as accompanying an inspector during an inspection visit. It is not realistic to expect one person to accompany an inspector and perform monitoring activities at the same time. It is preferable to fully explain the importance of monitoring procedures to a responsible line worker who can maintain the records and even take immediate action necessary when a deviation occurs. For example, a line worker on a final packaging line may be trained in monitoring activities at a metal detector. The individual can investigate detector rejections (kick outs) to determine cause, document findings, run calibration checks, etc. without direct involvement from supervisors. This person could even shut the line down if issues are identified and then inform supervisors for more in-depth investigations.

Individuals assigned to preventive controls monitoring activities must also receive food safety training on information discussed in Chapter 14: Record-keeping Procedures.

Monitoring Example

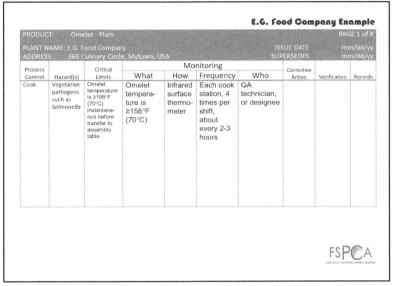

The E.G Food Company's Food Safety Team determined monitoring procedures for each of the two CCPs identified. The cook step is discussed here. Metal detection is available in Appendix 3.

As previously discussed, the critical limit for cooking the omelet was determined to be "Omelet surface temperature is ≥158°F (70°C) instantaneous before transfer to assembly table." Several elements of monitoring are associated with this CCP. Each omelet is cooked individually. A QA technician or designee (the Who) measures the surface temperature (the What) with an infrared surface thermometer (the How) for each cook station four times per shift (the When) and documents this on the form below.

E.G. Food Company Example

PRODUCT Omelet - Frozen		PAGE 27 of 34
PLANT NAME: E.G. Food Company	ISSUE DATE	09/20/2015
ADDRESS: 360 Culinary Circle, Mytown, USA	SUPERSEDES	08/06/2015

Cook Log

Hazard: Vegetative pathogens such as *Salmonella*

Parameters, values or critical limits: Omelet temperature is ≥158°F (70°C) instantaneous before transfer to assembly table.

Who, How, Frequency: QA technician or designee, checks an omelet temperature each cook station 4 times/shift (every 2-3 hr) using an infrared surface thermometer.

Corrective Action: Hold product back to the last good check and evaluate – rework, discard, or release. Determine root cause – retrain or correct as appropriate

Date:

Time	Cook Station	Cook name	Temperature (°F)	QA Tech (initials)

An example of a monitoring record is illustrated above. It provides space to record the data observed during the monitoring activity. While not required, it also includes information from the Process Control Form to ensure that the person who is doing the monitoring activity has the most current information and knows what to do. Monitoring record-keeping requirements are covered in Chapter 14: Record-keeping Procedures.

Corrective Actions and Corrections

Corrective Actions and Corrections

- Key discussion points
  - The definition of corrective action and corrections
  - Procedures for corrective actions
  - Record-keeping requirements for corrective actions

When something goes wrong, corrective actions or corrections must be performed depending on the hazard and the nature of the preventive control. Requirements vary for process, food allergen, sanitation and supply-chain program preventive controls. This section covers the definition of corrective action and corrections.

Deviations from process preventive controls frequently require corrective actions, thus corrective actions are addressed in this chapter, including basic information on record-keeping.

Definitions

Corrective action

- Procedures that must be taken if preventive controls are not properly implemented.
  - from 21 CFR 117.150(a)(1)

Correction

- An action to identify and correct a problem that occurred during the production of food, without other actions associated with a corrective action procedure (such as actions to reduce the likelihood that the problem will recur, evaluate all affected food for safety, and prevent affected food from entering commerce).
  - 21 CFR 117.3

Corrective actions and corrections are preventive control management components. Corrective actions are procedures that must be taken if preventive controls are not properly implemented, and involve documentation of the specific actions taken. Corrections apply when you take action in a timely manner to identify and correct a *minor and isolated problem* that *does not directly impact product safety*, such as identifying a food-contact surface that was not properly cleaned and re-cleaning it prior to production. Many sanitation preventive control lapses can be effectively managed through use of corrections. Conversely, many process preventive control lapses require corrective action procedures.

Corrective Actions

- Must be taken when process preventive controls are not properly implemented, resulting in a deviation
  - E.g., there is a deviation from a critical limit
- Unsafe product <u>may</u> have been produced
- Appropriate to the nature of the hazard and preventive control

A Food Safety Plan should be designed to ensure that critical limit deviations are rapidly identified and corrected. When a deviation occurs, it is possible that unsafe product may have been produced. The action take should be appropriate to the nature of the hazard and the preventive control. Thus, in some cases, you may be able to identify and correct a minor and isolated problem that does not directly impact product safety, in which case corrections may be adequate. The subsequent discussion focuses on corrective action.

Corrective Action Procedures

- Written procedures must describe steps to taken to:
  1. Identify and correct a problem with implementation
  2. Reduce likelihood of occurrence
  3. Evaluate affected food for safety
  4. Prevent affected food from entering commerce if you cannot ensure the food is not adulterated

The corrective action procedures must describe the steps to be taken to address the points noted above. The first requirement is to take appropriate action to identify and correct the problem with implementation of a preventive control. This could involve failure to meet a critical limit or a verification procedure indicating an issue.

Corrective actions may also be required for certain verification procedures, such as detection of pathogens. Process control must also be restored. Empowerment of employees to stop the line when they observe a process deviation can enhance food safety and minimize the amount of product that will be subject to review. This requires training and trust, but can be very useful to encourage a food safety-minded culture. Predetermined corrective actions in your Food Safety Plan provide a "how-to" guide that describes the steps to take when a preventive control is not properly implemented (e.g., a critical limit deviation occurs).

The second requirement is to take action to reduce the likelihood that the problem will recur, when appropriate. Root cause analysis may be useful to determine how to prevent recurrence. Corrective action examples may involve equipment repair, employee training and overall evaluation of the process for improvements. Sometimes this may be a simple readjustment of the process, but sometimes an alternate process is required. Alternate processes must be validated for effectiveness.

The third requirement is to evaluate all affected food for safety. Implicated product should be segregated and evaluated to determine if a food safety hazard exists. Product testing may or may not be required, depending on the nature of the hazard and the nature of the process.

The fourth requirement is to keep all affected food from entering into commerce unless you can ensure that the affected food is not adulterated (section 402 of the Federal Food Drug and Cosmetic Act) or misbranded with respect to allergen labeling (section 403(w) of the Federal Food Drug and Cosmetic Act). It is best to be cautious, but product destruction may not always be necessary. If a hazard exists, the affected product must be reworked or disposed in a manner to ensure it will not cause consumer illness.

Corrective Action Examples

Process Examples
- Immediate adjustment of process
- Employees stop line when deviation occurs
- Apply alternate process
- Repair equipment
- Retrain employees
- Evaluate operation

Product Examples
- Hold product
- Evaluate product
- Determine product disposition
  - Release, rework or destroy product

9-23

Examples of corrective action for the process include those listed above and others. Sometimes an immediate adjustment of the process may be possible; however, for many processes, constant "tweaking" can increase process variation, which reduces certainty of the overall effectiveness of the process. If an immediate adjustment is made frequently, a follow up study on the impact on the safety of the product overall may be warranted.

As previously mentioned, it may be appropriate for an employee to stop the line. This requires empowerment of the employee to take this action.

In some situations, an alternate process may have been validated to be effective at controlling the hazard. If this is the case, such a process may be implemented as a corrective action. For example, if a temperature drops below the critical limit, an alternate process that involves longer time at a lower temperature may be applied, provided it has been validated.

Equipment repairs may be required, as well as retraining employees on proper procedures. In some situations, an evaluation of the entire operation may be required to ensure that the product is capable of being produced under conditions that are essential for product safety.

Regarding corrective actions associated with the product, a product hold, however brief, is essential when a deviation occurs at a CCP and product has been produced. The product must be evaluated to determine the potential risk prior to making the decision to release, rework or destroy the product. This may include diverting the product to a different use where the hazard is not an issue, such as use as an ingredient that will be further processed or diverting it to animal food. Appropriate regulations must be followed.

Unanticipated Problems Include:

- Preventive control not properly implemented and a corrective action procedure has not been established
- One or more preventive controls are ineffective
- Review of records finds:
  - the records incomplete,
  - the activities did not follow the Food Safety Plan, or
  - corrective action decisions were not appropriate

Although it may not be possible to anticipate all the deviations that could happen, corrective actions need to be taken and fully documented even when an unanticipated situation occurs. Circumstances considered to be "unanticipated problems" include:

- A preventive control is not properly implemented and a corrective action procedure has not been established;

- A preventive control, combination of preventive controls or the food safety plan as a whole is found to be ineffective, such as when verification activities detect a pathogen in an RTE product.

- A review of records finds that they were not complete, activities were not conducted in accordance with the Food Safety Plan, or appropriate decisions were not made about corrective actions.

In such cases, in addition to taking the corrective actions already described, the Food Safety Plan (or applicable portion of the plan) must be reanalyzed to determine whether modifications to the plan are required.

Unanticipated Problems

- Required corrective action includes:
  1. Standard corrective action procedures
     ○ Identify and correct an implementation problem
     ○ Reduce the likelihood of occurrence
     ○ Evaluate all implicated product for safety
     ○ Prevent adulterated or misbranded product from entering commerce
  2. Reanalyze the Food Safety Plan
     ○ See Chapter 13 Verification and Validation Procedures

FSPCA

As with other product subject to a deviation, proper and thorough safety evaluation is necessary to determine the disposition of the product. Decisions related to the disposition of the affected product must be based on sound evidence. This evidence must be documented to support the decision. Like other corrective actions, if the product is rejected or destroyed, the processor needs to document that this has been done.

Whether the corrective action was planned or unanticipated, a preventive controls qualified individual must conduct or oversee review of records for the appropriateness of the corrective actions. Not every firm has an expert on staff who can evaluate the safety of

9-25

products involved in a deviation. It may be necessary to identify additional resources that can help with product safety evaluations.

Corrective Actions Required Records

1. Actions taken to identify and correct the problem,
2. Actions taken, when necessary, to reduce the likelihood that the problem will recur
3. Safety evaluation for all affected food
4. Records demonstrate that food that is potentially injurious to health did not enter commerce

---

First, records must document the actions taken to identify and correct the problem with implementation of the preventive control in order to reduce the likelihood that the problem will recur. Included in this requirement is a record of the actions taken to fix the problem that caused the deviation and to restore process control. Evaluation of historical corrective action records can help to identify recurring problems. When critical limit deviations frequently reoccur, the process and the Food Safety Plan may need reanalysis and modification. A formal process may be needed to manage major changes that need to be implemented. This may include reissuing forms, retraining employees, phasing in changes, managing label information, informing suppliers and other tasks, depending on the nature of the change.

Second, records must document how the safety of all affected food was evaluated. Specific technical expertise may be required for this evaluation, depending on the nature of the deviation.

Third, records must reflect that all affected food involved in a process deviation was prevented from entering commerce until it has been determined to be safe. This includes identifying the amount of product involved in the deviation, as well as records documenting the disposition of the product.

Corrective Action Form	E.G. Food Company Example PAGE 1 of X
PLANT NAME: E.G. Food Company ADDRESS: 360 Culinary Circle, Mytown, USA	
Date of Record:	Code or Lot Number:
Date and Time of Problem:	
Description of Problem and Root Cause:	
Actions Taken to Restore Order to the Process:	
Person Taking Action (name and signature) :	
Amount of Product Involved in Problem:	
Evaluation of Product Involved with Problem:	
Final Disposition of Product:	
Reviewed by (Name and Signature):	Date:

FSPCA

An example of a Corrective Action Form appears above. In some situations, corrective action activities may take place in a short period of time. In other, more complicated situations, corrective action activities may take place over several days, or possibly longer (e.g., capital improvement projects). It is important to have an accurate record of all corrective actions to protect both the public and the product. For example, failure to provide adequate rationale as to when the incident started and ended can lead to an expanded recall affecting a substantial amount of product.

Operating Limits and Critical Limits

Operating Limit Definition

- Criteria that are more stringent than critical limits and that are used by an operator to reduce the risk of a deviation.
  - National Seafood HACCP Alliance. 2011

FSPCA

Use of an operating limit allows the detection of a potential problem before a critical limit is violated because the value for the parameter is usually more stringent (or conservative) than the critical limit.

Operating limits should not be confused with critical limits. Operating limits are established so that the critical limit is achieved before the operating limit. The process may be adjusted when the operating limit is not met, which avoids violating the critical limit. These actions are called "process adjustments." A processor may use these adjustments to avoid loss of control resulting in a deviation and the need to take corrective action. Spotting a trend toward loss of control early and acting on it can save product re-work or, worse yet, product destruction.

Operating Limit Uses

- Operating limits may be established:
  - For quality reasons
  - To avoid deviating from a critical limit
  - To account for process variability

FSPCA

Operating limits may be selected for various reasons:

- For quality reasons – for example higher final temperatures than are needed to kill pathogens may enhance flavor or structure development, or may be necessary to control organisms that can cause spoilage. Shelf stable acidified foods present an example of a process in which operating limits are used, because the times and temperatures required to achieve commercial sterility generally exceed those needed to destroy pathogens that are potentially present.
- To avoid deviating from a critical limit – for example, a product that must be acidified to pH 4.6 for safety may have a more stringent operating limit of 4.4 to reduce the likelihood of exceeding the critical limit.
- To account for normal variability – for example, a fryer with a 5°F (2.8°C) variability should be set at least 5°F (2.8°C) above the critical limit to avoid violating it.

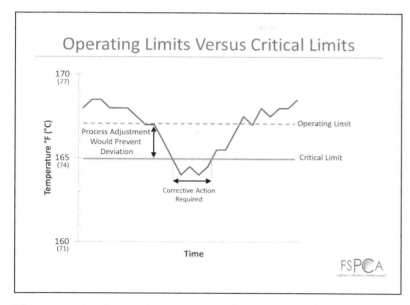

The example above illustrates two important points:
1) Operating limits and process adjustments, and
2) Critical limits and corrective actions.

In this example of a cooking process, a critical limit is established at 165°F (74°C) and it is clear that the temperature fell below that limit. Setting an operating limit above the critical limit, in this example at 167°F (75°C) could have alerted line personnel to make a process adjustment to bring the cook temperature back above the operating limit. If an adjustment is made before the temperature drops below the critical limit, no corrective action record is required. However, in this example, an adjustment was not made until after the temperature dropped below the critical limit of 165°F (74°C), thus appropriate corrective actions must be taken and a corrective action report must be written and included with preventive controls records.

Corrective Action Example

E.G. Food Company Example

PRODUCT: Omelet - Plain									PAGE 1 of X	
PLANT NAME: E.G. Food Company								ISSUE DATE		mm/dd/yy
ADDRESS: 360 Culinary Circle, Mytown, USA								SUPERSEDES		mm/dd/yy
Process Control	Hazard(s)	Critical Limits	Monitoring				Corrective Action	Verification	Records
			What	How	Frequency	Who			
Cook	Vegetative pathogens such as *Salmonella*	Omelet temperature is ≥158°F (70°C) instantaneous	Omelet temperature is ≥158°F (70°C)	Infrared surface thermometer	Each cook station, 4 times per shift, about every 2-3 hours	QA technician or designee	Hold product back to the last good check and evaluate - rework, discard, or release. Determine root cause - retrain or correct as appropriate		

FSPCA

The Cook step for E.G. Food Company's plain omelet has the following corrective action procedures: **Hold product back to the last good check and evaluate - rework, discard, or release. Determine root cause – retrain or correct as appropriate.**

This information is recorded in the Food Safety Plan.

Process Preventive Controls Summary

Process Preventive Controls Summary

- Procedures must be documented for the process-related hazards requiring a preventive control identified through the hazard analysis process.
  - These controls are usually CCPs.
  - Specific controls depend on the nature of the hazard and the nature of the preventive control.

continued

FSPCA

Process preventive controls focus on controls at process steps that are identified in the hazard analysis as steps where control can be applied to significantly minimize or prevent hazards requiring a preventive control. Process preventive controls are frequently called Critical Control Points. The specific controls depend on the nature of the hazard and the nature of the preventive control.

Process Preventive Controls Summary

- For each process-related preventive control identified, the following must be recorded, as appropriate:
  - Parameters and values (e.g., valid critical limits) that must be met
  - Monitoring procedures, including what, how, frequency and who
  - Corrective actions that identify the implicated product, determine its disposition, correct the cause and determine that the preventive controls are working again
    - Corrections may be appropriate in some situations
  - Verification and records (discussed in subsequent chapters)

Critical limits, i.e., a maximum and/or minimum value to which a process effectively controls a food safety hazard to an acceptable level must be determined at each process-related preventive control (e.g., CCPs) identified in the hazard analysis. Critical limits must be validated to ensure that the values established are effective in controlling the hazard. Monitoring procedures are required at each of these steps to ensure that the process is in control, e.g., that critical limits are met. Such procedures must specify what will be monitored, how it will take place, how often it will be done and who will do it. Corrective actions that describe what to do when critical limits are not met must also be determined, unless you are dealing with a minor and isolated problem that does not directly impact product safety.

Two additional requirements for process preventive controls are described in Chapter 13: Verification and Validation Procedures and Chapter 14: Record-keeping Procedures. Together these elements help to ensure the safety of food products.

Additional Reading

Canadian Food Inspection Agency. 2010. Guide to Food Safety Codex Alimentarius HACCP Documents

FDA. 2014. Dairy Grade A Voluntary HACCP.

Grocery Manufacturers Association. 2013. A Systems Approach Using Preventive Controls for Safe Food Production, GMA Science and Education Foundation, Washington, DC.

National Advisory Committee on Microbiological Criteria for Foods. 1998. Hazard Analysis and Critical Control Point Principles and Application Guidelines. Journal of Food Protection 61(9):1246-1259.

National Seafood HACCP Alliance. 2011. Hazard Analysis Critical Control Point - Training Curriculum, 5th Edition

NOTES:

CHAPTER 10.   Food Allergen Preventive Controls

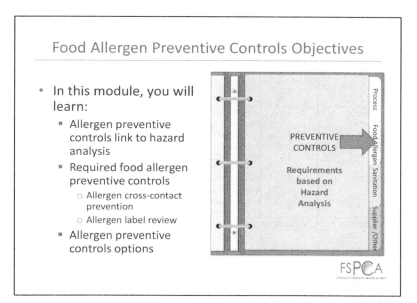

The *Preventive Controls for Human Food* regulation requires documented food allergen preventive controls to prevent allergen cross-contact and to ensure accurate allergen labeling is on finished food products. The need for specific food allergen controls is determined through the hazard analysis process. The specific allergen control practices required to manage food allergens depend on the specific product and manufacturing practices. Common causes for the presence of undeclared food allergens were discussed in Chapter 5: Chemical, Physical and Economically Motivated Food Safety Hazards. The required elements of allergen controls in a Food Safety Plan, i.e., accurate labeling to inform consumers and preventing allergen cross-contact, and the associated monitoring procedures are addressed in this chapter. A short discussion on allergen testing, which is a potential verification procedure, is also discussed in the context of allergen cross-contact. Other elements of verification are discussed in Chapter 13: Verification and Validation Procedures.

This is not intended to be a comprehensive chapter on allergen management, thus references are provided for further information at the end of the chapter.

Link to Hazard Analysis

Hazard Analysis Form					**E.G. Food Company Example**		
PRODUCT: Omelet – Plain, Cheese, and Cheese Biscuit						PAGE X of Y	
PLANT NAME	E.G. Food Company				ISSUE DATE	2/13/2016	
ADDRESS	360 Culinary Circle, Mytown, USA				SUPERSEDES	9/20/2015	
(1) Ingredient/ Processing Step	(2) Identify potential food safety hazards introduced, controlled or enhanced at this step	(3) Do any potential food safety hazards require a preventive control?		(4) Justify your decision for column 3	(5) What preventive control measure(s) can be applied to significantly minimize or prevent the food safety hazard? *Process including CCPs, Allergen, Sanitation, Supply-chain, other preventive control*	(6) Is the preventive control applied at this step?	
		Yes	No			Yes	No
Receiving frozen ingredients – biscuits *	C Allergen – wheat	X		Wheat is an allergen that must be labeled to inform consumers. Allergen cross-contact with other products must be controlled because some products do not contain wheat.	**Allergen Control – allergen labeling** at other steps *Sanitation Control* – at a subsequent step to **prevent allergen cross-contact**		X

*One of several Allergen Controls identified in the Hazard Analysis

FSPCA

As with process controls, Chapter 8: Hazard Analysis and Preventive Controls Determination describes the process of evaluating food allergen hazards to determine the allergen preventive controls that are required to be included in the Food Safety Plan. The slide above illustrates one of the steps identified in the E.G. Food Company omelet example as requiring an allergen preventive control. Biscuits have a wheat allergen, which is not present in their other products. The step illustrated, "Receiving frozen ingredients – biscuits" (Column 1), identifies the specific food allergen – wheat (Column 2) and concludes that a food safety hazard requiring a preventive control is present (Column 3). The justification (Column 4) includes two elements related to allergen control:

1) the need for allergen labeling to inform consumers and
2) the need to control allergen cross-contact because other products do not contain wheat.

Column 5 identifies two preventive controls to address the allergen concern:

1) allergen labeling at other steps and
2) sanitation to prevent allergen cross-contact at a subsequent step.

Neither of these are a CCP (they are not controlling a specific processing action) but both of them are preventive controls that **must** be addressed in the Food Safety Plan. The company should determine the best language to communicate the needs to the people performing the tasks involved in managing the control. Focus on *what must be done* to control the hazard, rather than what a specific step is called.

> The term "sanitation" may include both cleaning and sanitizing activities. Cleaning is necessary to control allergens. Sanitizing, which is intended to kill microorganisms, has little or no impact on allergens.

10-2

FALCPA* Required Food Allergen Labeling

- Milk
- Egg
- Peanut
- Tree nuts (species specific)

- Fish (species specific)
- Crustacean shellfish (species specific)
- Wheat
- Soy

* Food Allergen Labeling and Consumer Protection Act

Photo Sources: Microsoft Clip Art and KMJ Swanson (soybeans)

As discussed in Chapter 5: Chemical, Physical and Economically Motivated Food Safety Hazards, the food allergens listed on this slide contribute to about 90% of food allergic reactions in the U.S. The *Food Allergen Labeling and Consumer Protection Act* (FALCPA) mandates labeling for these food allergen groups if they are present in a food product, thus these are the allergens that you would identify as hazards requiring a preventive control during the hazard analysis if they are present in your product. When labeling a product containing a food allergen, the label must be specific to the allergen to inform the consumer who has an allergy to one food in a group. For example, if tree nuts are present, then the specific tree nut(s) must also be on the label. Similarly, individual species of fish and crustaceans must be labeled. A discussion of labeling is presented later in this section.

If all products produced in a given facility have identical food allergen profiles, then the allergen program needs to address only proper labeling because allergen cross-contact is not an issue. Sometimes a supply-chain program may be necessary, depending on the source and complexity of ingredients used in the product. For example, almond ingredients may come from a facility that processes other tree nuts; it will be important that the supplier has controls to address labeling and allergen cross-contact. See Chapter 12: Supply-chain Programs for more information on supply-chain programs.

10-3

Allergen Preventive Controls Requirements

Allergen Preventive Controls Requirements

1. Preventing allergen cross-contact
   - Clean shared equipment – potential sanitation controls
   - Properly manage rework
   - Avoid in-process or post-process allergen cross-contact
2. Accurate allergen labeling of finished food
   - Ensure labels are correct – potential supply-chain program
   - Ensure the correct label or package is used

- Human error can be involved – training is essential!

Allergen cross-contact can occur through a number of routes. Inadequate cleaning of equipment can leave residues that can introduce allergens from the equipment surface into product material. Allergen cross-contact can also occur during or after processing. For example, if two processing belts enter the same freezer, an allergenic component might fall from one line onto the other. Reworking material containing food allergens into a formula that does not have identical ingredients may also introduce allergens. If an allergen hazard is identified, an allergen preventive control must address these situations.

Incorrect labeling will occur if allergen cross-contact issues (discussed above) occur. In addition, other avenues of incorrect labeling exist. Formulation mistakes can introduce undeclared allergens into a product in a number of ways. Substituting ingredients, either intentionally or by mistake, can also lead to undeclared allergens in the product. Inadvertent use of the wrong package can occur in a number of ways. Label handling procedures and work processes can help to ensure that the right label goes on the right package. Undeclared allergens may also be present if an ingredient supplier does not manage their allergens effectively or if a label supplier does not print label stock accurately. Chapter 12: Supply-chain Program addresses relevant aspects of allergen control in a supply-chain program.

Human error can be involved in all of the common causes of undeclared allergens in food products. Because of this, training on the importance of allergen preventive control, including an awareness of the potential consequences of a mistake, is an important prerequisite for implementation of an effective allergen management program.

Allergen Cross-contact Prevention

Allergen Cross-contact Prevention Considerations

- Equipment cleaning and sanitary design
- Scheduling
- Manufacturing and engineering controls
- Allergenic ingredient control
- Rework management
- Personnel practices
- Employee training relevant to the above

Allergen preventive controls must document those procedures used to prevent allergen cross-contact when the hazard analysis process identifies allergens as hazards requiring a preventive control. Cleaning of equipment that is used to process different food allergens is typically a preventive control. However, certain practices such as scheduling and engineering controls, can minimize the frequency of such cleaning, and might be managed as a prerequisite program. A thorough understanding of where allergenic ingredients exist in the manufacturing environment, how they are managed and where they are introduced into the process can influence whether practices are managed as a prerequisite program or as a preventive control. Control of rework must also be considered and may require a preventive control. Personnel practices can also impact the likelihood of allergen cross-contact.

Whether or not the techniques mentioned above are a preventive control or prerequisite program depends on *how* the facility manages their system and the complexity of their allergen concerns.

The regulation does not require validation of allergen cleaning, but this is strongly encouraged. Numerous allergen recalls have occurred because equipment could not be adequately cleaned to remove allergen residues.

Equipment Cleaning

Equipment Cleaning
A Potential Preventive Control for Allergens

- Thorough cleaning between products with different allergens is required to prevent cross-contact
- Validation of allergen cleaning procedures is not required but may be useful
- Optional – Dedicate tools, surfaces and other devices for specific allergens

Effective cleaning is an essential element in an allergen management program. Food contact surfaces should be visibly clean as a starting point when products produced contain different allergens. Refer to Chapter 11: Sanitation Preventive Controls for information on cleaning procedure documentation requirements and Appendix 5: Sanitation Basics for more information on cleaning.

Equipment, tools and surfaces must be thoroughly cleaned prior to processing product that does not contain the same allergen profile. A record that documents cleaning between products that contain different allergens is required. This could be recorded on a sanitation record or an allergen scheduling record. Use a format that clarifies what must to be done to meet the needs of your operation.

Optional Techniques to Manage Cleaning
Dedicating specific tools and equipment, such as totes, bins, paddles, scoops and kettles, to specific allergens can reduce the frequency of allergen cleaning. Color-coded or labeled equipment is useful. Consider erecting a physical barrier (e.g., walls, curtains, partitions) between production lines in close proximity to reduce the risk of allergen cross-contact. Training of staff is very important for separating tools and utensils used with allergens. Line workers may incorrectly identify color codes for equipment if colors are not used in a consistent manner and the importance of dedicated tools and equipment is not emphasized.

Verification of Allergen Cleaning

- Visually clean
    - Minimum requirement
    - No residue, film or sheen
- Optional tests
    - Non-specific tests, e.g., ATP and protein
        - May not be sensitive enough to detect some allergens
    - Allergen test kits
        - Follow manufacturer's instructions!
    - Complex tests
        - Special situations

Verification that allergen cleaning procedures were performed is required by the *Preventive Controls for Human Food* regulation for hazards requiring a preventive control. Many companies use a standard of "visually clean" as the primary evidence of allergen cleaning. If you can see residue on the equipment, the equipment is not clean. This includes the presence of films or protein sheen. Use care with non-specific ATP and protein tests for verifying allergen cleaning. Some of these tests are not sensitive enough to detect levels of protein that could cause an allergic reaction. Validated allergen-specific test kits are available for some food allergens, and can be used to detect the presence of food allergens on food-contact surfaces using swabs. Push-through material can also be evaluated to establish safe times and volumes for such a procedure. If a surface cannot be effectively swabbed, final rinse water can be collected and tested, assuming the equipment and environment is suitable for wet cleaning, as discussed in Chapter 11: Sanitation Preventive Controls. While finished product can be tested, appropriate action is needed if allergens that are not on the label are detected.

Validation of allergen cleaning is not required. However, validation may be desirable for complex equipment the first time a unique allergen is introduced on a production line, or when major changes are made to product formulation to determine if cleaning procedures need to be adjusted.

Simple-to-clean equipment, such as a stainless steel table top, may not need validation if the surface is visibly clean (i.e., no residue or film) when cleaning procedures are followed.

Allergen Scheduling or Run Sequencing

Scheduling or Run Sequencing

- Minimize changeovers
- Run dedicated or designated systems as much as possible
- Schedule appropriate sanitation activities
- Control allergen addition

FSP©A

If a line is used to process both allergen-containing and non-allergen-containing products, the schedule sequence should run unique allergens toward the end. For example, vanilla ice cream might be scheduled first, followed by one with added pecans, followed by one with added pecans and almonds. If an allergen present in a product is not present in the next product scheduled to run, a sanitation protocol must be executed. Sanitation activities must be robust enough to remove all visible traces of an allergen residue prior to starting up the next product. If possible, only run products with the same allergen profile on the same production line.

E.G. Food Company Example

PRODUCT:	Omelet – Plain, Cheese and Cheese Biscuit								PAGE 1 of X
PLANT NAME: E.G. Food Company						ISSUE DATE		mm/dd/yy
ADDRESS: 360 Culinary Circle, Mytown, USA						SUPERSEDES		mm/dd/yy

Product Line Allergen Assessment

| Product Name | Production Line | Intentional Allergens | | | | | | | |
		Egg	Milk	Soy	Wheat	Tree Nut (market name)	Peanut	Fish (market name)	Crustacean Shellfish (market name)
Plain Omelet	1	X	X	X					
Cheese Omelet	1	X	X	X					
Cheese Omelet Biscuit	1	X	X	X	X Unique allergen				

Scheduling Implications:
Run the Plain and/or Cheese Omelet in the beginning of the shift and the Cheese Omelet Biscuit at the end of the shift to reduce the potential for allergen cross-contact.

Allergen Cleaning Implications:
An allergen clean is required AFTER production of Cheese Omelet Biscuit because it contains a unique allergen – wheat.

FSP©A

An example of a Production Line Allergen Assessment for the E.G. Food Company appears above. Only one product, the Cheese Omelet Biscuit, has a unique allergen. Scheduling implications and cleaning implications are noted.

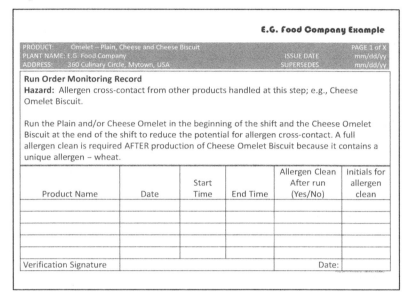

The E.G. Food Company chose to monitor run sequencing using the above form.

Manufacturing and Engineering Controls

Manufacturing and Engineering Controls

- Engineer the line to minimize mixing of allergenic products with non-allergenic products
- Use physical barriers to separate processing lines
- Minimize the reuse of water or oil

When engineering a production line, consider the potential for product crossing from one line to another. This may occur, for example, if an overhead conveyor spills product onto a conveyor below. Transfer via aerosols and dust may also occur when water sprays or air hoses are used. Engineering solutions may reduce the potential for transfer. In some cases, physical barriers such as curtains or walls between lines may be necessary to separate product streams containing different allergens. The potential for cross over can also exist in cooling water or frying oil that is reused. Because it is difficult to test cooking oil for the presence of allergens, the medium should not be reused unless sophisticated tests demonstrate that there is no carryover.

Maintenance and Engineering

- Sanitary design principles
- Monitor and reduce dust levels
- Minimize use of air compressors
- Maintain tools

It is important to design equipment that can be easily cleaned and inspected in all areas when products with different allergen profiles are made on a shared line. Dust collection systems should also be used to minimize the transfer of allergens between processing lines in a dusty processing environment. Socks should be cleaned and replaced as necessary. When cleaning, eliminate or minimize the use of compressed air, as its use may transfer allergenic material to already cleaned equipment. Maintenance employees should use dedicated tools in areas with allergens, to keep from spreading the residue.

Maps similar to the hygiene map discussed in Appendix 6: Hygienic Zoning and Environmental Monitoring may be appropriate to illustrate allergen flow through the facility. These maps may indicate where unique allergens are stored or handled. Small companies that have all of their operations in one room and handle only product with a common allergen profile may not need such a diagram.

Allergenic Ingredient Control

Allergenic Ingredient Control

- Develop a master list of allergenic ingredients used in the facility
  - Letters of guarantee from suppliers on the presence or absence of allergenic ingredients
  - Accessibility of master list at receiving dock
  - Use common names of allergens
- Apply careful handling at receiving to avoid allergen cross-contact
- Identify allergens with icons

Allergen icons can be useful, especially when different languages are spoken in a facility. You can develop them yourself of consider use of icons available through the International Association for Food Protection: http://www.foodprotection.org/resources/food-allergen-icons/

A master list of allergenic ingredients should be developed as part of allergen control. Frequently this can be managed by the individual in charge of developing and changing product formulations using information from supplier continuing guarantees. The list needs to be kept up to date, so it is important that any change information communicated from a supplier to the purchasing department, for example, gets to the person maintaining the master allergen list. Accessibility to the master allergen list at the loading dock is helpful so that allergenic materials can be placed in segregated storage. The master list should include the common name of the food allergen to ensure that allergens are properly identified. For example, some ingredient names do not directly identify the allergenic material, such as sodium caseinate (which contains a milk allergen) or lecithin (which may contain a soy allergen). Staff training could include allergen identification and assessment of ability to clearly segregate allergens. The master list of allergenic materials should also consider packaging, processing aids, colors, flavorings and lubricants. For example, wheat-derived or casein-derived agents in packaging material or lubricants can transfer to food products.

Considerations for handling and labeling of ingredients containing food allergens follow.

10-11

Receipt of Incoming Goods

- Review labels of incoming raw materials
- Include allergen check as a prerequisite program or in allergen preventive control for deliveries, depending on risk
- Color coding and pallet labeling useful
- Separate each type of tree nut, peanut, fish or crustacean shellfish species
- Consider separate area for each allergen
- Consider dedicated transportation vehicles for different allergens, depending on risk

FSPCA

Consider use of a documented check of allergens during receiving as a prerequisite program. This may be a preventive control in a facility that handles many allergens and produces many products with unique allergens. Identify allergens on raw material labels, use the common name and consider use of a color coding scheme or icon to reinforce the need for control within the facility. Color coding may be an issue for color blind people.

If bags or bins are opened to take test samples upon receipt, do not use the same knives to open bags of unlike allergens and ensure proper closure after samples are taken. Determine if controls are needed for fork lift drivers to prevent damage to packaging. Pierced or dropped bags and cracked or broken bins present allergen cross-contact opportunities that should be avoided.

Storage of Incoming Goods

- Separate allergenic ingredients from non-allergenic ingredients to prevent allergen cross-contact
  - Control traffic patterns also
- Use signage in areas used to store allergens
  - Maintain consistent allergen identifiers – color or image
- Store allergens in sealed, intact containers, as appropriate
- Do not store allergens above non-allergens on racks or pallets
- Store allergens with "like" allergens
- Have documented clean up procedures available

Separate allergen and non-allergen storage areas, and use dedicated pallets, combos or bins for allergenic material. If signage is used, consider whether the sign is needed in languages other than English. Storage of like allergens can simplify management. For example, milk and cheese can be stored together because they are both are dairy products. However, walnuts and almonds cannot be stored together, even though they are both tree nuts, because they have different allergens.

If signage is used on pallets, maintain uniform placement area on the pallet so the allergen label is visible when the pallet is opened and boxes are removed.

Allergen Cross-contact Prevention During Processing

- Requires segregation of unique allergenic material, e.g.:
  - Weigh powders containing unique allergens in a different area
  - Cover totes containing allergen-containing ingredients during transfer
  - Control ventilation over lines where protein powders are dumped
  - Consider dedicated tools and equipment
  - Proper use of containers that previously held food allergens

---

Segregation of allergenic foods and ingredients during handling helps to manage allergen cross-contact in the manufacturing setting. Preventive controls during processing start from the time a unique allergen is introduced into production, and control must extend beyond this point as well. For example, powders can easily disperse throughout an area through the air, thus weighing allergenic powders in a different room or area is useful. Covering totes that contain allergen-containing ingredients during transfer from one room to the next helps to prevent unintended allergen cross-contact. A review of ventilation systems over lines that handle powders may reveal a potential allergen cross-contact issue.

Sometimes an allergen may be the primary component of your product and thus does not present an allergen cross-contact risk because all products contain the ingredient. For example, in a dairy facility (e.g., fluid milk, ice cream, yogurt, cheese), milk allergens are present in all of the dairy products. Segregation becomes important when unique allergenic ingredients are used in some products and not in others. For example, if a dairy facility decides to put peanut clusters in ice cream, the peanut allergen in the cluster could be managed through segregation to prevent introducing peanut allergen into other dairy products not intended to contain peanuts. Likewise, if a dairy facility decides to pasteurize non-dairy soy milk on the same line, preventive measures are required to ensure that soy protein is not present in the dairy products *and* that dairy protein is not present in the soy product.

Depending on the number of major allergens in the plant, where they are introduced and the processes used, a facility may use some, all or none of these methods to prevent allergen cross-contact. Determining when preventive control is required is based on the outcome of the hazard analysis process.

Rework Management

Rework and Product on QA Hold

- Store allergen-containing rework or open product on QA hold to avoid cross-contact
- Clearly mark rework or open QA-hold material for the presence of allergens

---

Proper handling of rework and work in progress is critical. Use sturdy containers with secure covers, and interior disposable plastic liners where appropriate. Use dedicated containers, lids and pallets when feasible, or thoroughly wash and sanitize containers before reuse. Using containers that can be moved without use of equipment to hold allergen-containing materials (e.g., totes on wheels) makes it easier to segregate the material and reduces the potential for damage by fork lifts. Mark the rework bin properly with information such as:

- Name of the rework or QA hold product
- Name of the allergen
- Date/time of manufacture
- Date/time put into storage
- Date/time for using rework (if known)

Rework practices within a facility should be evaluated as part of the hazard analysis for allergens. If rework is identified as a possible risk for an undeclared allergen, consider the following control measures:

- Use rework for "exact into exact" applications.

- Label the containers appropriately for storage.
- The amount of allergen-containing rework generated and when and where it was used should be documented. This documentation helps reduce the risk of accidental product mixing.

Personnel Practices

Personnel Practices

- Manage employee outer clothing to avoid allergen cross-contact
- Consider keeping personnel who handle unique allergens out of non-allergen areas
- Training is essential!

Employees' outer clothing may accumulate residual allergen from the processing area. This situation should be managed. Approaches to consider include providing dedicated outer clothing (e.g., jacket or smock) that remains in the entrance to the processing area during breaks. Controlling traffic patterns to reduce allergen cross-contact, such as limiting the traffic of people and raw materials into and out of areas processing allergen-containing product is often effective. Avoid having employees work on a processing line that contains allergens and then move to a different processing line that does not contain the same allergen profile. Gloves can also be a potential source of allergen cross-contact. Disposable gloves should be discarded immediately after use to avoid allergen cross-contact issues.

10-15

Allergen Labeling Considerations

> ### Allergen Labeling Considerations
>
> - Label accuracy
>   - Accurate printing of allergen ingredients on the label
>   - The right label on the package
> - Supply-chain program
>   - Ingredients
>   - Labels
>
>

Procedures that ensure accurate allergen labeling are required in the Food Safety Plan when a product contains a food allergen. Supply-chain programs are also important to ensure that food ingredient suppliers accurately identify allergens in the products that they provide, and packaging suppliers accurately print ingredient information on labels.

Product Labeling

> ### Product Labeling and Packaging
>
> - Proper package labeling protects:
>   - Consumers
>   - Only way for them to know the allergen is in the product
>   - Companies
>   - Product recalls
>   - Regulatory inquiry
>   - Potential liability
> - Preventive controls for food labels and packages are as important as other food allergen management techniques!
>
>

Ensuring that a food product has the correct label and package is a key component in protecting the food allergic consumer because it is the only way for them to know the allergens that are in the product. Undeclared allergens can lead to illness and death. Moreover, labeling and packaging errors are leading causes of allergen-related recalls, which can cause brand damage, regulatory inquiry, manufacturing disruption, and potential liability when illness occurs.

Product Labeling Must Be Accurate

- Ensure all allergens are identified in compliance with appropriate law:
  - Food Allergen Labeling and Consumer Protection Act provides requirements for FDA-regulated foods

---

You must ensure that all allergens are properly identified on the product label. FALCPA (see Additional Reading) provides regulatory requirements that apply to ensure proper allergen labeling on FDA-regulated products.

Considerations for Food Labels and Packages

- Allergen labeling errors are a primary cause of food product recalls
- Consider controls that:
  - Ensure accurate printing
  - Ensure the right label or package is used for the product
  - Manage formula changes to ensure that the correct label is used during transition

---

As discussed in Chapter 5: Chemical, Physical and Economically Motivated Food Safety Hazards, labeling errors are a primary cause of recalls. Consider controls to check for printer's errors prior to labeling. In most facilities, a preventive control to ensure that the right label or package is applied to the product will be an allergen control.

Allergen Label Design Control Examples

Examples of procedures:

- Design and copy proofreading
- Written approval of label and package proofs
- Identity coding of printed labels and packages
- Lack of co-mingling when shipping labels and pre-printed packages

Proofreading label copy is a useful tool to prevent errors, and some organizations consider this a preventive control. If the label is complicated, use a couple of people during proofreading and consider developing a written approval process. Using an identity coding system for printed labels and packages (e.g., color codes that are easy to visualize) can help with effective label management on the production floor. Procedures that do not allow co-mingling of labels on the same pallet during shipping minimize the potential for the wrong label to be used in production.

Potential resources for determining labeling options when an ingredient has a precautionary label are:

- FDA's Guidance for Industry listed in Additional Reading and

- the Food Allergy Research and Resource Program (FARRP) http://farrp.unl.edu/

"May Contain" Labeling

- "May Contain" or similar labeling is NOT a substitute for appropriate GMPs
- Carefully consider label implications for ingredients with precautionary labels (e.g., "May Contain")

Precautionary labeling, such as "May Contain" or "Manufactured in a facility that produces…" a specific allergen is not a preventive control. While unintentional allergen cross-contact of food products with major food allergens can occur in the manufacturing process when product is exposed to the environment, precautionary labeling cannot be used to compensate for poor GMPs. When an ingredient has a precautionary label, you must determine how to handle this in regard to your allergen labeling requirements. Chapter 12: Supply-chain Program addresses requirements for supply-chain programs, which include documentation and verification procedures.

> Because applying a label to a package is part of a process, some companies may manage allergen labeling at a process control step and call it a CCP. Other companies may manage it in what they may call an "Allergen Control Plan." Either approach is fine as long as the allergens that are present in the food are declared on the label.

Allergen Preventive Controls for Labeling

* Preferable continuous review of label or wrap material during a processing run
  * E.g., bar code scanner
* Colored striping on edges of packages stacked flat in packaging machines reduces line operator errors
* Especially important when labels are applied to product held in unlabeled inventory

---

Ensuring that the correct label is applied to a product containing a food allergen is a required allergen preventive control. A variety of approaches may be used to help achieve this. Continuous monitoring, such as a bar code scanner, is most effective, but may not be affordable for some processors. Colored striping on stacked flat labels in packaging machines is another approach to reduce operator errors. This is particularly useful when the label supply runs out mid-production. Returning unused packaging materials to the warehouse, and not mixing them with other packaging materials helps avoid packaging mix-ups. It is best to store packaging (e.g., plastic cups, lids) in boxes that are sealed shut. Train line personnel to ensure product labels are switched properly at product changeover. This is especially important when labels are applied to product, such as cans, that are held in unlabeled inventory and labeled well after production.

A variety of other measures can help to reduce mistakes, such as a system to assure that out-of-date labels and packaging are removed and destroyed in a timely manner. Keeping accurate inventory records of labels and packaging can help – if the numbers do not match, it is likely that the wrong label was used on a packaging run. Stage packaging so that only those needed for current product are in the packaging area. Check packaging film labels for accuracy (e.g., by comparing the label to the formulation or recipe of the product being produced) before the roll is placed on the packaging machine. For on-site computer generated labels, verify that the correct electronic file is applied for each label, and have a system that lets only authorized personnel edit electronic label files.

Remember that the essential allergen preventive control is that product containers and labels applied during processing are monitored to ensure that allergen information on labels matches ingredient specifications of product.

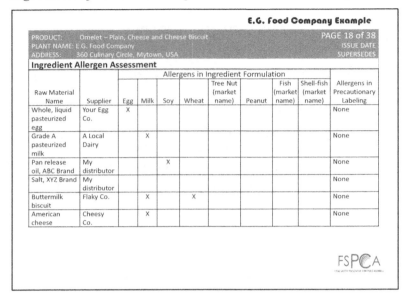

The fictitious E.G. Food Company's Ingredient Allergen Assessment, lists all of the raw materials used for products, along with the supplier name. There is also a column that is used only if precautionary labeling (e.g., "May Contain") labeling is used by their supplier. This information helps E.G. Food Company to identify the allergens that are in their products, depending on the ingredients used in each product.

Using their recipe sheets and the Ingredient Allergen Assessment, they document the allergen statements that must appear on labels for each product. As an allergen preventive control, they check the label upon receipt from the label manufacturer to prevent potential label shortages in case a mistake was made during printing and check the label number when labels are applied to product. Checking the label number when the label is applied involves less detailed review than reading the "contains" statement. They include the information used at two different steps on one form avoid potential errors if they tried to maintain two different documents with the same information.

E.G. Food Company Example

PRODUCT: Omelet - Plain									PAGE 1 of X
PLANT NAME: E.G. Food Company						ISSUE DATE			mm/dd/yy
ADDRESS: 360 Culinary Circle, Mytown, USA						SUPERSEDES			mm/dd/yy

Allergen Control	Hazard(s)	Criterion	Monitoring				Corrective Action	Verification	Records
			What	How	Frequency	Who			
Receiving packaging (labeled carton)	Undeclared allergens – egg, milk, soy (wheat in biscuit only)	All finished product labels must declare the allergens present in the formula per listing	Ingredient listing and allergen informa-tion matches product	Visual check of carton label to match product formula	Before release to production	Label coordi-nator	If label is incorrect, reject labels and return to supplier or destroy. Identify root cause and conduct training as needed to prevent recurrence	Review of Label verification, Corrective Action and Verification records within 7 working days	Allergen Label Verifica-tion listing; Allergen Label Verifica-tion log; Corrective Action records;

FSPCA

Label review could be done only at the labeling step, but many organizations perform two label reviews 1) upon receipt and 2) at labeling step. Complex labels require careful review by people trained in technical label wording requirements. Application of the label on line may be simply matching a label number to the product formula.

Training may be appropriate for a label developer, for example if a mistake is made on the copy sent to the printer.

The allergen preventive control for reviewing the label upon receipt is illustrated above and the preventive control for applying the label to the product is illustrated below. Upon receipt, the label coordinator matches the information on the label to the product formula information. This includes the allergen declaration as well as the listing of ingredients (we do not provide a complete listing of ingredients for the example).

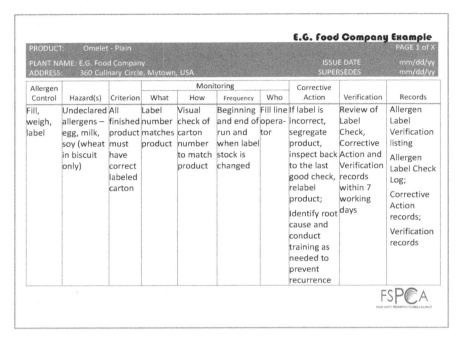

Allergen Control	Hazard(s)	Criterion	Monitoring				Corrective Action	Verification	Records
			What	How	Frequency	Who			
Fill, weigh, label	Undeclared allergens – egg, milk, soy (wheat in biscuit only)	All finished product must have correct labeled carton	Label number matches product	Visual check of carton number to match product	Beginning and end of run and when label stock is changed	Fill line opera-tor	If label is incorrect, segregate product, inspect back to the last good check, relabel product; Identify root cause and conduct training as needed to prevent recurrence	Review of Label Check, Corrective Action and Verification records within 7 working days	Allergen Label Verification listing; Allergen Label Check Log; Corrective Action records; Verification records

At the Fill, Weigh, Label step, the E.G. Food Company's Food Safety Plan states that "All finished product labels must have the correct label." The monitoring portion of their preventive controls for food allergens uses the same structure as that for process controls – identifying the what, how, when, and who. At this step, the fill line operator matches the label to the product number. Corrective action addresses what to do with the product as well as identification of the root cause and taking appropriate action to prevent recurrence.

As with process controls, the records associated with this preventive control procedure are verified – specifically the Label Check form and any corrective action or verification records.

Supply-chain Preventive Controls Related to Allergens

Allergen Control by Suppliers

- Understand allergens handled by suppliers
  - See Chapter 12: Supply-chain Preventive Controls
- Use caution with ingredient substitution

Definition:

Supplier: The establishment that manufactures/ processes the food, raises the animal, or grows the food that is provided to a receiving facility without further manufacturing/ processing by another establishment, except for further manufacturing/ processing that consists solely of the addition of labeling or similar activity of a <u>de minimis</u> nature. (21 CFR 117.3)

Whether or not you purchase your ingredients directly from a manufacturer, from a broker or from a retail store, the manufacturer (or grower) of the ingredient is "the supplier" by regulation (see text box). Carefully review the label for allergen information to determine if it provides the confidence needed for preventive controls. If not, follow up with the company that made the ingredient to obtain more information. This is especially relevant if "may contain" labeling is used on your ingredient.

It may be important to understand the level of allergen control exercised by the manufacturer, depending on the nature of the ingredient, the allergen profile of the product and other products produced by the supplier. Refer to Chapter 12: Supply-chain Program for a discussion of other relevant controls at the supplier level.

Allergen Training

> ### Allergen Training
>
> • Critical to implementation and execution of an Allergen Control Plan
> • Applies to a variety of personnel
> • Education and knowledge building
> • Empower individual role and responsibility
> • Reinforce commitment to food safety
> • Highlight changes or new development
>
> FSPCA

The University of Nebraska's Food Allergy Research and Resource Program (FARRP) provides resources and training relevant for food manufacturers.
http://farrp.unl.edu/workshopsandtraining

Other programs may also be available in your area.

Allergen awareness and control training is critical for the effective implementation of allergen preventive controls. Many food employees do not have food allergies and need to be made aware of the health hazards posed to consumers with allergies to certain foods. Training is useful for employees at all levels of the company. It not only provides an opportunity to build knowledge, but also communicates the importance of each employee's role in allergen management. Overall, training reinforces a commitment to food safety and highlights changes or improvements in production.

Supervisory personnel must be trained in the keys areas of allergen preventive controls so that they have the knowledge to train production workers. Food production workers must be trained in each of the areas relevant to their job responsibilities. Food allergen training at regular intervals reinforces proper practices and reminds workers of their importance to food allergic consumers.

The section on allergens in Chapter 5: Chemical, Physical and Economically Motivated Food Safety Hazards is a good starting point for allergen awareness training. Sanitation chemical providers frequently have training materials on allergens as well. It is important to know your culture and the type of training that works at your location. Budget constraints may limit the options, but good external training is available through recognized resources (see Additional Reading).

Food Allergen Preventive Controls Summary

Allergen Preventive Controls Summary

- Undeclared allergens present a risk :
  - Consumer reactions can be severe
  - Major cause of food recalls
- Allergen preventive controls required to:
  - Prevent allergen cross-contact
  - Accurately label product
- Allergen management best practices exist to:
  - Protect the allergic consumer
  - Reduce a company's risk
  - Make food safer for all to enjoy

Food allergens present a risk to consumer health and are a major cause of food safety recalls. Because of this, food allergen preventive controls are required to prevent allergen cross-contact with food allergenic material and ensure that products are accurately labeled. A variety of methods exist to reduce the potential for undeclared allergens to be present in food products. These include your supply-chain program, ingredient handling, allergen cross-contact prevention, accurate labeling and employee training. Additional training and information on food allergens is available through sources listed below and in Chapter 7: Resources for Food Safety Plans.

Additional Reading

FDA: Guidance for Industry: Questions and Answers Regarding Food Allergens, including the Food Allergen Labeling and Consumer Protection Act of 2004 (Edition 4); Final Guidance

Food Allergy Research and Resource Program (FARRP) and Food Allergy and Anaphylaxis Network. *Components of an Effective Allergen Control Plan – a Framework for Food Processors*

Gendel, S.M. and J. Zhu. 2014. 2013. Analysis of U.S. Food and Drug Administration food allergen recalls after implementation of the Food Allergen Labeling and Consumer Protection Act. J. Food Prot. 76(11) 1933-1938.

Gendel, S.M., J. Zhu. N. Nolan, K. Gombas. 2014. Learning from FDA food allergen recalls and reportable foods. Food Safety Magazine. April-May 2014:46-52, 80

Grocery Manufacturers Association (GMA). 2009. *Managing Allergens in Food Processing Establishments*

Jackson et al. 2008. Cleaning and other control and validation strategies to prevent allergen cross-contact in food-processing operations. J Food Prot. 71(2):445-458.

Pieretti, M.M., Chung, D., Pacenza, R., Slotkin, T., Sicherer, S.H. 2009. Audit of manufactured products: Use of allergen advisory labels and identification of labeling ambiguities. J Allergy Clin Immunol. 1242):337-41

NOTES:

CHAPTER 11. Sanitation Preventive Controls

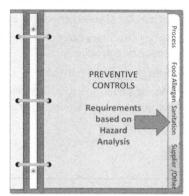

Sanitation is the beginning, not the end, of food processing. It establishes the basic hygienic conditions needed to produce safe and wholesome food. Without a clean operation to start, equipment and the environment can introduce potentially hazardous contamination. It can also contribute to loss of quality. Sanitation practices are required by Good Manufacturing Practices (GMP), including general cleaning, and washing and sanitizing of equipment, walls and floors (see Appendix 5: Sanitation Basics). Facilities must meet all applicable GMP requirements but documentation is required only for hazards requiring preventive controls. This chapter covers sanitation preventive controls identified through hazard analysis.

The *Preventive Controls for Human Food* regulation requires implementation of sanitation preventive controls, as appropriate to the facility and the food, to significantly minimize or prevent hazards such as environmental pathogens, biological hazards due to employee handing, and food allergen hazards. The hazard analysis identifies hazards requiring a preventive control.

This chapter begins with a review of sanitation-related food safety hazards and hazard analysis examples. Then preventive controls to assure cleanliness of food-contact surfaces, and prevention of allergen cross-contact and biological cross-contamination from objects and personnel in certain facilities are discussed. Finally, monitoring, corrections and verification requirements for sanitation preventive controls are addressed.

Definitions:

Allergen cross-contact: The unintentional incorporation of a food allergen into a food. (21 CFR 117.3)

Cross-contamination: The unintentional transfer of a foodborne pathogen from a food (where it may occur naturally) or insanitary object to another food (where it may present a hazard).

Food Safety Hazards Controlled by Sanitation Preventive Controls

> Hazards and Conditions Relevant to
> Sanitation Preventive Controls
>
> - Environmental pathogens when RTE product is exposed to the environment prior to packaging
>   - E.g., *Salmonella* and *L. monocytogenes*
> - Pathogens transferred through cross-contamination
>   - E.g., from insanitary objects or employees handling raw and processed product
> - Food allergen cross-contact
>   - Unintended milk, soy, egg, fish, crustacean shellfish, wheat, peanut or tree nut cross-contact
>
>

Environmental pathogens such as *Salmonella* and *Listeria monocytogenes* are major food safety hazards for many ready-to-eat products that are exposed to the processing environment prior to packaging. Sanitary facilities are essential to significantly minimize or prevent these hazards from contaminating RTE food.

Cross-contamination must be controlled to prevent pathogens from getting into the food. As discussed in Chapter 4: Biological Food Safety Hazards, foodborne pathogens can enter a facility on raw materials. Clean equipment and employee practices that minimize the transfer of these pathogens from raw ingredients to ready-to-eat products may be essential to effectively control these hazards.

Employee practices are also important to prevent allergen cross-contact between products that contain food allergens and those that do not. As discussed in Chapter 10: Food Allergen Preventive Controls, food allergens can also be transferred from equipment that is not cleaned to remove them before non-allergen containing products are handled.

GMPs That Support Cross-contamination and Cross-contact Prevention

- Employee hygiene practices
- Employee food handling practices
- Plant design and layout
- Packaging material storage and handling
- General cleaning and sanitizing
- Physical separation of:
  - Raw and ready-to-eat products
  - Unique food allergens

GMPs related to cleaning and sanitation are addressed in 117.35(d), (e), and (f). These can be managed as prerequisite programs unless the hazard analysis identifies hazards requiring a preventive control to address allergen cross-contact or cross-contamination.

For more information on basic cleaning and sanitation, see Appendix 5: Sanitation Basics.

GMPs and other prerequisite programs work together to establish a sound foundation for your food safety system. The considerations on the slide above are usually managed as GMPs. Employee hygiene, personnel practices and the design of the facility must prevent cross-contamination and allergen cross-contact. It is important for employees to understand that their actions can contribute to product contamination. Employees' hands or gloves, and equipment and utensils must be washed and sanitized, when necessary after being contaminated. For example, employees working in a raw product area should not work with a cooked finished product without washing and sanitizing their hands, gloves, equipment or utensils to avoid cross-contamination. Similarly, employees handing food allergens should wash their hands before handling food that does not contain those allergens to prevent allergen cross-contact.

Personal cleanliness is also important to prevent product contamination and is generally managed through GMPs. Workers must wear clean and appropriate attire, and must wash and sanitize their hands at appropriate intervals. When gloves are used, they are not a substitute for hand washing – leakage, cross-contamination and allergen cross-contact can occur.

Plant design must prevent potential contamination of stored ingredients and raw materials, food, and food contact surfaces, including separation of operations where contamination is likely to occur. This means separating raw product and unpackaged ready-to-eat product to avoid contamination. Similarly, separating foods that contain food allergens from those that do not contain the same food allergens helps to avoid allergen cross-contact. Food contact surfaces must be cleaned and sanitized, as appropriate, when contaminated. Packaging materials must be stored and handled properly so they do not become a source of contamination.

11-3

Hazard Analysis Example

		E.G. Food Company Example				

Hazard Analysis Worksheet		PRODUCT: Omelet – Plain, Cheese and Cheese Biscuit			PAGE X of Y	
PLANT NAME	E.G. Food Company			ISSUE DATE	mm/dd/yy	
ADDRESS	360 Culinary Circle, Mytown, USA			SUPERSEDES	mm/dd/yy	

(1) Ingredient/ Processing Step	(2) Identify potential food safety hazards introduced, controlled or enhanced at this step	(3) Do any potential food safety hazards require a preventive control? Yes / No	(4) Justify your decision for column 3	(5) What preventive control measure(s) can be applied to significantly minimize or prevent the food safety hazard? Process including CCPs, Allergen, Sanitation, Supply-chain, other preventive control	(6) Is the preventive control applied at this step? Yes / No
Assemble, wrap	B Introduction of environmental pathogens such as *L. monocytogenes*	X	Recontamination may occur if sanitation control is not in place.	**Sanitation Controls** – prevent recontamination	X
	C Allergen cross-contact from other products handled at this step; e.g., Cheese Omelet Biscuit	X	Biscuits could introduce wheat allergen to other products without control	**Sanitation and Allergen Controls** – prevent cross-contact	X

The hazard analysis process determines the hazards requiring a preventive control. Identifying specific hazards and preventive control procedures is required, and the procedures must be performed as designed on a continued basis to prevent the hazard. The E.G. Food Company's hazard analysis for omelets identified the Assemble, Wrap step as a step where a sanitation preventive control was necessary to prevent introduction of environmental pathogens such as *L. monocytogenes*. At this step the product has been cooked and then handled so cross-contamination could occur. No other step in the process would eliminate environmental pathogens that might be introduced through handling after the cook step.

The potential for allergen cross-contact from the wheat in the biscuit to non-biscuit containing products was also identified as a hazard requiring a preventive control at this step. The potential for allergen cross-contact can be significantly minimized or prevented through sanitation. Thus the slide above documents the sanitation preventive controls that are required to be addressed in the E.G. Food Company's Food Safety Plan. Other sanitation practices are handled through routine GMP procedures at the E.G. Food Company's plant. The rest of this chapter focuses on sanitation preventive controls requirements and not GMPs.

Sanitation Preventive Controls

Sanitation Preventive Controls*

- Procedures, practices and processes for:
  - Cleanliness of food-contact surfaces
  - Prevention of allergen cross-contact and cross-contamination
    - From insanitary objects and personnel to food, food packaging material, other food contact surfaces
    - From raw product to processed products

* When hazard analysis identifies a hazard requiring a preventive control

Lack of effective sanitation preventive controls has contributed to major recalls. When hazard analysis identifies a hazard requiring a sanitation preventive control, the procedures, practices and processes used to manage these hazards must be developed and documented. As appropriate to the food, facility and how the preventive control fits in the food safety system, this may involve procedures to ensure the cleanliness of food-contact surfaces, including food-contact surfaces of utensils and equipment. It may also involve procedures to significantly minimize or prevent allergen cross-contact and microbial cross-contamination.

Preventing hazard transfer from insanitary objects (such as dirty equipment and environmental sources) and from personnel to food, to food packaging material, and to other food contact surfaces may be appropriate depending on the operation. Preventing transfer from raw or unprocessed product to processed product may also be appropriate in some situations (e.g., from uncooked to cooked product, from unwashed to washed product, etc.).

Personnel can play a big role in preventing transfer of contamination. Food safety training is required by the *Preventive Controls for Human Food* regulations. This can help your employees to understand the important role they play in the food safety program. The E.G. Food Company example includes color-coded smocks for employees working in the Assemble, Wrap area as an example of a practice than can minimize transfer of environmental pathogens into this sensitive area IF employees understand why they are required to follow this procedure.

11-5

Sanitation Considerations for:

- Wet cleaning versus dry cleaning
- Personnel practices
- Hygienic zoning

Cleanliness of food-contact surfaces is a primary focus for sanitation preventive controls. However, prevention of allergen cross-contact and microbial cross-contamination requires consideration of sanitation practices for both food-contact and non-food contact surfaces because of environmental pathogens. For example, when manufacturing low-moisture foods such as chocolate and confectionary products, dry cleaning procedures facilitate control of environmental pathogens such as *Salmonella*. However, control of allergens may be easier when wet cleaning procedures are used. A facility must carefully consider when to use wet cleaning versus dry cleaning.

Food-contact surfaces used for low-moisture food *must* be in clean, dry and sanitary condition before use. When the surfaces are wet-cleaned, they must, when necessary, be sanitized and thoroughly dried before subsequent use. Moisture retained in environmental cracks and crevices can support pathogen growth, so use of wet-cleaning in dry environments should be avoided when possible and should **not** be a routine practice. See Appendix 5: Sanitation Basics for more information on wet versus dry cleaning.

Use of hygienic zoning to minimize transfer of hazards and considerations to minimize hazard transfer through personal practices may also be important, depending upon the process and the product. This is discussed below.

Hygienic Zoning

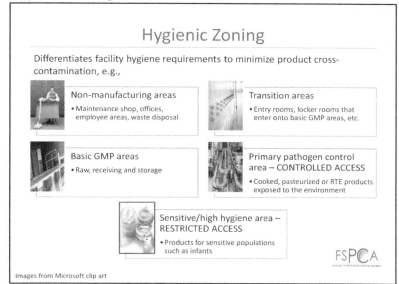

See Appendix 6: Hygienic Zoning and Environmental Monitoring for more information on this topic.

Sanitation is not the only control useful in preventing contamination of foods. The concept of hygienic zoning was developed for facilities where raw and ready-to-eat products are handled; however, similar concepts can be applied for allergen control and for dry versus wet cleaning areas. Every facility has different needs, depending on the product, the structure, traffic patterns and other factors involved with processing and handling food. Identifying areas that are specific to control of hazards requiring a preventive control and sanitation needs can reduce clean-up time if designed and implemented well.

The slide above discusses different types of hygiene areas. Non-manufacturing areas do not require the same level of sanitation as food processing areas. Transition areas into a GMP or processing space should be equipped with materials to minimize the potential for transferring potential pathogens into the facility. For example, smocks, footwear (if needed), hair covers etc. are typically available in transition areas, as well as hand-washing stations. Sanitation needs in basic GMP areas (such as receiving and storage areas and those that handle raw product) that are physically separated from sensitive areas (e.g., where an RTE food is exposed to the environment) typically are managed by GMP requirements and not preventive control requirements. More attention to sanitation and primary pathogen control is needed in areas that handle ready-to-eat products that are exposed to the environment. Even more diligent efforts are needed in areas that handle products for sensitive populations such as infants.

Control of traffic patterns between these areas with different levels of hygiene can minimize the transfer of hazards. Techniques that may be useful include:

- Dedicated equipment in different areas, especially when it is difficult to clean (e.g., carts, forklifts)
- Use of color-coded uniforms for people who work on the raw side and those who work on the cooked/ready-to-eat (RTE) side
- Linear flow through a facility, such that raw product does not enter the cooked/RTE product area.

It is understood that the above may not be practical in all situations. However, there is a requirement that efforts are made to prevent allergen cross-contact and cross-contamination when hazards requiring a preventive control are identified through hazard analysis. Preventive controls can address this through zoning and other means, as dictated by the situation at the facility.

Hygienic Zoning Considerations

- Infrastructure
- Personnel, materials and other traffic flow
- Cross-over areas
- Room air
- Compressed air, if used in direct product contact
- Adjacent and support areas

Each facility must determine the need for and scope of a sanitation preventive control program based on the potential for product contamination. The assessment should take into account the physical structure itself; personnel, packaging and ingredient traffic flows; and any cross-over areas. It should also consider potential contaminants from raw materials, air flow, support areas and activities taking place in the facility, which may include potential allergen and microbiological concerns. The sanitation preventive controls must address targeted environmental pathogens if relevant to the product being produced. A facility may choose to use zoning for allergens if this is determined to be a concern through hazard analysis.

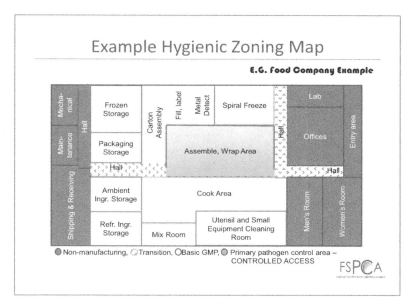

The map above is from the hygienic zoning example in Appendix 3: Food Safety Plan Example. The Assemble, Wrap Area is designated as a primary pathogen control area with controlled access because the cooked omelets are exposed to the environment prior to packaging.

Documenting Sanitation Preventive Controls

Documenting Sanitation Preventive Controls

- Document procedures, practices and processes to control identified hazards, including:
  - Cleanliness of food-contact surfaces
  - Prevention of allergen cross-contact and cross-contamination from:
    - Insanitary objects
    - Personnel to food, food packaging material, food-contact surfaces
    - Raw product to processed product
- Documentation required only for hazards a requiring preventive control

If the hazard analysis identifies a hazard requiring a sanitation preventive control, written procedures must be documented in the Food Safety Plan. This may include procedures, practices and processes needed to ensure the cleanliness of particular food-contact surfaces, including utensils and equipment. They also may include procedures to prevent cross-contamination or allergen cross-contact from insanitary objects, as well as from personnel to food, food packaging material and other food-contact surfaces. Procedures to

11-9

prevent cross-contamination from raw product to processed product are also included in the Food Safety Plan, when appropriate as identified in the hazard analysis.

Cleaning and Sanitizing Procedures

- Should identify:
    - Purpose
    - Frequency
    - Who
    - Procedure
    - Monitoring
    - Corrections
    - Verification
    - Records
    - Other special considerations

The most effective cleaning and sanitizing procedures contain the following elements:

- the purpose of doing the procedure to ensure that the operator understands why a sanitation preventive control procedure is so important
- the frequency or when the procedure needs to be conducted to be effective
- who is responsible for performing the procedure and other tasks listed
- the procedural instructions to accomplish the task, including identification of tools, chemicals, and specific steps, sometimes including pictures, especially if disassembly of equipment is required
- monitoring to provide a record that that the procedure was performed
- corrections, or what to do when inspection determines that the procedure was not adequate to produce a sanitary surface or area
- verification procedures
- the name of the form used to record monitoring activities

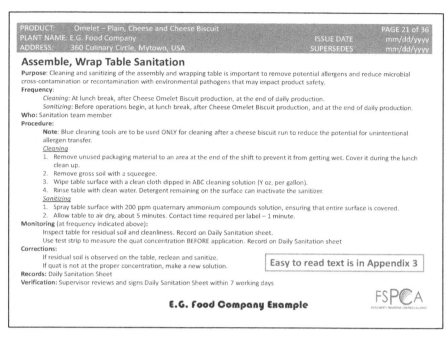

An example of the sanitation procedure for the E.G. Food Company's assembly table appears above. This is only an example of how a sanitation preventive control could be documented. The format used can vary considerably, and may even use photographs instead of words.

Sanitation Monitoring

Sanitation preventive controls must be monitored and results recorded as appropriates. The term *monitor* is defined in the *Preventive Controls for Human Food* regulation as "to conduct a planned sequence of observations or measurements to assess whether controls are operating as intended." As discussed above, procedures related to the sanitation process, as well as hygienic zoning, if used as a preventive control, require monitoring records. An example of the type of record that could be used for cleaning and sanitizing is illustrated below.

							E.G. Food Company Example	
PRODUCT: Omelet – Plain, Cheese and Cheese Biscuit							PAGE 31 of 36	
PLANT NAME: E.G. Food Company						ISSUE DATE	mm/dd/yyyy	
ADDRESS: 360 Culinary Circle, Mytown, USA						SUPERSEDES	mm/dd/yyyy	

Daily Sanitation Control Record – Omelet Line

DATE:

Sanitation Area and Goal	Pre-Op Time:	Start Time:	Lunch Break Time:	Post-Op Time:	Comments and Corrections	Operator Initials
Condition & Cleanliness of Food Contact Surfaces • Equipment cleaned and sanitized (S/U)* • Sanitizer type and strength: *Quaternary ammonium compound, 200 ppm*						
Omelet line (ppm)+						
Dish room dip tank (ppm)+						
Prevention of Cross-Contact • Cleaning after Cheese Omelet Biscuit (S/U/NA)&						
Condition & Cleanliness of Non-food Contact Surfaces • Floors and wall splash zones cleaned and sanitized (S/U) • Sanitizer type and strength: *Quaternary ammonium compound, 400-600 ppm*						
Floors and wall splash zones (ppm)+						

* S = Satisfactory, U = Unsatisfactory
+ Enter ppm measured per test strip
& NA = not applicable because Cheese Omelet Biscuit run after other products

Verification signature:	Date:

An E.G. Food Company example of a Daily Sanitation Control Record for its omelet line is illustrated above. It includes several monitoring activities on the same form. Visual observation of cleanliness is one type of monitoring activity, recorded as satisfactory or unsatisfactory on the initial observation. Recording the sanitizer concentration is another monitoring activity, which documents the specific concentration of the sanitizer used. Test strips are frequently used for this type of activity. Make sure that a test strip appropriate for the specific sanitizer is used.

It is entirely likely that a facility may want to use several different forms to record the information in order to locate the form where the cleaning takes place. For example, there could be a monitoring record located in the equipment cleaning room to record the sanitizer concentration in a tank used to submerge cleaned equipment parts (e.g., gaskets, cutter blades etc.). Other sanitation forms may be located in the production area next to the equipment being cleaned.

The facility must determine how frequently cleaning and sanitizing occurs, an important consideration to minimize the potential for environmental pathogens to become established and to prevent growth of pathogens on food residues remaining on surfaces. A chemical supplier can help provide guidelines for cleaning frequency in many situations. Note that not all sanitation procedures need to be included in a Food Safety Plan. Sanitation procedures conducted for quality reasons fall under GMPs rather than sanitation preventive controls and, thus, are not required to be documented in the Food Safety Plan.

The date, time (when appropriate), and intials of the operator performing the monitoring task must be included on a monitoring record each time they perform the task.

Corrections

Actions to Correct Sanitation Deficiencies

* Depend on situation and could include:
    * Re-clean
    * Re-sanitize
    * Re-train

When deficiencies at a sanitation preventive control are encountered, corrections must be made in a timely manner. The nature of the corrections depends on the specific situation. Sometimes corrections are relatively easy. For example, if food residue is observed on "clean" equipment, the equipment should be re-cleaned. If the sanitizer concentration is determined to be incorrect, a new sanitizer solution should be prepared and the equipment should be re-sanitized. Note that re-sanitizing equipment can be avoided if the sanitizer concentration is checked before it is used! The personnel cleaning the equipment may need to be re-trained.

Definition

Correction – An action to identify and correct a problem that occurred during the production of food, without other actions associated with a corrective action procedure (such as actions to reduce the likelihood that the problem will recur, evaluate all affected food for safety, and prevent affected food from entering commerce).

- 21 CFR 117.3 Definitions

Corrections versus Corrective Actions

Actions to correct conditions or practices related to cleanliness and prevention of cross-contamination and allergen cross-contact must be taken in a timely manner. When timely action is taken, "corrections" such as those described in the cleaning procedure, are adequate and, when appropriate, must be documented.

If action is not taken in a timely manner (e.g., unsanitary conditions exist for an extended period), full corrective action as described in 21 CFR 117.150 is required (e.g., product on hold, evaluate risk, etc.).

11-13

PRODUCT: Omelet – Plain, Cheese and Cheese Biscuit		PAGE 21 of 36	
PLANT NAME: E.G. Food Company		ISSUE DATE	mm/dd/yyyy
ADDRESS: 360 Culinary Circle, Mytown, USA		SUPERSEDES	mm/dd/yyyy

Assemble, Wrap Table Sanitation   **E.G. Food Company Example**

Purpose: Cleaning and sanitizing of the assembly and wrapping table is important to remove potential allergens and reduce microbial cross-contamination or recontamination with environmental pathogens that may impact product safety.

Frequency:
    Cleaning: At lunch break, after Cheese Omelet Biscuit production, at the end of daily production.
    Sanitizing: Before operations begin, at lunch break, after Cheese Omelet Biscuit production, and at the end of daily production.

Who: Sanitation team member

Procedure:
    Note: Blue cleaning tools are to be used ONLY for cleaning after a cheese biscuit run to reduce the potential for unintentional allergen transfer.
    Cleaning
    1. Remove unused packaging material to an area at the end of the shift to prevent it from getting wet. Cover it during the lunch clean up.
    2. Remove gross soil with a squeegee.
    3. Wipe table surface with a clean cloth dipped in ABC cleaning solution (Y oz. per gallon).
    4. Rinse table with clean water. Detergent remaining on the surface can inactivate the sanitizer.
    Sanitizing
    1. Spray table surface with 200 ppm quaternary ammonium compounds solution, ensuring that entire surface is covered.
    2. Allow table to air dry, about 5 minutes. Contact time required per label – 1 minute.

Monitoring (at frequency indicated above):
    Inspect table for residual soil and cleanliness. Record on Daily Sanitation sheet.
    Use test strip to measure the quat concentration BEFORE application. Record on Daily Sanitation sheet

Corrections:
1. If residual soil is observed on the table, reclean and sanitize.
2. If quat is not at the proper concentration, make a new solution.

Records: Daily Sanitation Sheet
Verification: Supervisor reviews and signs Daily Sanitation Sheet within 7 working days

FSPCA

Easy to read text is in Appendix 3

The example above from the E.G. Food Company example, illustrates how corrections can be described in a cleaning procedure. Other correction and corrective action procedure examples are in Appendix 3 for other sanitation preventive control procedures. This correction procedure informs operators the action that must be taken if procedures are not properly followed. Because these are correction procedures (and not corrective action procedures), completion of a corrective action report is not required.

Sanitation Verification

Sanitation Verification

- Activities that demonstrate that sanitation procedures are operating as intended
- Methods used can vary significantly depending on the food, the facility, and relevance in the food safety system
- Potential examples
  - Measuring chemical concentrations
  - ATP swabs, contact plates, microbial count swabs
  - Environmental monitoring for environmental pathogens
  - Record review

FSPCA

Verification is conducted to confirm that the sanitation preventive controls are properly implemented and the system is operating as intended. Review of sanitation preventive control records is also a required verification activity. Verification activities must be documented.

The specific verification activities depend on the facility and how the sanitation activities are set up. For example, some facilities prepare sanitizing solutions every day. Other facilities use an automated dosing system that includes a monitoring device. In the former, checking the sanitizer concentration right after you make it is a monitoring activity. However, if you periodically check the concentration of an automated system, this is a verification activity. In either case, this can be accomplished through test strip, titration or other methods frequently provided by the chemical supplier. The important thing is that the chemical concentration is checked and documented!

Some facilities may use quantitative microbiological swabs (e.g., swabbing a 3 × 3 inch (10 × 10 cm) area and plating) or indirect methods like ATP monitoring to provide quantitative verification of the effectiveness of sanitation procedures.

Environmental Monitoring

- If applicable, required to verify the effectiveness of preventive controls for environmental pathogens
  - E.g., facilities where ready-to-eat product is exposed to the environment
- Must be tailored to each facility
- A useful program diligently *tries to find* the organism and addresses issues identified!
- See Appendix 6 for more information

Environmental monitoring for an environmental pathogen or an appropriate indicator organism is required when an environmental pathogen is a hazard requiring a preventive control. This may be the case in facilities where ready-to-eat product is exposed to the environment before packaging.

An effective environmental monitoring program diligently tries to find the pathogen or indicator of concern so that corrections can be made *before* product is compromised. Environmental monitoring is a verification procedure for such a facility. Corrective actions

11-15

procedures (instead of corrections) must document actions to be taken when the environmental pathogen or an indicator organism is detected. See Chapter 13: Verification and Validation Procedures and Appendix 6: Hygienic Zoning and Environmental Monitoring Supplemental Information if it applies to your facility.

Sanitation Preventive Controls Summary

Sanitation Preventive Controls Summary

- Hazard analysis identifies hazards requiring a preventive control such as:
  - Environmental pathogens when RTE food is exposed to the environment prior to packaging
  - Pathogens transferred through cross-contamination
  - Allergens transferred through allergen cross-contact
- Sanitation preventive controls focus on:
  - Cleanliness of food-contact surfaces
  - Prevention of cross-contamination and allergen cross-contact
- Sanitation preventive controls describe:
  - Monitoring activities and frequency
  - Corrections to make when requirements are not met and corrective actions that apply for allergens and environmental pathogens
  - Verification activities appropriate to the facility

Sanitation is an element of GMPs that is required in all facilities. For some products and processes, the hazard analysis will identify specific instances where sanitation preventive controls are essential to protect consumers from contaminated product. Hazards requiring sanitation preventive controls depend on the facility and may include environmental pathogens when RTE food is exposed to the environment, pathogens transferred through cross-contamination and allergens transferred through allergen cross-contact. Sanitation preventive controls focus on the cleanliness of food-contact surfaces, and prevention of cross-contamination and allergen cross-contact. When identified in the hazard analysis process, these sanitation preventive control procedures must comply with preventive controls requirements and be documented in the Food Safety Plan. Required information includes monitoring activities and frequency; corrections for most procedures; corrective actions for allergens and environmental pathogens, if relevant; and verification activities.

Additional Reading

The FSPCA Website has many useful references on sanitation practices. In addition:

- See Appendix 5: Sanitation Basics and the FSPCA website for a wealth of references, including sanitary design checklists, basic sanitation and GMP training programs

- See Appendix 6: Hygienic Zoning and Environmental Monitoring for more detail and references on these topics.

NOTES:

CHAPTER 12.   Supply-chain Preventive Controls

Supplier Preventive Controls Objective

In this module, you will learn:

- That supply-chain preventive controls are linked to the hazard analysis
- Definitions of supplier, receiving facility and customer
- Supply-chain program contents
- Supply-chain program records

PREVENTIVE CONTROLS

Requirements based on Hazard Analysis

Process
Food Allergen
Sanitation
Supplier /Other

FSPCA

The safety of your product depends on much more than just what you control within your own facility. Use of an ingredient that has a history of association with a specific hazard may require a supply-chain program as a preventive control. In this course, the terms "supply-chain preventive control" and "supply-chain program" refer to requirements in Subpart G – Supply-chain Program in the *Preventive Controls for Human Food* regulation. Companies may have extensive supplier programs that encompass much more than food safety elements to manage their supplier expectations and performance. This chapter focuses on the requirements of the regulation for verifying measures for control of hazards prior to receipt and not a company's other supplier efforts.

Understanding the potential hazards associated with your supply chain helps to determine preventive controls needed to control those hazards, either within your facility or at the supplier. Some potential hazards have minimal food safety significance and can be addressed by GMP programs. Chapters 4 and 5 on Food Safety Hazards identify some ingredients that have a history of association with specific foodborne hazards. This chapter reviews definitions of supplier, receiving facility and customer as they apply to the *Preventive Controls for Human Food* regulation. Required contents for a regulatory compliant supply-chain program are discussed, as well as appropriate activities to verify control at the supplier level. Record requirements are also discussed.

> **NOTE:**
>
> For simplicity, the term *ingredients* may be used in place of the phrase "raw materials and other ingredients" used in the regulation.

If applicable to your operation, see the Foreign Supplier Verification Program requirements on FDA's website.

See the FSPCA website for information on the FSPCA Foreign Supplier Verification training program.

Special requirements for *Foreign Supplier Verification Programs (FSVP) for Importers of Food for Humans and Animals* are not covered in this chapter. However, if you import food products or ingredients you also need to comply with some additional requirements. Regardless of whether your ingredients come from a U.S. or a foreign supplier, the principles with respect to food safety are the same.

Link to Hazard Analysis

Link to Hazard Analysis

- The hazard analysis identifies hazards requiring a supply-chain-applied control
- An ingredient may not have a hazard requiring a preventive control; e.g., vinegar
- A hazard requiring a preventive control that is associated with an ingredient or raw material may not require a supply-chain program; e.g.,
  - Pathogens that will receive a validated kill step in your facility

The hazard analysis process (See Chapter 8: Hazard Analysis) determines when a hazard requiring a supply-chain-applied control exists. Some ingredients may not have hazards requiring a preventive control. For example, an ingredient like vinegar has not been associated with significant food safety issues. A vinegar processor must operate under GMPs, conduct their own hazard analysis and implement controls as necessary, but typically a receiver of vinegar may safely conclude that a food safety hazard requiring a supply-chain-applied control is not likely to be a concern.

Other ingredients, however, do have an association with specific food safety hazards. You do not need a supply-chain program if you implement a preventive control for the hazard within your facility. However, if you are a manufacturer/processor and the hazard is controlled before you receive the ingredient, a supply-chain program is required. To illustrate this point, let us look at different options that could have been used by the E.G. Food Company to address the hazard of *Salmonella* in eggs.

Hazard Analysis	PRODUCT: Omelet – Plain, Cheese and Cheese Biscuit					PAGE 9 of 36	
PLANT NAME	E.G. Food Company				ISSUE DATE	mm/dd/yyyy	
ADDRESS	360 Culinary Circle, Mytown, USA				SUPERSEDES	mm/dd/yyyy	

E.G. Food Company Example

(1) Ingredient/ Processing Step	(2) Identify potential food safety hazards introduced, controlled or enhanced at this step	(3) Do any potential food safety hazards require a preventive control?		(4) Justify your decision for column 3	(5) What preventive control measure(s) can be applied to significantly minimize or prevent the food safety hazard? *Process including CCPs, Allergen, Sanitation, Supply-chain, other preventive control*	(6) Is the preventive control applied at this step?	
		Yes	No			Yes	No
Receiving refrigerated ingredients – liquid pasteurized eggs	B Vegetative pathogens such as *Salmonella*	X		While pasteurization minimizes the likelihood of *Salmonella* USDA recommends the product be used in cooked foods. Experience has shown *Salmonella* occasionally occurs in this ingredient	Process Control – subsequent cook step		X

FSPCA
FOOD SAFETY PREVENTIVE CONTROLS ALLIANCE

The hazard analysis for the E.G. Food Company identified *Salmonella* as a hazard requiring a preventive control in the liquid pasteurized eggs that they receive. They chose to use a process preventive control to prevent the hazard from causing illness by the consuming public. However, they could have used other preventive controls approaches:

- E.G. Food Company could have used a supply-chain program instead of process control. This would require that they verify that the controls at the supplier (for pasteurization of the egg and for preventing recontamination) are adequate to control the hazard on an ongoing basis.

- Alternatively, the E.G. Food Company could have avoided applying a preventive control by informing their customers that the omelets are "not processed to control *Salmonella*" and by obtaining written assurance from all of their customers that they heat all omelets served to a validated temperature that would kill *Salmonella*.

In any of the three approaches the hazard (*Salmonella*) can be effectively inactivated to prevent illness. The E.G. Food Company can choose to apply any one of these approaches to ensure the hazard from *Salmonella* is controlled. The E.G. Food Company decided to use process control for the hazard of *Salmonella* in pasteurized liquid egg, perhaps because they thought it was more efficient to monitor their own process. Additionally, cooking the omelet will also address potential recontamination of the omelet batter during mixing. They handled pasteurized milk in a similar manner – using a process preventive control.

Hazard Analysis	PRODUCT: Omelet – Plain, Cheese and Cheese Biscuit					PAGE 10 of 36	
PLANT NAME	E.G. Food Company				ISSUE DATE	mm/dd/yyyy	
ADDRESS	360 Culinary Circle, Mytown, USA				SUPERSEDES	mm/dd/yyyy	

(1) Ingredient/ Processing Step	(2) Identify <u>potential</u> food safety hazards introduced, controlled or enhanced at this step	(3) Do any <u>potential</u> food safety hazards require a preventive control?		(4) Justify your decision for column 3	(5) What preventive control measure(s) can be applied to significantly minimize or prevent the food safety hazard? *Process including CCPs, Allergen, Sanitation, Supply-chain, other preventive control*	(6) Is the preventive control applied at this step?	
		Yes	No			Yes	No
Receiving refrigerated ingredients – pasteurized process cheese	B Vegetative and sporeforming pathogens such as *Salmonella*, pathogenic *E. coli*, *L. monocytogenes* and *C. botulinum*	X		Pathogens listed were identified as significant by ICMSF (2005) in process cheese. These hazards must be controlled when the cheese is made.	Supply-chain Control – approved supplier and 3rd party supplier audit by a qualified auditor	X	

FSPCA
FOOD SAFETY PREVENTIVE CONTROLS ALLIANCE

While the 3rd party audit is not conducted at receiving, the shipping clerk checks to assure that the material came from the approved supplier. Because the audit is not conducted at receiving then others may choose to check no.

Conversely, E.G. Food Company identified a supply-chain control for the biological hazards in pasteurized process cheese. In this example, the hazard analysis concluded that pasteurized process cheese has vegetative and sporeforming pathogen hazards requiring a supply-chain-applied control. The E.G. Food Company did not have processes in place to control these hazards because the cheese was just placed on the cooked omelet without any additional heat. They approve the supplier and use a third party audit to verify that controls are adequate. Other verification options are discussed later in this chapter.

The examples on this and the previous slide illustrate the flexibility that a company can use to ensure that hazards requiring a preventive control are controlled. Sometimes there are options, such as in the pasteurized egg example for the omelets. However, sometimes supply-chain control is the only option, such as in the pasteurized process cheese example.

Who Must Establish a Supply-chain Program

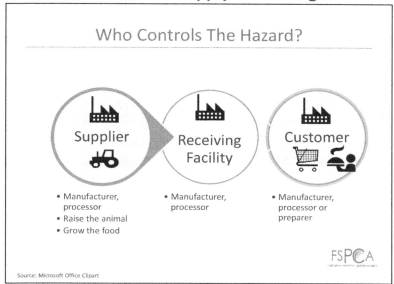

To understand supply-chain program requirements, it is important to understand the definition of supplier, receiving facility, and customer in the context of the regulation. Review the definitions in the textbox and the illustration above.

You (the manufacturer/processor) are the "receiving facility" for the raw material or other ingredient. Your "supplier" may be a manufacturer or processor of the food that you receive. Note that if you receive raw agricultural ingredients, your "supplier" is the entity that grows the food or raises the animal. For example, if Farmer Green grows a crop that is harvested and labeled by a regional harvesting organization, your supplier is still Farmer Green.

Your "customer" can be another manufacturer/processor or an entity that prepares the food, such as a foodservice or retail establishment, or other. The customer may or may not be subject to the *Preventive Controls for Human Food* regulation.

As the receiver, you must document and implement a supply-chain program when hazards requiring a supply-chain-applied control are identified through hazard analysis.

Definitions

Supplier: The establishment that manufacturers/ processes the food, raises the animal, or grows the food that is provided to a receiving facility without further manufacturing/ processing by another establishment, except for further manufacturing/ processing that consists solely of the addition of labeling or similar activity of a <u>de minimis</u> nature.
- 21 CFR 117.3

Receiving facility: A facility that is subject to subparts C [Preventive Controls] and G [Supply-chain Program] of this part and that manufactures/ processes a raw material or other ingredient that it receives from a supplier.
- 21 CFR 117.3

Customer: The entity the receiving facility sells to. May or may not be subject to the requirements for hazard analysis and risk-based preventive controls and may manufacture, process, or prepare the food in accordance with applicable food safety requirements.
- Based on 21 CFR 117.136

Supply-chain-applied control: A preventive control for a hazard in a raw material or other ingredient when the hazard in the raw material or other ingredient is controlled before its receipt.
- 21 CFR 117.3

12-5

Supply-chain Program **Not** Required:

1. When no hazards requiring a supply-chain-applied control exist

   OR

2. When you (the receiving facility) control the hazard

   OR

3. When a Customer or downstream entity provides written assurance that they control the hazard

---

A supply-chain program is not required in the following situations:

1. The hazard analysis concludes that there are no hazards requiring a supply-chain-applied control,

2. You control the hazards requiring a preventive control within your facility, or

3. You rely on your customer to control the hazard, you identify for your customer that the food has not been processed to control the hazard, and you have annual written assurance from your customer that they are following procedures to do so.

For example, Company A's hazard analysis determines *Salmonella* is a hazard in raw nuts that they receive raw from a farmer (the supplier). Company A sorts and shells the nuts for their customer, who then roasts the nuts using a validated process. Company A is not required to apply a preventive control for *Salmonella* if 1) they disclose in documents accompanying the shipment that the nuts were not processed to control *Salmonella* and 2) they obtain written assurance from their customer, on an annual basis, that *Salmonella* is being controlled along with information on how it is being controlled. Documentation requirements vary depending on whether or not the customer is subject to the *Preventive Controls for Human Food* regulation. Consult 21 CFR 117.136 for specific requirements if this situation applies to you.

Supply-Chain Program Exclusions

- An importer in compliance with the foreign supplier verification program for the ingredient
- Food supplied for research or evaluation use

FSP☾A

Two additional situations where the supply-chain program requirements do not apply are 1) when the receiving facility is an importer in compliance with the foreign supplier verification requirements (FSVP) and 2) when the food is supplied for research or evaluation use. A receiving facility that is an importer in compliance with FSVP requirements already has documentation that provides assurance that the hazards requiring a supply-chain-applied control have been significantly minimized or prevented.

Food that is supplied for research or evaluation use is not subject to supply-chain program requirements provided that:
- the food is not intended for retail sale and is not sold or distributed to the public;
- the food is labeled "Food for research or evaluation use;"
- the food is supplied in a small quantity consistent with a research, analysis or quality assurance purpose, it is used only for that purpose and unused food is properly disposed of; and
- the food is accompanied with documents stating that it will be used for research or evaluation and cannot be sold or distributed to the public.

General Requirements

General requirements for your supply-chain program when a supply-chain-applied control is identified are listed above. You must approve suppliers for these ingredients for which a supplier has applied the control for a hazard. You must determine the supplier verification activities that you will use to verify that the supplier is applying appropriate controls, and then you must ensure that these activities are conducted and documented. These activities will vary, depending on the food, the hazard and your food safety system. Each of these requirements is discussed below.

In some situations, the supply-chain-applied control may be conducted by an entity other than your supplier. For example, aflatoxin is a hazard associated with field corn. A milling company may have an aflatoxin control program for the dried corn they receive. A baking mix company may conduct verification activities at the miller to ensure that aflatoxin is controlled. If you receive cornbread muffin mix, you may verify the documentation from the baking mix company on their program for the miller.

Using Approved Suppliers

Using Approved Suppliers

- Applies to hazards requiring a supply-chain-applied control
- Approval required *before* receiving the ingredient
  - Temporary exception may be possible with justification
- Written procedures for receiving
- Receiving records required

You must approve suppliers of ingredients requiring a supply-chain-applied control before you receive the material. When necessary and appropriate, unapproved suppliers whose material is subjected to adequate verification activities before use (see verification discussion below) may be used on a temporary basis.

E.G. Food Company Example

Receiving Procedure Example

Receiving Procedure for Ingredients Requiring Supply-chain-applied Control

Purpose: Ensure that all ingredients requiring a supply-chain-applied preventive control are received from approved suppliers with appropriate preventive controls in place.

Frequency: Each delivery

Who: Receiving clerk

Procedure:
1. Verify that each load of Pasteurized Process Cheese was produced by Cheesy Co. located in Cowtown, USA by checking the bill of lading and manufacturer name on the cases received.
2. Document on receiving sheet

continued

See Appendix 3, page 25 for full procedure

Your supplier approval program must have written procedures for receiving the ingredients requiring supply-chain-applied controls. Additionally, records that document that material is indeed received from approved suppliers are required. You may use your existing receiving record system or add to it to record this information.

Determine Supplier Verification Activities

Definition

Verification: Those activities, other than monitoring, that establish the validity of the Food Safety Plan and that the system is operating according to the plan.

- 21 CFR 117.3 Definitions

Appropriate Supplier Verification Activities

Conduct one or more of the following verification activities *before* using and periodically thereafter:

- Onsite audit
- Sampling and testing
  - By the supplier or the receiving facility
- Review supplier's food safety records for the ingredient
- Other if applicable

Once approved suppliers are identified, you must identify and implement appropriate verification activities to ensure that the supplier actually controls the hazard requiring a supply-chain-applied control. Verification is usually not conducted at the same frequency as monitoring activities (see Chapter 13: Verification and Validation Procedures). Typically, verification is conducted after the fact as a check that the system is operating according to the plan. While some verification activities are performed for each lot (e.g., records review for in-house preventive controls), some supplier verification activities could be performed at a reduced frequency, depending on many factors, including the nature of the hazard and supplier performance.

Appropriate supplier verification activities are listed on the slide above. One or more of the following verification activities must be conducted before initial use and periodically thereafter for ingredients that require a supply-chain-applied control.

- An annual onsite audit of food safety practices conducted by a qualified auditor. This is required for hazards that can cause serious adverse health consequences or death unless you develop written justification for why less frequent auditing or another verification activity provides adequate assurance that the hazard is being controlled.
- Sampling and testing of the supplier's product for the hazard of concern. This may be done by the supplier or the receiving facility.
- A review of the supplier's relevant food safety records, such as processing times and temperatures.
- Other procedures based on the risk associated with the ingredient and the supplier.

The extent to which any of these activities is used must be risk-based and consistent with regulatory requirements.

Considerations for Appropriate Verification

- What does the hazard analysis suggest about the nature of the hazard?
- Are preventive controls applied by the supplier or the supplier's supplier?
- What are the supplier's procedures, processes and practices related to safety for the ingredient or raw material?
- Has FDA issued warning letters or import alerts related to the supplier's compliance?
- Do your historical test or audit results for the supplier indicate a trend – positive or negative?
- Have the supplier's corrective actions to past issues been appropriate and timely?
- Are the supplier's storage or transportation practices appropriate?

The verification activities used depend on the specific situation. The *Preventive Controls for Human Food* regulation requires consideration of the above in determining relevant verification activities. For example, when considering the hazard, is it likely to be present at high concentrations that would easily be detected by testing, or is the concentration expected to be so low that testing is unlikely to be reliable in detecting the hazard? This concept is discussed further in Chapter 13: Verification and Validation Procedures.

Where a preventive control is applied (e.g., at the supplier or at the supplier's supplier) may also impact verification procedures. For example, aflatoxin may be a hazard requiring a preventive control in cornmeal. The most effective controls for aflatoxin are applied during production, harvest and storage of the corn prior to milling. Thus upstream verification procedures for aflatoxin preventive controls may be applied by a miller who would also apply preventive controls in their operation based on risk. However, farther down the supply chain (e.g., companies using corn meal), a Certificate of Analysis (COA) from the cornmeal supplier or periodic testing for aflatoxin may be relevant.

Knowledge of your supplier's procedures, processes and practices related to food safety may also influence verification procedures. For example, a supplier that produces only peanuts would not be a major concern for non-peanut allergens because they only handle peanuts. However, a supplier that makes a variety of nut products with different kinds of nuts may present a higher risk because tree nuts of different varieties have different allergens present. Understanding how such a company controls allergens may be important to your supply-chain program.

Another consideration is a supplier's compliance history with FDA regulations. Warning letters and import alerts for a supplier may warrant taking extra precautions to verify that adequate controls are in place. Country of origin may be a consideration as well.

An ongoing relationship with a supplier is another important consideration. Some companies have many years of positive experience with a specific supplier, which may reduce the extent of verification activity needed. Conversely, constantly switching suppliers for an ingredient requiring a supply-chain applied control may warrant heightened verification activity to build confidence in the supplier's ability to meet your food safety requirements.

There may be other factors to consider, such as transportation and storage methods used by the supplier, e.g., when a food requires refrigeration for safety.

Supplier Verification Activity Exceptions

- Receiving facility does not need to conduct supplier verification for:
    - A very small business (qualified facility)
    - A farm that grows produce and is not covered under *Standards for Produce Safety* regulations
    - A shell egg producer that has <3,000 laying hens
- Must obtain written assurance that the supplier:
    - Retains its regulatory status
    - Complies with applicable food safety laws
      (see text for details)

For very small businesses, farms and shell egg producers (as defined by FDA), supplier verification activities are limited. The receiving facility must obtain written assurance that the supplier retains its regulatory status before approving the supplier and annually by December 31, and at least every two years thereafter obtain written assurance the qualified facility complies with applicable food safety regulations or that farms acknowledge that the food is subject to the adulteration provisions of the FD&C Act. If this applies to you, see 21 CFR 117.430 for specific requirements. For these suppliers, a receiving facility may use the absence of warning letters or other FDA compliance actions in determining whether to approve the supplier.

Conducting Supplier Verification Activities

Only the receiving facility can approve suppliers; however, other entities can determine and conduct other activities. The receiving facility must review and assess supplier verification activities that are determined by and/or conducted by another entity, and document the review and assessment activity. A supplier may provide test results for the lots that they send to you (the receiving facility) for your review and assessment as a supplier verification activity. However, you cannot rely on a supplier's determination of appropriate verification activities for its own product – you need to determine appropriate verification activities that are consistent with the food that you are producing. Thus, test results from a supplier are only acceptable if you have determined this is an appropriate verification activity for that food. Similarly, a supplier's self-audit or a supplier's review of their own records are not appropriate supplier verification activities. However, a supplier can provide an audit conducted by a qualified third-party auditor if you have determined this is an appropriate verification activity for that food.

As noted above, another entity, such as a broker, may perform supplier verification activities for review and assessment by the receiving facility. Remember, the *supplier* is the entity that manufactures the product, grows the food or raises the animal; thus a broker is not a supplier in regulatory terms. An entity other than the receiving facility may establish written procedures for receiving raw materials and ingredients from suppliers; document that the receiving procedures are followed; and determine, conduct and document appropriate supplier verification activities for those materials. The receiving facility may then review and assess the other entity's documentation to verify that the supply-chain-applied control was appropriate for their food safety system.

Onsite Audits

Onsite Audit Requirements

- For serious hazards requiring a supply-chain-applied control
  - Documented onsite audit *before* using the raw material
  - *At least annually* after the initial audit
- Exception
  - You document that other verification activities or less frequent auditing provides adequate assurance

---

Unless you have documentation justifying that other verification activities provide adequate assurance that hazards are controlled, an onsite audit is required when there is a reasonable probability that exposure to a serious hazard requiring a supply-chain-applied control will result in serious adverse health consequences or death. The audit is required before using the ingredient and at least annually thereafter.

You may be able to provide documentation that suggests why less frequent auditing is adequate to assure that controls are in place. For example, you may be able to demonstrate that an audit every two years combined with periodic testing provides adequate assurance that the supplier is controlling the hazard.

Definition:

Qualified auditor: A person who is a qualified individual as defined by this part and has technical expertise obtained through education, training, or experience (or a combination thereof) necessary to perform the auditing function required by 117.180(c)(2). Examples of qualified auditors include:

(1) A government employee, including a foreign government employee; and

(2) An audit agent of a certification body that is accredited in accordance with regulations of part 1, subpart M of this chapter [21 CFR].

- 21 CFR 117.3 Definitions

Onsite Audits – Who and What

- Must use a qualified auditor
- Review supplier's written HACCP or other Food Safety Plan and implementation documents for hazard identified in your hazard analysis

---

The audit must be conducted by a qualified auditor who has technical expertise to understand the hazard identified in your hazard analysis, the effectiveness of controls for that hazard and the requirements of the *Preventive Controls for Human Foods* regulation. It is important to ensure that audits include both records review and observation of practices for a complete picture. Comprehensive systems audits that include records reviews are more likely to reflect conditions throughout the year than an inspection focused only on the state of the facility at the time of the inspection. The audit must address process, allergen, sanitation and supply-chain-applied controls, as well as GMPs, as applicable, or, in some cases compliance to regulations such as the produce safety regulations. The audit must also address the specific hazards identified in your hazard analysis.

Some companies use their own qualified employees to audit suppliers (a "second party audit"). Such audits allow first hand review of the critical food safety programs and preventive controls in place at the site. One can obtain a sense for how effective programs are by diligently reviewing program records, observing activities and interviewing line workers. While this type of audit allows a company to verify that their specific requirements are being met, it requires internal resources and expertise that may not be feasible for some companies. Audits conducted by an independent third party may also be used. Your supplier may be able to provide a third party audit for your review.

> The Global Food Safety Initiative is an example of benchmarked auditing programs (aka "schemes") for food safety standards.

Some suppliers are routinely inspected by FDA or other recognized government agencies. Thus, you may be able to rely on the results of these inspections instead of a private party audit and obtain information on these inspections annually from the supplier. Keep in mind that these inspections may not occur annually.

Sampling and Testing

Sampling and Testing

- May be conducted:
  - by the supplier
  - at an outside lab or
  - upon receipt
- Can communicate results in a COA
- Methods used must be fit for purpose
- Consult references on appropriate tests for different types of products
  - Indicator tests may be more useful than pathogen tests to assess effectiveness of overall controls,
    - e.g., coliforms in dairy products

Testing of in-process materials, environmental samples or the food produced by the supplier, either at the supplier's facility, at an outside laboratory or in your facility may be appropriate if such testing provides meaningful results related to control of a hazard requiring a preventive control. This test information would be captured in a Certification of Analysis (COA). It is important to use methods that are fit for purpose and understand the limitations of testing due to sampling probability. Your approach should depend on the potential hazards and the controls in place for the specific product. Testing for new supplier approval is usually more extensive than for maintenance of approved supplier status.

It is advisable to consult a reference book (e.g., ICMSF, 2011), a technical expert or other credible source (see Chapter 7: Resources for Preparing Food Safety Plans) to determine appropriate testing and sampling plans for different types of food products. Sometimes indicator tests provide more useful information to verify process control than pathogen testing. For example, coliform testing is used by the dairy industry to verify the effectiveness of the overall pasteurization system, including sanitation, rather than testing for pathogens.

Other Verification Activities

Other Verification Activities

- Records reviews
- Requesting certificates of conformance
- Requesting continuing guarantees

Other activities that may be useful for supplier approval and verification depend on the hazards you are managing. Many companies require their vendors to provide a Continuing Product Guarantee certifying that the product meets company requirements, including legal, regulatory and conformance to specifications. These certificates generally cover multiple shipments or timeframes and should be reviewed and renewed at least annually or when requirements change. These generally do not serve as verification activities in the way that audits or testing (e.g., COAs) do, but may be suitable for certain ingredients, such as those with frequent government inspection. Further, they would not be the sole verification activity for compliance with the regulatory requirements. Copies of production records could also be reviewed to verify that the hazards were controlled and that material was produced to your specification.

Non-conformance

Actions Taken for Non-conformance

- Non-conformance actions focus on:
  - Identification of the issue
  - Steps taken to mitigate the effects of the issue
  - Steps taken to correct the issue
  - Identification of the root cause of the issue
  - Steps taken to modify the system to prevent reoccurrence
- Document all root cause and corrective actions
  - Ensure that corrective actions are implemented
- Records of actions taken for non-conformance are **required**

When an audit, other verification activity, relevant complaint or other information identifies a gap in supplier performance related to a hazard requiring a preventive control, you must ensure that the food you have manufactured is not adulterated or misbranded with respect to allergens as a result of the supplier not adequately controlling the hazard. Corrective actions will vary depending on the issue as previously discussed in the other chapters on other preventive controls.

Because system failures can occur in the supplier's process or procedures from time to time, the supplier must have a corrective action process for making modifications to prevent reoccurrence of an issue. You must ensure that the intended corrective action is actually implemented. In addition, you must evaluate all affected product for food safety to ensure that adulterated food did not enter into commerce. If adulterated product did enter commerce, then a recall would be required (see Chapter 15: Recall Plan). Corrective action is discussed in other chapters, including documentation requirements in Chapter14: Record-keeping Procedures.

Supply-chain Program Review

Supply-chain Program Review

- Compare findings from verification and non-conformance activities to spec and contract requirements
- Key points to consider:
  - Do the supplier contract and specifications clearly convey your product safety requirements?
  - Have all product safety issues been corrected?
  - Have changes or innovation at the supplier level impacted food safety? Any changes within your company?
- Adjust the program as needed to enhance safety

It is good business practice to evaluate your supply-chain program on a routine basis (typically annually). Comparing findings from your supplier approval, verification and corrective action processes against the safety requirements in the supplier specifications and contract may indicate the need for change. Raw material and other ingredient specifications should clearly communicate food safety requirements to the supplier, as well as identify these hazards for your own understanding and use in your supply-chain program.

If a food safety issue occurs with your product, review your supplier program, including verification activities, to ensure that program inadequacy was not the cause. For example, you may not have identified a hazard that is associated with an ingredient that needed to be controlled by the supplier. Also verify that the supplier took steps to prevent recurrence of issues, when applicable.

You or your supplier may create new formulations or new processes. Any ingredient change should be reviewed to ensure that food safety requirements are still met by the supplier if the ingredient is associated with a hazard requiring a preventive control. Similarly, new hazards are periodically identified – ensure that your supply-chain program is adequate to address new hazards associated with the raw material or other ingredient that the supplier provides.

Change Control Process

- Ensure supplier-initiated changes are communicated to the food safety team
- Ensure purchasing and others recognize resources required to manage supplier controls and verification
- Reanalysis of the Food Safety Plan may be needed

Change is a necessary part of the business process. Having procedures in place to accommodate changes can help avoid food safety or potentially disruptive supply-chain issues. Two aspects of change should be considered relative to suppliers – changes made by the supplier and changes made by the receiving facility. If suppliers make a change to the ingredients that they provide, the food safety team should be informed to allow reanalysis to determine if changes are needed to the Food Safety Plan or supply-chain program. Frequently supplier communications are handled by purchasing; thus the purchasing team must forward relevant information to the food safety team. The supplier must understand the importance of reporting all changes to customers so they can analyze the change with respect to their use of the ingredient.

Conversely, you or your purchasing team may identify a new supplier that can provide a similar ingredient. It is essential that purchasing not make a switch in suppliers of an ingredient or raw material associated with a hazard requiring a supply-chain control without the authorization of the food safety team. The new supplier must be approved if the ingredient is associated with a hazard requiring a supply-chain-applied control. Again, it is important to consider the resources needed to review supplier programs for new suppliers from a food safety perspective before switching suppliers. Reanalysis of the Food Safety Plan may also be relevant for company-initiated supplier changes, especially those for ingredients with hazards requiring a preventive control.

Documenting the Supply-chain Program

Supply-chain Program Documentation

- Written supply-chain program
- For import facilities, FSVP compliance documents
- Documentation of supplier approval
- Receiving procedures
- Receiving records
- Determination of appropriate supplier verification activities

continues on subsequent slides

Regulators, auditors and customers view records as the historical method for confirming a program is in place and functional. Without records, one cannot demonstrate supplier programs are implemented as designed and are effective in controlling hazards. This discussion is about records for your preventive controls supply-chain program.

A document on your supply-chain program is the starting point to describe how the facility develops and implements its supply-chain program. If the facility is an importer, then documentation that the facility is in compliance with the foreign supplier verification program requirements under 21 CFR 1 Subpart L is required.

You must maintain documentation of the approval of your supplier(s) that provide ingredients requiring a supply-chain-applied control. The receiving facility must also have written procedures for receiving raw materials and ingredients and maintain records that demonstrate that all raw materials and other ingredients with hazards requiring a supply-chain-applied control are received from approved suppliers.

You must document the determination of the appropriate supplier verification activities you will conduct for raw materials and other ingredients requiring a supply-chain-applied control. Onsite audits, sampling and testing, review of supplier's relevant food safety records or other approaches may be identified.

Onsite Audit Documentation

- Must include
  - Supplier name and location
  - Audit procedures
  - Audit dates
  - Audit conclusions
  - Corrective actions taken in response to significant deficiencies identified
  - Documentation that the audit was conducted by a qualified auditor

Records of the onsite audits for approved suppliers are required. The report must include the supplier name, audit procedures, the date(s) the audit was conducted, the conclusions, and corrective actions taken in response to significant deviations identified. Documentation that demonstrates that the audit was conducted by a qualified auditor is also required, which could be a receiving facility's employee if the employee meets the qualified auditor definition discussed previously.

Sampling and Testing Documentation

- Must include:
  - Identification of the raw material or other ingredient, including lot number, as appropriate, and number of samples tested
  - Test(s) conducted, including analytical method used
  - Date the test was conducted and date of the report
  - Results of the test
  - Corrective actions taken in response to detection of hazards
  - Identifying the laboratory conducting the test

Records of sampling and testing must identify the material tested, including the lot number as appropriate and number of samples tested. The tests conducted and analytical procedure used, the date the tests were conducted and the results must be documented, usually on the laboratory test form, which would also specify the laboratory

12-21

conducting the tests. Corrective actions, if any, must also be documented in response to the detection of hazards.

Additional Supply-chain Program Documents

- Review of supplier's relevant food safety records
- Other supplier verification activity records
- Support for reduced audit timing or other verification in lieu of audit
- Qualified facility documents
- Small Farm documents
- Small shell egg producer documents
- Government inspections in lieu of onsite audit
- Supplier non-conformance documents
- Documents from entity other than the receiving facility
- Review and assessment of other documents

When the receiving facility or audit team reviews a supplier's food safety records, the receiving facility must document the name of the facility, date of the review, conclusions of the review, corrective actions, if any, in response to deficiencies identified during review.

If verification activities other than those above are used, they must also be documented. The slide above lists other documents required if applicable to your facility. Supplier non-conformance documents would apply to all facilities. Refer to Chapter 14: Record-keeping Procedures for record retention requirements.

Supplier Controls Summary

Supply-chain Preventive Controls Summary

- Hazard analysis identifies hazards requiring a supply-chain-applied control
- Key definitions include:
  - A "supplier" manufactures the food, grows the food or raises the animal
  - A "receiving facility" is a manufacturer/processor
  - A "customer" may or may not be subject to preventive controls regulation

continued

In summary, a supplier program is an essential element of a food safety system. Your supplier is the entity that makes or grows the food or raises the animal you (the receiving facility) use to make your product. The hazard analysis process identifies hazards requiring a supply-chain-applied control for which a supply-chain program must be implemented.

Supply-chain Preventive Controls Summary

- Supply-chain program must include:
  - Using approved suppliers
  - Determining, conducting and documenting supply-chain verification activities
- Supplier verification activities may include:
  - Onsite audits, sampling and testing, review of the supplier's relevant food safety records, other activities based on risk
  - An annual onsite supplier audit is required for serious hazards unless another approach can be justified
- Documentation is a key element of supply-chain control

The supply-chain program must include using approved suppliers, and determining, conducting and documenting supply-chain verification activities. Verification activities may include onsite audits (required for serious hazards unless another approach is justified), sampling and testing, review of a supplier's relevant food safety records, and other activities based on risk. Records that document all of these activities must be maintained to demonstrate that your supplier program is operational and effective.

Additional Reading

FDA 2014, *Foreign Supplier Verification Programs (FSVP) for Importers of Food for Humans and Animals.*

FDA 2015. Interstate Milk Shippers List. Available at Interstate Milk Shippers

ICMSF (International Commission on Microbiological Specifications for Foods). 2011. *Microorganisms in Foods 8: Use of Data for Assessing Process Control and Product Acceptance.* Springer, New York

NOTES:

CHAPTER 13.   Verification and Validation Procedures

Verification and Validation Procedures
Objectives

In this module, you will learn:

- The definitions of verification and validation
- Preventive controls qualified individual involvement in validation and verification
- Verification procedure requirements for:
  - Calibration
  - Product sampling and testing
  - Monitoring, corrective actions and record review
- Food Safety Plan reanalysis requirements

Verification is another essential part of a preventive controls approach for food safety systems. This chapter explores the concepts of verification and validation, and procedures associated with these activities. Verification is an important component of supply-chain, sanitation, allergen and process preventive controls. It confirms that the Food Safety Plan is operating as intended. Validation confirms the effectiveness of the Food Safety Plan in controlling food safety hazards. The purpose of verification is to provide a level of confidence that the Food Safety Plan is 1) based on solid scientific principles that are adequate to control the hazards associated with the product and process, and 2) that the plan is being followed correctly every day of operation. A preventive controls qualified individual must perform or oversee validation and most verification activities. This chapter covers elements of verification, including validation, calibration, product sampling and testing, record review, and Food Safety Plan reanalysis. All of these are verification activities.

Verification Definitions 21 CFR 117.3

- Verification
  - "The application of methods, procedures, tests and other evaluations, in addition to monitoring, to determine whether a control measure or combination of control measures is or has been operating as intended and to establish the validity of the food safety plan." – 21 CFR 117.3
  - Are the controls in the Plan actually being properly implemented in a way to control the hazard?
- Validation
  - "Obtaining and evaluating scientific and technical evidence that a control measure, combination of control measures, or the food safety plan as a whole, when properly implemented, is capable of effectively controlling the identified hazards." – 21 CFR 117.3
  - Can the Plan, when implemented, actually control the identified hazards?

FSPCA

Both verification and validation are essential for an effective food safety system. Routine *verification* is an ongoing process to provide evidence that the plan is being properly implemented and operating as intended. *Validation* is demonstrating that following the plan will actually control the identified hazards. Thus, validation should be done before implementation of the Food Safety Plan. This is often described as an initial validation.

> Sometimes verification and monitoring activities can appear to be the same thing. For example, an operator that is cleaning equipment may record observing the equipment is visibly clean as a monitoring activity prior to completing their task. A supervisor may then visually inspect the equipment as a verification activity, confirming that the equipment was cleaned. The important thing is that the activity is done and recorded, rather than what it is called.

Potential Verification Procedures

In addition to records review for all preventive controls:

- Process verification
  - Validation of effectiveness
  - Checking equipment calibration
  - Targeted sampling and testing
- Allergen verification
  - Label review
  - Visual inspection of equipment

- Sanitation verification
  - Visual inspection of equipment
  - Environmental monitoring
- Supply-chain verification
  - 2nd and 3rd party audits
  - Targeted sampling and testing
- System verification
  - Food Safety Plan reanalysis
  - 3rd party audits
  - Internal audits

There are several types of verification activities and procedures, but requirements and application depend on the food, processes used and other factors. Validation (i.e., making sure that the process actually controls the hazard) is required for most process controls when hazards requiring a preventive control are identified. Validation, when required, is preferably done before the plan is implemented (discussion follows). Other elements of verification are typically ongoing procedures that may be regularly scheduled, such as calibration of equipment (e.g., the temperature monitoring device for the oven used to cook a product) or record reviews (e.g., to show that the oven temperature was at or above the temperature needed to kill the pathogen of concern). Some verification activities are done less frequently, such as periodic in-process or end product testing, internal audits, third-party audits and a reanalysis of the plan when changes are made or at a given frequency to ensure that the plan still reflects what happens at the facility. As with validation, required verification activities vary, depending on the food, facility and other factors. Regulatory inspections are yet another type of verification activity in which the inspector reviews the adequacy of the Food Safety Plan, determines if it is being properly implemented, and reviews records to see if parameters and values such as critical limits are continually met and corrective actions are adequate.

Validation

Validation Procedures

- Validation establishes the *scientific basis* for *process* preventive controls in the Food Safety Plan
- May include:
  - Using scientific principles and data
  - Use of expert opinion
  - Conducting in-plant observations or tests
  - Challenging the process at the limits of its operating controls
- Performed or overseen by a preventive controls qualified individual

> Validation → Does it actually control the hazard?
>
> Documentation is needed to demonstrate that procedures in place actually control the hazard.

The purpose of validation is to provide objective evidence that *process* preventive controls have a scientific basis and represent a "valid" approach to controlling the hazards associated with a specific product and process. This includes demonstrating that the equipment can deliver the process as designed and that the design parameters actually will control the hazard requiring a preventive control. Strategies that can be used to validate the Food Safety Plan include:

- using scientific principles and data from the literature
- relying on expert opinion
- conducting in-plant observations or tests at the limits of its operating controls
- using mathematical models

13-3

- incorporating regulatory guidelines

Because of the scientific concepts involved in validation, this element of preventive controls must be performed or overseen by a preventive controls qualified individual. This person does not have to be an employee of the company.

Required Validation Frequency

- Before the Food Safety Plan is implemented (ideally) or
- Within the first 90 calendar days of production or
- Within a reasonable timeframe with written justification by the preventive controls qualified individual
- When a change in control measure(s) could impact efficacy
- When reanalysis indicates the need

Ideally, an initial validation of process preventive controls should occur before the Food Safety Plan is implemented. This may not be possible in situations where process variation must be evaluated, thus continued validation activities may be necessary. The *Preventive Controls for Human Food* regulation requires that validation of process preventive control is completed within the first 90 calendar days of production. A longer period in a reasonable timeframe is allowed if the preventive controls qualified individual overseeing the validation provides written justification for the longer timeframe. Processors may want to hold product produced before validation data are complete to ensure that the process is effective in controlling identified hazards.

Revalidation may be required if the process or product is changed in a way that may impact the effectiveness of the process. Reanalysis (discussed later in the chapter) may also demonstrate the need for revalidation.

Validation Exceptions

- You do not need to validate:
  - Food allergen preventive controls
  - Sanitation preventive controls
  - Supply-chain program
  - Recall plan
  - Other preventive controls with written justification
- May be useful to validate some sanitation-related controls, e.g.,
  - How long a processing line can run between cleaning
  - Allergen controls for complex equipment

The *Preventive Controls for Human Food* regulation does not mandate validation of food allergen controls, sanitation controls, the supply-chain program or the recall plan. However, product recalls have been associated with undeclared allergens in products, thus validated cleaning procedures for difficult to clean equipment may be useful to assure that the procedures are effective in removing allergen residues.

Validation of the effectiveness of sanitizers to kill pathogens is conducted when the chemical manufacturer registers the product with the Environmental Protection Agency (EPA) or similar regulatory agencies in other countries. This validation demonstrates effectiveness of the sanitizer or sterilant when used according to label instructions and it is a violation of federal law to use such products in a manner that is not consistent with the label. Thus, following label instructions on registered sanitizers and sterilants is the first step in validation. Suppliers of cleaners and sanitizers often validate these products with respect to cleaning particular soils and eliminating certain pathogens, thus following their established procedures is also important. A facility may choose to validate that the frequency of cleaning is adequate to control hazards in their operation to prevent product safety issues.

Written justification that validation is not applicable to a preventive control may be prepared by the preventive controls qualified individual. This may be based on factors such as the nature of the hazard, the nature of the preventive control and its role in the food safety system.

The FSPCA website updates links to useful information for validation and other purposes.

Firms are responsible for confirming the applicability of this information to their specific situation.

Validation Information Sources

- FSPCA website links to scientific information such as:
  - Peer reviewed scientific literature
  - FDA Hazards Guides
    - Seafood, Juice etc.
  - Dairy Hazards and Controls Guide
  - FDA *Food Code* and Annexes
  - Validated microbial modeling programs
  - Trade association guidance
  - Internal and external scientific studies
  - Cooperative extension websites for many universities

A few sources of information that can be used for validation studies are listed above. The FSPCA website has links to information that may be useful. While companies that have technical experts are able to conduct validation studies themselves, many companies use external resources to obtain science-based validation data.

The IFT 2001 report also provides similar information for products that are heat treated in which only spores must be controlled.

Safe Harbor Example

pH and a_W combinations that inhibit growth of vegetative cells and spores

Critical a_W values	Critical pH values			
	<4.2	4.2 – 4.6	>4.6 – 5.0	>5.0
<0.88	No growth	No growth	No growth	No growth
0.88 – 0.90	No growth	No growth	No growth	?
>0.90 – 0.92	No growth	No growth	?	?
>0.92	No growth	?	?	?

? = Requires time/temperature control unless product testing demonstrates otherwise

Adapted from: IFT. 2001. Evaluation and Definition of Potentially Hazardous Foods, IFT/FDA Contract No. 223-98-2333.

An example of the type of information that may be used to substantiate validation activities is the above table from an Institute of Food Technologists report commissioned by FDA (IFT 2001). An accepted data source such as this is sometimes called a "safe harbor." The IFT table is based on a scientific evaluation of the potential for growth of or toxin formation by foodborne pathogens under otherwise ideal conditions. Products with a pH of <4.2 or a water activity (a_W) <0.88 are not reasonably likely to support foodborne pathogen growth even when products are held at optimum growth temperatures. Various combinations of pH and a_W may also inhibit growth, but combinations, such as a pH>5.0 and a_W>0.92 require further study to rule out growth, according to the table above.

Safe harbor data are useful but must be applied in the context of the product characteristics, the pathogens of significance and the process controls that are applied. A food establishment could use this table to support their conclusion that pathogen growth in their product is not likely if the product pH and a_W combination falls in the "No growth" area of the table. For some products, the pH and a_W parameters may be preventive controls that would require documentation (e.g., a formulated product). In others where this is a natural characteristic of the product (e.g., salt and sugar have a natural low water activity; vinegar has a naturally low pH), management as a process preventive control is not necessary.

E.G. Food Company Example

Validation Example – Egg Omelet

- Data sources for cook temperature
  - *FDA 2013 Food Code*
    - 158°F (70°C) for <1 second adequate for cooking raw egg-containing products that are not prepared for immediate service
  - Published study (Lowe 1937)
    - Egg coagulates at 158°F (70°C) and higher temperatures if milk is added
- Firm's data
  - Minimum actual temperature 162°F (72°C)
  - Set critical limit at ≥158°F (70°C)
- *See full validation study in Appendix 3*

The E.G. Food Company cooks their omelets to a temperature of ≥160°F (71°C) for quality reasons (an operating limit), because the omelet batter must be congealed in order to transfer it to the Assemble/Wrap table, where it is rolled and placed into a tray. The company worked with a consulting food safety expert to do a validation study for their cooking procedure. The consultant conducted studies that showed the temperature of the omelet was always above 158°F (70°C), as measured using an infrared thermometer, when the omelet batter was congealed. Their consultant wrote a report, which they included in their Food Safety Plan (see Appendix 3: Food Safety Plan Example – Omelet).

Verification Procedures

Verification Procedures

- Demonstrates that the Food Safety Plan is consistently being implemented as written
- Required as appropriate to the food, facility, and nature of the preventive control:
  - Calibration of process monitoring and verification instruments
  - Targeted testing:
    - Product testing
    - Environmental monitoring
  - Records review
    - Monitoring records
    - Corrective action records
    - Verification records
      - E.g., product testing, environmental monitoring, supplier program, when applicable

FSPCA

Verification provides evidence to demonstrate that the Food Safety Plan is working and being implemented as written. Several types of verification activities may be necessary for each preventive control to ensure that the procedures used are effective.

Ongoing verification actives such as calibration of monitoring instruments to ensure their accuracy and periodic in-process or end product testing to verify process control are important in showing that the Food Safety Plan works. As discussed in Chapter 11: Sanitation Preventive Controls, environmental monitoring is a verification activity to demonstrate that sanitation preventive controls are effective in facilities that produce ready-to-eat food that is exposed to the environment.

Supervisory review of monitoring, corrective action and verification (e.g., calibration and product testing) records is another type of verification that is used to demonstrate that the Food Safety Plan is being implemented as intended. Verification of supply-chain programs was discussed in Chapter 12: Supply-chain Program.

Calibration of Monitoring Equipment

Equipment Calibration

- Essential to assure that the data generated are correct
- Performed on equipment and instruments used to monitor or verify parameters in the Food Safety Plan
- Performed at a frequency that ensures equipment will provide an accurate measurement

FSPCA

Routine accuracy checks and periodic calibration of monitoring devices are verification activities used to ensure that the measurements taken by the monitoring devices are accurate and reliable. Accuracy checks and calibration are fundamental to the successful implementation and operation of the Food Safety Plan. If monitoring devices do not provide accurate measurements, then monitoring results are unreliable. If monitoring equipment is found to be out of calibration, a process preventive control should be considered out of control since the last documented acceptable accuracy check and calibration. Corrective action should be taken to evaluate the safety and determine appropriate disposition of the product (see Chapter 9: Process Control, Corrective Action section).

Calibration and Accuracy Check Examples

Calibration (Periodic)	Accuracy check (Routine)
Thermometer	
A dial thermometer is checked against an NIST* standardized thermometer for two or more temperatures	Thermometer used to monitor cold temperatures measures the correct temperature of an ice slurry (32°F (0°C))
pH Meter	
Meter is adjusted to read between two pH points of buffer standards	pH of a single standard near that of the product is measured correctly under plant conditions
Metal Detector	
Detector is adjusted by manufacturer to detect standardized metal slugs	Detector rejects product with metal standards

*NIST = National Institute of Standards and Technology

FSPCA

Calibration and accuracy checks are different but related concepts. Ideally a measurement device is both accurate (correct or true) and precise (repeatable or reproducible). The accuracy and precision of a measurement is usually established by measuring against a traceable reference standard. *Calibration* involves determining that the value of each reading on a particular measuring instrument is in fact correct, by measurement against a known calibrated instrument or comparison with two known standards. For example, a thermometer could be calibrated by comparing it to a National Institute of Standards (NIST) traceable thermometer at two different temperatures in the range (above and below) in which it will be used. *Accuracy* checks determine if the instrument is reading a true or correct value at a single point. Routine accuracy checks of a thermometer used to measure cold temperatures could involve immersing the probe in an ice-slurry to determine if the thermometer measures a temperature of 32°F (0°C). Boiling water could be used for a thermometer used to measure hot temperatures. Because the boiling point of water varies with altitude, the specific temperature needs to be determined.

Calibration is typically done less frequently than accuracy checks. Examples of calibration activities and accuracy checks are presented in the slide above.

Accuracy Check and Calibration Frequency

- Considerations:
  - Design of the monitoring device
  - Reliability and sensitivity of the device
  - Environment or conditions in which it is used

It is important to realize that the accuracy of monitoring devices can change, therefore it is important to conduct routine accuracy and periodic calibration checks to assure safety and to minimize the need to detain and evaluate product. A number of factors should be considered when determining the frequency of these activities for monitoring devices.

The design of the measuring instrument has to ensure that the device is capable of making accurate measurements when used within the expected environmental condition over some reasonable period of time. Calibration frequency depends on the type of device used, its condition and past performance, as well as the operating environment in which it will be used. For example, some instruments are affected by temperature or humidity. The reliability and sensitivity of the monitoring instrument should also be considered when determining the frequency of accuracy checks and calibration. Consistent temperature variations away from the actual value (drift) found during checks or calibrations of a temperature measuring device may indicate that more frequent calibration is needed or the device needs to be replaced, perhaps with a more durable device.

One of the most frequently used monitoring devices for food products is a thermometer. Some factors to consider when determining the frequency for thermometer accuracy checks and calibration include:

> See Flores and Boyle 2000 in Additional Reading for a reference on thermometer calibration, including forms.

- Inherent reliability: Daily accuracy checks may be needed for the least reliable instruments (i.e., dial thermometers and bi-metallic types). Periodic checks may be adequate for more reliable instruments (i.e., digital thermometers with a history of good performance).

- Manufacturer recommendations: The design and expected conditions of use for each individual product is considered when manufacturers make accuracy and calibration recommendations. This information should be used to determine the frequency that is needed for these activities in the Food Safety Plan.

Equipment Calibration Example
E.G. Food Company uses an infrared thermometer to measure the temperature of the cooked omelet as a verification activity. The accuracy of the thermometer is therefore important to check. The food safety team included the following verification activities in the Food Safety Plan to assure that the thermometer was accurate: **Daily accuracy check for thermometer. Annual calibration of thermometer**

See the FSPCA website for links to guides and posters for thermometer calibration.

Calibration and Accuracy Check Records

- Records must:
  - Document results of accuracy checks and calibration procedures
  - Be reviewed or review overseen by a preventive controls qualified individual
- Records should:
  - Provide a traceability to a reference device

Records must be kept to document the results of accuracy checks and calibrations of monitoring devices. These records must be reviewed by a person who has the training or experience necessary to evaluate the results and determine that all monitoring instruments are accurate and properly calibrated. The regulation does not require records to provide traceability to a reference device, but this is a useful practice. See the subsequent section on verification records review.

Product Sampling and Testing

Product Sampling and Testing

- Periodic verification **may** also include targeted sampling and laboratory testing of:
  - Ingredients
  - In-process materials
  - Finished products

Verification may also include targeted sampling, testing and other periodic activities. For example, supplier compliance with a standard may be verified by targeted periodic sampling and testing when a supply-chain program includes testing of an ingredient or raw material as verification of a supply-chain-applied control.

When a monitoring procedure does not involve a quantitative measurement, it should typically be coupled with a strong verification strategy. For example, visual observation of clean equipment could be verified through periodic testing using a method such as an ATP swab. Similar to calibration records, sample test results must be reviewed within a reasonable time after completing the reports. These reviews are part of the facility's verification activities.

Examples of periodic targeted sampling and testing for verification purposes may include:

- Coliform testing for pasteurized milk products to verify that the process meets requirements for safety and that sanitary practice is adequate.

- Testing dry corn for aflatoxin, especially when seasonal conditions increase the risk of aflatoxin production.

- Pesticide residue testing of raw fruits or vegetables used for further processing, especially from new suppliers.

> The E.G. Food Company Food Safety Plan includes a product testing example.

Product Testing Procedures Must...

- Be scientifically valid
- Identify:
  - The microorganism or analyte
  - Relationship to lots
  - The number of samples, frequency, and analytical unit
  - Analytical test method
  - Laboratory
  - Corrective action procedures

When the Food Safety Plan specifies product testing as a verification activity, you need to document the procedures to be followed. Ensure that the test methods are scientifically valid by using standard method published by international, regional or national standards-writing organizations such as the FDA, AOAC, ISO, etc. Documented procedures for the testing program must identify the information above.

- Identify the specific microorganism or analyte to be evaluated. Testing may be for pathogens or for relevant indicator organisms, which may provide quantitative information that

> Examples of organization that publish scientifically valid methods for examination of food include:
> - Official Methods of Analysis of AOAC International
> - American Public Health Association (APHA) Compendium of Methods for the Microbiological Examination of Foods
> - APHA Standard methods for the examination of Dairy Products
> - the Pesticide Analytical Manual (PAM)
> - the Food Additives Analytical Manual
> - the Food Chemicals Codex
> - FDA Bacteriological Analytical Manual (BAM)
> - FDA Macroanalytical Procedures Manual (MPM)
> - ORA Laboratory Information Bulletins (LIBs)
> - International Standards Organization (ISO) methods

is potentially more useful to assess the microbiological status of a lot. For example, the pasteurized milk industry has used coliforms as an indicator in milk products for many years rather than pathogen testing. Adequate pasteurization should destroy coliforms, thus detecting coliforms in a pasteurized milk product suggests post-process contamination or inadequate pasteurization conditions. A facility can act on this information, especially if data are analyzed over time to evaluate trends.

- Identify the specific lot or lots that the sample represents. For example, if the sample is an ingredient, preferably the analysis is done before the ingredient is used in a product. If not, then identify which lot(s) of product contained the ingredient. If it is a line sample, the sample may represent product made since the last clean up.

- Sampling plans frequently specify the number of samples to be taken throughout a lot. ICMSF (2011) provides considerations and recommends for microbiological sampling plans for a variety of food products.

- The actual test method used must be scientifically valid as discussed above. Ensure that the method has been validated for the specific food under consideration. Method providers may be of assistance in validating the test method.

- Your procedures must identify the laboratory that will conduct the test. You may conduct your own testing if you have the appropriate facilities and trained individuals. Many times an outside laboratory is used. Ensure that the laboratory has proficiency in working with food samples.

- Your procedures should identify corrective action procedures that will be followed if test results do not comply with your standards.

Environmental Monitoring

Environmental Monitoring

- Applies to RTE foods exposed to the environment after processing and before packaging
- Identify
  - Test microorganism(s)
  - Location and number of sites tested
  - Timing and frequency of sampling
  - Analytical method
  - Laboratory
  - Corrective action procedures

Definition

RTE (Ready-to-eat) food: Any food that is normally eaten in its raw state or any other food, including a processed food, for which it is reasonably foreseeable that the food will be eaten without further processing that would significantly minimize biological hazards.

- 21 CFR 117.3 Definitions

Environmental monitoring is used as a verification procedure for sanitation controls, especially in facilities that produce ready-to-eat products that are exposed to the environment. The procedures for environmental monitoring must document similar elements to those for product sampling, including the test microorganism(s), the location and number of sites tested, how often and when (e.g., during production, after cleaning or other timing), the analytical method, the laboratory used and corrective action procedures to be followed if a positive result is obtained. See Chapter 11: Sanitation Preventive Controls and Appendix 5B: Hygienic Zoning and Environmental Monitoring for more detail on environmental monitoring.

Verification Record Review

Verification Record Review

- All monitoring and corrective action records must be reviewed within seven (7) working days from the time they were created.
  - Preferably, prior to release of product
- Verification records, including calibration, product testing, environmental monitoring and supplier program records
  - Reviewed in a reasonable time
- Performed or overseen by a preventive controls qualified individual

When issues are identified during the review, corrective action is required

All monitoring and corrective action records should be reviewed under the oversight of a preventive controls qualified individual. This review is a verification activity. These records are valuable tools that document that the Food Safety Plan is operating within established safety parameters and that deviations are handled appropriately. However, records alone are meaningless unless someone reviews them on a periodic basis to "verify" that critical limits were met and the Food Safety Plan is being followed. Regulations require that monitoring and corrective action records be reviewed within seven (7) working days under the oversight of a preventive controls qualified individual. Preferably the records are reviewed prior to release of product to prevent potential recall and unintended consequences should a deviation be discovered during record review. Corrective action must be taken if the record review determines that a deviation has occurred. This may hold true for sanitation preventive controls records if, for example, the product is no longer in the establishment's control and the lack of proper implementation of the preventive control may lead to a hazard being likely to occur in the product.

The value of record review is maximized when the data are analyzed to look for trends. For example, are the verification results for one supplier the same as another supplier, or are there differences that warrant investigation? Are *Listeria* indicators isolated with greater frequency in one location? Do sanitation verification results indicate higher counts on one line or in one area? If a trend emerges during record review, adjustments may be warranted to minimize the potential for a future deviation. A rigorous verification program can be the basis for continuous improvement of operations and lead to a more effective food safety system.

Verification Example

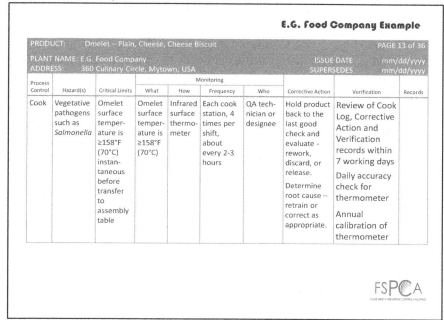

Process Control	Hazard(s)	Critical Limits	Monitoring				Corrective Action	Verification	Records
			What	How	Frequency	Who			
Cook	Vegetative pathogens such as *Salmonella*	Omelet surface temperature is ≥158°F (70°C) instantaneous before transfer to assembly table	Omelet surface temperature is ≥158°F (70°C)	Infrared surface thermometer	Each cook station, 4 times per shift, about every 2-3 hours	QA technician or designee	Hold product back to the last good check and evaluate - rework, discard, or release. Determine root cause – retrain or correct as appropriate.	Review of Cook Log, Corrective Action and Verification records within 7 working days. Daily accuracy check for thermometer Annual calibration of thermometer	

E.G. Food Company Example

PRODUCT: Omelet – Plain, Cheese, Cheese Biscuit   PAGE 13 of 36
PLANT NAME: E.G. Food Company
ADDRESS: 360 Culinary Circle, Mytown, USA   ISSUE DATE   mm/dd/yyyy   SUPERSEDES   mm/dd/yyyy

FSPCA

> The E.G. Food Company Food Safety Plan also includes other examples of verification for sanitation and allergen preventive controls.

An example of the Process Control verification activities performed by the E.G. Food Company is illustrated above. Verification activities include: 1) review of the Cook Log, corrective action and verification records within 7 working days and 2) daily accuracy and annual calibration checks of the thermometer used for verification checks. The procedures used to perform these validation activities should be documented.

Food Safety Plan Reanalysis

Food Safety Plan Reanalysis

- A food safety system changes with time
- Periodic reanalysis must be done to verify that the whole system works
- When
  - At least every three (3) years
  - Significant change in product or process
  - New information becomes available about potential hazards associated with the food
  - Unanticipated problem
  - Preventive control ineffective

FSPCA

In addition to the verification activities for CCPs and other preventive controls, strategies must be developed for scheduled reanalysis of the Food Safety Plan. Reanalysis is required at least every three (3) years or whenever there is a significant change in the product or process. Reanalysis is also required if information becomes available about a new hazard associated with the food (e.g., FDA issues an advisory notice) or if there is a failure with the system such as discovering an ineffective preventive control, an outbreak or similar situation. In addition, reanalysis is required when an unanticipated deviation occurs; i.e., a specific corrective action procedure has not been established. The preventive controls qualified individual is responsible for ensuring that this verification activity (reanalysis) is performed and they may contract with an independent third party to help conduct system-wide verification activities.

"Significant changes" may include construction events, new equipment installation and the like.

Significant Changes May Include:

- Changes in raw materials or suppliers
- Changes in product or process
- Adverse review findings
- Recurring deviations
- New scientific information on hazards or control measures relevant to the product
- New distribution or consumer handling practices

Significant changes in the product or process that may require reanalysis (and sometimes additional validation) include when an event or situation may alter the original conclusions. Examples include the following:

- Raw material changes, including a new supplier, may require reanalysis to determine if there is a potential for food safety related functional properties to be altered. For example, a new thickening agent may change the viscosity of a product, which could have an impact on heating characteristics for some products. Switching suppliers may also warrant review of the new supplier's allergen controls to assure that a new hazard is not introduced. The process may require reanalysis.

- Product or process changes may warrant reanalysis. For example, reducing the level of salt, which can alter microbial growth patterns, may require evaluation for some products. Intended shelf life, process requirements and other elements

13-18

© 2016 IIT IFSH

of the system may require reanalysis. If a new allergen is introduced on a line, reanalysis of the procedures used to clean the system may be warranted to validate that surfaces can be adequately cleaned to remove allergens.

- Increasing production volumes that lead to extended run times may provide more time for microbial growth for some processes. The adequacy of sanitation to maintain sanitary conditions during this extended time may require reanalysis.

- Adverse findings during reviews or observation of recurring deviations may suggest that the original validation is no longer adequate. This may trigger reanalysis of the full system, including validation of elements of the process that are not performing in a reliable manner.

- Emerging scientific information on hazards or control measures may also trigger reanalysis efforts. For example, when *E. coli* O157:H7 first emerged as a foodborne pathogen, it was observed that it tolerates higher levels of acid than many other foodborne pathogens. Reanalysis of process lethality was needed.

- New distribution or consumer-handling practices may also trigger reanalysis. For example, if an RTE product distributed to the general public though retail sales is subsequently marketed to infants, revalidation of controls to protect this more vulnerable population may be warranted.

Reanalysis Includes:

- Verifying that the Food Safety Plan, including the hazard analysis, is still accurate
- Reviewing records to identify trends and verify that the Food Safety Plan is being followed

---

Verifying that the Food Safety Plan is still applicable and relevant is the focus of reanalysis. This includes the hazard analysis. Reanalysis activities also include onsite observations and record reviews performed by the food safety team or other unbiased individuals not responsible for performing the monitoring activities. This is to verify that the Food Safety Plan is being followed and it may identify trends that need to be addressed. Reanalysis should occur at a frequency that ensures the Food Safety Plan is being followed continuously. This frequency depends on a number of conditions, such as the variability of the process and product. Activities that should be conducted during Food Safety Plan reanalysis include:

- Check the accuracy of the product description and flow diagram.
- Check for new guidance or scientific information related to critical limits or hazards that may require a change in the hazard analysis.
- Check that preventive controls are monitored as required by the Food Safety Plan.
- Check that processes are operating within established critical limits with few, if any, deviations.
- Check that appropriate corrective actions have been taken and verification activities have been completed.
- Check that records are completed accurately and at the time intervals required.
- Review consumer/customer complaints related to food safety.
- Check that corrective actions have been performed whenever monitoring indicated a deviation from critical limits.
- Check that equipment has been calibrated at the frequencies specified in the Food Safety Plan.
- Check that equipment has been maintained so that the process operates as originally designed.
- Check to be sure that all records are reviewed by a qualified person within 7 working days from the time they were created.

An independent third party audit can also be included in a system wide Food Safety plan verification. Third party auditors can provide an unbiased assessment to help determine if the plan is working properly. Experts may also need to be consulted to re-validate a particular processing step; e.g., when reanalysis identifies new information on a hazard that was not addressed in initial validation studies.

Verification and Validation Summary

Verification and Validation Summary

- Validation demonstrates that the Food Safety Plan will effectively control the identified hazards
- Verification demonstrates that the Food Safety Plan is properly implemented by those involved
- Validation is overseen by a preventive controls qualified individual
- Verification activities are conducted at a frequency identified in the Plan
- Reanalysis is conducted as needed and at least every 3 years.

Verification and validation are essential elements of an effective Food Safety Plan. Initial and any subsequent validation of the Plan must be overseen by a preventive controls qualified individual to ensure that the controls identified will control the hazards that are likely to be present in the food without such controls. Verification activities are conducted to audit and document that the Food Safety Plan is being implemented as designed, that people are doing what is expected, and that records are available to demonstrate ongoing performance. These activities must also be performed or overseen by a preventive controls qualified individual. Reanalysis is required as needed and at least every 3 years.

Additional Reading

Brackett, R.E. et al. (2014) Validation and Verification: A Practical, Industry-driven Framework Developed to Support the Requirements of the Food Safety Modernization Act (FSMA) of 2011. Food Protection Trends November/December 2014: 410-425.

Flores N.C. and E.A.E. Boyle. 2000 Thermometer Calibration Guide. Kansas State University.

ICMSF (International Commission on Microbiological Specifications for Foods) 2011. Microorganisms in Foods 8: Use of Data for Assessing Process Control and Product Acceptance. Springer, New York

IFT (Institute of Food Technologists) 2001. Evaluation and Definition of Potentially Hazardous Foods.

NACMCF (National Advisory Committee on Microbiological Criteria for Foods) 2004. Requisite scientific parameters for establishing the equivalence of alternative methods of pasteurization.

NOTES:

CHAPTER 14.   Record-keeping Procedures

Record-keeping Procedures Objectives

In this module, you will learn:
- What records are required
- General information required on records
- Implementation record requirements and examples
- How to conduct a record review
- Record retention and availability

Accurate record-keeping is an essential part of a successful preventive controls system. This chapter covers records that are required under the *Preventive Controls for Human Food* regulation, general information required on these records, examples of implementation records, how to review records and record keeping logistics. Regulatory implications related to use of computerized records are also addressed.

The chapter does not cover records that may be required by other regulations, customers, auditors or business needs.

What Records Are Required?

In general, there are two types of required records in the *Preventive Controls for Human Food* regulation – 1) the Food Safety Plan itself and 2) implementation records. All of these documents are subject to review and copying by regulatory personnel.

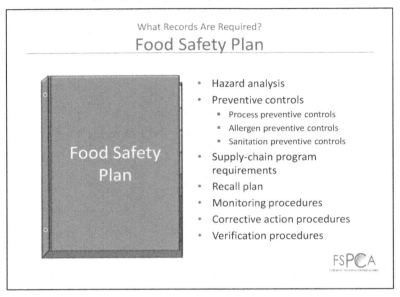

The components of the Food Safety Plan were discussed in earlier chapters. Essentially, these Food Safety Plan records document what you need to do.

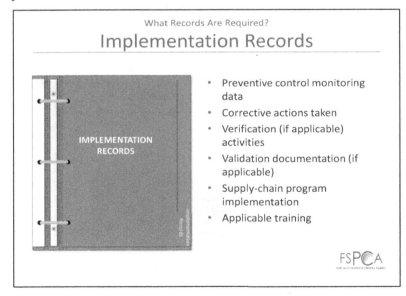

This chapter focuses on implementation records. Implementation records document the actual implementation of the Food Safety Plan. In other words, implementation records demonstrate that you did what you were supposed to do. Examples of implementation records include, where applicable, records that document the actual monitoring of preventive controls, corrective actions taken, different verification activities performed, validation activities performed (if needed), the supply-chain program checks and applicable training records.

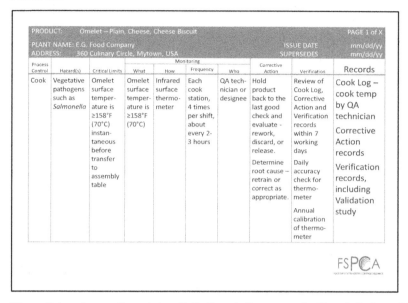

Process Control	Hazard(s)	Critical Limits	Monitoring				Corrective Action	Verification	Records
			What	How	Frequency	Who			
Cook	Vegetative pathogens such as *Salmonella*	Omelet surface temperature is ≥158°F (70°C) instantaneous before transfer to assembly table	Omelet surface temperature is ≥158°F (70°C)	Infrared surface thermometer	Each cook station, 4 times per shift, about every 2-3 hours	QA technician or designee	Hold product back to the last good check and evaluate - rework, discard, or release. Determine root cause – retrain or correct as appropriate.	Review of Cook Log, Corrective Action and Verification records within 7 working days Daily accuracy check for thermometer Annual calibration of thermometer	Cook Log – cook temp by QA technician Corrective Action records Verification records, including Validation study

PRODUCT: Omelet – Plain, Cheese, Cheese Biscuit   PAGE 1 of X

PLANT NAME: E.G. Food Company   ISSUE DATE mm/dd/yy

ADDRESS: 360 Culinary Circle, Mytown, USA   SUPERSEDES mm/dd/yy

FSPCA

The slide above from the E.G. Food Company's Food Safety Plan in Appendix 3: Food Safety Plan Example, illustrates how implementation records could be referenced in a Food Safety Plan. The name of the record for recording monitoring activity is included. Corrective action and verification records are also referenced, including the validation study for the cook step. These types of records are discussed later in this chapter following an overview of the general requirements for all records.

General Requirements for Records

General Requirements for Records

- Form
  - Original, true copies or electronic
- Content
  - Actual values or observations
  - Accurate, permanent (e.g., in ink) and legible
  - Real time recording
  - Adequate detail

All records must be kept as originals or true copies (i.e., photocopies, pictures, scanned copies, microfilm, microfiche or other accurate reproductions of originals) or in an electronic format.

Monitoring and verification records associated with the Food Safety Plan must include the actual values or observation. For example, if a temperature is being measured, the actual temperature must be recorded rather than a checkmark indicating that the temperature complied with the critical limit. All record entries must be accurately recorded in a permanent manner that can be read. For example, records cannot be recorded in pencil because they can be changed.

The information must be recorded at the time it is observed. In other words, it is not acceptable to walk out on to the production floor, observe practices and then go back to an office to record the observations. To comply with the regulations, the information needs to be recorded at the same time the activity is being performed. The records need to include enough detail to provide a history of the work performed.

Computerized Records

- Must be equivalent to paper records and hand written signatures
- An electronic record-keep system must:
  - Be authentic, accurate and protected
  - Provide accurate and complete copies of records
  - Protect records for later retrieval
  - Limit access to authorized individuals
  - Provide a secure record audit trail
  - Be reviewed by a trained individual

Electronic or computerized records are acceptable in a preventive controls system as long as they are equivalent to paper records and electronic signatures are equivalent to traditional handwritten signatures. Controls are necessary to ensure that records are authentic, accurate and protected from unauthorized changes. If a firm intends to implement an electronic record-keeping system, factors that must be considered in the design and implementation of the system include:

- Electronic records must be authentic, accurate and protected from unauthorized changes
- They must be reviewed by management with adequate frequency to ensure the facility's Food Safety Plan is being followed.
- They must be available for review and copying by public health authorities, if necessary.

If a facility decides to use an electronic or computerized record-keeping system, the system should be validated just like any other process or piece of equipment. Recent advances in electronic communications makes the use of portable electronic devices attractive to reduce the amount of paper records that must be kept in a food safety system. Again, any system that is used must ensure that the electronic records are equivalent to paper records and the electronic signatures are equivalent to traditional handwritten signatures.

> ### Owner / Agent In Charge Must be Informed
>
> - The Food Safety Plan must be signed and dated by owner, operator or agent-in-charge
>   - Upon initial completion
>   - After modifications are made
> - Intent is to keep management informed of changes
>
> FSPCA

A Food Safety Plan cover sheet that is signed and dated by the responsible individual is sufficient.

The Food Safety Plan must be signed and dated by the owner, operator or agent in charge of the facility. This must take place when the Food Safety Plan is initially completed and any time there is a modification. This ensures management is informed of changes and indicates support of implementation.

Examples of forms with all of this information follow.

> ### Basic Information on Records
>
> - Name of record
> - Name and location of facility
> - Date and, when appropriate, time of activity documented
> - Actual measurement or observation taken, as applicable
> - Product identification, if applicable
> - Signature or initials of the person performing the monitoring activity
> - Signature or initials of the person reviewing the record, and date of the review
>
> FSPCA

All Food Safety Plan and implementation records must include basic information to provide a history of what happened. Basic information includes the name of the record; the name and, when necessary, location of the facility; the date, and when appropriate, time that the activity was documented; and the actual measurements or observations made, when applicable. For many records, product identification and a lot code may be relevant, but for some processes, such as pre-operational sanitation records, the time and the date are adequate. Initials or signatures of individuals performing monitoring and verification activities are also required.

Implementation Record Requirements and Examples

Implementation Records

- Monitoring records for preventive controls
- Corrective action records
- Verification records, when required
  - Validation
  - Verification of monitoring and corrective action
  - Calibration of monitoring and verification instruments
  - Product testing
  - Environmental monitoring
  - Records reviews
  - Reanalysis
- Supply-chain program and supporting documentation
- Training records, as appropriate

Food Safety Plan implementation records demonstrate that the activities described in your plan were carried out. These include monitoring, corrective action, several types of verification activities, your supply-chain program activities and training records. Examples of some of these records are discussed below.

Other implementation records may include information used for validation and decision making during hazard analysis, such as published scientific studies, in-plant studies done by technical experts, and data from other experts such as trade associations, equipment manufacturers or sanitation chemical providers.

Documentation of verification activities associated with the supply-chain program, such as ingredient testing, supplier audits, also represent implementation records. This includes written assurances from customers that they control a hazard requiring a preventive control, if relevant to your organization.

Organizing these implementation records in a logical manner is recommended to facilitate retrieval during inspection or when an incident occurs.

Monitoring Records

- Records used to document that food safety hazards have been controlled by preventive controls
- Information required:
  - Standard information required for all records
  - Signature or initials of the individual reviewing the record, and date of the review

Monitoring records can be routinely used by an operator or manager to determine if a process or procedure is approaching a parameter and associated value or critical limit that suggests the situation is not under control. This enables the operator to make adjustments before unacceptable results are observed. This adjustment can allow a process change before a deviation occurs, which can reduce or eliminate the labor and material costs associated with corrective actions.

As previously mentioned, all monitoring information must be recorded at the time the observation is made. Accurate record-keeping provides documentation that food safety hazards are being controlled. False or inaccurate records filled out before the actual operation takes place or those that are completed later may lead to regulatory and legal actions, especially if found to be fraudulent.

Each monitoring record must be designed to capture the measurements or observations for parameters and associated values, such as critical limits, for the preventive control. The record must have an identifier (e.g., a title or number) that corresponds to the record written in the Food Safety Plan. The actual measurement or observation that is taken must also be recorded on the record, along with the time (if appropriate) and date that the measurement or observation was made, and the signature or initials of the person who made the observation. A signature or initials from the person who verified that the record complied with required parameters and associated values, as well as the date of the review is also required. These verification procedures were discussed in Chapter 13: Verification and Validation Procedures.

Because conditions in each facility are different, there is no single form that is appropriate for all operations. The following monitoring record examples are generic records that illustrate a basic design that can be used in a food safety preventive controls program.

Periodic Monitoring of Cooking Example

Form Title: Daily Cooker Temperature Log						
Firm Name:				Firm Location:		
Product Identification:						
Critical Limits:						
Date	Time	Line Number, Lot Code	Cooker Temp (°F)	Cook Time (minutes)	Critical Limit Met (Yes/No)	Line Operator (Initials)
Verification Reviewer Signature:				Date of Review:		
Date issued: dd/mm/yy				Supersedes issue: dd/mm/yy		

FSP©A

Example forms include a box for a verification reviewer signature. Either a signature or initials can be used for this purpose.

This form documents the periodic monitoring of time and temperature under normal operating conditions of a cooker.

Periodic Monitoring of Continuous Temperature Record

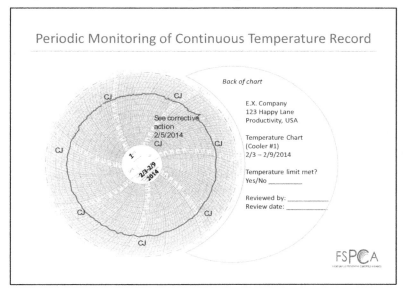

Back of chart

E.X. Company
123 Happy Lane
Productivity, USA

Temperature Chart
(Cooler #1)
2/3 – 2/9/2014

Temperature limit met?
Yes/No _____

Reviewed by: _____
Review date: _____

See corrective action
2/5/2014

FSP©A

Remember that the verification activity should include more than just signing the chart. Observation of trends by comparing different days is very useful for identifying issues BEFORE corrective action is required.

This record is used to continuously monitor the operations of a refrigerated storage unit. The record is periodically checked visually by the operator to ensure compliance with the critical limit. Notice the back of the chart is used to record the information required on all monitoring records, such as the name and location of the company, the name of the form, the date and verification review.

Allergen Label Check Monitoring Log Example

Form Title: Allergen Label Check Monitoring Log					
Firm Name:				Firm Location:	
Product Identification:					

Parameters: All finished product labels must declare the allergens present in the formula:
    Product A: list allergens
    Product B: list allergens					

Date	Time	Lot Code	Lot Number	Proper Label Applied (Yes/No)	Line Operator (Initials)
Verification Reviewer Signature:				Date of Review:	
Date issued: dd/mm/yy				Supersedes issue: dd/mm/yy	

FSP©A

This form documents the use of labels that identify allergens in the product or the product ingredients. The facility could affix one copy of the current label used to the report. Other formats can be used. The monitoring record could look very different for facilities that use a different approach to monitoring labels, for example if a barcode scanner was used.

Corrective Action Records

- Records that document the root cause and corrective actions taken in response to a deviation from the Food Safety Plan
- For each event, information required includes:
  - Product identification and volume on hold, if applicable
  - Description of deviation from parameters
  - Actions taken to prevent recurrence
  - Final disposition of product
  - Evaluation or testing results, if relevant
  - Corrective action verification

A corrective action record describes the deviation that triggered corrective action and captures the following:

- Product identification such as the product description, lot codes covered and amount of product on hold,
- Summary of the root cause of the deviation and actions taken to prevent further occurrences,

- Results of the evaluation or testing of product placed on hold, if necessary and the final disposition of the product,
- Name and signature of the person responsible for the corrective action(s), and
- Name and signature of the person reviewing the corrective action(s) report.

Corrective Action Example

Corrective Action Form		
Date of Record: 6 February 2015	Code or Lot Number: AY123	
Date and Time of Deviation:	2:15 pm, 5 February 2015	
Description of Deviation: Labels for product A were applied to product B because the operator selected the wrong stack of labels. The issue was discovered by the operator loading packages into cases.		
Actions Taken to Restore Order to the Process: 1. Production was halted when error was discovered. 2. Product was segregated back to the last good check. 3. Product was relabeled with the correct label 4. Line operator was retrained on how to check the label before placing a new stack on the line and the importance of doing so. The procedure was emphasized with all operators as a teachable moment.		
Person (name and signature) of Person Taking Action:	P.K. Lead Pat K. Lead	
Amount of Product Involved in Deviation:	50 cases	
Evaluation of Product Involved with Deviation: All relabeled product was double checked to ensure that the correct label was in place.		
Final Disposition of Product: Released		
Reviewed by (Name and Signature):	Date of Review:	

A sample corrective action record is illustrated above. This form can also be used to record corrective actions for preventive controls, if relevant. Keep in mind that for sanitation, some corrections may not require the level of detail needed for process and allergen controls. For example, if equipment is not clean prior to start up, then re-cleaning the equipment is the appropriate corrective action with no implications for product hold.

The example above involved mislabeling of product in regard to allergen hazards. The information on the form describes when the incident occurred, what happened, what was done to correct the situation, as well as what happened to the product. More specific information may be added in a real situation.

Verification Records

- As appropriate for the nature of the preventive control and its role in the food safety system, document the results of:
  - Validation studies
  - Verification of monitoring and corrective action records
  - Accuracy checks and calibration of process-monitoring instruments
  - Product testing
  - Environmental monitoring
  - Supply-chain program verification
  - Reanalysis

Records of verification activities must be kept to demonstrate that the Food Safety Plan has been implemented properly, monitoring measurements or observations are accurate and reliable, and the food safety system is working as intended. Different records may be needed to capture the verification information that is specified in the Food Safety Plan.

Examples of records with frequent verification activities might include:

- Logs that document the results of checks to verify the accuracy of thermometers, pH meters or other instruments used to monitor critical limits and other parameters.

- Monitoring records by a trained individual under the oversight of a preventive controls qualified individual to verify that parameters were met and appropriate corrective actions were taken.

Examples of less frequent, but also important records for verification activities might include:

- Logs that document calibration activities for the thermometers, pH meters and other instruments mentioned above.
- Results of microbiological, chemical or physical tests of raw materials, in-process products, finished products or the plant environment
- Results of equipment evaluation tests, heat penetration or temperature distribution for ovens, fryers or other equipment.
- Audit records verifying supplier compliance with food safety requirements

> Records generated by third parties must also meet the requirements for records. Examples on this slide may include validation studies, calibration records, product testing, and environmental monitoring when conducted by a consultant or outside lab.

- Results from third party audits or regulatory agency inspections
- Reanalysis activities such as a report describing modifications made to the Food Safety Plan because of a change in products, ingredients, formulations, processes, packaging or distribution methods

---

Validation Records, When Applicable

- Potential information used to support decisions made in the Food Safety Plan
  - Process authority validation records
  - In-plant studies or challenge studies
  - Information on emerging hazards
  - Recognized academic or research institution studies
  - Peer reviewed journal articles
  - Industry or regulatory guidance documents
  - Lack of customer and consumer complaints related to food safety

---

As discussed in Chapter 13: Verification and Validation Procedures, validation provides evidence that the parameters and preventive controls in the Food Safety Plan will control relevant hazards. Validation answers questions such as: Are we doing what we should be doing? Are the preventive controls (and the parameters and values or critical limits at CCPs) adequate to significantly minimize or prevent food safety concerns? Is there new information the facility should consider regarding the safety of their products, like emerging hazards? Does lack of customer or consumer complaints (when you have a system to collect them) suggest that there is history of a food safety concern?

Many sources of information can be used to validate a Food Safety Plan. These include validation studies done by process authorities, in-plant or challenge studies conducted on your specific product, trade association summaries on emerging hazards, university or research institution reports and studies, peer reviewed journal articles, and regulatory or other guidance documents. Records supporting validation decisions made by the facility must be maintained.

Thermometer Accuracy Record Example

Form Title: Daily Thermometer Accuracy Verification Log

Firm Name:			Firm Location:		
Product Identification:					

Verification: Check each thermometer daily for accuracy. Temperature must be ± x°F from the standard.

Date	Time	Instrument Number	Boiling Water Check	Within Specification (Yes/No)	Line Operator (Initials)

Verification Reviewer Signature:			Date of Review:		
Date issued: dd/mm/yy			Supersedes issue: dd/mm/yy		

FSPCA

This form could be used to document daily accuracy checks of all thermometers used in the daily process monitoring operations. The form could be modified to include a procedure number for the work instructions used. Otherwise, the method or procedure number could be written in the Method column. Note that the thermometer sensitivity should be based on thermometer manufacturer's stated sensitivity. An ice bath would be appropriate to check thermometers used for cold temperatures. If boiling water is used, the temperature for the altitude at the location should be indicated. Instead of heading the column "Boiling Water Check" a standard operating procedure could be referenced or other descriptive terminology.

Thermometer Calibration Record Example

Form Title: Quarterly Thermometer Calibration Log

Firm Name:			Firm Location:		
Product Identification:					

Verification: Check each thermometer quarterly against a thermometer traced to a recognized standard. Temperature must be ±x°F from the standard.

Date of Calibration	Instrument Number(s)	Method of Calibration	Calibration Results	Within Specification (Yes/No)	Line Operator (Initials)

Verification Reviewer Signature:			Date of Review:		
Date issued: dd/mm/yy			Supersedes issue: dd/mm/yy		

FSPCA

This form could be used to document the calibration check of thermometers. As mentioned in the verification chapter, the facility needs to determine the frequency with which such activities are conducted. Thermometer calibration may occur on a quarterly basis, a monthly basis, an annual basis or other frequency deemed appropriate for the type of thermometer and other considerations.

Product Testing and Environmental Monitoring Records

- Applies to microbiological and chemical tests specified as verification activities in the Food Safety Plan
- Keep original record from laboratory
  - Name of lab
  - Sample identification (including date sampled)
  - Location of sampling (e.g., finished product, in-process, etc.)
  - Date of test
  - What you are testing for
  - Method used
  - Results per unit volume (e.g., per gram, per milliliter, or per unit of analytical unit for presence absence)
- Format can vary considerably

NOTE: A result that says "Negative" or "Not detected" must also include the analytical unit (e.g., grams, milliliter, per swab, etc.) in order to determine the sensitivity of the test.

Chapter 13: Verification and Validation Procedures discussed procedures for product testing for verification. The results of those tests are verification records. Data from in-house or outside testing should be maintained in original records that document:
- the laboratory conducting the test,
- sample identification (including date of sampling, lot number, etc. where applicable),
- location of sampling (e.g., finished product, in-process, environmental sample site, etc.),
- date of test,
- target microorganism or chemical,
- methods used and
- results of the test per unit volume (e.g., per gram, per milliliter or per analytical unit for presence/absence tests).

An example is not provided because the types of tests and the acceptable limits vary substantially.

Record Review Example

Corrective Action Form

Date of Record: 6 February 2015	Code or Lot Number: AY128
Date and Time of Deviation:	2:15 pm, 5 February 2015

Description of Deviation: Labels for product A were applied to product B because the operator selected the wrong stack of labels. The issue was discovered by the operator loading packages into cases.

Actions Taken to Restore Order to the Process:
1. Production was halted when error was discovered.
2. Product was segregated back to the last good check.
3. Product was relabeled with the correct label
4. Line operator was retrained on how to check the label before placing a new stack on the line ... ce of doing so. The procedure was emphasized with all operators as a teachable moment.

Person (name and signature) of Person Taking Action: Sig N Ture   Sig N Ture

Amount of Product Involved in Deviation: XXXX

Evaluation of Product Involved with Deviation: All relabeled product was double checke... ...l was in place.

Final Disposition of Product: Released

Reviewed by: F.S. Leader Fred S. Leader (Name and Signature)	Date of Review: 13 Feb 2015
Date issued: dd/mm/yy	Supersedes: dd/mm/yy

Verification or review of monitoring and corrective action records is another element of record-keeping. This review should ensure that the information is complete and that procedures were followed appropriately. After the record is reviewed, it is signed and dated by the reviewer. The example above uses the corrective action record discussed previously. F.S. Leader reviewed the information entered by the packaging line supervisor to ensure that the description of the incident was clear and that the corrective actions taken were consistent with those described in the allergen preventive control chart. Verification of monitoring records follows the same process.

Food Safety Plan Reanalysis Checklist

Reason for reanalysis:

Task	Date Reviewed and initials	Is Update Needed? (yes/no)	Date Task Completed	Signature or Initials of Person Completing the Task
List of Food Safety Team with individual responsibilities				
Product flow diagrams				
Hazard analysis				
Process Preventive Controls				
Food Allergen Preventive Controls				
Sanitation Preventive Controls				
Supply-chain Program				
Recall Plan				
Updated Food Safety Plan implemented				
Updated Food Safety Plan signed by owner or agent in charge				
Reviewer Signature:			Date Review:	
Date issued: dd/mm/yy	Supersedes: dd/mm/yy			

This form is not required but may be a useful starting point. Reanalysis must be documented as discussed in the verification chapter.

As discussed in Chapter 13: Verification and Validation Procedures, records of reanalysis of the Food Safety Plan are required when unanticipated deviations occur, when there are repetitive deviations, at least every three (3) years or if a significant change in activities or new information (e.g., FDA determination) creates a reasonable potential for a new hazard requiring a preventive control or an increase in a previously identified hazard. For example, reanalysis is required in a situation such as a recall when a preventive control is found to be ineffective or not properly implemented. This form could be used to document this reanalysis. Forms should be developed to meet the needs of the organization. While a flow diagram is not required by regulations, it is very useful to include a review during reanalysis because flow diagrams provide a high level overview of the process. A summary of changes made is a useful accompaniment to this checklist.

Employee Training Record

- Records could be kept in individual personnel files and summarized for easy access as follows:

Form Title: Employee Training Record

Employee Name: Name		Hire Date: dd/mm/yyyy
Employee Training Course	**Location**	**Date Completed**
FSPCA Food Safety Preventive Controls for Human Food course	Local University Extension	November 15, 2015
Sanitation in the processing plant, 4-hour course	Chemical supplier in house	February 28, 2015
Good manufacturing practices (GMPs) online course	Cornell University Distance Learning Center	March 15, 2015
Allergen labels and cleaning control procedures	On the job training	March 1, 2015
Date issued: dd/mm/yy	Supersedes: dd/mm/yy	

This report is an example of how employee training activities could be documented. Other training records could include attendance lists or training documents maintained in individual personnel files. The approach is flexible.

Record Retention and Availability

Record Retention and Availability

- Required records must be retained at least 2 years
- Records that must be retained, e.g., at the facility
  - Food Safety Plan
  - Records on general adequacy of equipment and processes used, including scientific studies
  - Electronic records considered onsite if they can be accessed onsite
- Other than the Food Safety Plan, records may be stored offsite IF accessible within 24 hours
- All required records must be made available to regulatory personnel upon oral or written request

The *Preventive Controls for Human Food* regulation requires that food safety related records must be retained for a minimum of 2 years from the date the record was created. Records that relate to the general adequacy of the equipment or processes being used, including the scientific studies and evaluations, must be kept at the facility for at least 2 years after their use is discontinued (e.g., because the Food Safety Plan has been updated). The Food Safety Plan must be retained onsite. Electronic records are considered to be onsite if they are accessible from onsite. Other records, such as monitoring records, may be stored offsite if they are readily available within 24 hours, when requested for official review (e.g., by FDA). All records associated with the Food Safety Plan are available to FDA regulatory personnel, or their designate.

Having organized and accessible records is important to demonstrate that you have effectively implemented your Food Safety Plan.

Record-keeping Summary

> ### Record-keeping Summary
>
> - Required records include the Food Safety Plan and implementation records, as appropriate to the control:
>   - Monitoring records, corrective action records, verification records, supply-chain assurances, training records
> - Records must be permanent, recorded at the time the activity occurred and identify the facility, date, time (as appropriate) and appropriate signatures
> - Records must be verified and must be accessible upon request by the regulatory authority
> - Organized and accessible records facilitate implementation, audits and inspections
>
>

Records are an essential component of a food safety preventive controls system. They establish the history of past activity and can be used to demonstrate the effectiveness of your food safety program. The written Food Safety Plan and implementation records such as monitoring records, corrective action records, verification records and applicable training records are required. Supply-chain verification activities and assurances are also required.

Monitoring records must be recorded as the activity takes place. All records must be permanent (e.g., in ink with no erasures) and electronic records can be used if they meet requirements. Required records must be verified by an individual under the oversight of a preventive controls qualified individual. Upon request all records associated with the Food Safety Plan must be made available for inspection by FDA or their designee.

Additional Reading

Canadian Food Inspection Agency, 2010. Guide to Food Safety

FDA. 2003. *Guidance for Industry: Part 11, Electronic Records; Electronic Signatures – Scope and Application*

FSPCA Food Safety Plan Forms

Grocery Manufacturer's Association 2013 *A Systems Approach Using Preventive Controls for Safe Food Production*

National Conference on Milk Shipment worksheets for milk plant use

National Seafood HACCP Alliance 2011. *Hazard Analysis Critical Control Point – Training Curriculum* 5th Edition

NACMCF and Codex forms

NOTES:

CHAPTER 15.   Recall Plan

The *Preventive Controls for Human Food* regulation requires the development of a written Recall Plan when a hazard analysis identifies a hazard requiring a preventive control. This module reviews definitions of recall classes, required elements of a Recall Plan, who to notify when a recall is necessary, how to conduct effectiveness checks and methods that can be used to dispose of affected product.

See Additional Reading for guidance on FDA's mandatory recall authority.

Recalls are actions taken by an establishment to remove an adulterated, misbranded or violative product from the market. In other words, a product for which FDA or a state could take legal action against the company would be subject to recall. If a company withdraws a product that does not violate food law or the product has not entered the marketplace, these situations dealing with quality issues are not usually considered recalls but may be considered a stock recovery or market withdrawal.

Three classes of recalls are defined based on the potential health effects.

- A Class I recall is the most serious and involves product that has a reasonable probability of causing serious injury, illness or death.
- Class II recalls may cause temporary illness that typically resolves in full recovery. For Class II recalls, death and other serious consequences are not likely.
- Class III recalls are not likely to cause illness but are still in violation of the law.

Typically, a company voluntarily conducts a product recall, either on their own accord or at the request of FDA or a state. FDA has the authority to require a company to conduct a recall in Class I situations.

Recall Plan Requirements

- Required for any food with a hazard requiring a preventive control
- Must be written
- Must describe steps to take and assign responsibility to:
  - Notify direct customers and consignees
  - Notify the public, when appropriate
  - Conduct effectiveness checks
  - Execute disposition of food

A Recall Plan must be written and in place before an adverse event takes place to ensure that actions taken to recall a food are conducted efficiently and as soon as possible. A rapid response is especially important for Class I and Class II recalls for which public health is at risk.

The written Recall Plan must include procedures that describe the steps to take and assign responsibility for taking those steps. Some people can be assigned to multiple tasks, but their role should be predetermined to support a quick response. The required procedures include:

1) direct customer notification, when required (see text box), about the food being recalled, including how to return or dispose of the affected product,
2) public notification about any hazard presented by the food, when appropriate to protect public health,
3) effectiveness checks to verify that the recall was carried out, and
4) appropriate disposition of the food through reprocessing, reworking, diverting to a use that does not present a safety concern or destroying the food.

> Notification of customers is required for Class 1 recalls and sometimes for Class 2 recalls when there is a threat to public health. Decisions on when notification is necessary can be determined through discussions with FDA. FDA has the authority to initiate a recall in class I situations, but typically a company voluntarily issues the recall notice.

Recall Plan Common Elements

- Defined roles and responsibilities
- Contact lists for external notification
  - Regulators, customers, public
- Lot identification and verification information
- Effectiveness check procedures during a recall
- Product disposition procedures

FSPCA

The *Preventive Controls for Human Food* regulation does not specify how a facility should carry out the procedures discussed above. Common industry practices include:

- predefined roles and responsibilities;
- procedures to determine if a recall is needed;
- contact lists for external notification of regulators, customers, and the public;
- lot identification descriptions;
- effectiveness check procedures to be used during a recall;
- forms to record information; and
- draft notices to complete in the event of a recall.

A brief discussion of these elements follows.

Define Recall Roles

- Identify and document a recall coordinator and recall team
- Describe duties and roles of the team in the recall plan

- Recall team may include:
  - Recall coordinator
  - Operations manager
  - Publicity and public relations
  - Sales and marketing
  - Logistics and receiving
  - Quality assurance
  - Accountant
  - Scientific advisor
  - Attorney
  - Administrative support
  - FDA recall coordinator
  - State recall coordinator

The owner, operator or agent in charge of a facility is accountable for the safety of the food and must ensure that a Recall Plan is written. A recall coordinator and recall team are typically identified ahead of time. The recall coordinator generally has the following duties:

- Directs all product recalls
- Directs the recall team and coordinates all actions and communications during a product recall scenario
- Ensures that all appropriate documentation relating to the manufacture and shipment of the affected product is collected; e. g., processing records, laboratory testing records, ingredient batch sheets, inventory reports, shipping manifests etc. depending on the incident.
- Determines (e.g., from inventory management and shipping records) exact location and quantity of affected product involved in the recall
- Reports the status, findings and recommendations related to all product recall situations to senior management if they are not part of the recall team
- Notifies all pertinent regulatory agencies
- Maintains the establishment's written policy, Recall Plan and all associated recall activities

The recall team should include all functions necessary to collect accurate and complete information. For example, production, shipping, quality assurance, sales and administrative personnel should be considered as members of the recall team. If the firm has multiple locations, the team may include corporate team members from different departments (e.g., safety, quality assurance, distribution, etc.). Each recall team member should have clearly defined roles.

Define and Assign Responsibility

- Define details of each step in the recall process and person responsible for each item
  - Scope of recall
  - Regulatory agency communication
  - Recall initiation
  - Customer notification
  - Information and data compilation
  - Document gathering
  - Securing inventory of affected lot(s) in your control
  - Product disposition
  - Documentation

FSPCA

The Recall Plan should define each step of the recall process and clearly describe what needs to be done and who is responsible for carrying out the task. Knowing this ahead of time and practicing reduces confusion and helps to support an organized response. Job responsibility (who is responsible) should be clearly defined for who will initiate the recall and who will notify external customers.

Clear documentation helps to define the extent of the recall. While several people may be involved in gathering different types of documents, compiling the information and data gathered ultimately should be done by one individual to ensure that a complete picture of the situation is available. Assign responsibility for each of the types of documents needed to ensure that everything is completed.

When recalls occur, frequently some of the affected product is still in the company's control and some of the product is in the hands of customers or in route. In addition to notifying customers, assign responsibility and define procedures for securing inventory that is still within your control to avoid increasing the problem by inadvertently shipping product that would be subject to recall.

External Notification

- Notify regulatory agencies
  - FDA and state recall coordinator
- Contact customers affected by the recall
  - Identify product and how to return or dispose of it
- Notify the public when appropriate
  - Required for Class I and some Class II recalls

When it is determined that a recall is necessary, notify the appropriate regulatory agencies. In addition to FDA contacts (see text box), many states have recall coordinators. It is useful to include their contact information in your Recall Plan. In some cases, an agency may notify you first, for example if a foodborne illness is traced back to your product. In other cases, you may need to initiate the contact, such as if you receive several calls from consumers regarding an allergic reaction to your product and you determine that the product has an allergen that was not listed on the label.

The Recall Plan must include procedures for notification of outside customers/consignees who received product. You should inform your customers of the type of product, quantities of affected product they received, dates product was shipped and reason for the recall. Also tell customers to immediately put product on hold. Once information is gathered, product disposition will be determined, as well as effectiveness of the recall effort.

A press release is usually used to inform the public of a recall that has a public health issue. While a detailed press release cannot be developed until an incident occurs, a Recall Plan can include templates that describe the information that would be inserted and should identify where to send a press release if this is necessary. FDA must approve the press release and has model press release examples available (see Additional Reading).

Identification and Verification of Lot Information

- Identify product involved in a recall with specific markings
  - Inner packaging (where appropriate)
  - Outer packaging (where appropriate)
  - Case
- Identify quantities of product involved in a recall
  - Facilitates metrics involved in the recovery of suspect product

---

Lots involved in a recall must be accurately identified. How this is done is dictated by how materials are tracked from incoming goods through the process and in distribution, as well as how a lot is defined. Recall efforts involve identifying specific lots that might be implicated and then tracing those products through the distribution system to ensure that all product that has not already been consumed is recovered.

Specific information on how lots are identified should be easily understood by all the stakeholders that receive this information during a recall investigation. Unclear or poorly identified lots hamper the effectiveness of any recall effort and increase the amount of time and resources needed to complete the recall. It is critical that lot records are clearly identified and stored so that they are rapidly accessible in the event of a recall. Be sure to consider how rework is used in a facility – if rework from an implicated batch is used in subsequent batches, the amount of product involved in a recall can expand beyond the implicated batch.

All information should be cross checked against multiple sources and through multiple people so that the accuracy can be verified prior to initiation of the recall. Incomplete or erroneous information causes confusion and delays in transmitting information that is needed by the recovery team. It cannot be overemphasized that correct information, based on accurate records, is a critical requirement for efficient recall activities. Government agencies will review these records and lack of organization can slow down the process.

Effectiveness Checks

- Daily reconciliation of quantity recovered versus total
- Consignee response and follow up
- Recall effectiveness
  - ○ 100 × (# cases recovered / total cases shipped)
- Regulatory effectiveness audits

The recalling establishment must determine whether its recall is progressing satisfactorily. The firm has an obligation to conduct effectiveness checks as part of its recall process. These checks are used to verify that all affected consignees were notified about a recall and have taken appropriate action. Your Recall Plan should describe how you will conduct effectiveness checks during a recall. Most establishments follow up daily with consignees via phone calls or email to ensure they are progressing in locating and segregating all affected material. In some cases onsite assistance may be necessary at consignee locations. See the example at the end of the chapter for ideas on how this might be structured.

Product Disposition

- Determined based on the hazard, the food and other factors
- May include
  - Reconditioning
  - Reworking
  - Relabeling
  - Diverting to a use that does not present safety concern
  - Destruction

It may be possible to divert product for animal food use. See the discussion on GMPs for animal food use and the *Preventive Controls for Animal Food* regulation for more information.

The Recall Plan must include procedures that describe the steps taken to determine the appropriate disposition of the recalled product.

Depending upon the hazard and the food, sometimes a product can be reconditioned or reworked to eliminate the hazard. Diverting the product to another use, such as animal food production, may also be an option if it does not present a safety concern. As discussed in Chapter 3: GMPs and Other Prerequisite Programs, if you plan to divert the product to animal food use, the food must comply with the *Preventive Controls for Animal Food* regulation – plan ahead if you want to consider this option. Destruction of the food is the final option and is sometime necessary.

Procedures for product disposition need to consider both product that is in-house (and thus under the establishment's control), as well as product that is returned from customers. In some cases, you may have customers destroy product instead of returning it. Such situations could be described in your plan. In any case, a clear accounting of the amount of product available and its ultimate disposition is needed to close out a recall.

Corrective Action Related to Recalls

- Reanalysis of the Food Safety Plan is required
- May result in:
  - Modification of the Food Safety Plan
  - Retraining to enhance implementation effectiveness
  - Other actions to prevent recurrence of the problem
- Maintain a log of decisions made throughout recall
- After recall is completed, conduct review meeting

When a food safety recall occurs, reanalysis (see Chapter 13: Verification and Validation Procedures) of the Food Safety Plan is required to determine how to prevent a recurring situation. In some cases, modification of the Food Safety Plan may be required. For example, if a new hazard is identified, then the hazard analysis should be updated to include that hazard and preventive controls should be modified or added to ensure ongoing control. In other cases, the Food Safety Plan may be adequate, but implementation of the plan may need to be improved through enhanced training, equipment upgrades or other relevant corrections. In any case, the food safety team should strive to determine the root cause of the problem and act quickly to take corrective actions, as appropriate.

Refer to previous chapters on process, allergen and sanitation preventive controls, as well as on supply-chain programs and record-keeping for information on corrective action documentation requirements. Keep a log of all decisions made throughout the recall and maintain this as part of your recall records. This includes a summary of actions taken at the final recall review meeting.

The references and resources at the end of this chapter and in Chapter 7: Resources for Food Safety Plans provide examples and templates that can be used to construct a Recall Plan and associated records to support these efforts. You will also find an example Recall Plan at the end of this chapter and a template that provides forms and considerations to help you develop a Recall Plan specific to your operation.

Periodically Test the System

- Verify information in the recall plan
  - Contact information, product descriptions, templates, customer lists, supplier lists, etc.
- Test the recall team
  - Can they determine if a recall would be needed?
  - Are the right people on the team and are there alternates?
  - Do they know how to contact technical help if needed?
  - Can they trace product one-step forward and one-step back?
  - Can they create records, logs, product descriptions, press releases, etc.?

FSPCA

Once the recall plan is developed, it is important to periodically test the system to ensure that it will work if a recall is necessary. This is sometimes referred to a "mock recall." These mock recalls typically include verifying that the information in the recall plan is current, and testing the recall team to determine if they can do what needs to be done if there was a recall. Tracing products and ingredients one-step forward and one-step back in the supply chain is a common element of a mock recall, however, actual customers and suppliers are <u>not</u> typically contacted to avoid confusion.

Traceability checks are an important part of a mock recall. These checks determine how long it takes identify where a specific lot of product was sent (one step forward) and to identify the source and lot code(s) of all ingredients used in the production lot (one step back). In addition, it is useful to test the recall team to see if they can determine if a recall is actually necessary, if they know who and how to contact for technical help if needed, if they can create the required documentation to perform a recall.

A test of the system can be performed over time (e.g., verifying contact information), but the importance of conducting trials should not be overlooked. Being prepared can same time, money and lives.

Recall Plan Summary

Recall Plan Summary

- Recall Plan required when a hazard requiring a preventive control is identified
- Recalls can involve food safety or quality issues
- Predefined Recall Plans are required to define who and how to:
  - Notify direct customers and consignees
  - Notify the public, when appropriate
- How to conduct effectiveness checks is part of the recall plan
- Mock recalls are useful to verify that the plan is current
- Proper disposition of product will be determined with FDA and regulatory authorities

A Recall Plan is required when hazard analysis identifies a hazard requiring a preventive control, and it is a good idea to have one even if you do not identify such a hazard. A predefined food safety Recall Plan enables rapid response to remove contaminated product from the marketplace if it contains a hazard that can cause illness or injury. Your Recall Plan should define who to contact if a recall is necessary to minimize the impact of the recall on public health and on your business. Effectiveness checks are required when a recall occurs. Mock recalls are useful to ensure that the plan is current and that people understand their roles. A rapid and efficient response can reduce the number of illnesses and protect your business. FDA and other regulatory authorizes like state officials will work with you on proper disposition of the product.

Additional Reading

A recall plan template follows the additional reading list. This can be used to develop your own recall plan. The template is available on the FSPCA website. Other references provide recall plan examples, templates or additional information.

Association of Food and Drug Officials (AFDO) Directory of state and local officials (DSLO) – a directory of regulatory officials involved with food, animal feed, animal health, and food defense.

FDA 2012. Guidance for Industry: Product Recalls, Including Removals and Corrections.

FDA 2013. Chapter 7 Recall Procedures, in *Regulatory Procedures Manual*

FDA 2013. Monitoring and Auditing Recall Effectiveness.

FDA 2014. ORA District and Headquarters Recall Coordinators.

FDA 2014. Reportable Food Registry (RFR) At a Glance

Grocery Manufacturers Association 2008. *Food Supply Chain Handbook*.

Institute of Food Technologists. 2015. Global Food Traceability Center, Resource Library

University of Florida, IFAS Extension. 2008. *The Food Recall Manual*

NOTES:

Recall Plan Template and Teaching Example

[Company Name]
Recall Plan

Reviewed by: *Signature*, Title

Date: September 14, 2015

> This model Recall Plan identifies information that is either required or recommended to facilitate an effective and efficient recall. While a Recall Plan is required by the *Preventive Controls for Human Food* regulation, no specific format and content is specified. This model contains questions and templates that can be used to develop an individualized Recall Plan. A Recall Plan must be developed as part of your Food Safety Plan records.

Table of Contents

Recall Team

[Add, combine or delete rows to accommodate your operation]

Assignment	Person	Contact Information
Senior Operations Manager Alternate:		Office: Mobile: Home:
Publicity and Public Relations Alternate:		Office: Mobile: Home:
Sales & Marketing Alternate:		Office: Mobile: Home:
Scientific Advisor Alternate:		Office: Mobile: Home:
Logistics and Receiving Alternate:		Office: Mobile: Home:
Quality Assurance Alternate:		Office: Mobile: Home:
Accountant Alternate:		Office: Mobile: Home:
Attorney Alternate:		Office: Mobile: Home:
Administrative Support		Office: Mobile: Home:
FDA Recall Coordinator		Office:

Determining if a Recall Action Necessary

Problem reported by	Initial Action	Decisions	Actions
Regulatory Agency believe your product is causing illness	Assemble recall team and ask agency if recall is recommended	Evaluate situation; decide if, what and how much product to recall	**If no recall is needed:** Document why not and action.
News media story on problem with a type of food you produce	Assemble recall team, review internal records		**If recall is needed:** • Assign responsibilities • Gather evidence • Analyze evidence • Get word out • Monitor recall • Dispose of product • Apply for termination of recall • Assemble recall team and debrief • Prepare for legal issues
Internal QC or customer information suggest a potential problem	Assemble recall team and review internal records		
Health Department believes your produce is causing illness	Assemble recall team, contact appropriate regulatory agency		

Information Templates for FDA Communication

PRODUCT INFORMATION:

Modify the "Product Description, Distribution, Consumers and Intended Use" form as needed to reflect only the product involved, including:

- Product name (including brand name and generic name)
- Product number/UPC or product identification
- Remove any names of products that are not involved in the recall

Assemble TWO COMPLETE SETS OF ALL labeling to the Local FDA District Recall Coordinator. Include:

- Product labeling (including ALL private labels)
- Individual package label
- Case label (photocopy acceptable)
- Package Inserts
- Directions for Use
- Promotional Material (if applicable)

CODES (Lot Identification Numbers):

- UPC code(s) involved: _____

- Lot number(s) involved: _____

- Lot numbers coding system: *Describe how to read your product code:* -
  _____

  _____

- Expected shelf life of product: _____

RECALLING FIRM Contacts

Provide this information to FDA for clear communication:

Manufacturer name: [Name and address]

Position	Name, Title	Contact Information
RECALL coordinator		Office: Mobile: Fax: email:
Most responsible individual		Office: Mobile: Fax: email:
Public contact:	*May be one of the above or another individual. If possible, it is useful to name a different individual to allow the coordinator focus on retrieving product and resolving the issue*	Office: Mobile: Fax: email:

REASON FOR THE RECALL:

Explain in detail how product is defective or violative	
Explain how the defect affects the performance and safety of the product, including an assessment of a health risk associated with the deficiency, if any.	
If the recall is due to the presence of a foreign object, describe the foreign objects' size, composition, hardness, and sharpness.	
If the recall is due to the presence of a contaminant (cleaning fluid, machine oil, paint vapors), explain the level of contaminant in the product. Provide labeling, a list of ingredients and the Material Safety Data Sheet for the contaminant.	
If the recall is due to failure of the product to meet product specifications, provide the specifications and report all test results. Include copies of any sample analysis.	
If the recall is due to a label/ingredient issue, provide and identify the correct and incorrect label(s), description(s), and formulation(s).	
Explain how the problem occurred and the date(s) it occurred.	
Explain if the problem/defect affects ALL units subject to recall, or just a portion of the units in the lots subject to recall.	
Explain why this problem affects only those products/lots subject to recall.	
Provide detailed information on complaints associated with the product/problem: • Date of complaint • Description of complaint -include details of any injury or illness • Lot Number involved	
If a State agency is involved in this recall, identify Agency and contact.	

15-19

VOLUME OF RECALLED PRODUCT:

Total quantity produced	
Date(s) produced	
Quantity distributed	
Date(s) distributed	
Quantity on HOLD	
Indicate how the product is being quarantined	
Estimate amount remaining in marketplace • distributor level	
• customer level	
Provide the status/disposition of marketed product, if known, (e.g., used, used in further manufacturing, or destroyed).	

DISTRIBUTION PATTERN:

Number of DIRECT accounts (customers you sell directly to) by type

Type	Number
▪ wholesalers/distributors	
▪ repackers	
▪ manufacturers	
▪ retail	
▪ consumers (internet or catalog sales)	
▪ federal government consignees	
▪ foreign consignees (specify whether they are wholesale distributors, retailers, or users)	
▪ Geographic areas of distribution, including foreign countries	

CONSIGNEE LIST

Provide this list to the local District Recall Coordinator. Include US customers, foreign customers, and federal government consignees (e.g., USDA, Veterans Affairs, Department of Defense)

Commercial customers

Name	Street Address	City	State	Recall contact name	Contact phone number	Recalled product **was** shipped?	Recalled product **was** sold?	Recalled product **may have** been shipped or sold

Was product sold under Government Contract?

Yes _____ No _____

If yes, include contact name and information above AND complete information below.

Contracting Agency	Contract Number	Contract date	Implementation date

School Lunch Program:

If product was sold to federal, state or local agency for the school lunch program, complete table and notify "ship to" (so they can retrieve product) and "bill to" customers (so they can initiate the sub-recall).

Consignee	Quantity	Sale date	Shipment date

RECALL STRATEGY:

Level in the distribution chain

Level	Included		Rationale if "No"
	Yes	No	
Wholesale/distributor			
Retail			

Instructions for Consignee Notification

Write instructions on how consignees will be notified (i.e., by mail, phone, facsimile, e-mail). NOTE: It is advisable to include a written notification so customers will have a record of the recall and your instructions. Include instructions such as:

- How letters will be sent to customers (e.g., overnight mail, first class mail, certified mail, facsimile)
- Draft phone script if you decide to use phone. NOTE: If initial notification is by phone, be prepared to provide a copy of the phone script to FDA.
- Draft recall notification (see example on last page) for website and instructions for posting it, if applicable. NOTE: The web is not recommended as a sole means of customer notification.
- Draft instructions for consignees on what to do with recalled product. If there is a recall, FDA will want a copy of final instructions.
- Consider what to do for out-of-business distributors.

Effectiveness Checks

Effectiveness checks by account – Consider filling in the Consignee's recall contact name and information to make it easier to contact them in the event of a recall.

Consignee	Recall contact		Date contacted	Method of contact				Date if response	Number of products returned or corrected
	Name	Contact info		Phone	Email	Fax	Letter		

Effectiveness check summary – to be provided to FDA periodically

Date of notification	Method of notification	Number of consignees notified	Number of consignees responding	Quantity of product on hand when notification received	Number of consignees not responding, and action taken	Quantity accounted for	Estimated completion date

Product destruction/ reconditioning

o Provide a proposed method of destruction, if applicable.

o If the product is to be "reconditioned", explain how and where the reconditioning will take place. It is recommended that you provide details of the reconditioning plan to your local FDA District Recall Coordinator before implementation. All reconditioning must be conducted under any applicable GMPs.

o Describe how reconditioned product will be identified so it is not confused with recalled (pre-reconditioned) product.

o It is recommended that you contact your local FDA District Recall Coordinator prior to product destruction. FDA will review your proposed method of destruction and may choose to witness the destruction.

o You and your customers should keep adequate documentation of product destruction (and whether or not destruction was witnessed by an FDA investigator).

o Field corrections, like product relabeling, be performed by recalling firm representatives, or under their supervision and control. Contact your local FDA District Recall Coordinator prior to release of reconditioned goods.

DRAFT Recall Notice

[Company Name] Voluntarily Recalls [insert summary info] Representing [X quantity]
[--No Other Products Affected--]

Contact
Consumer:
[insert phone number]

Media Contact:
[insert phone number]

FOR IMMEDIATE RELEASE – [date] – [Company name] is voluntarily recalling [X] Lot Codes of [COMPANY/BRAND name] [insert specific product name and description], representing [insert quantity]. [Insert reason for recall].

This action relates only to [COMPANY NAME] products with any of these Lot Codes printed on the package:

- **[insert lot codes]**

No other Lot Codes, or any other [COMPANY NAME] products, are involved in this action.

Only these specific lot codes are impacted. Customers are asked to remove all product with codes listed below out of distribution immediately. Customers may call the number listed or visit our website for instructions on what to do with the product.

PRODUCT	LOT CODE	ITEM NO.
[Company Name] [insert product name(s)]	[insert product codes(s)]	[insert item number(s)]

[Company Name] is conducting this voluntary recall because [insert product name(s)] [modify as necessary. We have not received any reports of illness associated with this product, but we are voluntarily recalling this product out of an abundance of caution.]

For more information or assistance, please contact us at [insert phone number] (Monday to Friday, 9:30 a.m. to 5 p.m. EST) or via our website at [insert website address].

CHAPTER 16.   Regulation Overview – cGMP, Hazard Analysis, and Risk-based Preventive Controls for Human Food

You can submit questions about this regulation to FDA's FSMA Technical Assistance Network using a web form at http://www.fda.gov/FSMA.

This form provides FSMA Technical Assistance Network subject matter experts with the information needed to give accurate and timely responses.

Regulation Overview Objective

In this module, you will develop an awareness of:

* The requirements of the *Current Good Manufacturing Practice, Hazard Analysis, and Risk-based Preventive Controls for Human Food* regulation

On September 17, 2015, FDA's final regulation on *Current Good Manufacturing Practice, Hazard Analysis, and Risk-based Preventive Controls for Human Food* was published. The regulation focuses on a preventive approach to food safety and is known as the *Preventive Controls for Human Food* regulation. We refer to it as "the regulation" for the rest of this chapter. A copy of the entire text of the regulation is found in Appendix 1 of this manual.

This course was developed to assist food establishments with developing and implementing risk-based preventive controls that comply with the regulation. In some sections of the course, the information provided goes beyond what is in the regulation to assist with implementation of a robust Food Safety Plan. This module focuses on the specific requirements of the regulation. It contains the specific provisions and regulatory citations for the regulatory requirements. This is an overview of the regulation. If you have specific questions on interpretation, you can use the FSMA Technical Assistance Network (see Text Box) or legal counsel.

21 CFR Part 117 – Current Good Manufacturing Practice, Hazard
Analysis, and Risk-based Preventive Controls for Human Food

Subpart A – General Provisions

Subpart B – Current Good Manufacturing Practice

Subpart C – Hazard Analysis and Risk-based Preventive Controls

Subpart D – Modified Requirements

Subpart E – Withdrawal of a Qualified Facility Exemption

Subpart F – Requirements Applying to Records That Must be
Established and Maintained

Subpart G – Supply-chain Program

The regulation is Part 117 in Title 21 of the *Code of Federal Regulations*
and contains seven subparts:

A. general provisions such as definitions and exemptions;
B. current Good Manufacturing Practice requirements;
C. hazard analysis and risk-based preventive controls, which is
    the main focus for this course;
D. modified requirements for certain facilities;
E. withdrawal of a qualified facility exemption;
F. requirements for records that must be established and
    maintained; and
G. requirements for a supply-chain program.

Subpart A – General Provisions

21 CFR Part 117 – Current Good Manufacturing Practice, Hazard
Analysis, and Risk-based Preventive Controls for Human Food

Subpart A – General Provisions

§ 117.1 Applicability and status

§ 117.3 Definitions

§ 117.4 Qualifications of individuals who manufacture, process,
pack, or hold food

§ 117.5 Exemptions

§ 117.7 Applicability of subparts C, D and G to a facility solely
engaged in the storage of unexposed packaged food

§ 117.8 Applicability of subpart B of this part to the off-farm
packing and holding of raw agricultural commodities

§ 117.9 Records required for this subpart

Subpart A discusses applicability of the regulation to different facilities; defines terms used in the regulation; addresses qualifications for individuals who manufacture, process, pack or hold food; and identifies exemptions from specific regulatory requirements for certain situations. It also updates definitions in other parts of the *Code of Federal Regulations* such as clarifying what constitutes on-farm manufacturing, packing and holding of food in 21 CFR Part 1. It also defines a small and very small business, which have different compliance dates. These updates were required by the Food Safety Modernization Act's section 103.

Who is Covered
by the *Preventive Controls for Human Food Regulation?*

- Facilities that manufacture, process, pack or hold human food (§ 117.1)
- In general, facilities required to register with FDA under sec. 415 of the FD&C Act
  - Not farms or retail food establishments
- Applies to domestic and imported food
- Some exemptions and modified requirements apply

The National Sustainable Agriculture Coalition has information designed to help farmers, small food businesses, and the organizations that work with them understand whether the FSMA rules apply to them and, if so, what requirements apply. Look for "Who is Affected" page on their website.
http://sustainableagriculture.net/fsma/who-is-affected/

Facilities can register on FDA's website.

Facilities covered by the preventive controls requirements in 21 CFR 117 are those that manufacture, process, pack or hold human food. In general, facilities required to register with FDA under current regulations are covered. This applies to both domestic and foreign food processors exporting food covered by 21 CFR 117 to the U.S. Farms and retail food establishments are not covered. There are some exemptions and modified requirements, which are covered later.

---

§ 117.4 Qualifications of Individuals
Who Manufacture, Process, Pack, or Hold Food

- Must have the education/ training/ experience necessary to manufacture, process, pack, or hold clean and safe food as appropriate to the individual's assigned duties
- *Must receive training in the principles of food hygiene and food safety*, as appropriate to the food, the facility and the individual's assigned duties
- Records required for food hygiene and food safety training, as appropriate

---

The regulation requires that all individuals that manufacture, process, pack or hold food must have the education, training or experience necessary to perform their jobs in a manner to keep the food clean and safe. Individuals need specific training in the principles of food hygiene and food safety as appropriate to the individual's assigned duties. The level of training varies based on duties. For example, training for a fork lift operator may vary from that for an operator handling unpackaged ready-to-eat food. Supervisors must also have the education, training or experience necessary to supervise the production of clean and safe food. Records must be maintained for the food hygiene and food safety training.

Exemptions and Modified Requirements -1

- "Qualified" facilities (§ 117.5(a))
  - Very small businesses (less than $1 million in total annual sales of human food plus the value of food held without sale)

  OR

  - Food sales averaging less than $500,000 per year during the last three years AND
  - Sales to qualified end-users must exceed sales to others
- Exempt from hazard analysis and risk-based preventive controls when certain documentation is provided

---

Most exemptions are with respect to the hazard analysis and risk-based preventive controls provisions. The first example of an exemption is for "qualified facilities," which include:

- Very small businesses (less than $1 million in total annual sales of human food plus the value of food manufactured, processed, packed or held without sale (e.g., for a fee)) or
- Food sales averaging less than $500,000 per year during the last three years and sales to qualified end-users must exceed sales to others.

"Qualified end-users" are consumers in any location, and restaurants and retail food establishments in the same state (or Indian reservation) or within 275 miles of the facility that purchase the food for sale directly to consumers. Qualified facilities are exempt from hazard analysis and preventive controls requirements (including supply-chain programs) but certain documentation is required. They are still subject to the GMP regulations.

Exemptions and Modified Requirements – 2
(§ 117.5)

The following are exempt from preventive controls requirements as noted:

- Foods subject to HACCP regulations (seafood – Part 123 and juice – Part 120)
- Foods subject to low-acid canned food regulations (only microbiological hazards regulated under Part 113)
- Dietary supplements (Part 111)
- Alcoholic beverages

The regulation provides an exemption for the following:

- Food subject to HACCP (seafood and juice - 117.5(b) and c))
- Food subject to low-acid canned food regulations (only with respect to microbiological hazards) (117.5(d))
- Dietary supplements (117.5(e))
- Food subject to produce safety requirements (117.5(f))
- Alcoholic beverages (117.5(i))

The types of businesses listed are exempt from Food Safety Plan requirements provided that (with the exception of alcoholic beverages) they are in compliance with the applicable regulations referenced above. These businesses are not exempt from GMP requirements and low-acid canned foods manufacturers must conduct a hazard analysis to determine if chemical and physical hazards are an issue, and document the analysis.

Exemptions and Modified Requirements - 3

- Facilities, such as warehouses, that only store unexposed packaged food (§117.7)
  - Certain packaged food for which refrigeration is required for safety must have temperature controls, monitoring, verification and records (§117.206)
  - GMPs apply

Facilities such as warehouses that store only unexposed packaged food are exempt from the requirements for hazard analysis and risk-based preventive controls, with one exception. That is, certain packaged food for which refrigeration is required for safety must have temperature controls, monitoring, verification and records.

Exemptions and Modified Requirements- 4
(§117.5(j))

- Certain storage facilities such as grain elevators and warehouses that only store raw agricultural commodities (other than fruits and vegetables) intended for further distribution or processing are exempt.
- Facilities such as warehouses that store raw agricultural commodities that are fruits and vegetables are NOT exempt from hazard analysis and risk-based preventive controls.

Certain storage facilities such as grain elevators and warehouses that only store raw agricultural commodities (other than fruits and vegetables) intended for further distribution or processing are exempt from hazard analysis and risk-based preventive controls.

FSMA provided FDA with authority to exempt or modify requirements for storage of raw agricultural commodities (RACs) intended for further distribution or processing, but specifically excluded storage of fruits and vegetables.

The "RAC Exemption" (§117.5(k))

- Subpart B (GMPs) does not apply to holding or transportation of raw agricultural commodities (RACs)
    - This exemption is not new.
- GMPs apply to packaging, packing and holding of certain dried raw agricultural commodities
    - Compliance can be achieve by complying with subpart B or requirements for packing and holding in 21 CFR 112
    - A similar approach can be used for off-farm packaging, packing and holding of produce RACs (§117.8)

---

21 CFR 117 Subpart B (GMPs) does not apply to farms and activities of farm mixed-type facilities, fishing vessels, establishments solely engaged in holding or transportation of raw agricultural commodities, and establishments solely engaged in hulling, shelling, drying, packing, and/or holding nuts without additional processing. This is based on an existing provision in the GMPs (21 CFR 110.19(a)) known as the "RAC exemption."

GMPs apply to packaging, packing and holding of certain dried raw agricultural commodities such as raisins made from grapes. Compliance may be achieved by complying with Subpart B or the applicable requirements for packing and holding in part 112. Similarly, off-farm packaging, packing and holding of raw agricultural commodities are subject to the GMPs; if these commodities are produce (as defined in 21 CFR part 112) compliance may be achieved by complying with Subpart B or the applicable requirements for packing and holding in part 112.

Farm-Related Exemptions (§§117.5 (f), (g) and (h))

- Activities within the definition of "farm," including farm activities that are covered by the produce rule
- Certain low-risk manufacturing/processing, packing and holding activities conducted by small/very small businesses on farms for specific foods

Farm-related exemptions are activities within the definition of "farm" in 21 CFR 1.227, including farm activities that are covered by the produce regulation, and certain low-risk manufacturing/ processing activities conducted by small/very small businesses on farms for specific foods. The regulation includes an exhaustive list and the exemption only applies if these are the only activities they conduct that were subject to the registration requirement.

Subpart B – Current Good Manufacturing Practice

21 CFR Part 117 – Current Good Manufacturing Practice, Hazard Analysis, and Risk-based Preventive Controls for Human Food

Subpart B – Current Good Manufacturing Practice

§117.10 Personnel

§117.20 Plant and grounds

§117.35 Sanitary operations

§117.37 Sanitary facilities and controls

§117.40 Equipment and utensils

§117.80 Processes and controls

§117.93 Warehousing and distribution

§117.95 Holding and distribution of human food by-products for use as animal food

§117.110 Defect action levels

Updated GMPs are part of the regulation (moved from 21 CFR 110 to 21 CFR 117). Requirements for personnel, plant and grounds, sanitary operations, sanitary facilities and controls, equipment and utensils, processes and controls, warehousing and distribution, and defect action levels are addressed under GMP provisions. In addition, a new provision was added for holding and distribution of human food by-products for use as animal food. GMP provisions are not the focus of this course on hazard analysis and preventive controls, but an update follows.

Updated Good Manufacturing Practices

- Protection against allergen cross-contact
- Updated language (e.g., "must" instead of "shall")
- Certain provisions containing recommendations were deleted
- Requires cleaning of non-food contact surfaces as frequently as necessary to protect against allergen cross-contact and contamination of food, food-contact surfaces and food packaging.
- GMPs for holding and distributing human food by-products for use as animal food are new

---

The GMPs were modified to clarify that certain provisions requiring protection against contamination of food also require protection against allergen cross-contact. Further, language in the regulation was updated, such as using "must" instead of "shall," and "manufacturing/processing" in place of "manufacturing" for consistency with definitions. Certain provisions containing recommendations were deleted and may be added to guidance (e.g., previous provisions using "should" or "compliance may be achieved by").

The GMP regulations now require cleaning of non-food-contact surfaces as frequently as necessary to protect against contamination of food and food-contact surfaces. Additionally, the holding and distribution of human food by-products for use as animal food is not subject to the *Preventive Controls for Animal Food* regulation if the human food facility complies with the human food GMPs and does not further manufacture the by-products. Facilities that hold and distribute human food by-products for use as animal food must comply with 21 CFR 117.95.

Subpart C – Preventive Controls

21 CFR Part 117 – Current Good Manufacturing Practice, Hazard Analysis, and Risk-based Preventive Controls for Human Food

Subpart C – Hazard Analysis and Risk-based Preventive Controls

§ 117.126 Food safety plan

§ 117.130 Hazard analysis

§ 117.135 Preventive controls

§ 117.136 Circumstances in which... facility is not required to implement a preventive control

§ 117.137 Provisions of assurances required under § 117.136...

§ 117.139 Recall plan

§ 117.140 Preventive control management components

§ 117.145 Monitoring

§ 117.150 Corrective actions and corrections

§ 117.155 Verification

§ 117.160 Validation

§ 117.165 Verification of implementation and effectiveness

§ 117.170 Reanalysis

§ 117.180 Requirements applicable to a preventive controls qualified individual and qualified auditor

§ 117.190 Implementation records required for this subpart

The focus of this training program is on 21 CFR 117 Subpart C: *Hazard Analysis and Risk-based Preventive Controls for Human Food* (referred to as *"Preventive Controls for Human Food* regulation" in this document) and Subpart G: *Supply-Chain Program.* Each facility is required to implement a written Food Safety Plan that focuses on preventing hazards in foods (21 CFR 117.126).

Hazard Analysis (§ 117.130)

- Must be written regardless of outcome
- Hazard identification must consider known or reasonably foreseeable biological, chemical and physical hazards.
  - Could occur naturally, be unintentionally introduced or be intentionally introduced for economic gain.

The regulation focuses on identifying hazards requiring a preventive control, thus a written hazard analysis is required. The first part of hazard analysis is identification of biological, chemical (including radiological) and physical hazards that may be associated with the facility or the food. These hazards may occur naturally, may be unintentionally introduced or may be intentionally introduced for economic gain.

Examples of biological hazards include pathogenic bacteria (including environmental pathogens), viruses, parasites and other pathogens. Chemical hazard examples include radiological hazards, substances such as pesticide and drug residues, natural toxins, certain decomposition products, unapproved food or color additives, and food allergens. Physical hazards examples include stones, glass or metal fragments that could inadvertently be introduced into food. Hazards introduced for economic gain must also be considered.

Hazard Evaluation

- Determine if the known or reasonably foreseeable hazards require a preventive control
  - Must consider severity of illness/injury and probability of occurrence in absence of a preventive control
- Must include an evaluation of environmental pathogens when:
  - A ready-to-eat food is exposed to the environment prior to packaging and
  - Packaged product is not treated after packaging

During the hazard analysis process, the hazard evaluation is conducted to determine the hazards requiring a preventive control. This evaluation includes an assessment of the severity of the illness or injury that would result if the hazard was in the food. Potential contamination from the food handling environment, as well as from food ingredients, must be considered for ready-to-eat foods that are exposed to the environment prior to packaging if the packaged food does not receive a treatment or otherwise include a control measure (such as a formulation lethal to the pathogen) that would significantly minimize the pathogen.

16-11

Hazard Evaluation Considerations

- Formulation of the food
- Facility and equipment
- Raw materials and ingredients
- Transportation practices
- Manufacturing/processing procedures
- Packaging and labeling activities
- Storage and distribution
- Intended or reasonably foreseeable use
- Sanitation, including employee hygiene
- Other relevant factors

The hazard evaluation must consider the effect of the following on the safety of the finished food for the intended consumer:

- Formulation of the food;
- Condition, function and design of the facility and equipment;
- Raw materials and ingredients;
- Transportation practices;
- Manufacturing/processing procedures;
- Packaging activities and labeling activities;
- Storage and distribution;
- Intended or reasonably foreseeable use;
- Sanitation, including employee hygiene; and
- Any other relevant factors, such as weather-related concerns in regard to formation of some natural toxins.

Preventive Controls (§ 117.135(c))

Required, if relevant, for hazards requiring a preventive control

- Process controls
- Food allergen controls
- Sanitation controls
- Supply-chain controls
- Recall plan
- Other controls

The preventive controls required depend on which, if any, hazards are determined to require a preventive control. When a hazard requiring a preventive control is associated with the production of the food, an appropriate preventive control for the hazard must be addressed in the Food Safety Plan. Potential preventive controls for the identified hazard may be process controls, food allergen controls, sanitation controls, supply-chain controls, other controls. A recall plan is required whenever a hazard requiring a preventive control is identified.

The preventive controls required include only those appropriate to the facility and the food, as determined by hazard analysis. Preventive controls may or may not be at critical control points (CCPs). Process controls are similar to controls addressed through HACCP CCPs. Required food allergen preventive controls are those determined through hazard analysis as necessary to protect food from allergen cross-contact and to ensure that all food allergens are properly labeled.

Required sanitation preventive controls are those determined through hazard analysis as necessary to significantly minimize or prevent 1) environmental pathogens in a ready-to-eat (RTE) food exposed to the environment prior to packaging where the packaged food does not receive a treatment that would significantly minimize the pathogen; 2) biological hazards in an RTE food due to employee handling; and 3) food allergen hazards. Other aspects of sanitation such as pest control, safety of water and employee health do not need to be in a Food Safety Plan unless they are determined to be hazards requiring a preventive control.

Supply-chain controls, implemented through a supply-chain program, are required for ingredients or raw materials for which the receiving facility's hazard analysis identified a hazard requiring a supply-chain-applied control. Other preventive controls may be identified as appropriate based on the hazard analysis.

16-13

Preventive Control – Not Required
(§§ 117.136 & 117.137)

- Not required when an identified hazard requiring a preventive control is controlled by another entity later in the distribution chain IF you:
  - Disclose that food has not been processed to control an identified hazard
  - Obtain written assurances that the hazard will be controlled later in the food chain

There are certain circumstances in which you are not required to implement a preventive control even when you identify a hazard requiring a preventive control (identified hazard). These include:

- You determine that the type of food made could not be consumed without applying an appropriate control. Examples may include raw agricultural commodities such as cocoa beans, coffee beans and grains. You must document the considerations that lead to this conclusion.

- You rely on a customer to ensure that the identified hazard is significantly minimized or prevented. For this to apply, you must:
  - disclose in documents that accompany the food, in a manner consistent with the practice of trade, that it is "not processed to control [identified hazard]".
  - obtain annual written assurance that the hazard is being controlled.

This can apply whether or not your customer is subject to the preventive controls regulations. If your customer does not control the hazard (e.g., they send it on for further processing), additional assurances are required. Refer to the regulation for specifics.

A facility providing the type of written assurance described above must document the action taken to control the hazard.

Recall Plan (§ 117.139)

- Written procedures that describe steps to
  - Directly notify the direct consignees of the food being recalled;
  - Notify the public when appropriate to protect public health;
  - Conduct effectiveness checks to verify that the recall is carried out; and
  - Appropriately dispose of recalled food

A recall plan is required when a hazard requiring a preventive control is identified for a food. It includes written procedures to follow when a recall is needed and assigns responsibilities to do so. These procedures include how you will:

1) inform customers that the food is being recalled, including how to return or dispose of the affected food;
2) notify the public about any hazard presented by the food when appropriate to protect public health,
3) conduct effectiveness checks to verify that your customers received notification and removed the recalled product, and
4) appropriately dispose of the recalled food through reprocessing, reworking, diverting to a use that does not present a safety concern, or destroying the food.

Preventive Control Management Components (§ 117.140)

As appropriate to ensure the effectiveness of the preventive controls, taking into account the nature of the preventive control and its role in the facility's food safety system

- Process, food allergen and sanitation preventive controls
  - Monitoring
  - Corrective actions and corrections
  - Verification (including records review)
- Supplier preventive controls
  - Corrective actions and corrections
  - Records review
  - Reanalysis

Note that reanalysis is also required for other preventive controls in 21 CFR 117.170.

Process, food allergen and sanitation preventive controls all require monitoring, as appropriate, to ensure effectiveness of the preventive control. Predefined corrective actions, or corrections for certain sanitation issues (e.g., observation of unclean equipment before use), and verification are also required, as appropriate, to ensure preventive controls are effective.

Supply-chain programs do not require monitoring; however, corrective actions or corrections (as appropriate) are required as necessary and a review of records of supplier verification activities must be conducted. As with other preventive controls, reanalysis may be needed for supply-chain programs when issues are identified, when a new ingredient is added or when a new supplier replaces a current supplier for the same ingredient.

The recall plan is not subject to these management components.

Monitoring (§ 117.145)

As appropriate to the nature of the preventive control and its role in the facility's food safety system:

- Facility must have written procedures, including frequency they are to be performed, for monitoring the preventive controls
- Monitoring must be documented in records subject to verification
- Exception records allowed for refrigeration, and potentially other systems

---

Written procedures on how you monitor preventive controls are required as appropriate to the preventive control. The procedures must describe the frequency of monitoring.

Refrigeration temperature monitoring records may be either affirmation records (demonstrating that the temperature is controlled in the required limits) or exception records (demonstrating loss of temperature control). An example of an exception record other than refrigeration is x-ray detection for foreign material. No record is generated when no foreign material is present – the record is only generated when foreign material is present, thus it is an exception.

Monitoring records for preventive controls must be verified under the direction of a preventive controls qualified individual.

Corrective Actions (§ 117.150(a)(2))

As appropriate to the nature of the preventive control and its role in the facility's food safety system:

- Facility must establish and implement written corrective action procedures to:
  - Identify and correct a problem with implementation of a preventive control
  - When necessary, reduce the likelihood that the problem will recur
  - Ensure affected food is evaluated for safety
  - Ensure adulterated food is prevented from entering into commerce
- Records of corrective actions taken are required

Corrective action procedures vary depending on the nature of the preventive control and how it fits into the food safety system. For each preventive control requiring a corrective action procedure (typically for a process preventive control), written procedures are required. These corrective actions have four elements:

1) identifying the problem and correcting it,
2) when necessary, reducing the likelihood that the problem will recur,
3) ensuring that affected food is evaluated for safety, and
4) ensuring that adulterated food does not enter commerce. If it does, a recall is warranted.

All corrective actions taken must be documented in records and the records are subject to verification and record review.

Corrective Actions (§ 117.150(a)(1)) Pathogens

- Establish and implement written procedures to:
  - Respond to detection of a pathogen or appropriate indicator organism in an RTE product subject to verification testing
  - Respond to the presence of an environmental pathogen or appropriate indicator organism detected through environmental monitoring
- Response may vary as appropriate to the nature of the preventive control and its role in the facility's food safety system

Corrective action provisions also require written procedures to address the action to take in response to detection of a pathogen or indicator organism in an RTE product that is being tested for verification. Similarly, procedures to respond to detection of an environmental pathogen or indicator organism must be documented. The response to these situations will vary depending on the preventive control itself, the facility, the food and the overall food safety system.

Corrective Actions – Unanticipated Problem (§ 117.150(b))

- Follow corrective action procedures previously discussed
- Perform reanalysis (§ 117.170) to determine if the Food Safety Plan needs to be modified

---

If there is an unanticipated problem and a specific corrective action procedure has not been established, or a preventive control is found to be ineffective (e.g., the process for the product is found to be inadequate), the Food Safety Plan must be reanalyzed to determine whether it should be modified.

Corrections (§ 117.150(c))

- If action is taken in a timely manner, full corrective action procedures are not required for:
  - Food allergen cross-contact controls (§ 117.135(c)(2)(i)
  - Sanitation controls (§ 117.170(c)(3)(i)and (ii))
  - A minor and isolated problem that does not directly impact product safety
- Keep records of corrections made, as appropriate to the situation

---

In some situations you may use corrections in place of corrective action if you take action in a timely manner to identify and correct a minor and isolated problem that does not directly impact product safety. For example, if equipment with a potential food allergen residue is observed before production starts and the surface is cleaned before production begins, a correction is appropriate.

Verification (§ 117.155)

- As appropriate to the nature of the preventive control and its role in the facility's food safety system, must include:
  - Validation (§ 117.160)
  - Verification that monitoring is being conducted
  - Verification that corrective action decisions are appropriate
  - Verification of implementation and effectiveness (§ 117.165)
    - Calibration, product testing, environmental monitoring, review of records
  - Reanalysis

Verification activities are required to ensure that preventive controls are consistently implemented and effective. They include validation, and verification that monitoring is being conducted and that appropriate corrective action decisions are being made. Verification of implementation and effectiveness includes review of calibration, product testing and environmental monitoring records. Reanalysis of the Food Safety Plan is another verification activity.

Validation (§ 117.160)

Documented scientific and technical evidence that the preventive control will effectively control the hazard

- Required for process controls
- Performed or overseen by a preventive controls qualified individual
  - Prior to implementation OR
  - Within first 90 days of production OR
  - Reasonable time with written justification

- Not required for:
  - Food allergen controls
  - Sanitation controls
  - Supply-chain program
  - Recall plan

Validation is "the process of obtaining and evaluating scientific and technical evidence that a control measure, combination of control measures, or the food safety plan as a whole, when properly implemented, is capable of effectively controlling the identified hazards." Preferably, validation is conducted before production; however, it is recognized that on-line validation may be necessary, for example to account for process variation. In any case, validation must be complete within the first 90 days of production or a reasonable amount of time with written justification by a preventive controls qualified individual.

Validation is not required for food allergen, sanitation or supply-chain program controls, but may be useful. Validation is not required for the recall plan.

Verification of Implementation and Effectiveness (§ 117.165)

- Verification of implementation and effectiveness includes, <u>as appropriate</u> to the facility, the food and the nature of the preventive control
  - Calibration
  - Product testing for a pathogen or appropriate indicator or other hazard
  - Environmental monitoring if an environmental hazard requiring a preventive control is identified
  - Review of records

Verification of implementation and effectiveness includes, as appropriate to the facility, the food and the nature of the preventive control, activities such as calibration, product testing, environmental monitoring and records review. These are activities that help you assess whether what you are doing is controlling the hazards.

Calibration is required for instruments used for process monitoring and verification. Product testing for a pathogen (or appropriate indicator) or other hazard is required for hazards requiring a preventive control when appropriate for verification. Environmental monitoring is a required verification activity when an environmental pathogen is identified as a hazard requiring a preventive control.

Review of Records (§ 117.165(a)(4))

- Within 7 working days after records were created
  - Monitoring records
  - Corrective action records
  - Preventive controls qualified individual may provide written justification for a longer "reasonable timeframe"
- Within a reasonable timeframe after records were created
  - Calibration
  - Product and environmental monitoring testing
  - Supplier and supply-chain verification activities
  - Other verification activities

Review of monitoring and corrective action records is required within seven working days after the record was created unless a preventive controls qualified individual prepares or oversees written justification for a longer reasonable timeframe. Calibration records, product testing records and environment monitoring records, when applicable, must be reviewed within a reasonable time after the records were created. Review of relevant supplier and supply-chain verification records is also required in a reasonable timeframe.

Verification Written Procedures (§ 117.165(b))

Must have written procedures as appropriate to the facility, the food, the nature of the preventive control, and role in the food safety system

- Method and frequency of calibration (or accuracy checks) for monitoring and verification instruments
- Product testing:
  - Scientifically valid procedures
  - Identify test microorganism(s) or other analyte(s)
  - Procedures to identify sample and relation to production lot(s)
  - Procedures for sampling (number and frequency)
  - Test(s) conducted and method(s) used
  - Laboratory conducting the testing
  - Corrective action procedures
- Environmental monitoring
  - Scientifically valid procedures
  - Identify test microorganism(s)
  - Identify sample locations, number of sites tested – must be adequate to determine whether preventive controls are effective
  - Timing and frequency for collecting and testing
  - Test(s) conducted and method(s) used
  - Laboratory conducting the testing
  - Corrective action procedures

Written procedures required for Food Safety Plans vary depending on the facility, the food, the nature of the preventive control and the role of that control in the facility's food safety system. Written procedures are required for calibrating monitoring and verification equipment in the plan, as well as the frequency of calibration. When product testing is required, scientifically valid procedures must be used and identified. Written procedures must identify the test microorganisms or analytes, how the samples relate to the lot, the number and frequency of taking samples, the tests conducted and methods used, the laboratory conducting the test, and corrective action procedures to implement for results that do not meet requirements. Similar procedures are required when environmental monitoring is required.

Reanalysis (§ 117.170(a) and (b)) – When

- A verification activity must be conducted for the full plan:
  - At least every 3 years
  - When FDA determines it is necessary to respond to new hazards
- Applicable sections of the plan:
  - When there is a significant change that creates the potential for a new hazard or a significant increase in one previously identified
  - When you become aware of new information about potential hazards associated with a food
  - When appropriate after an unanticipated food safety problem (§ 117.150(b))
  - When you find that a preventive control, combination of preventive controls or the Food Safety Plan as a whole is ineffective

---

Reanalysis of the Food Safety Plan is another verification activity. The full plan must be reviewed at least every 3 years to ensure that it still accurately reflects the preventive controls needed. FDA may also determine that reanalysis is necessary in response to new hazards and developments in scientific understanding.

Reanalysis of applicable sections of the plan is also required when there is a significant change in the operation or in current knowledge that may increase concern regarding a new or previously identified hazard. Reanalysis may also be required after an unanticipated food safety problem occurs or when a preventive control, combination of preventive controls or the Food Safety Plan itself is ineffective.

Reanalysis (§ 117.170(c), (d) and (e))

- Complete the reanalysis BEFORE you make any changes OR (when necessary) within 90 days (or a reasonable timeframe with written justification) after production first begins
- You must:
  - Revise the Food Safety Plan if significant changes occur that create a reasonable potential for a new or significant increase in an identified hazard OR
  - Document the basis for concluding that no change is needed
- A preventive controls qualified individual must perform or oversee the reanalysis

When reanalysis is conducted, in most cases it must take place before any changes are made to the Food Safety Plan. When necessary to demonstrate control measures can be implemented as designed, validation activities needed as a result of the reanalysis may take place in the first 90 days of production. If your reanalysis indicates an increased food safety risk, your Food Safety Plan must be revised. If you determine that no revision is necessary, the basis for that decision must also be documented. A preventive controls qualified individual must perform or oversee reanalysis of the Food Safety Plan.

Preventive Controls Qualified Individual Responsibilities (§ 117.180(a))

- Oversees or performs
  - Preparation of the Food Safety Plan
  - Validation of the preventive controls
    - Justification for validation timeframe exceeding 90 days
    - Determination that validation is not required
  - Review of records
    - Justification for review of monitoring and corrective action records timeframe exceeding 7 working days
  - Reanalysis of the Food Safety Plan
    - Determining that the timeframe for reanalysis and additional preventive controls validation can exceed the first 90 days of production

A preventive controls qualified individual is required to develop or oversee development of the Food Safety Plan, validation of the preventive controls used in the plan, review of records and reanalysis of the Food Safety Plan. Additional tasks that must be performed or overseen by a preventive controls qualified individual involve written justification in situations where expected timeframes for certain activities are not met. These include justification for completing validation activities after 90 days of first production or determining that validation is not required, justification for review of monitoring and corrective action records exceeding 7 working days, and determining that it is appropriate to perform reanalysis and validation of additional preventive controls in a period longer than the first 90 days of production.

Preventive Controls Qualified Individual (§ 117.180(c)(1))

- Must have <u>successfully completed training</u> in the development and application of risk-based preventive controls
  - At least equivalent to that received under a standardized curriculum recognized as adequate by FDA
- <u>Or be otherwise qualified</u> through job experience to develop and apply a food safety system.
- Can be an external consultant
- Training must be documented in records – date, type of training, person(s) trained

---

Certain activities for preventive controls must be overseen by a preventive controls qualified individual. There are essentially two ways for an individual to achieve this recognition. The first way is to successfully complete training in the development and application of risk-based preventive controls, such as attending this training class and successfully completing the exercises. Training must be documented in records, including the date, type of training, person trained etc.

The second way is for an individual to be qualified through job experience. These individuals will need to understand the specific regulatory requirements of the *Preventive Controls for Human Food* regulation, which differ somewhat from requirements in other food safety regulations and standards.

Some organizations may have one or more people on staff that can perform all of the functions that require oversight by a preventive controls qualified individual. Other organizations may choose to engage a technical expert to help with certain aspects, such as development of the hazard analysis, validating preventive controls and other highly technical aspects of this role. This can vary considerably depending on the complexity of the product and the potential food safety hazards for the food and facility.

Qualified Auditor (§ 117.180(b) and (c)(2))

- Must conduct onsite audits, when required
- Must have technical expertise obtained by education, training and experience in the auditing function
- Training must be documented in records – date, type of training, person(s) trained

Auditing may be a required verification activity, for example for a supply-chain program. The auditor must be a qualified individual and be qualified to do the audit through a combination of education, auditing experience (including an understanding of the commodity involved) and auditing training. Records of such experience are required.

Implementation Records (§ 117.190)

- Records required by 117.136 regarding not implementing a preventive control in your facility
- Records that document monitoring of the preventive controls
- Records that document corrective actions
- Records that document verification
- Records that document the supply-chain program
- Records that document training for the preventive controls qualified individual and the qualified auditor

The *Preventive Controls for Human Food* regulation also has specific requirements for implementation records. You may recall that 21 CFR 117.136 described situations where a preventive control is not required to be implemented, such as when the food could not be consumed without application of an appropriate control or when the processing facility receives assurances that their customer will apply the control. Records documenting these situations are required. Other records that are more common include those that document monitoring activities of the preventive controls identified in the hazard analysis; records of corrective actions associated with preventive controls; records documenting training in the principles of food hygiene and food safety for individuals engaged in manufacturing, processing, packing or holding food; records for the supply-chain program, records of training for preventive controls qualified individuals and qualified auditors, and several different types of verification activities. Records that document verification include, as applicable:

- validation records that establish the scientific and technical basis of the preventive controls,
- verification of monitoring records to ensure that critical limits and other parameters were met,
- verification of corrective action records to ensure that appropriate actions were carried out and completed,
- calibration of process monitoring and verification instruments to ensure that the data they provide are accurate,
- records of product testing,
- records of environmental monitoring,
- record to document record review, and
- reanalysis of the Food Safety Plan.

Subpart D – Modified Requirements

21 CFR Part 117 – Current Good Manufacturing Practice, Hazard Analysis, and Risk-based Preventive Controls for Human Food

Subpart D – Modified Requirements

§ 117.201 Modified requirements that apply to a qualified facility

§ 117.206 Modified requirements that apply to a facility solely engaged in the storage of unexposed packaged food

There are modified requirements for certain facilities such as very small businesses (i.e., a qualified facility) or warehouses that solely engage in storage of unexposed packaged food. These modified requirements are addressed in 21 CFR 117 Subpart D. Consult this section if you are a qualified facility. A brief discussion of requirements that apply to facilities solely engaged in storage of unexposed packaged food follows.

Storage of Unexposed Packaged Food (§ 117.206)

- Modified requirements apply to refrigerated foods that require refrigeration for safety
  - Implement temperature controls for pathogens
  - Monitor temperatures
  - Take corrective actions when there are temperature control problems
  - Verify temperature controls
    - Calibrate temperature monitoring and recording devices
    - Review monitoring and corrective action records

For facilities that store *refrigerated* packaged food (e.g., refrigerated storage warehouses), there are requirements for time/temperature control if the product can support pathogen growth or toxin production. These include monitoring temperatures and taking corrective action when appropriate. Verification activities related to temperature monitoring also apply.

Subpart E – Withdrawal of a Qualified Facility Exemption

---

21 CFR Part 117 – Current Good Manufacturing Practice, Hazard Analysis, and Risk-based Preventive Controls for Human Food

Subpart E – Withdrawal of a Qualified Facility Exemption
§ 117.251 Circumstances that may lead FDA to withdraw a qualified facility exemption
§ 117.254 Issuance of an order to withdraw a qualified facility exemption
§ 117.257 Contents of an order to withdraw a qualified facility exemption
§ 117.260 Compliance with, or appeal of, an order to withdraw a qualified facility exemption
§ 117.264 Procedure for submitting an appeal
§ 117.267 Procedure for requesting an informal hearing
§ 117.270 Requirements applicable to an informal hearing
§ 117.274 Presiding officer for an appeal and for an informal hearing
§ 117.277 Timeframe for issuing a decision on an appeal
§ 117.280 Revocation of an order to withdraw a qualified facility exemption
§ 117.284 Final agency action
§ 117.287 Reinstatement of a qualified facility exemption that was withdrawn

---

21 CFR 117 Subpart E describes the circumstances, procedures and requirements for withdrawing a qualified facility exemption. If you believe that you are a qualified facility, you should become familiar

with the provisions for withdrawal and reinstatement of the exemption for qualified facilities. When such situations arise, other assistance is needed, including from legal counsel, to assure that the legal requirements are fulfilled.

Subpart F - Records

21 CFR Part 117 – Current Good Manufacturing Practice, Hazard Analysis, and Risk-based Preventive Controls for Human Food

Subpart F – Requirements Applying to Records That Must be Established and Maintained

§ 117.301 Records subject to the requirements of this subpart

§ 117.305 General requirements applying to records

§ 117.310 Additional requirements applying to the food safety plan

§ 117.315 Requirements for record retention

§ 117.320 Requirements for official review

§ 117.325 Public disclosure

§ 117.330 Use of existing records

§ 117.335 Special requirements applicable to a written assurance

21 CFR 117 Subpart F describes requirements for records. Records must be kept as original records, true copies (e.g., photocopies, pictures, scanned copies, microfilm, microfiche or other accurate reproductions of the original) or electronic records. They must contain the actual values and observations obtained during monitoring and, as appropriate, during verification activities. Records must be accurate, indelible, legible and created concurrently with the activity being documented. Records must be as detailed as necessary to provide a history of the work performed, including:

- adequate information to identify the plant or facility (e.g., the name and when necessary the location of the facility),
- the date and, when appropriate, time of the activity documented,
- the signature or initials of the person performing the activity and
- where appropriate, the identity of the product and the lot code, if any.

The Food Safety Plan must be signed and dated by the owner, operator or agent in charge of the facility upon initial completion and upon any modification.

All required records must be retained at the facility for at least 2 years after the date they were prepared. Records related to the general adequacy of the equipment or processes being used by the facility, including scientific studies and evaluations, must be retained for at least 2 years after their use is discontinued. This applies to Food Safety Plans that are no longer used because they have been updated, validation records for processes no longer used, and potentially other records.

Except for the Food Safety Plan, offsite storage of required records is permitted if they can be retrieved and provided onsite within 24 hours of the request for official review. Electronic records are considered onsite if they can be accessed from an onsite location. All records required must be made promptly available for official review and copying upon oral or written request. Records required are subject to disclosure requirements under 21 CFR Part 20.

Existing records, such as records kept to comply with other federal, state or local regulations or any other reason, may be used if they contain all the required information. You can supplement existing records if they are missing some of the required elements. You do not have to keep your records as one set of records – any new information not on an existing record can be kept separately or combined with the existing records.

Any required written assurance (21 CFR 117.335) related to application of a preventive control elsewhere in the supply-chain (see 21 CFR 117.136 and 117.430) must contain the effective date, printed names and signatures of authorized officials, and relevant information regarding acknowledgement of legal responsibility. Read the section carefully if it applies to your facility.

Subpart G – Supply-chain Program

21 CFR Part 117 – Current Good Manufacturing Practice, Hazard Analysis, and Risk-based Preventive Controls for Human Food

Subpart G – Supply-chain Program

§ 117.405 Requirement to establish and implement a supply-chain program

§ 117.410 General requirements applicable to a supply-chain program

§ 117.415 Responsibilities of the receiving facility

§ 117.420 Using approved suppliers

§ 117.425 Determining appropriate supplier verification activities (including determining the frequency of conducting the activity)

§ 117.430 Conducting supplier verification activities for raw materials and other ingredients

§ 117.435 Onsite audit

§ 117.475 Records documenting the supply-chain program

Hazards requiring a preventive control for which you rely on supplier efforts are managed through your supply-chain program. 21 CFR 117 Subpart G covers requirements to establish and implement a supply-chain program, general requirements, responsibilities of the receiving

facility, using approved suppliers, determining appropriate verification activities, conducting those activities, onsite audits and records required for your supply-chain program.

Requirement to Establish and Implement a Supply-chain Program (§ 117.405)

- Receiving facility must have a risk-based supply-chain program for raw materials and other ingredients identified as having a hazard requiring a supply-chain applied control unless
  - Does not apply to importers meeting FSVP requirements or ingredients for research or evaluation
- Must be written
- Must maintain records to demonstrate implementation

FSPCA

A supply-chain program is required to address only those ingredients and raw materials that present potential hazards requiring a supply-chain applied control (i.e., the hazard is controlled before receipt). Your supply-chain program must be written and you must have records to demonstrate that the program is implemented.

Supply-chain Program General Requirements (§ 117.410)

- Use approved suppliers
- Determine appropriate supplier verification activities
- Conduct and document supplier verification activities
- If a supply-chain-applied control is applied by an entity other than your supplier
  - Verify that the control was applied by someone other than the supplier OR
  - Obtain documentation of verification by another entity
- Take prompt action and document it when issues are identified

FSPCA

For these ingredients, you must use approved suppliers. For these suppliers, you must determine the appropriate supplier verification activities, then conduct and document those activities. Sometimes a supply-chain-applied control is applied by an entity other than the receiving facility's supplier (e.g., when a "non-supplier" applies controls to certain produce (i.e., produce subject to the produce safety rule), because growing, harvesting, and packing activities are under different management). The receiving facility must (1) verify the supply-chain-applied control; or (2) obtain documentation of verification from another entity (e.g., supplier produce distributor) using one of the verification procedures that is discussed in the next slide.

Supplier Verification Activities (§ 117.410(b))

- Onsite audits
- Sampling and testing
- Review of relevant food safety records
- Other as appropriate

The activities listed above are appropriate supplier verification activities for raw materials and other ingredients requiring supply-chain-applied control. In determining which approach to use, consider:

- the results of the hazard analysis including the nature of the hazard requiring a supply-chain-applied control;
- the supplier's procedures, processes and practices related to the safety of the ingredient;
- relevant FDA food safety regulations and information such as warning letters and import alerts related to the food and the supplier's compliance with these;
- the supplier's food safety history including applicable test results, audit results, response to correct problems, etc., and
- storage and transportation practices.

Onsite audits must be performed by a qualified auditor and must include review of the supplier's written plan (e.g., HACCP plan or other Food Safety Plan if the supplier is subject to an FDA food safety regulation). An appropriate inspection conducted by FDA (or other specified agency officials) for compliance with FDA food safety regulations may be substituted for an onsite audit. If this applies to one of your suppliers, refer to the regulation for details.

If you determine through verification activities that the supplier is not controlling the hazard, you must take action and document the action taken to ensure that your food is not adulterated or misbranded.

Regulation Overview Summary

- The full regulation, *21 CFR Part 117 – Current Good Manufacturing Practice, Hazard Analysis, and Risk-based Preventive Controls for Human Food*, is in Appendix 1
- Sections include
  - Subpart A – General Provisions
  - Subpart B – Current Good Manufacturing Practice
  - Subpart C – Hazard Analysis and Risk-based Preventive Controls
  - Subpart D – Modified Requirements
  - Subpart E – Withdrawal of a Qualified Facility Exemption
  - Subpart F – Requirements Applying to Records That Must be Established and Maintained
  - Subpart G – Supply-chain Program

The *Current Good Manufacturing Practice, Hazard Analysis, and Risk-Based Preventive Controls for Human Food* regulation is intended to focus preventive controls where they matter most. GMPs are required for all facilities unless an exemption exists. This course focuses on 21 CFR 117 Subpart C – Hazard Analysis and Risk-based Preventive Controls for Human Food and Subpart G – Supply-chain Program. More detailed information on other provisions can be obtained through other means, such as reading the regulation (see Appendix 1), through other training programs or through legal counsel.

Where to Go for Help

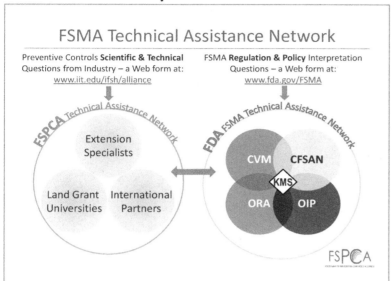

Remember that Chapter 7 discussed the FSPCA and the FDA Technical Assistance Networks and provided the links to both the FSPCA Website (www.iit.edu/ifsh/alliance) and the FDA Website at (www.fda.gov/FSMA). These networks will work together – with FDA addressing answers to regulation and policy interpretation questions and FSPCA addressing scientific and technical questions, as appropriate.

NOTES:

APPENDIX 1: FDA Regulation on cGMP, Hazard Analysis, and Risk-based Preventive Controls for Human Food

NOTE: NOT an official version. Provided for reference only.
Includes technical amendments (22 January 2016) and corrections (25 January 2016).

Title 21 of the Code of Federal Regulation Part 117—Current Good Manufacturing Practice, Hazard Analysis, and Risk-based Preventive Controls for Human Food

Subpart A – General Provisions

§ 117.1 Applicability and status.
(a) The criteria and definitions in this part apply in determining whether a food is:
  (1) Adulterated within the meaning of:
     (i) Section 402(a)(3) of the Federal Food, Drug, and Cosmetic Act in that the food has been manufactured under such conditions that it is unfit for food; or
     (ii) Section 402(a)(4) of the Federal Food, Drug, and Cosmetic Act in that the food has been prepared, packed, or held under insanitary conditions whereby it may have become contaminated with filth, or whereby it may have been rendered injurious to health; and
  (2) In violation of section 361 of the Public Health Service Act (42 U.S.C. 264).
(b) The operation of a facility that manufactures, processes, packs, or holds food for sale in the United States if the owner, operator, or agent in charge of such facility is required to comply with, and is not in compliance with, section 418 of the Federal Food, Drug, and Cosmetic Act or subpart C, D, E, F, or G of this part is a prohibited act under section 301(uu) of the Federal Food, Drug, and Cosmetic Act.
(c) Food covered by specific current good manufacturing practice regulations also is subject to the requirements of those regulations.

§ 117.3 Definitions.
The definitions and interpretations of terms in section 201 of the Federal Food, Drug, and Cosmetic Act apply to such terms when used in this part. The following definitions also apply:

Acid foods or acidified foods means foods that have an equilibrium pH of 4.6 or below.

Adequate means that which is needed to accomplish the intended purpose in keeping with good public health practice.

Affiliate means any facility that controls, is controlled by, or is under common control with another facility.

Allergen cross-contact means the unintentional incorporation of a food allergen into a food.

Audit means the systematic, independent, and documented examination (through observation, investigation, records review, discussions with employees of the audited entity, and, as appropriate, sampling and laboratory analysis) to assess an entity's food safety processes and procedures.

Batter means a semifluid substance, usually composed of flour and other ingredients, into which principal components of food are dipped or with which they are coated, or which may be used directly to form bakery foods.

Blanching, except for tree nuts and peanuts, means a prepackaging heat treatment of foodstuffs for an adequate time and at an adequate temperature to partially or completely inactivate the naturally occurring enzymes and to effect other physical or biochemical changes in the food.

Calendar day means every day shown on the calendar.

Correction means an action to identify and correct a problem that occurred during the production of food, without other actions associated with a corrective action procedure (such as actions to reduce the likelihood that the problem will recur, evaluate all affected food for safety, and prevent affected food from entering commerce).

Critical control point means a point, step, or procedure in a food process at which control can be applied and is essential to prevent or eliminate a food safety hazard or reduce such hazard to an acceptable level.

Defect action level means a level of a non-hazardous, naturally occurring, unavoidable defect at which FDA may regard a food product "adulterated" and subject to enforcement action under section 402(a)(3) of the Federal Food, Drug, and Cosmetic Act.

Environmental pathogen means a pathogen capable of surviving and persisting within the manufacturing, processing, packing, or holding environment such that food may be contaminated and may result in foodborne illness if that food is

© 2016 IIT IFSH

consumed without treatment to significantly minimize the environmental pathogen. Examples of environmental pathogens for the purposes of this part include <u>Listeria monocytogenes</u> and <u>Salmonella</u> spp. but do not include the spores of pathogenic sporeforming bacteria.

<u>Facility</u> means a domestic facility or a foreign facility that is required to register under section 415 of the Federal Food, Drug, and Cosmetic Act, in accordance with the requirements of part 1, subpart H of this chapter.

<u>Farm</u> means farm as defined in § 1.227 of this chapter.

<u>FDA</u> means the Food and Drug Administration.

<u>Food</u> means food as defined in section 201(f) of the Federal Food, Drug, and Cosmetic Act and includes raw materials and ingredients.

<u>Food allergen</u> means a major food allergen as defined in section 201(qq) of the Federal Food, Drug, and Cosmetic Act.

<u>Food-contact surfaces</u> are those surfaces that contact human food and those surfaces from which drainage, or other transfer, onto the food or onto surfaces that contact the food ordinarily occurs during the normal course of operations. "Food-contact surfaces" includes utensils and food-contact surfaces of equipment.

<u>Full-time equivalent employee</u> is a term used to represent the number of employees of a business entity for the purpose of determining whether the business qualifies for the small business exemption. The number of full-time equivalent employees is determined by dividing the total number of hours of salary or wages paid directly to employees of the business entity and of all of its affiliates and subsidiaries by the number of hours of work in 1 year, 2,080 hours (i.e., 40 hours x 52 weeks). If the result is not a whole number, round down to the next lowest whole number.

<u>Harvesting</u> applies to farms and farm mixed-type facilities and means activities that are traditionally performed on farms for the purpose of removing raw agricultural commodities from the place they were grown or raised and preparing them for use as food. Harvesting is limited to activities performed on raw agricultural commodities, or on processed foods created by drying/dehydrating a raw agricultural commodity without additional manufacturing/processing, on a farm. Harvesting does not include activities that transform a raw agricultural commodity into a processed food as defined in section 201(gg) of the Federal Food, Drug, and Cosmetic Act. Examples of harvesting include cutting (or otherwise separating) the edible portion of the raw agricultural commodity from the crop plant and removing or trimming part of the raw agricultural commodity (e.g., foliage, husks, roots or stems). Examples of harvesting also include cooling, field coring, filtering, gathering, hulling, shelling, sifting, threshing, trimming of outer leaves of, and washing raw agricultural commodities grown on a farm.

<u>Hazard</u> means any biological, chemical (including radiological), or physical agent that has the potential to cause illness or injury.

<u>Hazard requiring a preventive control</u> means a known or reasonably foreseeable hazard for which a person knowledgeable about the safe manufacturing, processing, packing, or holding of food would, based on the outcome of a hazard analysis (which includes an assessment of the severity of the illness or injury if the hazard were to occur and the probability that the hazard will occur in the absence of preventive controls), establish one or more preventive controls to significantly minimize or prevent the hazard in a food and components to manage those controls (such as monitoring, corrections or corrective actions, verification, and records) as appropriate to the food, the facility, and the nature of the preventive control and its role in the facility's food safety system.

<u>Holding</u> means storage of food and also includes activities performed incidental to storage of a food (e.g., activities performed for the safe or effective storage of that food, such as fumigating food during storage, and drying/dehydrating raw agricultural commodities when the drying/dehydrating does not create a distinct commodity (such as drying/dehydrating hay or alfalfa)). Holding also includes activities performed as a practical necessity for the distribution of that food (such as blending of the same raw agricultural commodity and breaking down pallets), but does not include activities that transform a raw agricultural commodity into a processed food as defined in section 201(gg) of the Federal Food, Drug, and Cosmetic Act. Holding facilities could include warehouses, cold storage facilities, storage silos, grain elevators, and liquid storage tanks.

<u>Known or reasonably foreseeable hazard</u> means a biological, chemical (including radiological), or physical hazard that is known to be, or has the potential to be, associated with the facility or the food.

<u>Lot</u> means the food produced during a period of time and identified by an establishment's specific code.

<u>Manufacturing/processing</u> means making food from one or more ingredients, or synthesizing, preparing, treating, modifying or manipulating food, including food crops or ingredients. Examples of manufacturing/processing activities include: Baking, boiling, bottling, canning, cooking, cooling, cutting, distilling, drying/dehydrating raw agricultural commodities to create a distinct commodity (such as drying/dehydrating grapes to produce raisins), evaporating, eviscerating, extracting juice, formulating, freezing, grinding, homogenizing, irradiating, labeling, milling, mixing, packaging (including modified atmosphere packaging), pasteurizing, peeling, rendering, treating to manipulate ripening, trimming, washing, or waxing. For farms and farm mixed-type facilities, manufacturing/processing does not include activities that are part of harvesting, packing, or holding.

<u>Microorganisms</u> means yeasts, molds, bacteria, viruses, protozoa, and microscopic parasites and includes species that are pathogens. The term "undesirable microorganisms" includes those microorganisms that are pathogens, that subject food to decomposition, that indicate that food is contaminated with filth, or that otherwise may cause food to be adulterated.

A1-2

Mixed-type facility means an establishment that engages in both activities that are exempt from registration under section 415 of the Federal Food, Drug, and Cosmetic Act and activities that require the establishment to be registered. An example of such a facility is a "farm mixed-type facility," which is an establishment that is a farm, but also conducts activities outside the farm definition that require the establishment to be registered.

Monitor means to conduct a planned sequence of observations or measurements to assess whether control measures are operating as intended.

Packing means placing food into a container other than packaging the food and also includes re-packing and activities performed incidental to packing or re-packing a food (e.g., activities performed for the safe or effective packing or re-packing of that food (such as sorting, culling, grading, and weighing or conveying incidental to packing or re-packing)), but does not include activities that transform a raw agricultural commodity into a processed food as defined in section 201(gg) of the Federal Food, Drug, and Cosmetic Act.

Pathogen means a microorganism of public health significance.

Pest refers to any objectionable animals or insects including birds, rodents, flies, and larvae.

Plant means the building or structure or parts thereof, used for or in connection with the manufacturing, processing, packing, or holding of human food.

Preventive controls means those risk-based, reasonably appropriate procedures, practices, and processes that a person knowledgeable about the safe manufacturing, processing, packing, or holding of food would employ to significantly minimize or prevent the hazards identified under the hazard analysis that are consistent with the current scientific understanding of safe food manufacturing, processing, packing, or holding at the time of the analysis.

Preventive controls qualified individual means a qualified individual who has successfully completed training in the development and application of risk-based preventive controls at least equivalent to that received under a standardized curriculum recognized as adequate by FDA or is otherwise qualified through job experience to develop and apply a food safety system.

Qualified auditor means a person who is a qualified individual as defined in this part and has technical expertise obtained through education, training, or experience (or a combination thereof) necessary to perform the auditing function as required by § 117.180(c)(2). Examples of potential qualified auditors include:

(1) A government employee, including a foreign government employee; and

(2) An audit agent of a certification body that is accredited in accordance with regulations in part 1, subpart M of this chapter.

Qualified end-user, with respect to a food, means the consumer of the food (where the term consumer does not include a business); or a restaurant or retail food establishment (as those terms are defined in § 1.227 of this chapter) that:

(1) Is located:

(i) In the same State or the same Indian reservation as the qualified facility that sold the food to such restaurant or establishment; or

(ii) Not more than 275 miles from such facility; and

(2) Is purchasing the food for sale directly to consumers at such restaurant or retail food establishment.

Qualified facility means (when including the sales by any subsidiary; affiliate; or subsidiaries or affiliates, collectively, of any entity of which the facility is a subsidiary or affiliate) a facility that is a very small business as defined in this part, or a facility to which both of the following apply:

(1) During the 3-year period preceding the applicable calendar year, the average annual monetary value of the food manufactured, processed, packed or held at such facility that is sold directly to qualified end-users (as defined in this part) during such period exceeded the average annual monetary value of the food sold by such facility to all other purchasers; and

(2) The average annual monetary value of all food sold during the 3-year period preceding the applicable calendar year was less than $500,000, adjusted for inflation.

Qualified facility exemption means an exemption applicable to a qualified facility under § 117.5(a).

Qualified individual means a person who has the education, training, or experience (or a combination thereof) necessary to manufacture, process, pack, or hold clean and safe food as appropriate to the individual's assigned duties. A qualified individual may be, but is not required to be, an employee of the establishment.

Quality control operation means a planned and systematic procedure for taking all actions necessary to prevent food from being adulterated.

Raw agricultural commodity has the meaning given in section 201(r) of the Federal Food, Drug, and Cosmetic Act.

Ready-to-eat food (RTE food) means any food that is normally eaten in its raw state or any other food, including a processed food, for which it is reasonably foreseeable that the food will be eaten without further processing that would significantly minimize biological hazards.

Receiving facility means a facility that is subject to subparts C and G of this part and that manufactures/processes a raw material or other ingredient that it receives from a supplier.

Rework means clean, unadulterated food that has been removed from processing for reasons other than insanitary conditions or that has been successfully reconditioned by reprocessing and that is suitable for use as food.

Safe-moisture level is a level of moisture low enough to prevent the growth of undesirable microorganisms in the finished product under the intended conditions of manufacturing, processing, packing, and holding. The safe moisture level for a food is related to its water activity (a_w). An a_w will be considered safe for a food if adequate data are available that demonstrate that the food at or below the given a_w will not support the growth of undesirable microorganisms.

Sanitize means to adequately treat cleaned surfaces by a process that is effective in destroying vegetative cells of pathogens, and in substantially reducing numbers of other undesirable microorganisms, but without adversely affecting the product or its safety for the consumer.

Significantly minimize means to reduce to an acceptable level, including to eliminate.

Small business means, for purposes of this part, a business (including any subsidiaries and affiliates) employing fewer than 500 full-time equivalent employees.

Subsidiary means any company which is owned or controlled directly or indirectly by another company.

Supplier means the establishment that manufactures/processes the food, raises the animal, or grows the food that is provided to a receiving facility without further manufacturing/processing by another establishment, except for further manufacturing/processing that consists solely of the addition of labeling or similar activity of a de minimis nature.

Supply-chain-applied control means a preventive control for a hazard in a raw material or other ingredient when the hazard in the raw material or other ingredient is controlled before its receipt.

Unexposed packaged food means packaged food that is not exposed to the environment.

Validation means obtaining and evaluating scientific and technical evidence that a control measure, combination of control measures, or the food safety plan as a whole, when properly implemented, is capable of effectively controlling the identified hazards.

Verification means the application of methods, procedures, tests and other evaluations, in addition to monitoring, to determine whether a control measure or combination of control measures is or has been operating as intended and to establish the validity of the food safety plan.

Very small business means, for purposes of this part, a business (including any subsidiaries and affiliates) averaging less than $1,000,000, adjusted for inflation, per year, during the 3-year period preceding the applicable calendar year in sales of human food plus the market value of human food manufactured, processed, packed, or held without sale (e.g., held for a fee).

Water activity (a_w) is a measure of the free moisture in a food and is the quotient of the water vapor pressure of the substance divided by the vapor pressure of pure water at the same temperature.

Written procedures for receiving raw materials and other ingredients means written procedures to ensure that raw materials and other ingredients are received only from suppliers approved by the receiving facility (or, when necessary and appropriate, on a temporary basis from unapproved suppliers whose raw materials or other ingredients are subjected to adequate verification activities before acceptance for use).

You means, for purposes of this part, the owner, operator, or agent in charge of a facility.

§ 117.4 Qualifications of individuals who manufacture, process, pack, or hold food.

(a) Applicability.

(1) The management of an establishment must ensure that all individuals who manufacture, process, pack, or hold food subject to subparts B and F of this part are qualified to perform their assigned duties.

(2) The owner, operator, or agent in charge of a facility must ensure that all individuals who manufacture, process, pack, or hold food subject to subpart C, D, E, F, or G of this part are qualified to perform their assigned duties.

(b) Qualifications of all individuals engaged in manufacturing, processing, packing, or holding food. Each individual engaged in manufacturing, processing, packing, or holding food (including temporary and seasonal personnel) or in the supervision thereof must:

(1) Be a qualified individual as that term is defined in § 117.3--i.e., have the education, training, or experience (or a combination thereof) necessary to manufacture, process, pack, or hold clean and safe food as appropriate to the individual's assigned duties; and

(2) Receive training in the principles of food hygiene and food safety, including the importance of employee health and personal hygiene, as appropriate to the food, the facility and the individual's assigned duties.

(c) Additional qualifications of supervisory personnel. Responsibility for ensuring compliance by individuals with the requirements of this part must be clearly assigned to supervisory personnel who have the education, training, or experience (or a combination thereof) necessary to supervise the production of clean and safe food.

(d) Records. Records that document training required by paragraph (b)(2) of this section must be established and maintained.

§ 117.5 Exemptions.

(a) Except as provided by subpart E of this part, subparts C and G of this part do not apply to a qualified facility. Qualified facilities are subject to the modified requirements in §117.201.

(b) Subparts C and G of this part do not apply with respect to activities that are subject to part 123 of this chapter (Fish and Fishery Products) at a facility if you are required to comply with, and are in compliance with, part 123 of this chapter with respect to such activities.

(c) Subparts C and G of this part do not apply with respect to activities that are subject to part 120 of this chapter (Hazard Analysis and Critical Control Point (HACCP) Systems) at a facility if you are required to comply with, and are in compliance with, part 120 of this chapter with respect to such activities.

(d) (1) Subparts C and G of this part do not apply with respect to activities that are subject to part 113 of this chapter (Thermally Processed Low-Acid Foods Packaged in Hermetically Sealed Containers) at a facility if you are required to comply with, and are in compliance with, part 113 of this chapter with respect to such activities.

(2) The exemption in paragraph (d)(1) of this section is applicable only with respect to the microbiological hazards that are regulated under part 113 of this chapter.

(e) Subparts C and G do not apply to any facility with regard to the manufacturing, processing, packaging, or holding of a dietary supplement that is in compliance with the requirements of part 111 of this chapter (Current Good Manufacturing Practice in Manufacturing, Packaging, Labeling, or Holding Operations for Dietary Supplements) and section 761 of the Federal Food, Drug, and Cosmetic Act (Serious Adverse Event Reporting for Dietary Supplements).

(f) Subparts C and G of this part do not apply to activities of a facility that are subject to section 419 of the Federal Food, Drug, and Cosmetic Act (Standards for Produce Safety).

(g)(1) The exemption in paragraph (g)(3) of this section applies to packing or holding of processed foods on a farm mixed-type facility, except for processed foods produced by drying/dehydrating raw agricultural commodities to create a distinct commodity (such as drying/dehydrating grapes to produce raisins, and drying/dehydrating fresh herbs to produce dried herbs), and packaging and labeling such commodities, without additional manufacturing/processing (such as chopping and slicing), the packing and holding of which are within the "farm" definition in § 1.227 of this chapter. Activities that are within the "farm" definition, when conducted on a farm mixed-type facility, are not subject to the requirements of subparts C and G of this part and therefore do not need to be specified in the exemption.

(2) For the purposes of paragraphs (g)(3) and (h)(3) of this section, the following terms describe the foods associated with the activity/food combinations. Several foods that are fruits or vegetables are separately considered for the purposes of these activity/food combinations (i.e., coffee beans, cocoa beans, fresh herbs, peanuts, sugarcane, sugar beets, tree nuts, seeds for direct consumption) to appropriately address specific hazards associated with these foods and/or processing activities conducted on these foods.

(i) <u>Dried/dehydrated fruit and vegetable products</u> includes only those processed food products such as raisins and dried legumes made without additional manufacturing/processing beyond drying/dehydrating, packaging, and/or labeling.

(ii) <u>Other fruit and vegetable products</u> includes those processed food products that have undergone one or more of the following processes: acidification, boiling, canning, coating with things other than wax/oil/resin, cooking, cutting, chopping, grinding, peeling, shredding, slicing, or trimming. Examples include flours made from legumes (such as chickpea flour), pickles, and snack chips made from potatoes or plantains. Examples also include dried fruit and vegetable products made with additional manufacturing/processing (such as dried apple slices; pitted, dried plums, cherries, and apricots; and sulfited raisins). This category does not include dried/dehydrated fruit and vegetable products made without additional manufacturing/processing as described in paragraph (g)(2)(i) of this section. This category also does not include products that require time/temperature control for safety (such as fresh-cut fruits and vegetables).

(iii) <u>Peanut and tree nut products</u> includes processed food products such as roasted peanuts and tree nuts, seasoned peanuts and tree nuts, and peanut and tree nut flours.

(iv) <u>Processed seeds for direct consumption</u> include processed food products such as roasted pumpkin seeds, roasted sunflower seeds, and roasted flax seeds.

(v) <u>Dried/dehydrated herb and spice products</u> includes only processed food products such as dried intact herbs made without additional manufacturing/processing beyond drying/dehydrating, packaging, and/or labeling.

(vi) <u>Other herb and spice products</u> includes those processed food products such as chopped fresh herbs, chopped or ground dried herbs (including tea), herbal extracts (e.g., essential oils, extracts containing more than 20 percent ethanol, extracts containing more than 35 percent glycerin), dried herb- or spice-infused honey, and dried herb- or spice-infused oils and/or vinegars. This category does not include dried/dehydrated herb and spice products made without additional manufacturing/processing beyond drying/dehydrating, packaging, and/or labeling as described in paragraph (g)(2)(v) of this section. This category also does not include products that require time/temperature control for safety, such as fresh herb-infused oils.

(vii) <u>Grains</u> include barley, dent- or flint-corn, sorghum, oats, rice, rye, wheat, amaranth, quinoa, buckwheat and oilseeds for oil extraction (such as cotton seed, flax seed, rapeseed, soybeans, and sunflower seed).

(viii) <u>Milled grain products</u> include processed food products such as flour, bran, and corn meal.

(ix) <u>Baked goods</u> include processed food products such as breads, brownies, cakes, cookies, and crackers. This category does not include products that require time/temperature control for safety, such as cream-filled pastries.

(x) <u>Other grain products</u> include processed food products such as dried cereal, dried pasta, oat flakes, and popcorn. This category does not include milled grain products as described in paragraph (g)(2)(viii) of this section or baked goods as described in paragraph (g)(2)(ix) of this section.

(3) Subparts C and G of this part do not apply to on-farm packing or holding of food by a small or very small business, and § 117.201 does not apply to on-farm packing or holding of food by a very small business, if the only packing and holding activities subject to section 418 of the Federal Food, Drug, and Cosmetic Act that the business conducts are the following low-risk packing or holding activity/food combinations--i.e., packing (or re-packing) (including weighing or conveying incidental to packing or re-packing); sorting, culling, or grading incidental to packing or storing; and storing (ambient, cold and controlled atmosphere) of:

(i) Baked goods (e.g., bread and cookies);

(ii) Candy (e.g., hard candy, fudge, maple candy, maple cream, nut brittles, taffy, and toffee);

(iii) Cocoa beans (roasted);

(iv) Cocoa products;

(v) Coffee beans (roasted);

(vi) Game meat jerky;

(vii) Gums, latexes, and resins that are processed foods;

(viii) Honey (pasteurized);

(ix) Jams, jellies, and preserves;

(x) Milled grain products (e.g., flour, bran, and corn meal);

(xi) Molasses and treacle;

(xii) Oils (e.g., olive oil and sunflower seed oil);

(xiii) Other fruit and vegetable products (e.g., flours made from legumes; pitted, dried fruits; sliced, dried apples; snack chips);

(xiv) Other grain products (e.g., dried pasta, oat flakes, and popcorn);

(xv) Other herb and spice products (e.g., chopped or ground dried herbs, herbal extracts);

(xvi) Peanut and tree nut products (e.g., roasted peanuts and tree nut flours);

(xvii) Processed seeds for direct consumption (e.g., roasted pumpkin seeds);

(xviii) Soft drinks and carbonated water;

(xix) Sugar;

(xx) Syrups (e.g., maple syrup and agave syrup);

(xxi) Trail mix and granola;

(xxii) Vinegar; and

(xxiii) Any other processed food that does not require time/temperature control for safety (e..g., vitamins, minerals, and dietary ingredients (e.g., bone meal) in powdered, granular, or other solid form).

(h)(1) The exemption in paragraph (h)(3) of this section applies to manufacturing/processing of foods on a farm mixed-type facility, except for manufacturing/processing that is within the "farm" definition in § 1.227 of this chapter. Drying/dehydrating raw agricultural commodities to create a distinct commodity (such as drying/dehydrating grapes to produce raisins, and drying/dehydrating fresh herbs to produce dried herbs), and packaging and labeling such commodities, without additional manufacturing/processing (such as chopping and slicing), are within the "farm" definition in § 1.227 of this chapter. In addition, treatment to manipulate ripening of raw agricultural commodities (such as by treating produce with ethylene gas), and packaging and labeling the treated raw agricultural commodities, without additional manufacturing/processing, is within the "farm" definition. In addition, coating intact fruits and vegetables with wax, oil, or resin used for the purpose of storage or transportation is within the "farm" definition. Activities that are within the "farm" definition, when conducted on a farm mixed-type facility, are not subject to the requirements of subparts C and G of this part and therefore do not need to be specified in the exemption.

(2) The terms in paragraph (g)(2) of this section describe certain foods associated with the activity/food combinations in paragraph (h)(3) of this section.

(3) Subparts C and G of this part do not apply to on-farm manufacturing/processing activities conducted by a small or very small business for distribution into commerce, and §117.201 does not apply to on-farm manufacturing/processing activities conducted by a very small business for distribution into commerce, if the only manufacturing/processing activities subject to section 418 of the Federal Food, Drug, and Cosmetic Act that the business conducts are the following low-risk manufacturing/processing activity/food combinations:

(i) Boiling gums, latexes, and resins;

(ii) Chopping, coring, cutting, peeling, pitting, shredding, and slicing acid fruits and vegetables that have a pH less than 4.2 (e.g., cutting lemons and limes), baked goods (e.g., slicing bread), dried/dehydrated fruit and vegetable products (e.g., pitting dried plums), dried herbs and other spices (e.g., chopping intact, dried basil), game meat jerky, gums/latexes/resins, other grain products (e.g., shredding dried cereal), peanuts and tree nuts, and peanut and tree nut products (e.g., chopping roasted peanuts);

(iii) Coating dried/dehydrated fruit and vegetable products (e.g., coating raisins with chocolate), other fruit and vegetable products except for non-dried, non-intact fruits and vegetables (e.g., coating dried plum pieces, dried pitted cherries, and dried pitted apricots with chocolate are low-risk activity/food combinations but coating apples on a stick with caramel is not a low-risk activity/food combination), other grain products (e.g., adding caramel to popcorn or adding seasonings to popcorn provided that the seasonings have been treated to significantly minimize pathogens, peanuts and tree nuts (e.g., adding seasonings provided that the seasonings have been treated to significantly minimize pathogens), and peanut and tree nut products (e.g., adding seasonings provided that the seasonings have been treated to significantly minimize pathogens);

(iv) Drying/dehydrating (that includes additional manufacturing or is performed on processed foods) other fruit and vegetable products with pH less than 4.2 (e.g., drying cut fruit and vegetables with pH less than 4.2), and other herb and spice products (e.g., drying chopped fresh herbs, including tea);

(v) Extracting (including by pressing, by distilling, and by solvent extraction) dried/dehydrated herb and spice products (e.g., dried mint), fresh herbs (e.g., fresh mint), fruits and vegetables (e.g., olives, avocados), grains (e.g., oilseeds), and other herb and spice products (e.g., chopped fresh mint, chopped dried mint);

(vi) Freezing acid fruits and vegetables with pH less than 4.2 and other fruit and vegetable products with pH less than 4.2 (e.g., cut fruits and vegetables);

(vii) Grinding/cracking/crushing/milling baked goods (e.g., crackers), cocoa beans (roasted), coffee beans (roasted), dried/dehydrated fruit and vegetable products (e.g., raisins and dried legumes), dried/dehydrated herb and spice products (e.g., intact dried basil), grains (e.g., oats, rice, rye, wheat), other fruit and vegetable products (e.g., dried, pitted dates), other grain products (e.g., dried cereal), other herb and spice products (e.g., chopped dried herbs), peanuts and tree nuts, and peanut and tree nut products (e.g., roasted peanuts);

(viii) Labeling baked goods that do not contain food allergens, candy that does not contain food allergens, cocoa beans (roasted), cocoa products that do not contain food allergens), coffee beans (roasted), game meat jerky, gums/latexes/resins that are processed foods, honey (pasteurized), jams/jellies/preserves, milled grain products that do not contain food allergens (e.g., corn meal) or that are single-ingredient foods (e.g., wheat flour, wheat bran), molasses and treacle, oils, other fruit and vegetable products that do not contain food allergens (e.g., snack chips made from potatoes or plantains), other grain products that do not contain food allergens (e.g., popcorn), other herb and spice products (e.g., chopped or ground dried herbs), peanut or tree nut products,(provided that they are single-ingredient, or are in forms in which the consumer can reasonably be expected to recognize the food allergen(s) without label declaration, or both (e.g., roasted or seasoned whole nuts, single-ingredient peanut or tree nut flours)), processed seeds for direct consumption, soft drinks and carbonated water, sugar, syrups, trail mix and granola (other than those containing milk chocolate and provided that peanuts and/or tree nuts are in forms in which the consumer can reasonably be expected to recognize the food allergen(s) without label declaration), vinegar, and any other processed food that does not require time/temperature control for safety and that does not contain food allergens (e.g., vitamins, minerals, and dietary ingredients (e.g., bone meal) in powdered, granular, or other solid form);

(ix) Making baked goods from milled grain products (e.g., breads and cookies);

(x) Making candy from peanuts and tree nuts (e.g., nut brittles), sugar/syrups (e.g., taffy, toffee), and saps (e.g., maple candy, maple cream);

(xi) Making cocoa products from roasted cocoa beans;

(xii) Making dried pasta from grains;

(xiii) Making jams, jellies, and preserves from acid fruits and vegetables with a pH of 4.6 or below;

(xiv) Making molasses and treacle from sugar beets and sugarcane;

(xv) Making oat flakes from grains;

(xvi) Making popcorn from grains;

(xvii) Making snack chips from fruits and vegetables (e.g., making plantain and potato chips);

(xviii) Making soft drinks and carbonated water from sugar, syrups, and water;

(xix) Making sugars and syrups from fruits and vegetables (e.g., dates), grains (e.g., rice, sorghum), other grain products (e.g., malted grains such as barley), saps (e.g., agave, birch, maple, palm), sugar beets, and sugarcane;

(xx) Making trail mix and granola from cocoa products (e.g., chocolate), dried/dehydrated fruit and vegetable products (e.g., raisins), other fruit and vegetable products (e.g., chopped dried fruits), other grain products (e.g., oat flakes), peanut and tree nut products, and processed seeds for direct consumption, provided that peanuts, tree nuts, and processed seeds are treated to significantly minimize pathogens;

(xxi) Making vinegar from fruits and vegetables, other fruit and vegetable products (e.g., fruit wines, apple cider), and other grain products (e.g., malt);

(xxii) Mixing baked goods (e.g., types of cookies), candy (e.g., varieties of taffy), cocoa beans (roasted), coffee beans (roasted), dried/dehydrated fruit and vegetable products (e.g., dried blueberries, dried currants, and raisins), dried/dehydrated herb and spice products (e.g., dried, intact basil and dried, intact oregano), honey (pasteurized), milled grain products (e.g., flour, bran, and corn meal), other fruit and vegetable products (e.g., dried, sliced apples and dried, sliced peaches), other grain products (e.g., different types of dried pasta), other herb and spice products (e.g., chopped or ground dried herbs, dried herb- or spice-infused honey, and dried herb- or spice-infused oils and/or vinegars), peanut and tree nut products, sugar, syrups, vinegar, and any other processed food that does not require time/temperature control for safety (e.g., vitamins, minerals, and dietary ingredients (e.g., bone meal) in powdered, granular, or other solid form);

(xxiii) Packaging baked goods (e.g., bread and cookies), candy, cocoa beans (roasted), cocoa products, coffee beans (roasted), game meat jerky, gums/latexes/resins that are processed foods, honey (pasteurized), jams/jellies/preserves, milled grain products (e.g., flour, bran, corn meal), molasses and treacle, oils, other fruit and vegetable products (e.g., pitted, dried fruits; sliced, dried apples; snack chips), other grain products (e.g., popcorn), other herb and spice products (e.g., chopped or ground dried herbs), peanut and tree nut products, processed seeds for direct consumption, soft drinks and carbonated water, sugar, syrups, trail mix and granola, vinegar, and any other processed food that does not require time/temperature control for safety (e.g., vitamins, minerals, and dietary ingredients (e.g., bone meal) in powdered, granular, or other solid form);

(xxiv) Pasteurizing honey;

(xxv) Roasting and toasting baked goods (e.g., toasting bread for croutons);

(xxvi) Salting other grain products (e.g., soy nuts), peanut and tree nut products, and processed seeds for direct consumption; and

(xxvii) Sifting milled grain products (e.g., flour, bran, corn meal), other fruit and vegetable products (e.g., chickpea flour), and peanut and tree nut products (e.g., peanut flour, almond flour).

(i)(1) Subparts C and G of this part do not apply with respect to alcoholic beverages at a facility that meets the following two conditions:

(i) Under the Federal Alcohol Administration Act (27 U.S.C. 201 et seq.) or chapter 51 of subtitle E of the Internal Revenue Code of 1986 (26 U.S.C. 5001 et seq.) the facility is required to obtain a permit from, register with, or obtain approval of a notice or application from the Secretary of the Treasury as a condition of doing business in the United States, or is a foreign facility of a type that would require such a permit, registration, or approval if it were a domestic facility; and

(ii) Under section 415 of the Federal Food, Drug, and Cosmetic Act the facility is required to register as a facility because it is engaged in manufacturing, processing, packing, or holding one or more alcoholic beverages.

(2) Subparts C and G of this part do not apply with respect to food that is not an alcoholic beverage at a facility described in paragraph (i)(1) of this section, provided such food:

(i) Is in prepackaged form that prevents any direct human contact with such food; and

(ii) Constitutes not more than 5 percent of the overall sales of the facility, as determined by the Secretary of the Treasury.

(j) Subparts C and G of this part do not apply to facilities that are solely engaged in the storage of raw agricultural commodities (other than fruits and vegetables) intended for further distribution or processing.

(k)(1) Except as provided by paragraph (k)(2) of this section, subpart B of this part does not apply to any of the following:

(i) "Farms" (as defined in § 1.227 of this chapter);

(ii) Fishing vessels that are not subject to the registration requirements of part 1, subpart H of this chapter in accordance with § 1.226(f) of this chapter;

(iii) Establishments solely engaged in the holding and/or transportation of one or more raw agricultural commodities;

(iv) Activities of "farm mixed-type facilities" (as defined in § 1.227 of this chapter) that fall within the definition of "farm"; or

(v) Establishments solely engaged in hulling, shelling, drying, packing, and/or holding nuts (without additional manufacturing/processing, such as roasting nuts).

(2) If a "farm" or "farm mixed-type facility" dries/dehydrates raw agricultural commodities that are produce as defined in part 112 of this chapter to create a distinct commodity, subpart B of this part applies to the packaging, packing, and holding of the dried commodities. Compliance with this requirement may be achieved by complying with subpart B of this part or with the applicable requirements for packing and holding in part 112 of this chapter.

§ 117.7 Applicability of subparts C, D, and G of this part to a facility solely engaged in the storage of unexposed packaged food.

(a) Applicability of subparts C and G. Subparts C and G of this part do not apply to a facility solely engaged in the storage of unexposed packaged food.

(b) Applicability of subpart D. A facility solely engaged in the storage of unexposed packaged food, including unexposed packaged food that requires time/temperature control to significantly minimize or prevent the growth of, or toxin production by, pathogens is subject to the modified requirements in § 117.206 for any unexposed packaged food that requires time/temperature control to significantly minimize or prevent the growth of, or toxin production by, pathogens.

§ 117.8 Applicability of subpart B of this part to the off-farm packing and holding of raw agricultural commodities.
Except as provided by §117.5(k)(1), subpart B of this part applies to the off- farm packaging, packing, and holding of raw agricultural commodities. Compliance with this requirement for raw agricultural commodities that are produce as defined in part 112 of this chapter may be achieved by complying with subpart B of this part or with the applicable requirements for packing and holding in part 112 of this chapter.

§ 117.9 Records required for this subpart.
(a) Records that document training required by § 117.4(b)(2) must be established and maintained.
(b) The records that must be established and maintained are subject to the requirements of subpart F of this part.

Subpart B – Current Good Manufacturing Practice
§ 117.10 Personnel.
The management of the establishment must take reasonable measures and precautions to ensure the following:
(a) <u>Disease control</u>. Any person who, by medical examination or supervisory observation, is shown to have, or appears to have, an illness, open lesion, including boils, sores, or infected wounds, or any other abnormal source of microbial contamination by which there is a reasonable possibility of food, food-contact surfaces, or food-packaging materials becoming contaminated, must be excluded from any operations which may be expected to result in such contamination until the condition is corrected, unless conditions such as open lesions, boils, and infected wounds are adequately covered (e.g., by an impermeable cover). Personnel must be instructed to report such health conditions to their supervisors.
(b) <u>Cleanliness</u>. All persons working in direct contact with food, food-contact surfaces, and food-packaging materials must conform to hygienic practices while on duty to the extent necessary to protect against allergen cross-contact and against contamination of food. The methods for maintaining cleanliness include:
    (1) Wearing outer garments suitable to the operation in a manner that protects against allergen cross-contact and against the contamination of food, food-contact surfaces, or food-packaging materials.
    (2) Maintaining adequate personal cleanliness.
    (3) Washing hands thoroughly (and sanitizing if necessary to protect against contamination with undesirable microorganisms) in an adequate hand-washing facility before starting work, after each absence from the work station, and at any other time when the hands may have become soiled or contaminated.
    (4) Removing all unsecured jewelry and other objects that might fall into food, equipment, or containers, and removing hand jewelry that cannot be adequately sanitized during periods in which food is manipulated by hand. If such hand jewelry cannot be removed, it may be covered by material which can be maintained in an intact, clean, and sanitary condition and which effectively protects against the contamination by these objects of the food, food-contact surfaces, or food-packaging materials.
    (5) Maintaining gloves, if they are used in food handling, in an intact, clean, and sanitary condition.
    (6) Wearing, where appropriate, in an effective manner, hair nets, headbands, caps, beard covers, or other effective hair restraints.
    (7) Storing clothing or other personal belongings in areas other than where food is exposed or where equipment or utensils are washed.
    (8) Confining the following to areas other than where food may be exposed or where equipment or utensils are washed: eating food, chewing gum, drinking beverages, or using tobacco.
    (9) Taking any other necessary precautions to protect against allergen cross-contact and against contamination of food, food-contact surfaces, or food-packaging materials with microorganisms or foreign substances (including perspiration, hair, cosmetics, tobacco, chemicals, and medicines applied to the skin).

§ 117.20 Plant and grounds.
(a) <u>Grounds</u>. The grounds about a food plant under the control of the operator must be kept in a condition that will protect against the contamination of food. The methods for adequate maintenance of grounds must include:
    (1) Properly storing equipment, removing litter and waste, and cutting weeds or grass within the immediate vicinity of the plant that may constitute an attractant, breeding place, or harborage for pests.
    (2) Maintaining roads, yards, and parking lots so that they do not constitute a source of contamination in areas where food is exposed.
    (3) Adequately draining areas that may contribute contamination to food by seepage, foot-borne filth, or providing a breeding place for pests.
    (4) Operating systems for waste treatment and disposal in an adequate manner so that they do not constitute a source of contamination in areas where food is exposed.
    (5) If the plant grounds are bordered by grounds not under the operator's control and not maintained in the manner described in paragraphs (a)(1) through (4) of this section, care must be exercised in the plant by inspection, extermination, or other means to exclude pests, dirt, and filth that may be a source of food contamination.
(b) <u>Plant construction and design</u>. The plant must be suitable in size, construction, and design to facilitate maintenance and sanitary operations for food-production purposes (i.e., manufacturing, processing, packing, and holding). The plant must:

(1) Provide adequate space for such placement of equipment and storage of materials as is necessary for maintenance, sanitary operations, and the production of safe food.

(2) Permit the taking of adequate precautions to reduce the potential for allergen cross-contact and for contamination of food, food-contact surfaces, or food-packaging materials with microorganisms, chemicals, filth, and other extraneous material. The potential for allergen cross-contact and for contamination may be reduced by adequate food safety controls and operating practices or effective design, including the separation of operations in which allergen cross-contact and contamination are likely to occur, by one or more of the following means: location, time, partition, air flow systems, dust control systems, enclosed systems, or other effective means.

(3) Permit the taking of adequate precautions to protect food in installed outdoor bulk vessels by any effective means, including:

    (i) Using protective coverings.

    (ii) Controlling areas over and around the vessels to eliminate harborages for pests.

    (iii) Checking on a regular basis for pests and pest infestation.

    (iv) Skimming fermentation vessels, as necessary.

(4) Be constructed in such a manner that floors, walls, and ceilings may be adequately cleaned and kept clean and kept in good repair; that drip or condensate from fixtures, ducts and pipes does not contaminate food, food-contact surfaces, or food-packaging materials; and that aisles or working spaces are provided between equipment and walls and are adequately unobstructed and of adequate width to permit employees to perform their duties and to protect against contaminating food, food-contact surfaces, or food-packaging materials with clothing or personal contact.

(5) Provide adequate lighting in hand-washing areas, dressing and locker rooms, and toilet rooms and in all areas where food is examined, manufactured, processed, packed, or held and where equipment or utensils are cleaned; and provide shatter-resistant light bulbs, fixtures, skylights, or other glass suspended over exposed food in any step of preparation or otherwise protect against food contamination in case of glass breakage.

(6) Provide adequate ventilation or control equipment to minimize dust, odors and vapors (including steam and noxious fumes) in areas where they may cause allergen cross-contact or contaminate food; and locate and operate fans and other air-blowing equipment in a manner that minimizes the potential for allergen cross-contact and for contaminating food, food-packaging materials, and food-contact surfaces.

(7) Provide, where necessary, adequate screening or other protection against pests.

§ 117.35 Sanitary operations.

(a) <u>General maintenance</u>. Buildings, fixtures, and other physical facilities of the plant must be maintained in a clean and sanitary condition and must be kept in repair adequate to prevent food from becoming adulterated. Cleaning and sanitizing of utensils and equipment must be conducted in a manner that protects against allergen cross-contact and against contamination of food, food-contact surfaces, or food-packaging materials.

(b) <u>Substances used in cleaning and sanitizing; storage of toxic materials</u>.

    (1) Cleaning compounds and sanitizing agents used in cleaning and sanitizing procedures must be free from undesirable microorganisms and must be safe and adequate under the conditions of use. Compliance with this requirement must be verified by any effective means, including purchase of these substances under a letter of guarantee or certification or examination of these substances for contamination. Only the following toxic materials may be used or stored in a plant where food is processed or exposed:

        (i) Those required to maintain clean and sanitary conditions;

        (ii) Those necessary for use in laboratory testing procedures;

        (iii) Those necessary for plant and equipment maintenance and operation; and

        (iv) Those necessary for use in the plant's operations.

    (2) Toxic cleaning compounds, sanitizing agents, and pesticide chemicals must be identified, held, and stored in a manner that protects against contamination of food, food-contact surfaces, or food-packaging materials.

(c) <u>Pest control</u>. Pests must not be allowed in any area of a food plant. Guard, guide, or pest-detecting dogs may be allowed in some areas of a plant if the presence of the dogs is unlikely to result in contamination of food, food-contact surfaces, or food-packaging materials. Effective measures must be taken to exclude pests from the manufacturing, processing, packing, and holding areas and to protect against the contamination of food on the premises by pests. The use of pesticides to control pests in the plant is permitted only under precautions and restrictions that will protect against the contamination of food, food-contact surfaces, and food-packaging materials.

(d) <u>Sanitation of food-contact surfaces</u>. All food-contact surfaces, including utensils and food-contact surfaces of equipment, must be cleaned as frequently as necessary to protect against allergen cross-contact and against contamination of food.

    (1) Food-contact surfaces used for manufacturing/processing, packing, or holding low-moisture food must be in a clean, dry, sanitary condition before use. When the surfaces are wet-cleaned, they must, when necessary, be sanitized and thoroughly dried before subsequent use.

    (2) In wet processing, when cleaning is necessary to protect against allergen cross-contact or the introduction of microorganisms into food, all food-contact surfaces must be cleaned and sanitized before use and after any

interruption during which the food-contact surfaces may have become contaminated. Where equipment and utensils are used in a continuous production operation, the utensils and food-contact surfaces of the equipment must be cleaned and sanitized as necessary.

(3) Single-service articles (such as utensils intended for one-time use, paper cups, and paper towels) must be stored, handled, and disposed of in a manner that protects against allergen cross-contact and against contamination of food, food-contact surfaces, or food-packaging materials.

(e) Sanitation of non-food-contact surfaces. Non-food-contact surfaces of equipment used in the operation of a food plant must be cleaned in a manner and as frequently as necessary to protect against allergen cross-contact and against contamination of food, food-contact surfaces, and food-packaging materials.

(f) Storage and handling of cleaned portable equipment and utensils. Cleaned and sanitized portable equipment with food-contact surfaces and utensils must be stored in a location and manner that protects food-contact surfaces from allergen cross-contact and from contamination.

§ 117.37 Sanitary facilities and controls.

Each plant must be equipped with adequate sanitary facilities and accommodations including:

(a) Water supply. The water supply must be adequate for the operations intended and must be derived from an adequate source. Any water that contacts food, food-contact surfaces, or food-packaging materials must be safe and of adequate sanitary quality. Running water at a suitable temperature, and under pressure as needed, must be provided in all areas where required for the processing of food, for the cleaning of equipment, utensils, and food-packaging materials, or for employee sanitary facilities.

(b) Plumbing. Plumbing must be of adequate size and design and adequately installed and maintained to:
(1) Carry adequate quantities of water to required locations throughout the plant.
(2) Properly convey sewage and liquid disposable waste from the plant.
(3) Avoid constituting a source of contamination to food, water supplies, equipment, or utensils or creating an unsanitary condition.
(4) Provide adequate floor drainage in all areas where floors are subject to flooding-type cleaning or where normal operations release or discharge water or other liquid waste on the floor.
(5) Provide that there is not backflow from, or cross-connection between, piping systems that discharge waste water or sewage and piping systems that carry water for food or food manufacturing.

(c) Sewage disposal. Sewage must be disposed of into an adequate sewerage system or disposed of through other adequate means.

(d) Toilet facilities. Each plant must provide employees with adequate, readily accessible toilet facilities. Toilet facilities must be kept clean and must not be a potential source of contamination of food, food-contact surfaces, or food-packaging materials.

(e) Hand-washing facilities. Each plant must provide hand-washing facilities designed to ensure that an employee's hands are not a source of contamination of food, food-contact surfaces, or food-packaging materials, by providing facilities that are adequate, convenient, and furnish running water at a suitable temperature.

(f) Rubbish and offal disposal. Rubbish and any offal must be so conveyed, stored, and disposed of as to minimize the development of odor, minimize the potential for the waste becoming an attractant and harborage or breeding place for pests, and protect against contamination of food, food-contact surfaces, food-packaging materials, water supplies, and ground surfaces.

§ 117.40 Equipment and utensils.

(a)(1) All plant equipment and utensils used in manufacturing, processing, packing, or holding food must be so designed and of such material and workmanship as to be adequately cleanable, and must be adequately maintained to protect against allergen cross-contact and contamination.
(2) Equipment and utensils must be designed, constructed, and used appropriately to avoid the adulteration of food with lubricants, fuel, metal fragments, contaminated water, or any other contaminants.
(3) Equipment must be installed so as to facilitate the cleaning and maintenance of the equipment and of adjacent spaces.
(4) Food-contact surfaces must be corrosion-resistant when in contact with food.
(5) Food-contact surfaces must be made of nontoxic materials and designed to withstand the environment of their intended use and the action of food, and, if applicable, cleaning compounds, sanitizing agents, and cleaning procedures.
(6) Food-contact surfaces must be maintained to protect food from allergen cross-contact and from being contaminated by any source, including unlawful indirect food additives.

(b) Seams on food-contact surfaces must be smoothly bonded or maintained so as to minimize accumulation of food particles, dirt, and organic matter and thus minimize the opportunity for growth of microorganisms and allergen cross-contact.

(c) Equipment that is in areas where food is manufactured, processed, packed, or held and that does not come into contact with food must be so constructed that it can be kept in a clean and sanitary condition.

A1-11

(d) Holding, conveying, and manufacturing systems, including gravimetric, pneumatic, closed, and automated systems, must be of a design and construction that enables them to be maintained in an appropriate clean and sanitary condition.
(e) Each freezer and cold storage compartment used to store and hold food capable of supporting growth of microorganisms must be fitted with an indicating thermometer, temperature-measuring device, or temperature-recording device so installed as to show the temperature accurately within the compartment.
(f) Instruments and controls used for measuring, regulating, or recording temperatures, pH, acidity, water activity, or other conditions that control or prevent the growth of undesirable microorganisms in food must be accurate and precise and adequately maintained, and adequate in number for their designated uses.
(g) Compressed air or other gases mechanically introduced into food or used to clean food-contact surfaces or equipment must be treated in such a way that food is not contaminated with unlawful indirect food additives.

§ 117.80 Processes and controls.
(a) _General_. (1) All operations in the manufacturing, processing, packing, and holding of food (including operations directed to receiving, inspecting, transporting, and segregating) must be conducted in accordance with adequate sanitation principles.
(2) Appropriate quality control operations must be employed to ensure that food is suitable for human consumption and that food-packaging materials are safe and suitable.
(3) Overall sanitation of the plant must be under the supervision of one or more competent individuals assigned responsibility for this function.
(4) Adequate precautions must be taken to ensure that production procedures do not contribute to allergen cross-contact and to contamination from any source.
(5) Chemical, microbial, or extraneous-material testing procedures must be used where necessary to identify sanitation failures or possible allergen cross-contact and food contamination.
(6) All food that has become contaminated to the extent that it is adulterated must be rejected, or if appropriate, treated or processed to eliminate the contamination.
(b) _Raw materials and other ingredients_.
(1) Raw materials and other ingredients must be inspected and segregated or otherwise handled as necessary to ascertain that they are clean and suitable for processing into food and must be stored under conditions that will protect against allergen cross-contact and against contamination and minimize deterioration. Raw materials must be washed or cleaned as necessary to remove soil or other contamination. Water used for washing, rinsing, or conveying food must be safe and of adequate sanitary quality. Water may be reused for washing, rinsing, or conveying food if it does not cause allergen cross-contact or increase the level of contamination of the food.
(2) Raw materials and other ingredients must either not contain levels of microorganisms that may render the food injurious to the health of humans, or they must be pasteurized or otherwise treated during manufacturing operations so that they no longer contain levels that would cause the product to be adulterated.
(3) Raw materials and other ingredients susceptible to contamination with aflatoxin or other natural toxins must comply with FDA regulations for poisonous or deleterious substances before these raw materials or other ingredients are incorporated into finished food.
(4) Raw materials, other ingredients, and rework susceptible to contamination with pests, undesirable microorganisms, or extraneous material must comply with applicable FDA regulations for natural or unavoidable defects if a manufacturer wishes to use the materials in manufacturing food.
(5) Raw materials, other ingredients, and rework must be held in bulk, or in containers designed and constructed so as to protect against allergen cross-contact and against contamination and must be held at such temperature and relative humidity and in such a manner as to prevent the food from becoming adulterated. Material scheduled for rework must be identified as such.
(6) Frozen raw materials and other ingredients must be kept frozen. If thawing is required prior to use, it must be done in a manner that prevents the raw materials and other ingredients from becoming adulterated.
(7) Liquid or dry raw materials and other ingredients received and stored in bulk form must be held in a manner that protects against allergen cross-contact and against contamination.
(8) Raw materials and other ingredients that are food allergens, and rework that contains food allergens, must be identified and held in a manner that prevents allergen cross-contact.
(c) _Manufacturing operations_.
(1) Equipment and utensils and food containers must be maintained in an adequate condition through appropriate cleaning and sanitizing, as necessary. Insofar as necessary, equipment must be taken apart for thorough cleaning.
(2) All food manufacturing, processing, packing, and holding must be conducted under such conditions and controls as are necessary to minimize the potential for the growth of microorganisms, allergen cross-contact, contamination of food, and deterioration of food.
(3) Food that can support the rapid growth of undesirable microorganisms must be held at temperatures that will prevent the food from becoming adulterated during manufacturing, processing, packing, and holding.

(4) Measures such as sterilizing, irradiating, pasteurizing, cooking, freezing, refrigerating, controlling pH, or controlling a_w that are taken to destroy or prevent the growth of undesirable microorganisms must be adequate under the conditions of manufacture, handling, and distribution to prevent food from being adulterated.

(5) Work-in-process and rework must be handled in a manner that protects against allergen cross-contact, contamination, and growth of undesirable microorganisms.

(6) Effective measures must be taken to protect finished food from allergen cross-contact and from contamination by raw materials, other ingredients, or refuse. When raw materials, other ingredients, or refuse are unprotected, they must not be handled simultaneously in a receiving, loading, or shipping area if that handling could result in allergen cross-contact or contaminated food. Food transported by conveyor must be protected against allergen cross-contact and against contamination as necessary.

(7) Equipment, containers, and utensils used to convey, hold, or store raw materials and other ingredients, work-in-process, rework, or other food must be constructed, handled, and maintained during manufacturing, processing, packing, and holding in a manner that protects against allergen cross-contact and against contamination.

(8) Adequate measures must be taken to protect against the inclusion of metal or other extraneous material in food.

(9) Food, raw materials, and other ingredients that are adulterated:

  (i) Must be disposed of in a manner that protects against the contamination of other food; or

  (ii) If the adulterated food is capable of being reconditioned, it must be:

   (A) Reconditioned (if appropriate) using a method that has been proven to be effective; or

   (B) Reconditioned (if appropriate) and reexamined and subsequently found not to be adulterated within the meaning of the Federal Food, Drug, and Cosmetic Act before being incorporated into other food.

(10) Steps such as washing, peeling, trimming, cutting, sorting and inspecting, mashing, dewatering, cooling, shredding, extruding, drying, whipping, defatting, and forming must be performed so as to protect food against allergen cross-contact and against contamination. Food must be protected from contaminants that may drip, drain, or be drawn into the food.

(11) Heat blanching, when required in the preparation of food capable of supporting microbial growth, must be effected by heating the food to the required temperature, holding it at this temperature for the required time, and then either rapidly cooling the food or passing it to subsequent manufacturing without delay. Growth and contamination by thermophilic microorganisms in blanchers must be minimized by the use of adequate operating temperatures and by periodic cleaning and sanitizing as necessary.

(12) Batters, breading, sauces, gravies, dressings, dipping solutions, and other similar preparations that are held and used repeatedly over time must be treated or maintained in such a manner that they are protected against allergen cross-contact and against contamination, and minimizing the potential for the growth of undesirable microorganisms.

(13) Filling, assembling, packaging, and other operations must be performed in such a way that the food is protected against allergen cross-contact, contamination and growth of undesirable microorganisms.

(14) Food, such as dry mixes, nuts, intermediate moisture food, and dehydrated food, that relies principally on the control of a_w for preventing the growth of undesirable microorganisms must be processed to and maintained at a safe moisture level.

(15) Food, such as acid and acidified food, that relies principally on the control of pH for preventing the growth of undesirable microorganisms must be monitored and maintained at a pH of 4.6 or below.

(16) When ice is used in contact with food, it must be made from water that is safe and of adequate sanitary quality in accordance with § 117.37(a), and must be used only if it has been manufactured in accordance with current good manufacturing practice as outlined in this part.

§ 117.93 Warehousing and distribution.

Storage and transportation of food must be under conditions that will protect against allergen cross-contact and against biological, chemical (including radiological), and physical contamination of food, as well as against deterioration of the food and the container.

§ 117.95 Holding and distribution of human food by-products for use as animal food.

(a) Human food by-products held for distribution as animal food without additional manufacturing or processing by the human food processor, as identified in § 507.12 of this chapter, must be held under conditions that will protect against contamination, including the following:

  (1) Containers and equipment used to convey or hold human food by-products for use as animal food before distribution must be designed, constructed of appropriate material, cleaned as necessary, and maintained to protect against the contamination of human food by-products for use as animal food;

  (2) Human food by-products for use as animal food held for distribution must be held in a way to protect against contamination from sources such as trash; and

  (3) During holding, human food by-products for use as animal food must be accurately identified.

(b) Labeling that identifies the by-product by the common or usual name must be affixed to or accompany human food by-products for use as animal food when distributed.

(c) Shipping containers (e.g., totes, drums, and tubs) and bulk vehicles used to distribute human food by-products for use as animal food must be examined prior to use to protect against contamination of the human food by-products for use as animal food from the container or vehicle when the facility is responsible for transporting the human food by-products for use as animal food itself or arranges with a third party to transport the human food by-products for use as animal food.

§ 117.110 Defect action levels.

(a) The manufacturer, processor, packer, and holder of food must at all times utilize quality control operations that reduce natural or unavoidable defects to the lowest level currently feasible.

(b) The mixing of a food containing defects at levels that render that food adulterated with another lot of food is not permitted and renders the final food adulterated, regardless of the defect level of the final food. For examples of defect action levels that may render food adulterated, see the Defect Levels Handbook, which is accessible at http://www.fda.gov/pchfrule and at http://www.fda.gov.

Subpart C– Hazard Analysis and Risk-Based Preventive Controls

§ 117.126 Food safety plan.

(a) Requirement for a food safety plan.

(1) You must prepare, or have prepared, and implement a written food safety plan.

(2) The food safety plan must be prepared, or its preparation overseen, by one or more preventive controls qualified individuals.

(b) Contents of a food safety plan. The written food safety plan must include:

(1) The written hazard analysis as required by § 117.130(a)(2);

(2) The written preventive controls as required by § 117.135(b);

(3) The written supply-chain program as required by subpart G of this part;

(4) The written recall plan as required by § 117.139(a); and

(5) The written procedures for monitoring the implementation of the preventive controls as required by § 117.145(a)(1);

(6) The written corrective action procedures as required by § 117.150(a)(1); and

(7) The written verification procedures as required by § 117.165(b).

(c) Records. The food safety plan required by this section is a record that is subject to the requirements of subpart F of this part.

§ 117.130 Hazard analysis.

(a) Requirement for a hazard analysis.

(1) You must conduct a hazard analysis to identify and evaluate, based on experience, illness data, scientific reports, and other information, known or reasonably foreseeable hazards for each type of food manufactured, processed, packed, or held at your facility to determine whether there are any hazards requiring a preventive control.

(2) The hazard analysis must be written regardless of its outcome.

(b) Hazard identification. The hazard identification must consider:

(1) Known or reasonably foreseeable hazards that include:

(i) Biological hazards, including microbiological hazards such as parasites, environmental pathogens, and other pathogens;

(ii) Chemical hazards, including radiological hazards, substances such as pesticide and drug residues, natural toxins, decomposition, unapproved food or color additives, and food allergens; and

(iii) Physical hazards (such as stones, glass, and metal fragments); and

(2) Known or reasonably foreseeable hazards that may be present in the food for any of the following reasons:

(i) The hazard occurs naturally;

(ii) The hazard may be unintentionally introduced; or

(iii) The hazard may be intentionally introduced for purposes of economic gain.

(c) Hazard evaluation.

(1)(i) The hazard analysis must include an evaluation of the hazards identified in paragraph (b) of this section to assess the severity of the illness or injury if the hazard were to occur and the probability that the hazard will occur in the absence of preventive controls.

(ii) The hazard evaluation required by paragraph (c)(1)(i) of this section must include an evaluation of environmental pathogens whenever a ready-to-eat food is exposed to the environment prior to packaging and the packaged food does not receive a treatment or otherwise include a control measure (such as a formulation lethal to the pathogen) that would significantly minimize the pathogen.

(2) The hazard evaluation must consider the effect of the following on the safety of the finished food for the intended consumer:

(i) The formulation of the food;

(ii) The condition, function, and design of the facility and equipment;

(iii) Raw materials and other ingredients;

(iv) Transportation practices;

(v) Manufacturing/processing procedures;

(vi) Packaging activities and labeling activities;

(vii) Storage and distribution;

(viii) Intended or reasonably foreseeable use;

(ix) Sanitation, including employee hygiene; and

(x) Any other relevant factors, such as the temporal (e.g., weather-related) nature of some hazards (e.g., levels of some natural toxins).

§ 117.135 Preventive controls.

(a)(1) You must identify and implement preventive controls to provide assurances that any hazards requiring a preventive control will be significantly minimized or prevented and the food manufactured, processed, packed, or held by your facility will not be adulterated under section 402 of the Federal Food, Drug, and Cosmetic Act or misbranded under section 403(w) of the Federal Food, Drug, and Cosmetic Act.

(2) Preventive controls required by paragraph (a)(1) of this section include:

(i) Controls at critical control points (CCPs), if there are any CCPs; and

(ii) Controls, other than those at CCPs, that are also appropriate for food safety.

(b) Preventive controls must be written.

(c) Preventive controls include, as appropriate to the facility and the food:

(1) Process controls. Process controls include procedures, practices, and processes to ensure the control of parameters during operations such as heat processing, acidifying, irradiating, and refrigerating foods. Process controls must include, as appropriate to the nature of the applicable control and its role in the facility's food safety system:

(i) Parameters associated with the control of the hazard; and

(ii) The maximum or minimum value, or combination of values, to which any biological, chemical, or physical parameter must be controlled to significantly minimize or prevent a hazard requiring a process control.

(2) Food allergen controls. Food allergen controls include procedures, practices, and processes to control food allergens. Food allergen controls must include those procedures, practices, and processes employed for:

(i) Ensuring protection of food from allergen cross-contact, including during storage, handling, and use; and

(ii) Labeling the finished food, including ensuring that the finished food is not misbranded under section 403(w) of the Federal Food, Drug, and Cosmetic Act.

(3) Sanitation controls. Sanitation controls include procedures, practices, and processes to ensure that the facility is maintained in a sanitary condition adequate to significantly minimize or prevent hazards such as environmental pathogens, biological hazards due to employee handling, and food allergen hazards. Sanitation controls must include, as appropriate to the facility and the food, procedures, practices, and processes for the:

(i) Cleanliness of food-contact surfaces, including food-contact surfaces of utensils and equipment;

(ii) Prevention of allergen cross-contact and cross-contamination from insanitary objects and from personnel to food, food packaging material, and other food-contact surfaces and from raw product to processed product.

(4) Supply-chain controls. Supply-chain controls include the supply-chain program as required by subpart G of this part.

(5) Recall plan. Recall plan as required by § 117.139.

(6) Other controls. Preventive controls include any other procedures, practices, and processes necessary to satisfy the requirements of paragraph (a) of this section. Examples of other controls include hygiene training and other current good manufacturing practices.

§ 117.136 Circumstances in which the owner, operator, or agent in charge of a manufacturing/processing facility is not required to implement a preventive control.

(a) <u>Circumstances</u>. If you are a manufacturer/processor, you are not required to implement a preventive control when you identify a hazard requiring a preventive control (identified hazard) and any of the following circumstances apply:

(1) You determine and document that the type of food (e.g., raw agricultural commodities such as cocoa beans, coffee beans, and grains) could not be consumed without application of an appropriate control.

(2) You rely on your customer who is subject to the requirements for hazard analysis and risk-based preventive controls in this subpart to ensure that the identified hazard will be significantly minimized or prevented and you:

(i) Disclose in documents accompanying the food, in accordance with the practice of the trade, that the food is "not processed to control [identified hazard]"; and

(ii) Annually obtain from your customer written assurance, subject to the requirements of § 117.137, that the customer has established and is following procedures (identified in the written assurance) that will significantly minimize or prevent the identified hazard.

A1-15

(3) You rely on your customer who is not subject to the requirements for hazard analysis and risk-based preventive controls in this subpart to provide assurance it is manufacturing, processing, or preparing the food in accordance with applicable food safety requirements and you:

(i) Disclose in documents accompanying the food, in accordance with the practice of the trade, that the food is "not processed to control [identified hazard]"; and

(ii) Annually obtain from your customer written assurance that it is manufacturing, processing, or preparing the food in accordance with applicable food safety requirements.

(4) You rely on your customer to provide assurance that the food will be processed to control the identified hazard by an entity in the distribution chain subsequent to the customer and you:

(i) Disclose in documents accompanying the food, in accordance with the practice of the trade, that the food is "not processed to control [identified hazard]"; and

(ii) Annually obtain from your customer written assurance, subject to the requirements of § 117.137, that your customer:

(A) Will disclose in documents accompanying the food, in accordance with the practice of the trade, that the food is "not processed to control [identified hazard]"; and

(B) Will only sell to another entity that agrees, in writing, it will:

(1) Follow procedures (identified in a written assurance) that will significantly minimize or prevent the identified hazard (if the entity is subject to the requirements for hazard analysis and risk-based preventive controls in this subpart) or manufacture, process, or prepare the food in accordance with applicable food safety requirements (if the entity is not subject to the requirements for hazard analysis and risk-based preventive controls in this subpart); or

(2) Obtain a similar written assurance from the entity's customer, subject to the requirements of § 117.137, as in paragraphs (a)(4)(ii)(A) and (B) of this section, as appropriate; or

(5) You have established, documented, and implemented a system that ensures control, at a subsequent distribution step, of the hazards in the food you distribute and you document the implementation of that system.

(b) Records. You must document any circumstance, specified in paragraph (a) of this section, that applies to you, including:

(1) A determination, in accordance with paragraph (a) of this section, that the type of food could not be consumed without application of an appropriate control;

(2) The annual written assurance from your customer in accordance with paragraph (a)(2) of this section;

(3) The annual written assurance from your customer in accordance with paragraph (a)(3) of this section;

(4) The annual written assurance from your customer in accordance with paragraph (a)(4) of this section; and

(5) Your system, in accordance with paragraph (a)(5) of this section, that ensures control, at a subsequent distribution step, of the hazards in the food you distribute.

§ 117.137 Provision of assurances required under § 117.136(a)(2), (3), and (4).
A facility that provides a written assurance under § 117.136(a)(2), (3), or (4) must act consistently with the assurance and document its actions taken to satisfy the written assurance.

§ 117.139 Recall plan.
For food with a hazard requiring a preventive control:

(a) You must establish a written recall plan for the food.

(b) The written recall plan must include procedures that describe the steps to be taken, and assign responsibility for taking those steps, to perform the following actions as appropriate to the facility:

(1) Directly notify the direct consignees of the food being recalled, including how to return or dispose of the affected food;

(2) Notify the public about any hazard presented by the food when appropriate to protect public health;

(3) Conduct effectiveness checks to verify that the recall is carried out; and

(4) Appropriately dispose of recalled food--e.g., through reprocessing, reworking, diverting to a use that does not present a safety concern, or destroying the food.

§ 117.140 Preventive control management components.
(a) Except as provided by paragraphs (b) and (c) of this section, the preventive controls required under § 117.135 are subject to the following preventive control management components as appropriate to ensure the effectiveness of the preventive controls, taking into account the nature of the preventive control and its role in the facility's food safety system:

(1) Monitoring in accordance with § 117.145;

(2) Corrective actions and corrections in accordance with § 117.150; and

(3) Verification in accordance with § 117.155.

(b) The supply-chain program established in subpart G of this part is subject to the following preventive control management components as appropriate to ensure the effectiveness of the supply-chain program, taking into account the nature of the hazard controlled before receipt of the raw material or other ingredient:

(1) Corrective actions and corrections in accordance with § 117.150, taking into account the nature of any supplier non-conformance;

(2) Review of records in accordance with § 117.165(a)(4); and

(3) Reanalysis in accordance with § 117.170.

(c) The recall plan established in § 117.139 is not subject to the requirements of paragraph (a) of this section.

§ 117.145 Monitoring.

As appropriate to the nature of the preventive control and its role in the facility's food safety system:

(a) <u>Written procedures</u>. You must establish and implement written procedures, including the frequency with which they are to be performed, for monitoring the preventive control; and

(b) <u>Monitoring</u>. You must monitor the preventive controls with adequate frequency to provide assurance that they are consistently performed.

(c) <u>Records</u>.

(1) <u>Requirement to document monitoring</u>. You must document the monitoring of preventive controls in accordance with this section in records that are subject to verification in accordance with § 117.155(a)(2) and records review in accordance with § 117.165(a)(4)(i).

(2) <u>Exception records</u>.

(i) Records of refrigeration temperature during storage of food that requires time/temperature control to significantly minimize or prevent the growth of, or toxin production by, pathogens may be affirmative records demonstrating temperature is controlled or exception records demonstrating loss of temperature control.

(ii) Exception records may be adequate in circumstances other than monitoring of refrigeration temperature.

§ 117.150 Corrective actions and corrections.

(a) <u>Corrective action procedures</u>. As appropriate to the nature of the hazard and the nature of the preventive control, except as provided by paragraph (c) of this section:

(1) You must establish and implement written corrective action procedures that must be taken if preventive controls are not properly implemented, including procedures to address, as appropriate:

(i) The presence of a pathogen or appropriate indicator organism in a ready-to-eat product detected as a result of product testing conducted in accordance with § 117.165(a)(2); and

(ii) The presence of an environmental pathogen or appropriate indicator organism detected through the environmental monitoring conducted in accordance with § 117.165(a)(3).

(2) The corrective action procedures must describe the steps to be taken to ensure that:

(i) Appropriate action is taken to identify and correct a problem that has occurred with implementation of a preventive control;

(ii) Appropriate action is taken, when necessary, to reduce the likelihood that the problem will recur;

(iii) All affected food is evaluated for safety; and

(iv) All affected food is prevented from entering into commerce, if you cannot ensure that the affected food is not adulterated under section 402 of the Federal Food, Drug, and Cosmetic Act or misbranded under section 403(w) of the Federal Food, Drug, and Cosmetic Act.

(b) <u>Corrective action in the event of an unanticipated food safety problem</u>.

(1) Except as provided by paragraph (c) of this section, you are subject to the requirements of paragraphs (b)(2) of this section if any of the following circumstances apply:

(i) A preventive control is not properly implemented and a corrective action procedure has not been established;

(ii) A preventive control, combination of preventive controls, or the food safety plan as a whole is found to be ineffective; or

(iii) A review of records in accordance with § 117.165(a)(4) finds that the records are not complete, the activities conducted did not occur in accordance with the food safety plan, or appropriate decisions were not made about corrective actions.

(2) If any of the circumstances listed in paragraph (b)(1) of this section apply, you must:

(i) Take corrective action to identify and correct the problem, reduce the likelihood that the problem will recur, evaluate all affected food for safety, and, as necessary, prevent affected food from entering commerce as would be done following a corrective action procedure under paragraphs (a)(2)(i) through (iv) of this section; and

(ii) When appropriate, reanalyze the food safety plan in accordance with § 117.170 to determine whether modification of the food safety plan is required.

(c) <u>Corrections</u>. You do not need to comply with the requirements of paragraphs (a) and (b) of this section if:

(1) You take action, in a timely manner, to identify and correct conditions and practices that are not consistent with the food allergen controls in § 117.135(c)(2)(i) or the sanitation controls in § 117.135(c)(3)(i) or (ii); or

A1-17

(2) You take action, in a timely manner, to identify and correct a minor and isolated problem that does not directly impact product safety.

(d) <u>Records</u>. All corrective actions (and, when appropriate, corrections) taken in accordance with this section must be documented in records. These records are subject to verification in accordance with §117.155(a)(3) and records review in accordance with §117.165(a)(4)(i).

§ 117.155 Verification.

(a) <u>Verification activities</u>. Verification activities must include, as appropriate to the nature of the preventive control and its role in the facility's food safety system:

(1) Validation in accordance with § 117.160.

(2) Verification that monitoring is being conducted as required by § 117.140 (and in accordance with § 117.145).

(3) Verification that appropriate decisions about corrective actions are being made as required by § 117.140 (and in accordance with § 117.150).

(4) Verification of implementation and effectiveness in accordance with § 117.165; and

(5) Reanalysis in accordance with § 117.170.

(b) <u>Documentation</u>. All verification activities conducted in accordance with this section must be documented in records.

§ 117.160 Validation.

(a) You must validate that the preventive controls identified and implemented in accordance with § 117.135 are adequate to control the hazard as appropriate to the nature of the preventive control and its role in the facility's food safety system.

(b) The validation of the preventive controls:

(1) Must be performed (or overseen) by a preventive controls qualified individual:

(i)(A) Prior to implementation of the food safety plan; or

(B) When necessary to demonstrate the control measures can be implemented as designed:

(<u>1</u>) Within 90 calendar days after production of the applicable food first begins; or

(<u>2</u>) Within a reasonable timeframe, provided that the preventive controls qualified individual prepares (or oversees the preparation of) a written justification for a timeframe that exceeds 90 calendar days after production of the applicable food first begins;

(ii) Whenever a change to a control measure or combination of control measures could impact whether the control measure or combination of control measures, when properly implemented, will effectively control the hazards; and

(iii) Whenever a reanalysis of the food safety plan reveals the need to do so;

(2) Must include obtaining and evaluating scientific and technical evidence (or, when such evidence is not available or is inadequate, conducting studies) to determine whether the preventive controls, when properly implemented, will effectively control the hazards; and

(c) You do not need to validate:

(1) The food allergen controls in § 117.135(c)(2);

(2) The sanitation controls in § 117.135(c)(3);

(3) The recall plan in § 117.139;

(4) The supply-chain program in subpart G of this part; and

(5) Other preventive controls, if the preventive controls qualified individual prepares (or oversees the preparation of) a written justification that validation is not applicable based on factors such as the nature of the hazard, and the nature of the preventive control and its role in the facility's food safety system.

§ 117.165 Verification of implementation and effectiveness.

(a) <u>Verification activities</u>. You must verify that the preventive controls are consistently implemented and are effectively and significantly minimizing or preventing the hazards. To do so you must conduct activities that include the following, as appropriate to the facility, the food, and the nature of the preventive control and its role in the facility's food safety system:

(1) Calibration of process monitoring instruments and verification instruments (or checking them for accuracy);

(2) Product testing, for a pathogen (or appropriate indicator organism) or other hazard;

(3) Environmental monitoring, for an environmental pathogen or for an appropriate indicator organism, if contamination of a ready-to-eat food with an environmental pathogen is a hazard requiring a preventive control, by collecting and testing environmental samples; and

(4) Review of the following records within the specified timeframes, by (or under the oversight of) a preventive controls qualified individual, to ensure that the records are complete, the activities reflected in the records occurred in accordance with the food safety plan, the preventive controls are effective, and appropriate decisions were made about corrective actions:

(i) Records of monitoring and corrective action records within 7 working days after the records are created or within a reasonable timeframe, provided that the preventive controls qualified individual prepares (or oversees the preparation of) a written justification for a timeframe that exceeds 7 working days; and

(ii) Records of calibration, testing (e.g., product testing, environmental monitoring), supplier and supply-chain verification activities, and other verification activities within a reasonable time after the records are created; and

(5) Other activities appropriate for verification of implementation and effectiveness.

(b) <u>Written procedures</u>. As appropriate to the facility, the food, the nature of the preventive control, and the role of the preventive control in the facility's food safety system, you must establish and implement written procedures for the following activities:

(1) The method and frequency of calibrating process monitoring instruments and verification instruments (or checking them for accuracy) as required by paragraph (a)(1) of this section.

(2) Product testing as required by paragraph (a)(2) of this section. Procedures for product testing must:

(i) Be scientifically valid;

(ii) Identify the test microorganism(s) or other analyte(s);

(iii) Specify the procedures for identifying samples, including their relationship to specific lots of product;

(iv) Include the procedures for sampling, including the number of samples and the sampling frequency;

(v) Identify the test(s) conducted, including the analytical method(s) used;

(vi) Identify the laboratory conducting the testing; and

(vii) Include the corrective action procedures required by § 117.150(a)(1).

(3) Environmental monitoring as required by paragraph (a)(3) of this section. Procedures for environmental monitoring must:

(i) Be scientifically valid;

(ii) Identify the test microorganism(s);

(iii) Identify the locations from which samples will be collected and the number of sites to be tested during routine environmental monitoring. The number and location of sampling sites must be adequate to determine whether preventive controls are effective;

(iv) Identify the timing and frequency for collecting and testing samples. The timing and frequency for collecting and testing samples must be adequate to determine whether preventive controls are effective;

(v) Identify the test(s) conducted, including the analytical method(s) used;

(vi) Identify the laboratory conducting the testing; and

(vii) Include the corrective action procedures required by § 117.150(a)(1).

§ 117.170 Reanalysis.

(a) You must conduct a reanalysis of the food safety plan as a whole at least once every 3 years;

(b) You must conduct a reanalysis of the food safety plan as a whole, or the applicable portion of the food safety plan:

(1) Whenever a significant change in the activities conducted at your facility creates a reasonable potential for a new hazard or creates a significant increase in a previously identified hazard;

(2) Whenever you become aware of new information about potential hazards associated with the food;

(3) Whenever appropriate after an unanticipated food safety problem in accordance with § 117.150(b); and

(4) Whenever you find that a preventive control, combination of preventive controls, or the food safety plan as a whole is ineffective.

(c) You must complete the reanalysis required by paragraphs (a) and (b) of this section and validate, as appropriate to the nature of the preventive control and its role in the facility's food safety system, any additional preventive controls needed to address the hazard identified:

(1) Before any change in activities (including any change in preventive control) at the facility is operative; or

(2) When necessary to demonstrate the control measures can be implemented as designed:

(i) Within 90 calendar days after production of the applicable food first begins; or

(ii) Within a reasonable timeframe, provided that the preventive controls qualified individual prepares (or oversees the preparation of) a written justification for a timeframe that exceeds 90-calendar days after production of the applicable food first begins.

(d) You must revise the written food safety plan if a significant change in the activities conducted at your facility creates a reasonable potential for a new hazard or a significant increase in a previously identified hazard or document the basis for the conclusion that no revisions are needed.

(e) A preventive controls qualified individual must perform (or oversee) the reanalysis.

(f) You must conduct a reanalysis of the food safety plan when FDA determines it is necessary to respond to new hazards and developments in scientific understanding.

§ 117.180 Requirements applicable to a preventive controls qualified individual and a qualified auditor.

(a) One or more preventive controls qualified individuals must do or oversee the following:

(1) Preparation of the food safety plan (§ 117.126(a)(2));

(2) Validation of the preventive controls (§ 117.160(b)(1));

(3) Written justification for validation to be performed in a timeframe that exceeds the first 90 calendar days of production of the applicable food;

(4) Determination that validation is not required (§ 117.160(c)(5));

(5) Review of records (§ 117.165(a)(4));

(6) Written justification for review of records of monitoring and corrective actions within a timeframe that exceeds 7 working days;

(7) Reanalysis of the food safety plan (§ 117.170(d)); and

(8) Determination that reanalysis can be completed, and additional preventive controls validated, as appropriate to the nature of the preventive control and its role in the facility's food safety system, in a timeframe that exceeds the first 90 calendar days of production of the applicable food.

(b) A qualified auditor must conduct an onsite audit (§ 117.435(a)).

(c)(1) To be a preventive controls qualified individual, the individual must have successfully completed training in the development and application of risk-based preventive controls at least equivalent to that received under a standardized curriculum recognized as adequate by FDA or be otherwise qualified through job experience to develop and apply a food safety system. Job experience may qualify an individual to perform these functions if such experience has provided an individual with knowledge at least equivalent to that provided through the standardized curriculum. This individual may be, but is not required to be, an employee of the facility.

(2) To be a qualified auditor, a qualified individual must have technical expertise obtained through education, training, or experience (or a combination thereof) necessary to perform the auditing function.

(d) All applicable training in the development and application of risk-based preventive controls must be documented in records, including the date of the training, the type of training, and the person(s) trained.

§ 117.190 Implementation records required for this subpart.

(a) You must establish and maintain the following records documenting implementation of the food safety plan:

(1) Documentation, as required by § 117.136(b), of the basis for not establishing a preventive control in accordance with § 117.136(a);

(2) Records that document the monitoring of preventive controls;

(3) Records that document corrective actions;

(4) Records that document verification, including, as applicable, those related to:

(i) Validation;

(ii) Verification of monitoring;

(iii) Verification of corrective actions;

(iv) Calibration of process monitoring and verification instruments;

(v) Product testing;

(vi) Environmental monitoring;

(vii) Records review; and

(viii) Reanalysis;

(5) Records that document the supply-chain program; and

(6) Records that document applicable training for the preventive controls qualified individual and the qualified auditor.

(b) The records that you must establish and maintain are subject to the requirements of subpart F of this part.

Subpart D – Modified Requirements

§ 117.201 Modified requirements that apply to a qualified facility.

(a) <u>Attestations to be submitted</u>. A qualified facility must submit the following attestations to FDA:

(1) An attestation that the facility is a qualified facility as defined in § 117.3. For the purpose of determining whether a facility satisfies the definition of qualified facility, the baseline year for calculating the adjustment for inflation is 2011; and

(2)(i) An attestation that you have identified the potential hazards associated with the food being produced, are implementing preventive controls to address the hazards, and are monitoring the performance of the preventive controls to ensure that such controls are effective; or

(ii) An attestation that the facility is in compliance with State, local, county, tribal, or other applicable non-Federal food safety law, including relevant laws and regulations of foreign countries, including an attestation based on licenses, inspection reports, certificates, permits, credentials, certification by an appropriate agency (such as a State department of agriculture), or other evidence of oversight.

(b) <u>Procedure for submission</u>. The attestations required by paragraph (a) of this section must be submitted to FDA by one of the following means:

(1) <u>Electronic submission</u>. To submit electronically, go to http://www.fda.gov/furls and follow the instructions. This Web site is available from wherever the Internet is accessible, including libraries, copy centers, schools, and Internet cafes. FDA encourages electronic submission.

(2) <u>Submission by mail</u>.

(i) You must use Form FDA 3942a. You may obtain a copy of this form by any of the following mechanisms:

(A) Download it from http://www.fda.gov/pchfrule;

(B) Write to the U.S. Food and Drug Administration (HFS-681), 5100 Paint Branch Parkway, College Park, MD 20740; or

(C) Request a copy of this form by phone at 1-800-216-7331 or 301-575-0156.

(ii) Send a paper Form FDA 3942a to the U.S. Food and Drug Administration (HFS-681), 5100 Paint Branch Parkway, College Park, MD 20740. We recommend that you submit a paper copy only if your facility does not have reasonable access to the Internet.

(c) Frequency of determination of status and submission.

(1) A facility must determine and document its status as a qualified facility on an annual basis no later than July 1 of each calendar year.

(2) The attestations required by paragraph (a) of this section must be:

(i) Submitted to FDA initially:

(A) By December 17, 2018, for a facility that begins manufacturing, processing, packing, or holding food before September 17, 2018;

(B) Before beginning operations, for a facility that begins manufacturing, processing, packing, or holding food after September 17, 2018; or

(C) By July 31 of the applicable calendar year, when the status of a facility changes from "not a qualified facility" to "qualified facility" based on the annual determination required by paragraph (c)(1) of this section; and

(ii) Beginning in 2020, submitted to FDA every 2 years during the period beginning on October 1 and ending on December 31.

(3) When the status of a facility changes from "qualified facility" to "not a qualified facility" based on the annual determination required by paragraph (c)(1) of this section, the facility must notify FDA of that change in status using Form 3942a by July 31 of the applicable calendar year.

(d) Timeframe for compliance with subparts C and G of this part when the facility status changes to "not a qualified facility." When the status of a facility changes from "qualified facility" to "not a qualified facility," the facility must comply with subparts C and G of this part no later than December 31 of the applicable calendar year unless otherwise agreed to by FDA and the facility.

(e) Notification to consumers. A qualified facility that does not submit attestations under paragraph (a)(2)(i) of this section must provide notification to consumers as to the name and complete business address of the facility where the food was manufactured or processed (including the street address or P.O. box, city, state, and zip code for domestic facilities, and comparable full address information for foreign facilities), as follows:

(1) If a food packaging label is required, the notification required by paragraph (e) of this section must appear prominently and conspicuously on the label of the food.

(2) If a food packaging label is not required, the notification required by paragraph (e) of this section must appear prominently and conspicuously, at the point of purchase, on a label, poster, sign, placard, or documents delivered contemporaneously with the food in the normal course of business, or in an electronic notice, in the case of Internet sales.

(f) Records.

(1) A qualified facility must maintain those records relied upon to support the attestations that are required by paragraph (a) of this section.

(2) The records that a qualified facility must maintain are subject to the requirements of subpart F of this part.

§ 117.206 Modified requirements that apply to a facility solely engaged in the storage of unexposed packaged food.

(a) If a facility that is solely engaged in the storage of unexposed packaged food stores any such refrigerated packaged food that requires time/temperature control to significantly minimize or prevent the growth of, or toxin production by, pathogens, the facility must conduct the following activities as appropriate to ensure the effectiveness of the temperature controls:

(1) Establish and implement temperature controls adequate to significantly minimize or prevent the growth of, or toxin production by, pathogens;

(2) Monitor the temperature controls with adequate frequency to provide assurance that the temperature controls are consistently performed;

(3) If there is a loss of temperature control that may impact the safety of such refrigerated packaged food, take appropriate corrective actions to:

(i) Correct the problem and reduce the likelihood that the problem will recur;

(ii) Evaluate all affected food for safety; and

(iii) Prevent the food from entering commerce, if you cannot ensure the affected food is not adulterated under section 402 of the Federal Food, Drug, and Cosmetic Act;

(4) Verify that temperature controls are consistently implemented by:

(i) Calibrating temperature monitoring and recording devices (or checking them for accuracy);

A1-21

(ii) Reviewing records of calibration within a reasonable time after the records are created; and
(iii) Reviewing records of monitoring and corrective actions taken to correct a problem with the control of temperature within 7 working days after the records are created or within a reasonable timeframe, provided that the preventive controls qualified individual prepares (or oversees the preparation of) a written justification for a timeframe that exceeds 7 working days;
(5) Establish and maintain the following records:
(i) Records (whether affirmative records demonstrating temperature is controlled or exception records demonstrating loss of temperature control) documenting the monitoring of temperature controls for any such refrigerated packaged food;
(ii) Records of corrective actions taken when there is a loss of temperature control that may impact the safety of any such refrigerated packaged food; and
(iii) Records documenting verification activities.
(b) The records that a facility must establish and maintain under paragraph (a)(5) of this section are subject to the requirements of subpart F of this part.

Subpart E – Withdrawal of a Qualified Facility Exemption
§ 117.251 Circumstances that may lead FDA to withdraw a qualified facility exemption.
(a) FDA may withdraw a qualified facility exemption under § 117.5(a):
(1) In the event of an active investigation of a foodborne illness outbreak that is directly linked to the qualified facility; or
(2) If FDA determines that it is necessary to protect the public health and prevent or mitigate a foodborne illness outbreak based on conditions or conduct associated with the qualified facility that are material to the safety of the food manufactured, processed, packed, or held at such facility.
(b) Before FDA issues an order to withdraw a qualified facility exemption, FDA:
(1) May consider one or more other actions to protect the public health or mitigate a foodborne illness outbreak, including a warning letter, recall, administrative detention, suspension of registration, refusal of food offered for import, seizure, and injunction;
(2) Must notify the owner, operator, or agent in charge of the facility, in writing, of circumstances that may lead FDA to withdraw the exemption, and provide an opportunity for the owner, operator, or agent in charge of the facility to respond in writing, within 15 calendar days of the date of receipt of the notification, to FDA's notification; and
(3) Must consider the actions taken by the facility to address the circumstances that may lead FDA to withdraw the exemption.

§ 117.254 Issuance of an order to withdraw a qualified facility exemption.
(a) An FDA District Director in whose district the qualified facility is located (or, in the case of a foreign facility, the Director of the Office of Compliance in the Center for Food Safety and Applied Nutrition), or an FDA official senior to either such Director, must approve an order to withdraw the exemption before the order is issued.
(b) Any officer or qualified employee of FDA may issue an order to withdraw the exemption after it has been approved in accordance with paragraph (a) of this section.
(c) FDA must issue an order to withdraw the exemption to the owner, operator, or agent in charge of the facility.
(d) FDA must issue an order to withdraw the exemption in writing, signed and dated by the officer or qualified employee of FDA who is issuing the order.

§ 117.257 Contents of an order to withdraw a qualified facility exemption.
An order to withdraw a qualified facility exemption under § 117.5(a) must include the following information:
(a) The date of the order;
(b) The name, address, and location of the qualified facility;
(c) A brief, general statement of the reasons for the order, including information relevant to one or both of the following circumstances that leads FDA to issue the order:
(1) An active investigation of a foodborne illness outbreak that is directly linked to the facility; or
(2) Conditions or conduct associated with a qualified facility that are material to the safety of the food manufactured, processed, packed, or held at such facility.
(d) A statement that the facility must either:
(1) Comply with subparts C and G of this part on the date that is 120 calendar days after the date of receipt of the order, or within a reasonable timeframe, agreed to by FDA, based on a written justification, submitted to FDA, for a timeframe that exceeds 120 calendar days from the date of receipt of the order; or
(2) Appeal the order within 15 calendar days of the date of receipt of the order in accordance with the requirements of § 117.264.
(e) A statement that a facility may request that FDA reinstate an exemption that was withdrawn by following the procedures in § 117.287;
(f) The text of section 418(l) of the Federal Food, Drug, and Cosmetic Act and of this subpart;

(g) A statement that any informal hearing on an appeal of the order must be conducted as a regulatory hearing under part 16 of this chapter, with certain exceptions described in § 117.270;

(h) The mailing address, telephone number, email address, and facsimile number of the FDA district office and the name of the FDA District Director in whose district the facility is located (or, in the case of a foreign facility, the same information for the Director of the Office of Compliance in the Center for Food Safety and Applied Nutrition); and

(i) The name and the title of the FDA representative who approved the order.

§ 117.260 Compliance with, or appeal of, an order to withdraw a qualified facility exemption.

(a) If you receive an order under § 117.254 to withdraw a qualified facility exemption, you must either:

(1) Comply with applicable requirements of this part within 120 calendar days of the date of receipt of the order, or within a reasonable timeframe, agreed to by FDA, based on a written justification, submitted to FDA, for a timeframe that exceeds 120 calendar days from the date of receipt of the order; or

(2) Appeal the order within 15 calendar days of the date of receipt of the order in accordance with the requirements of § 117.264.

(b) Submission of an appeal, including submission of a request for an informal hearing, will not operate to delay or stay any administrative action, including enforcement action by FDA, unless the Commissioner of Food and Drugs, as a matter of discretion, determines that delay or a stay is in the public interest.

(c) If you appeal the order, and FDA confirms the order:

(1) You must comply with applicable requirements of this part within 120 calendar days of the date of receipt of the order, or within a reasonable timeframe, agreed to by FDA, based on a written justification, submitted to FDA, for a timeframe that exceeds 120 calendar days from the date of receipt of the order; and

(2) You are no longer subject to the modified requirements in § 117.201.

§ 117.264 Procedure for submitting an appeal.

(a) To appeal an order to withdraw a qualified facility exemption, you must:

(1) Submit the appeal in writing to the FDA District Director in whose district the facility is located (or, in the case of a foreign facility, the Director of the Office of Compliance in the Center for Food Safety and Applied Nutrition), at the mailing address, email address, or facsimile number identified in the order within 15 calendar days of the date of receipt of confirmation of the order; and

(2) Respond with particularity to the facts and issues contained in the order, including any supporting documentation upon which you rely.

(b) In a written appeal of the order withdrawing an exemption provided under § 117.5(a), you may include a written request for an informal hearing as provided in § 117.267.

§ 117.267 Procedure for requesting an informal hearing.

(a) If you appeal the order, you:

(1) May request an informal hearing; and

(2) Must submit any request for an informal hearing together with your written appeal submitted in accordance with § 117.264 within 15 calendar days of the date of receipt of the order.

(b) A request for an informal hearing may be denied, in whole or in part, if the presiding officer determines that no genuine and substantial issue of material fact has been raised by the material submitted. If the presiding officer determines that a hearing is not justified, written notice of the determination will be given to you explaining the reason for the denial.

§ 117.270 Requirements applicable to an informal hearing.

If you request an informal hearing, and FDA grants the request:

(a) The hearing will be held within 15 calendar days after the date the appeal is filed or, if applicable, within a timeframe agreed upon in writing by you and FDA.

(b) The presiding officer may require that a hearing conducted under this subpart be completed within 1-calendar day, as appropriate.

(c) FDA must conduct the hearing in accordance with part 16 of this chapter, except that:

(1) The order withdrawing an exemption under §§ 117.254 and 117.257, rather than the notice under § 16.22(a) of this chapter, provides notice of opportunity for a hearing under this section and is part of the administrative record of the regulatory hearing under § 16.80(a) of this chapter.

(2) A request for a hearing under this subpart must be addressed to the FDA District Director (or, in the case of a foreign facility, the Director of the Office of Compliance in the Center for Food Safety and Applied Nutrition) as provided in the order withdrawing an exemption.

(3) Section 117.274, rather than § 16.42(a) of this chapter, describes the FDA employees who preside at hearings under this subpart.

(4) Section 16.60(e) and (f) of this chapter does not apply to a hearing under this subpart. The presiding officer must prepare a written report of the hearing. All written material presented at the hearing will be attached to the report. The presiding officer must include as part of the report of the hearing a finding on the credibility of witnesses (other

than expert witnesses) whenever credibility is a material issue, and must include a proposed decision, with a statement of reasons. The hearing participant may review and comment on the presiding officer's report within 2-calendar days of issuance of the report. The presiding officer will then issue the final decision.

(5) Section 16.80(a)(4) of this chapter does not apply to a regulatory hearing under this subpart. The presiding officer's report of the hearing and any comments on the report by the hearing participant under § 117.270(c)(4) are part of the administrative record.

(6) No party shall have the right, under § 16.119 of this chapter to petition the Commissioner of Food and Drugs for reconsideration or a stay of the presiding officer's final decision.

(7) If FDA grants a request for an informal hearing on an appeal of an order withdrawing an exemption, the hearing must be conducted as a regulatory hearing under a regulation in accordance with part 16 of this chapter, except that § 16.95(b) of this chapter does not apply to a hearing under this subpart. With respect to a regulatory hearing under this subpart, the administrative record of the hearing specified in §§ 16.80(a)(1) through (3) and (a)(5) of this chapter and 117.270(c)(5) constitutes the exclusive record for the presiding officer's final decision. For purposes of judicial review under § 10.45 of this chapter, the record of the administrative proceeding consists of the record of the hearing and the presiding officer's final decision.

§ 117.274 Presiding officer for an appeal and for an informal hearing.

The presiding officer for an appeal, and for an informal hearing, must be an FDA Regional Food and Drug Director or another FDA official senior to an FDA District Director.

§ 117.277 Timeframe for issuing a decision on an appeal.

(a) If you appeal the order without requesting a hearing, the presiding officer must issue a written report that includes a final decision confirming or revoking the withdrawal by the 10th calendar day after the appeal is filed.

(b) If you appeal the order and request an informal hearing:

(1) If FDA grants the request for a hearing and the hearing is held, the presiding officer must provide a 2-calendar day opportunity for the hearing participants to review and submit comments on the report of the hearing under § 117.270(c)(4), and must issue a final decision within 10-calendar days after the hearing is held; or

(2) If FDA denies the request for a hearing, the presiding officer must issue a final decision on the appeal confirming or revoking the withdrawal within 10 calendar days after the date the appeal is filed.

§ 117.280 Revocation of an order to withdraw a qualified facility exemption.

An order to withdraw a qualified facility exemption is revoked if:

(a) You appeal the order and request an informal hearing, FDA grants the request for an informal hearing, and the presiding officer does not confirm the order within the 10-calendar days after the hearing, or issues a decision revoking the order within that time; or

(b) You appeal the order and request an informal hearing, FDA denies the request for an informal hearing, and FDA does not confirm the order within the 10-calendar days after the appeal is filed, or issues a decision revoking the order within that time; or

(c) You appeal the order without requesting an informal hearing, and FDA does not confirm the order within the 10-calendar days after the appeal is filed, or issues a decision revoking the order within that time.

§ 117.284 Final agency action.

Confirmation of a withdrawal order by the presiding officer is considered a final agency action for purposes of 5 U.S.C. 702.

§ 117.287 Reinstatement of a qualified facility exemption that was withdrawn.

(a) If the FDA District Director in whose district your facility is located (or, in the case of a foreign facility, the Director of the Office of Compliance in the Center for Food Safety and Applied Nutrition) determines that a facility has adequately resolved any problems with the conditions and conduct that are material to the safety of the food manufactured, processed, packed, or held at the facility and that continued withdrawal of the exemption is not necessary to protect public health and prevent or mitigate a foodborne illness outbreak, the FDA District Director in whose district your facility is located (or, in the case of a foreign facility, the Director of the Office of Compliance in the Center for Food Safety and Applied Nutrition) will, on his own initiative or on the request of a facility, reinstate the exemption.

(b) You may ask FDA to reinstate an exemption that has been withdrawn under the procedures of this subpart as follows:

(1) Submit a request, in writing, to the FDA District Director in whose district your facility is located (or, in the case of a foreign facility, the Director of the Office of Compliance in the Center for Food Safety and Applied Nutrition); and

(2) Present data and information to demonstrate that you have adequately resolved any problems with the conditions and conduct that are material to the safety of the food manufactured, processed, packed, or held at your facility, such that continued withdrawal of the exemption is not necessary to protect public health and prevent or mitigate a foodborne illness outbreak.

(c) If your exemption was withdrawn under § 117.251(a)(1) and FDA later determines, after finishing the active investigation of a foodborne illness outbreak, that the outbreak is not directly linked to your facility, FDA will reinstate your exemption under § 117.5(a), and FDA will notify you in writing that your exempt status has been reinstated.

(d) If your exemption was withdrawn under both § 117.251(a)(1) and (2) and FDA later determines, after finishing the active investigation of a foodborne illness outbreak, that the outbreak is not directly linked to your facility, FDA will inform you of this finding, and you may ask FDA to reinstate your exemption under § 117.5(a) in accordance with the requirements of paragraph (b) of this section.

Subpart F--Requirements Applying to Records That Must Be Established and Maintained
§ 117.301 Records subject to the requirements of this subpart.
(a) Except as provided by paragraphs (b) and (c) of this section, all records required by this part are subject to all requirements of this subpart.
(b) The requirements of § 117.310 apply only to the written food safety plan.
(c) The requirements of § 117.305(b), (d), (e), and (f) do not apply to the records required by § 117.201.

§ 117.305 General requirements applying to records.
Records must:
(a) Be kept as original records, true copies (such as photocopies, pictures, scanned copies, microfilm, microfiche, or other accurate reproductions of the original records), or electronic records;
(b) Contain the actual values and observations obtained during monitoring and, as appropriate, during verification activities;
(c) Be accurate, indelible, and legible;
(d) Be created concurrently with performance of the activity documented;
(e) Be as detailed as necessary to provide history of work performed; and
(f) Include:
> (1) Information adequate to identify the plant or facility (e.g., the name, and when necessary, the location of the plant or facility);
> (2) The date and, when appropriate, the time of the activity documented;
> (3) The signature or initials of the person performing the activity; and
> (4) Where appropriate, the identity of the product and the lot code, if any.

(g) Records that are established or maintained to satisfy the requirements of this part and that meet the definition of electronic records in § 11.3(b)(6) of this chapter are exempt from the requirements of part 11 of this chapter. Records that satisfy the requirements of this part, but that also are required under other applicable statutory provisions or regulations, remain subject to part 11 of this chapter.

§ 117.310 Additional requirements applying to the food safety plan.
The owner, operator, or agent in charge of the facility must sign and date the food safety plan:
(a) Upon initial completion; and
(b) Upon any modification.

§ 117.315 Requirements for record retention.
(a)(1) All records required by this part must be retained at the plant or facility for at least 2 years after the date they were prepared.
> (2) Records that a facility relies on during the 3-year period preceding the applicable calendar year to support its status as a qualified facility must be retained at the facility as long as necessary to support the status of a facility as a qualified facility during the applicable calendar year.

(b) Records that relate to the general adequacy of the equipment or processes being used by a facility, including the results of scientific studies and evaluations, must be retained by the facility for at least 2 years after their use is discontinued (e.g., because the facility has updated the written food safety plan (§ 117.126) or records that document validation of the written food safety plan (§ 117.155(b)));
(c) Except for the food safety plan, offsite storage of records is permitted if such records can be retrieved and provided onsite within 24 hours of request for official review. The food safety plan must remain onsite. Electronic records are considered to be onsite if they are accessible from an onsite location.
(d) If the plant or facility is closed for a prolonged period, the food safety plan may be transferred to some other reasonably accessible location but must be returned to the plant or facility within 24 hours for official review upon request.

§ 117.320 Requirements for official review.
All records required by this part must be made promptly available to a duly authorized representative of the Secretary of Health and Human Services for official review and copying upon oral or written request.

§ 117.325 Public disclosure.
Records obtained by FDA in accordance with this part are subject to the disclosure requirements under part 20 of this chapter.

§ 117.330 Use of existing records.
(a) Existing records (e.g., records that are kept to comply with other Federal, State, or local regulations, or for any other reason) do not need to be duplicated if they contain all of the required information and satisfy the requirements of this subpart. Existing records may be supplemented as necessary to include all of the required information and satisfy the requirements of this subpart.
(b) The information required by this part does not need to be kept in one set of records. If existing records contain some of the required information, any new information required by this part may be kept either separately or combined with the existing records.

§ 117.335 Special requirements applicable to a written assurance.
(a) Any written assurance required by this part must contain the following elements:
    (1) Effective date;
    (2) Printed names and signatures of authorized officials;
    (3) The applicable assurance under:
        (i) Section 117.136(a)(2);
        (ii) Section 117.136(a)(3);
        (iii) Section 117.136(a)(4);
        (iv) Section 117.430(c)(2);
        (v) Section 117.430(d)(2); or
        (vi) Section 117.430(e)(2);
(b) A written assurance required under § 117.136(a)(2), (3), or (4) must include:
    (1) Acknowledgement that the facility that provides the written assurance assumes legal responsibility to act consistently with the assurance and document its actions taken to satisfy the written assurance; and
    (2) Provision that if the assurance is terminated in writing by either entity, responsibility for compliance with the applicable provisions of this part reverts to the manufacturer/processor as of the date of termination.

Subpart G--Supply-Chain Program
§ 117.405 Requirement to establish and implement a supply-chain program.
(a)(1) Except as provided by paragraphs (a)(2) and (3) of this section, the receiving facility must establish and implement a risk-based supply-chain program for those raw materials and other ingredients for which the receiving facility has identified a hazard requiring a supply-chain-applied control.
    (2) A receiving facility that is an importer, is in compliance with the foreign supplier verification program requirements under part 1, subpart L of this chapter, and has documentation of verification activities conducted under § 1.506(e) of this chapter (which provides assurance that the hazards requiring a supply-chain-applied control for the raw material or other ingredient have been significantly minimized or prevented) need not conduct supplier verification activities for that raw material or other ingredient.
    (3) The requirements in this subpart do not apply to food that is supplied for research or evaluation use, provided that such food:
        (i) Is not intended for retail sale and is not sold or distributed to the public;
        (ii) Is labeled with the statement "Food for research or evaluation use";
        (iii) Is supplied in a small quantity that is consistent with a research, analysis, or quality assurance purpose, the food is used only for this purpose, and any unused quantity is properly disposed of; and
        (iv) Is accompanied with documents, in accordance with the practice of the trade, stating that the food will be used for research or evaluation purposes and cannot be sold or distributed to the public.
(b) The supply-chain program must be written.
(c) When a supply-chain-applied control is applied by an entity other than the receiving facility's supplier (e.g., when a non-supplier applies controls to certain produce (i.e., produce covered by part 112 of this chapter), because growing, harvesting, and packing activities are under different management), the receiving facility must:
    (1) Verify the supply-chain-applied control; or
    (2) Obtain documentation of an appropriate verification activity from another entity, review and assess the entity's applicable documentation, and document that review and assessment.

§ 117.410 General requirements applicable to a supply-chain program.
(a) The supply-chain program must include:
    (1) Using approved suppliers as required by § 117.420;
    (2) Determining appropriate supplier verification activities (including determining the frequency of conducting the activity) as required by § 117.425;
    (3) Conducting supplier verification activities as required by §§ 117.430 and 117.435;
    (4) Documenting supplier verification activities as required by § 117.475; and
    (5) When applicable, verifying a supply-chain-applied control applied by an entity other than the receiving facility's supplier and documenting that verification as required by § 117.475, or obtaining documentation of an appropriate

verification activity from another entity, reviewing and assessing that documentation, and documenting the review and assessment as required by § 117.475.

(b) The following are appropriate supplier verification activities for raw materials and other ingredients:

(1) Onsite audits;

(2) Sampling and testing of the raw material or other ingredient;

(3) Review of the supplier's relevant food safety records; and

(4) Other appropriate supplier verification activities based on supplier performance and the risk associated with the raw material or other ingredient.

(c) The supply-chain program must provide assurance that a hazard requiring a supply-chain-applied control has been significantly minimized or prevented.

(d)(1) Except as provided by paragraph (d)(2) of this section, in approving suppliers and determining the appropriate supplier verification activities and the frequency with which they are conducted, the following must be considered:

(i) The hazard analysis of the food, including the nature of the hazard controlled before receipt of the raw material or other ingredient, applicable to the raw material and other ingredients;

(ii) The entity or entities that will be applying controls for the hazards requiring a supply-chain-applied control;

(iii) Supplier performance, including:

(A) The supplier's procedures, processes, and practices related to the safety of the raw material and other ingredients;

(B) Applicable FDA food safety regulations and information relevant to the supplier's compliance with those regulations, including an FDA warning letter or import alert relating to the safety of food and other FDA compliance actions related to food safety (or, when applicable, relevant laws and regulations of a country whose food safety system FDA has officially recognized as comparable or has determined to be equivalent to that of the United States, and information relevant to the supplier's compliance with those laws and regulations); and

(C) The supplier's food safety history relevant to the raw materials or other ingredients that the receiving facility receives from the supplier, including available information about results from testing raw materials or other ingredients for hazards, audit results relating to the safety of the food, and responsiveness of the supplier in correcting problems; and

(iv) Any other factors as appropriate and necessary, such as storage and transportation practices.

(2) Considering supplier performance can be limited to the supplier's compliance history as required by paragraph (d)(1)(iii)(B) of this section, if the supplier is:

(i) A qualified facility as defined by § 117.3;

(ii) A farm that grows produce and is not a covered farm under part 112 of this chapter in accordance with § 112.4(a), or in accordance with §§ 112.4(b) and 112.5; or

(iii) A shell egg producer that is not subject to the requirements of part 118 of this chapter because it has less than 3,000 laying hens.

(e) If the owner, operator, or agent in charge of a receiving facility determines through auditing, verification testing, document review, relevant consumer, customer or other complaints, or otherwise that the supplier is not controlling hazards that the receiving facility has identified as requiring a supply-chain-applied control, the receiving facility must take and document prompt action in accordance with § 117.150 to ensure that raw materials or other ingredients from the supplier do not cause food that is manufactured or processed by the receiving facility to be adulterated under section 402 of the Federal Food, Drug, and Cosmetic Act or misbranded under section 403(w) of the Federal Food, Drug, and Cosmetic Act.

§ 117.415 Responsibilities of the receiving facility.

(a)(1) The receiving facility must approve suppliers.

(2) Except as provided by paragraphs (a)(3) and (4) of this section, the receiving facility must determine and conduct appropriate supplier verification activities, and satisfy all documentation requirements of this subpart.

(3) An entity other than the receiving facility may do any of the following, provided that the receiving facility reviews and assesses the entity's applicable documentation, and documents that review and assessment:

(i) Establish written procedures for receiving raw materials and other ingredients by the entity;

(ii) Document that written procedures for receiving raw materials and other ingredients are being followed by the entity; and

(iii) Determine, conduct, or both determine and conduct the appropriate supplier verification activities, with appropriate documentation.

(4) The supplier may conduct and document sampling and testing of raw materials and other ingredients, for the hazard controlled by the supplier, as a supplier verification activity for a particular lot of product and provide such documentation to the receiving facility, provided that the receiving facility reviews and assesses that documentation, and documents that review and assessment.

(b) For the purposes of this subpart, a receiving facility may not accept any of the following as a supplier verification activity:

(1) A determination by its supplier of the appropriate supplier verification activities for that supplier;

(2) An audit conducted by its supplier;

(3) A review by its supplier of that supplier's own relevant food safety records; or

(4) The conduct by its supplier of other appropriate supplier verification activities for that supplier within the meaning of § 117.410(b)(4).

(c) The requirements of this section do not prohibit a receiving facility from relying on an audit provided by its supplier when the audit of the supplier was conducted by a third-party qualified auditor in accordance with §§ 117.430(f) and 117.435.

§ 117.420 Using approved suppliers.

(a) _Approval of suppliers._ The receiving facility must approve suppliers in accordance with the requirements of § 117.410(d), and document that approval, before receiving raw materials and other ingredients received from those suppliers;

(b) Written procedures for receiving raw materials and other ingredients.

(1) Written procedures for receiving raw materials and other ingredients must be established and followed;

(2) The written procedures for receiving raw materials and other ingredients must ensure that raw materials and other ingredients are received only from approved suppliers (or, when necessary and appropriate, on a temporary basis from unapproved suppliers whose raw materials or other ingredients are subjected to adequate verification activities before acceptance for use); and

(3) Use of the written procedures for receiving raw materials and other ingredients must be documented.

§ 117.425 Determining appropriate supplier verification activities (including determining the frequency of conducting the activity).

Appropriate supplier verification activities (including the frequency of conducting the activity) must be determined in accordance with the requirements of § 117.410(d).

§ 117.430 Conducting supplier verification activities for raw materials and other ingredients.

(a) Except as provided by paragraph (c), (d), or (e) of this section, one or more of the supplier verification activities specified in § 117.410(b), as determined under § 117.410(d), must be conducted for each supplier before using the raw material or other ingredient from that supplier and periodically thereafter.

(b)(1) Except as provided by paragraph (b)(2) of this section, when a hazard in a raw material or other ingredient will be controlled by the supplier and is one for which there is a reasonable probability that exposure to the hazard will result in serious adverse health consequences or death to humans:

(i) The appropriate supplier verification activity is an onsite audit of the supplier; and

(ii) The audit must be conducted before using the raw material or other ingredient from the supplier and at least annually thereafter.

(2) The requirements of paragraph (b)(1) of this section do not apply if there is a written determination that other verification activities and/or less frequent onsite auditing of the supplier provide adequate assurance that the hazards are controlled.

(c) If a supplier is a qualified facility as defined by § 117.3, the receiving facility does not need to comply with paragraphs (a) and (b) of this section if the receiving facility:

(1) Obtains written assurance that the supplier is a qualified facility as defined by § 117.3:

(i) Before first approving the supplier for an applicable calendar year; and

(ii) On an annual basis thereafter, by December 31 of each calendar year, for the following calendar year; and

(2) Obtains written assurance, at least every 2 years, that the supplier is producing the raw material or other ingredient in compliance with applicable FDA food safety regulations (or, when applicable, relevant laws and regulations of a country whose food safety system FDA has officially recognized as comparable or has determined to be equivalent to that of the United States). The written assurance must include either:

(i) A brief description of the preventive controls that the supplier is implementing to control the applicable hazard in the food; or

(ii) A statement that the facility is in compliance with State, local, county, tribal, or other applicable non-Federal food safety law, including relevant laws and regulations of foreign countries.

(d) If a supplier is a farm that grows produce and is not a covered farm under part 112 of this chapter in accordance with § 112.4(a), or in accordance with §§ 112.4(b) and 112.5, the receiving facility does not need to comply with paragraphs (a) and (b) of this section for produce that the receiving facility receives from the farm as a raw material or other ingredient if the receiving facility:

(1) Obtains written assurance that the raw material or other ingredient provided by the supplier is not subject to part 112 of this chapter in accordance with § 112.4(a), or in accordance with §§ 112.4(b) and 112.5:

(i) Before first approving the supplier for an applicable calendar year; and

(ii) On an annual basis thereafter, by December 31 of each calendar year, for the following calendar year; and

(2) Obtains written assurance, at least every 2 years, that the farm acknowledges that its food is subject to section 402 of the Federal Food, Drug, and Cosmetic Act (or, when applicable, that its food is subject to relevant laws and regulations of a country whose food safety system FDA has officially recognized as comparable or has determined to be equivalent to that of the United States).

(e) If a supplier is a shell egg producer that is not subject to the requirements of part 118 of this chapter because it has less than 3,000 laying hens, the receiving facility does not need to comply with paragraphs (a) and (b) of this section if the receiving facility:

(1) Obtains written assurance that the shell eggs produced by the supplier are not subject to part 118 because the shell egg producer has less than 3,000 laying hens:

(i) Before first approving the supplier for an applicable calendar year; and

(ii) On an annual basis thereafter, by December 31 of each calendar year, for the following calendar year; and

(2) Obtains written assurance, at least every 2 years, that the shell egg producer acknowledges that its food is subject to section 402 of the Federal Food, Drug, and Cosmetic Act (or, when applicable, that its food is subject to relevant laws and regulations of a country whose food safety system FDA has officially recognized as comparable or has determined to be equivalent to that of the United States).

(f) There must not be any financial conflicts of interests that influence the results of the verification activities listed in § 117.410(b) and payment must not be related to the results of the activity.

§ 117.435 Onsite audit.

(a) An onsite audit of a supplier must be performed by a qualified auditor.

(b) If the raw material or other ingredient at the supplier is subject to one or more FDA food safety regulations, an onsite audit must consider such regulations and include a review of the supplier's written plan (e.g., Hazard Analysis and Critical Control Point (HACCP) plan or other food safety plan), if any, and its implementation, for the hazard being controlled (or, when applicable, an onsite audit may consider relevant laws and regulations of a country whose food safety system FDA has officially recognized as comparable or has determined to be equivalent to that of the United States).

(c)(1) The following may be substituted for an onsite audit, provided that the inspection was conducted within 1 year of the date that the onsite audit would have been required to be conducted:

(i) The written results of an appropriate inspection of the supplier for compliance with applicable FDA food safety regulations by FDA, by representatives of other Federal Agencies (such as the United States Department of Agriculture), or by representatives of State, local, tribal, or territorial agencies; or

(ii) For a foreign supplier, the written results of an inspection by FDA or the food safety authority of a country whose food safety system FDA has officially recognized as comparable or has determined to be equivalent to that of the United States.

(2) For inspections conducted by the food safety authority of a country whose food safety system FDA has officially recognized as comparable or determined to be equivalent, the food that is the subject of the onsite audit must be within the scope of the official recognition or equivalence determination, and the foreign supplier must be in, and under the regulatory oversight of, such country.

(d) If the onsite audit is solely conducted to meet the requirements of this subpart by an audit agent of a certification body that is accredited in accordance with regulations in part 1, subpart M of this chapter, the audit is not subject to the requirements in those regulations.

§ 117.475 Records documenting the supply-chain program.

(a) The records documenting the supply-chain program are subject to the requirements of subpart F of this part.

(b) The receiving facility must review the records listed in paragraph (c) of this section in accordance with § 117.165(a)(4).

(c) The receiving facility must document the following in records as applicable to its supply-chain program:

(1) The written supply-chain program;

(2) Documentation that a receiving facility that is an importer is in compliance with the foreign supplier verification program requirements under part 1, subpart L of this chapter, including documentation of verification activities conducted under § 1.506(e) of this chapter;

(3) Documentation of the approval of a supplier;

(4) Written procedures for receiving raw materials and other ingredients;

(5) Documentation demonstrating use of the written procedures for receiving raw materials and other ingredients;

(6) Documentation of the determination of the appropriate supplier verification activities for raw materials and other ingredients;

(7) Documentation of the conduct of an onsite audit. This documentation must include:

(i) The name of the supplier subject to the onsite audit;

(ii) Documentation of audit procedures;

(iii) The dates the audit was conducted;

(iv) The conclusions of the audit;

(v) Corrective actions taken in response to significant deficiencies identified during the audit; and

(vi) Documentation that the audit was conducted by a qualified auditor;

(8) Documentation of sampling and testing conducted as a supplier verification activity. This documentation must include:

(i) Identification of the raw material or other ingredient tested (including lot number, as appropriate) and the number of samples tested;

(ii) Identification of the test(s) conducted, including the analytical method(s) used;

(iii) The date(s) on which the test(s) were conducted and the date of the report;

(iv) The results of the testing;

(v) Corrective actions taken in response to detection of hazards; and

(vi) Information identifying the laboratory conducting the testing;

(9) Documentation of the review of the supplier's relevant food safety records. This documentation must include:

(i) The name of the supplier whose records were reviewed;

(ii) The date(s) of review;

(iii) The general nature of the records reviewed;

(iv) The conclusions of the review; and

(v) Corrective actions taken in response to significant deficiencies identified during the review;

(10) Documentation of other appropriate supplier verification activities based on the supplier performance and the risk associated with the raw material or other ingredient;

(11) Documentation of any determination that verification activities other than an onsite audit, and/or less frequent onsite auditing of a supplier, provide adequate assurance that the hazards are controlled when a hazard in a raw material or other ingredient will be controlled by the supplier and is one for which there is a reasonable probability that exposure to the hazard will result in serious adverse health consequences or death to humans;

(12) The following documentation of an alternative verification activity for a supplier that is a qualified facility:

(i) The written assurance that the supplier is a qualified facility as defined by § 117.3, before approving the supplier and on an annual basis thereafter; and

(ii) The written assurance that the supplier is producing the raw material or other ingredient in compliance with applicable FDA food safety regulations (or, when applicable, relevant laws and regulations of a country whose food safety system FDA has officially recognized as comparable or has determined to be equivalent to that of the United States);

(13) The following documentation of an alternative verification activity for a supplier that is a farm that supplies a raw material or other ingredient and is not a covered farm under part 112 of this chapter:

(i) The written assurance that supplier is not a covered farm under part 112 of this chapter in accordance with § 112.4(a), or in accordance with §§ 112.4(b) and 112.5, before approving the supplier and on an annual basis thereafter; and

(ii) The written assurance that the farm acknowledges that its food is subject to section 402 of the Federal Food, Drug, and Cosmetic Act (or, when applicable, that its food is subject to relevant laws and regulations of a country whose food safety system FDA has officially recognized as comparable or has determined to be equivalent to that of the United States);

(14) The following documentation of an alternative verification activity for a supplier that is a shell egg producer that is not subject to the requirements established in part 118 of this chapter because it has less than 3,000 laying hens:

(i) The written assurance that the shell eggs provided by the supplier are not subject to part 118 of this chapter because the supplier has less than 3,000 laying hens, before approving the supplier and on an annual basis thereafter; and

(ii) The written assurance that the shell egg producer acknowledges that its food is subject to section 402 of the Federal Food, Drug, and Cosmetic Act (or, when applicable, that its food is subject to relevant laws and regulations of a country whose safety system FDA has officially recognized as comparable or has determined to be equivalent to that of the United States);

(15) The written results of an appropriate inspection of the supplier for compliance with applicable FDA food safety regulations by FDA, by representatives of other Federal Agencies (such as the United States Department of Agriculture), or by representatives from State, local, tribal, or territorial agencies, or the food safety authority of another country when the results of such an inspection is substituted for an onsite audit;

(16) Documentation of actions taken with respect to supplier non-conformance;

(17) Documentation of verification of a supply-chain-applied control applied by an entity other than the receiving facility's supplier; and

(18) When applicable, documentation of the receiving facility's review and assessment of:

(i) Applicable documentation from an entity other than the receiving facility that written procedures for receiving raw materials and other ingredients are being followed;

(ii) Applicable documentation, from an entity other than the receiving facility, of the determination of the appropriate supplier verification activities for raw materials and other ingredients;

(iii) Applicable documentation, from an entity other than the receiving facility, of conducting the appropriate supplier verification activities for raw materials and other ingredients;

(iv) Applicable documentation, from its supplier, of:

    (A) The results of sampling and testing conducted by the supplier; or

    (B) The results of an audit conducted by a third-party qualified auditor in accordance with §§ 117.430(f) and 117.435; and

(v) Applicable documentation, from an entity other than the receiving facility, of verification activities when a supply-chain-applied control is applied by an entity other than the receiving facility's supplier.

~~~~~~

NOTES:

Appendix 2. Food Safety Plan Worksheets

Worksheets are recommended to document the product description, hazard analysis and preventive controls. The hazard analysis form should contain information to justify the identification of the hazards requiring preventive controls and the types of preventive controls applied. Information in the Food Safety Plan must explain the details for each preventive control.

There is no standardized or mandated format for these worksheets, but the information should be arranged in a progressive manner that clearly explains the thought process for the hazard analysis and the individual steps in the Food Safety Plan. Forms used for process preventive controls may be adapted for allergen preventive controls, but other formats are entirely acceptable if it works for your organization and contains all of the required information.

The following worksheets are provided as examples. The information is arranged in a similar manner, but the layouts are in either a landscape or a portrait form to suit individual preferences. Other forms can be adapted from those in the Food Safety Plan example.

Special Note: These worksheets can be copied for routine use, but if they are used for official use, they must include details that identify the commercial firm and related information. The additional information must include:

- Firm name and location
- Dates and, when appropriate, the time of the activity
- Product identification
- Usually, record review signature (or initial) and date

> All forms can be adapted or modified as needed. There is NO required form.

PLANT NAME	ISSUE DATE	PAGE
ADDRESS	SUPERSEDES	PRODUCT CODE

Product Description Distribution, Consumers and Intended Use

Product Name(s)	
Product Description, including Important Food Safety Characteristics	
Ingredients	
Packaging Used	
Intended Use	
Intended Consumers	
Shelf Life	
Labeling Instructions related to Safety	
Storage and Distribution	

Approved: Signature: Print name:	Date:

PLANT NAME	ISSUE DATE	PAGE
ADDRESS	SUPERSEDES	PRODUCT CODE

Hazard identification (column 2) considers those that may be present in the food because the hazard occurs naturally, the hazard may be unintentionally introduced, or the hazard may be intentionally introduced for economic gain.

B = Biological hazards including bacteria, viruses, parasites, and environmental pathogens

C = Chemical (including radiological) hazards, food allergens, substances such as pesticides and drug residues, natural toxins, decomposition, and unapproved food or color additives

P = Physical hazards include potentially harmful extraneous matter that may cause choking, injury or other adverse health effects

Hazard Analysis

(1) Ingredient / Processing Step	(2) Identify potential food safety hazards introduced, controlled or enhanced at this step		(3) Do any potential food safety hazards require a preventive control?		(4) Justify your decision for column 3	(5) What preventive control measure(s) can be applied to significantly minimize or prevent the food safety hazard? *Process including CCPs, Allergen, Sanitation, Supply-chain, other preventive control*	(6) Is the preventive control applied at this step?	
			Yes	No			Yes	No
	B							
	C							
	P							
	B							
	C							
	P							
	B							
	C							
	P							

A2-3

PLANT NAME	ISSUE DATE	PAGE
ADDRESS	SUPERSEDES	PRODUCT CODE

Process Preventive Controls – Landscape Layout

Process Controls	Hazard(s)	Parameters, values or critical limits	Monitoring				Corrective Action	Verification	Records
			What	How	Frequency	Who			

PLANT NAME		ISSUE DATE	PAGE
ADDRESS		SUPERSEDES	PRODUCT CODE

Process Preventive Controls – Portrait Format

[This is an alternate layout for process preventive control.]

Process Control Step				
Hazard(s)				
Parameters, values or critical limits				
Monitoring	What			
	How			
	Frequency			
	Who			
Corrective Action				
Verification				
Records				

A2-5

PLANT NAME	ISSUE DATE	PAGE
ADDRESS	SUPERSEDES	PRODUCT CODE

Form Name: Food Allergen Preventive Controls

Allergen Control	Hazard(s)	Criterion	Monitoring				Corrective Action	Verification	Records
			What	How	Frequency	Who			

PLANT NAME	ISSUE DATE	PAGE
ADDRESS	SUPERSEDES	PRODUCT CODE

Form Name: Food Allergen Ingredient Analysis

Raw Material Name	Supplier	Food Allergens in Ingredient Formulation								Allergens in Precautionary Labeling
		Egg	Milk	Soy	Wheat	Tree Nut (market name)	Peanut	Fish (market name)	Shellfish (market name)	

NOTE:
The above format is an alternative for an allergen specific hazard analysis. If you choose to use a form like this, then there is no need to duplicate allergen considerations in your hazard analysis chart. Duplication of information in multiple forms can create extra work and may lead to inconsistencies.

Some organizations may even choose to do an ingredient hazard analysis that considers not only allergens, but also other hazards. This may be a useful option for you.

How to Use the Chart
List all ingredients received in the facility. Identify allergens contained in each ingredient by reviewing ingredient labels or contacting the manufacturer. Any allergens listed in "May contain" or other precautionary labeling on ingredients should be listed in the last column and reviewed to determine if allergen labeling is needed on the finished product.

A2-7

PLANT NAME	ISSUE DATE	PAGE
ADDRESS	SUPERSEDES	PRODUCT CODE

Form Name: Food Allergen Label Verification Listing

Product	Allergen Statement

PLANT NAME	ISSUE DATE	PAGE
ADDRESS	SUPERSEDES	PRODUCT CODE

Form Name: Production Line Food Allergen Assessment

		Intentional Allergens							
Product Name	**Production Line**	Egg	Milk	Soy	Wheat	Tree Nut (market name)	Peanut	Fish (market name)	Shellfish (market name)

Scheduling Implications:

Allergen Cleaning Implications: (Required)

How to Use This Form

Complete for each production line. Identify each allergen contained in each product produced on the line. Identify any allergens unique to a specific product, then indicate scheduling information (i.e., run unique allergens last) and allergen cleaning information (i.e., full allergen clean before running cheese or plain omelets after a biscuit run.

A2-9

PLANT NAME	ISSUE DATE	PAGE
ADDRESS	SUPERSEDES	PRODUCT CODE

Form Name: Sanitation Preventive Controls

Location	
Purpose	
Frequency	
Who	
Procedure	
Monitoring	
Corrections	
Records	
Verification	Date

PLANT NAME	ISSUE DATE	PAGE
ADDRESS	SUPERSEDES	PRODUCT CODE

Corrective Action Form

Date of Record:	Code or Lot Number:
Date and Time of Deviation:	

Description of Deviation:

Actions Taken to Restore Order to the Process:

Person (name and signature) of Person Taking Action:	
Amount of Product Involved in Deviation:	

Evaluation of Product Involved with Deviation:

Final Disposition of Product:

Reviewed by (Name and Signature):	Date of Review:

A2-11

PLANT NAME	ISSUE DATE	PAGE
ADDRESS	SUPERSEDES	PRODUCT CODE

Food Safety Plan Reanalysis Checklist

Reason for reanalysis:

Task	Date Reviewed and Initials	Is Update Needed? (yes/no)	Date Task Completed	Signature or Initials of Person Completing the Task
List of Food Safety Team with individual responsibilities				
Product flow diagrams				
Hazard analysis				
Process Preventive Controls				
Food Allergen Preventive Controls				
Sanitation Preventive Controls				
Supply-chain Program				
Recall Plan				
Updated Food Safety Plan implemented				
Updated Food Safety Plan signed by owner or agent in charge				
Reviewer Signature:			Date Review:	
Date issued: dd/mm/yy		Supersedes: dd/mm/yy		

Appendix 3: Model Food Safety Plan Teaching Example

Food Safety Plan

for

Frozen Omelets

Reviewed by: *I. N. Charge*, Plant Manager

Date: February 13, 2016

The information in this example is for training purposes only and does not represent any specific operation. Development of a Food Safety Plan is site specific, thus it is highly unlikely that this plan can be adapted to another operation without significant modification.

This teaching model includes required and optional information to illustrate how a Food Safety Plan might be documented. The format may vary significantly for each specific company.

- The **Background Information** section is not required, but is highly useful for organizing the plan and explaining its organization to others. It is essential for a teaching example to clarify underlying assumptions in decisions that are made.
- The **Hazard Analysis** section is required for all Food Safety Plans subject to the *Preventive Controls for Human Food* regulation.
- The Preventive Controls sections (Process, Allergen, Sanitation and Supply-chain) are required ONLY for hazards requiring a preventive control identified by the hazard analysis.
- A Recall Plan is required ONLY when a hazard requiring a preventive control is identified by the hazard analysis.
- Implementation Records are required only for hazards requiring a preventive control.
    - A validation study is required only for process preventive controls.

Table of Contents

Background Information

Company Overview and Food Safety Team

E.G. Food Company's ~150 employees produce egg-based products, including plain omelets, cheese omelets and cheese omelet biscuits. Product is made 5 days a week in one 8 hour production shift, followed by 4 hours for sanitation. Cleaning and sanitizing of all processing equipment is conducted per a master sanitation schedule, which also includes cleaning and sanitizing between different products if needed for allergen control. Municipal water, which is treated and tested per EPA requirements by the city, is used throughout the facility. The company practices hygienic zoning to prevent cooked product exposure to environmental pathogens and employees working in the high hygiene areas wear color coded smocks and dedicated footwear. These employees are instructed on proper hand washing procedures, glove use, and importance of zoning.

Food Safety Team

Name	Position	Training (Records are in personnel file)
I.N. Charge	Plant Manager	In plant training
F.S. Leader*	QA manager and food safety team leader	FSPCA class
E.F. Ency	Production supervisor	In plant training
I.M. Clean	Sanitation supervisor	In plant training
P.H. Books*	Consultant, PH Books Consulting Service	M.S. & Ph.D. in Food Science and FSPCA lead instructor

*Preventive controls qualified individual

A3-3

Product Description, Distribution, Consumers and Intended Use

Product Name(s)	Omelet – Plain, Cheese and Cheese Biscuit
Product Description, including Important Food Safety Characteristics	Frozen, cooked egg omelet, with or without cheese filling and a wheat biscuit bun pH 7.1 - 7.9, water activity >0.98, no preservatives
Ingredients	Plain: Eggs, milk, pan release oil, salt Cheese: Eggs, milk, cheese, pan release oil, salt Cheese Biscuit: Eggs, milk, cheese, biscuit, pan release oil, salt
Packaging Used	Paperboard trays wrapped with plastic wrap and inserted in a corrugated case.
Intended Use	The product is considered ready-to-eat, but is typically heated to hot holding temperatures (135°F (57°C)) or above for palatability. Heating is typically conducted using microwaves or convection oven. End user may thaw at refrigeration temperatures overnight to reduce cooking time. End users may also add toppings or fillings. Sold for foodservice applications. *Potential abuse:* Some establishments may hold thawed product for longer than the recommended 24 hours.
Intended Consumers	General public
Shelf Life	1 year frozen
Labeling Instructions	Keep frozen or thaw under refrigeration (<41°F (5°C)) for <24 hours before cooking.
Storage and Distribution	Frozen
Approved:* Signature: F.S. Leader Print name: F.S. Leader	Date: April 11, 2015

*Signature may just be on plan, or may be on each page.

Flow Diagram

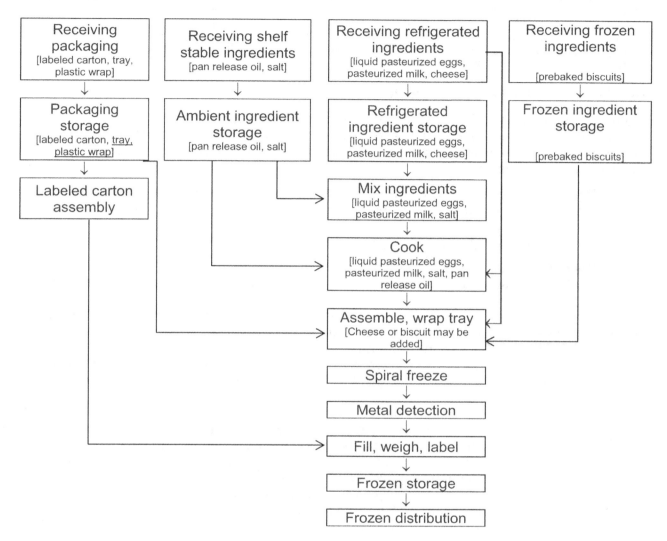

NOTE: Text in [square brackets] optional and for teaching purposes

Verified by: F.S. Leader April 11, 2015

Process Description

This Process Narrative was developed for teaching purposes to create a common vision of this hypothetical process among course participants. There is no requirement for an establishment to create such a document; however, a Process Narrative may be useful to guide hazard analysis and to orient auditors. Other company documents outside of the Food Safety Plan may substitute for a Process Narrative, such as ingredient specifications, product specifications, production instructions, standard operating procedures, etc. This Process Narrative does not represent any existing process.

Receiving Ingredients and Packaging:

Ingredients and raw materials are purchased from reputable suppliers that comply with internationally recognized food safety and quality systems. For each ingredient, the same brand is used consistently to minimize variation. Ingredients are stored according to manufacturers' recommendations when specified.

- **Receiving packaging**: Corrugated shippers, paperboard trays and plastic wrap are received in bulk. Specifications require food grade material for trays and plastic wrap that is compatible with frozen storage of food products. Labeled cartons are reviewed for conformance with product allergen requirements and ingredients.

- **Receiving shelf stable ingredients**:
  - *Salt*: Received in 10-pound bags from our distributor. Specifications require food grade salt.
  - *Pan release oil*: The pan release oil contains soybean oil, soy lecithin and natural flavor. It is received from our distributor in 10-gallon jugs.
- **Receiving refrigerated ingredients**:
  - *Eggs*: Refrigerated, pasteurized liquid eggs, processed to meet USDA requirements, are received in 20-pound, bag-in-box containers from our sole source supplier, in refrigerated trucks.
  - *Milk*: Pasteurized Grade A milk is received from a local dairy in 20-pound bag-in-crate containers in refrigerated trucks. The supplier's letter of guarantee states that production practices are in compliance with Pasteurized Milk Ordinance requirements for pasteurized milk products, including animal drug residue testing.
  - *Cheese:* Pre-sliced, pasteurized process cheese is received in 3-pound cases from our sole source supplier. The cheese contains cultured pasteurized milk and skim milk, buttermilk, milkfat, salt, sodium phosphate, tricalcium phosphate, lactic acid, milk protein concentrate, artificial color, and enzymes.

- **Receiving frozen ingredients:**
  - *Biscuits*: Pre-sliced, wheat biscuits are received frozen in 16-pound cases (5 trays of 20 biscuits per case) from our distributor. The biscuits contain enriched bleached flour (wheat flour, niacin, iron, thiamine mononitrate, riboflavin, folic acid), water, shortening (palm oil, mono and diglycerides, polysorbate 60, citric acid), buttermilk solids, sugar, baking powder (sodium acid pyrophosphate, sodium bicarbonate, cornstarch, calcium sulfate, monocalcium phosphate), and salt.

Storing Ingredients and Packaging:

- **Packaging storage**: Labeled cartons and trays are stored in the dry storage room in the packaging area. Plastic wrap is stored in sealed containers to protect from contamination. Packaging is used First-In-First-Out.

- **Ambient ingredient storage**: Salt and pan release oil are stored in the dry storage room in the ingredient area, arranged by ingredient code number. All containers are sealed to avoid allergen cross-contact and cross-contamination during storage. Ingredients containing food allergens are identified and stored in specific locations with like allergenic ingredients, unless allergen cross-contact is not reasonably likely to occur.

- **Refrigerated ingredient storage**: Pasteurized liquid eggs and pasteurized fluid milk are stored in separate designated areas in a cooler that is kept at ≤40°F (≤4.4°C) and used within code date. No open containers are returned to the cooler to minimize the potential for allergen cross-contact with either milk or egg allergens.

- **Frozen ingredient storage**: Frozen biscuits are stored in a designated area separate from finished goods storage. The freezer is maintained at <0°F (-18°C). A partially used case may be resealed and returned to the freezer after use on the line.

Mix ingredients: Eggs, milk and salt are combined in the mixing room using a commercial mixer with a wire whip. The batch size is used within 30 minutes. The temperature of the omelet batter is ≤40°F (≤4.4°C) after mixing. Mixing bowls are taken to the cook line for dispensing. Bowls are moved to a separate room for cleaning at the morning break, at lunch break and after the shift.

Cook: Pan-release oil is used to grease the omelet pans as needed to prevent sticking. Approximately one cup of omelet batter is deposited manually into omelet pans on high heat setting. The pan is swirled and edges of the omelet are lifted with a spatula to allow uncooked (liquid) batter to flow under the cooked portion. Surface temperatures (the coolest point) are periodically measured with an infrared thermometer and are typically >162°F (72°C) when the omelet is fully congealed, the surface is not shiny and thus cooking is complete. A congealed omelet is required to enable assembly. All omelet batter prepared is cooked or discarded – there is no rework.

Assemble, wrap: Cooked omelets are transferred to a table with the cooking spatula. The same table is used to assemble all products.

- *Plain omelets* are folded or rolled by hand to desired shape. Plain omelets are the first product made each day.

- *Cheese omelet* production begins after plain omelet numbers have been prepared. Cheese is brought to the line just in time for production in sufficient quantity to be used in <2 hours. Plain omelets are prepared, and a slice of cheese is placed in the center of the omelet prior to folding or rolling. All cheese is used for product or very small amounts are discarded at the end of the day.

- *Cheese biscuit omelets* are the last item made each day and only prepared when orders require. The required number of biscuits is brought to the line and trays containing 20 biscuits each placed on assembly tables. A folded plain omelet is placed on the bottom biscuit half, a slice of cheese is placed on the omelet, which is then topped with the biscuit top. All biscuit trays removed from a case are used for production or discarded at the end of the day. A partial case (i.e., 1-4 full trays) may be resealed, dated, returned to the freezer and used for the next production.

Twelve (12) omelets or six (6) cheese biscuit omelets are placed on a tray and plastic wrap is applied to cover the tray. Packaging does not reduce the oxygen level.

A3-7

Spiral freeze: Wrapped trays are placed on a belt that carries the omelets though a spiral freezer. Freezing takes place rapidly, with temperatures dropping from >135°F (57°C) to <41°F (5°C) in <1 hour from the time the omelet is placed on the assembly table. Product exiting freezer is frozen solid, with temperatures continuing to drop to <10°F (-12°C) in frozen storage.

Metal detection: Frozen product in trays is passed through a metal detector. All rejected product is examined for the presence of metal.

Labeled carton assembly: Labeled cartons are assembled as needed at the 'Fill, Weigh, Label' step.

Fill, weigh, label: Four trays of frozen omelets are placed in labeled cartons. Labeled cartons are weighed and sealed, and the lot code is applied. This step takes place in <30 minutes for each case.

Frozen storage: Finished product is stored at <10°F (-12°C) until distributed.

Frozen shipping: Product is shipped in freezer trucks to customers at <10°F (-12°C).

A3-8

Hazard Analysis

Hazard identification (column 2) considers those that may be present in the food because the hazard occurs naturally, the hazard may be unintentionally introduced, or the hazard may be intentionally introduced for economic gain.

- B = Biological hazards including bacteria, viruses, parasites, and environmental pathogens
- C = Chemical (including radiological) hazards, food allergens, substances such as pesticides and drug residues, natural toxins, decomposition, and unapproved food or color additives
- P = Physical hazards include potentially harmful extraneous matter that may cause choking, injury or other adverse health effects

(1) Ingredient/ Processing Step	(2) Identify potential food safety hazards introduced, controlled or enhanced at this step		(3) Do any potential food safety hazards require a preventive control?		(4) Justify your decision for column 3	(5) What preventive control measure(s) can be applied to significantly minimize or prevent the food safety hazard? *Process including CCPs, Allergen, Sanitation, Supply-chain, other preventive control*	(6) Is the preventive control applied at this step?	
			Yes	No			Yes	No
Receiving packaging	B	None						
	C	Undeclared allergens – egg, milk, soy (wheat in biscuit only)	X		Labeled cartons must declare allergens present in the product and print errors have occurred	Allergen Control – label review for allergen information	X	
	P	None			**NOTE:** Label review could be done only at the labeling step, but many organizations perform this upon receipt because individuals with different skills are needed.			
Receiving shelf stable ingredients – salt	B	None						
	C	None						
	P	None						
Receiving shelf stable ingredients – pan release oil	B	None						
	C	Allergen – soy	X		Soy lecithin may contain soy allergen that must be labeled to inform consumers. Allergen cross-contact is not an issue – all products contain soy.	Allergen Control – allergen labeling at other steps		X
	P	None						
Receiving refrigerated ingredients – liquid pasteurized eggs	B	Vegetative pathogens such as *Salmonella*	X		While pasteurization minimizes the likelihood of *Salmonella* USDA recommends the product be used in cooked foods. Experience has shown *Salmonella* occasionally occurs in this ingredient.	Process Control - subsequent cook step		X
	C	Allergen – egg	X		Egg is an allergen that must be labeled to inform consumers. Allergen cross-contact is not an issue – all products contain egg.	Allergen Control – allergen labeling at other steps		X
Continued	P	None						

(1) Ingredient/ Processing Step	(2) Identify potential food safety hazards introduced, controlled or enhanced at this step		(3) Do any potential food safety hazards require a preventive control?		(4) Justify your decision for column 3	(5) What preventive control measure(s) can be applied to significantly minimize or prevent the food safety hazard? *Process including CCPs, Allergen, Sanitation, Supply-chain, other preventive control*	(6) Is the preventive control applied at this step?	
			Yes	No			Yes	No
Receiving refrigerated ingredients – pasteurized Grade A milk	B	Vegetative pathogens such as *Salmonella*	X		Raw milk has a history of association with *Salmonella*. Pasteurization by the supplier or our cook step can control the hazard.	Process Control - subsequent cook step		X
	C	Allergen – milk	X		Milk is an allergen that must be labeled to inform consumers. Allergen cross-contact is not an issue – all products contain milk.	Allergen Control – allergen labeling at other steps		X
	P	None						
Receiving refrigerated ingredients – pasteurized process cheese	B	Vegetative and sporeforming pathogens such as *Salmonella*, pathogenic *E. coli*, *L. monocytogenes* and *C. botulinum*	X		Pathogens listed were identified as significant by ICMSF (2005) in process cheese. These hazards must be controlled when the cheese is made.	Supply-chain Control – approved supplier and 3rd party supplier audit by a qualified auditor	X	
	C	Allergen – milk	X		Milk is an allergen that must be labeled to inform consumers. Allergen cross-contact is not an issue – all products contain milk.	Allergen Control – allergen labeling at other steps		X
	P	None						
Receiving frozen ingredients – biscuits	B	None						
	C	Allergen - wheat	X		Wheat is an allergen that must be labeled to inform consumers. Allergen cross-contact with other products must be controlled because some products produced on the line do not contain wheat.	Allergen Control – allergen labeling at other steps Sanitation Control – at a subsequent step to prevent allergen cross-contact		X
	P	None						
Storage – Pack-aging & dry ingredients [pan release oil, salt]	B	None						
	C	None						
	P	None						
Continued								

A3-10

(1) Ingredient/ Processing Step	(2) Identify <u>potential</u> food safety hazards introduced, controlled or enhanced at this step		(3) Do any <u>potential</u> food safety hazards require a preventive control?		(4) Justify your decision for column 3	(5) What preventive control measure(s) can be applied to significantly minimize or prevent the food safety hazard? *Process including CCPs, Allergen, Sanitation, Supply-chain, other preventive control*	(6) Is the preventive control applied at this step?	
			Yes	No			Yes	No
Refrigerated ingredient storage [eggs, milk]	B	Vegetative pathogens such as *Salmonella*		X	Pathogen growth to levels that render the cook step ineffective is not likely to occur			
	C	None						
	P	None						
Frozen ingredient storage [biscuits]	B	None						
	C	None						
	P	None						
Labeled carton assembly	B	None						
	C	None						
	P	None						
Mix ingredients [eggs, milk, salt]	B	None						
	C	None						
	P	Metal	X		Mixer has metal-on-metal contact	Process Control – subsequent metal detection		X
Cook [eggs, milk, salt, pan release oil]	B	Survival of vegetative pathogens such as *Salmonella*	X		Thorough cooking is required to kill vegetative pathogens	Process Control – cooking to achieve a lethal temperature	X	
	C	None						
	P	None						
Assemble, wrap	B	Introduction of environmental pathogens such as *L. monocytogenes*	X		Recontamination may occur if sanitation controls are not in place	Sanitation Controls – prevent recontamination	X	
		Growth of vegetative pathogens such as *Salmonella* and *L. monocytogenes*		X	Time is too short for growth to be reasonably likely.			
	C	Allergen cross-contact from other products handled at this step; e.g., Cheese Omelet Biscuit	X		Biscuits could introduce wheat allergen to other products without control	Sanitation and Allergen Controls – prevent allergen cross-contact	X	
	P	None						

Continued

(1) Ingredient/ Processing Step	(2) Identify potential food safety hazards introduced, controlled or enhanced at this step		(3) Do any potential food safety hazards require a preventive control?		(4) Justify your decision for column 3	(5) What preventive control measure(s) can be applied to significantly minimize or prevent the food safety hazard? *Process including CCPs, Allergen, Sanitation, Supply-chain, other preventive control*	(6) Is the preventive control applied at this step?	
			Yes	No			Yes	No
Spiral freeze	B	Growth of vegetative pathogens such as *Salmonella* and *L. monocytogenes*		X	Time is too short for growth to be reasonably likely			
	C	None						
	P	None						
Metal detection	B	None						
	C	None						
	P	Metal	X		Metal-on-metal contact on the line may introduce metal fragments	Process Control – metal detection	X	
Fill, weigh, label	B	None						
	C	Undeclared allergens – egg, milk, soy (wheat in biscuit only)	X		All products contain egg, milk and soy allergens. The cheese biscuit also contains wheat	Allergen Control – correct labeled carton for product	X	
	P	None						
Frozen storage	B	None						
	C	None						
	P	None						
Frozen distribution	B	None						
	C	None						
	P	None						

A3-12

Process Preventive Control

Process Control	Hazard(s)	Critical Limits	Monitoring				Corrective Action	Verification	Records
			What	How	Frequency	Who			
Cook	Vegetative pathogens such as *Salmonella*	Omelet temperature is ≥158°F (70°C) instantaneous before transfer to assembly table	Omelet surface temperature is ≥158°F (70°C)	Infrared surface thermometer	Each cook station, 4 times per shift, about every 2-3 hours	QA technician or designee	Hold product back to the last good check and evaluate – rework, discard, or release. Determine root cause – retrain or correct as appropriate	Review of Cook Log, Corrective Action and Verification records within 7 working days. Daily accuracy check for thermometer. Annual calibration of thermometer	Cook Log – cook temp by QA technician. Corrective Action records. Verification records, including validation study

A3-13

Cook Validation Study

P.H. Books Consulting Services
123 Research Way, Infoville USA

E.G. Food Company Omelet Cook Validation Study

Determination of lethal cook temperatures for *Salmonella* in egg products

Section 3-401.11 (A) (2) of the *Food Code* (a credible source for science-based recommendations) identifies the following time and temperature combinations as adequate for cooking raw egg-containing products:

- 145°F(63°C) for 3 minutes
- 150°F(66°C) for 1 minute
- 155°F(68°C) for 15 seconds
- 158°F(70°C) for <1 second (instantaneous)

Conclusion: A critical limit of ≥158°F (70°C) for <1 second (instantaneous) will effectively manage the risk of *Salmonella* in omelets based on the *Food Code*. Use of pasteurized eggs adds an extra margin of safety.

Determination that a congealed omelet is a valid visual cue for achieving a lethal temperature

It is well established that coagulation of eggs protein is a function of temperature. Lowe[1] reported that whole egg coagulates at 158°F (70°C), but commented that addition of milk can elevate the coagulation temperature. Stadelman and Cotterill[2] also discuss the influence of non-egg components on elevation of coagulation temperature. Therefore a study was conducted to determine temperatures achieved when omelets coagulated under routine operating conditions and to determine the frequency of temperature measurements.

A calibrated infrared thermometer was used to measure the temperature of the surface of omelets when they were cooked to desired doneness by 10 operators – 5 omelets for each of 10 operators on 3 separate days, for a total of 150 measurements. The omelet batter for each of the 3 separate days used different lots of eggs and milk. Omelets were prepared using standard procedures – one cup of omelet batter was deposited into oiled omelet pans on the high heat setting. Each pan was swirled and edges of the omelet were lifted with a spatula to allow uncooked (liquid) batter to flow under the cooked portion until coagulation was complete, no liquid batter is present, and the surface is no longer shiny.

Conclusion: The minimum temperature observed was 162°F (72°C), which is more than adequate to assure temperatures are above the critical limit of ≥158°F (70°C). The maximum temperature observed was 170°F (77°C). Temperatures will be monitored four (4) times per shift to provide ongoing documentation.

Signed: *P.H. Books*   Date: 9 September 2014

Principle Consultant

---

[1] Lowe, B. 1937. Experimental Cookery from the Chemical and Physical Standpoint. John Wiley & Sons. Egg section available at http://chestofbooks.com/food/science/Experimental-Cookery/index.html#.Uqol39vnYiR Accessed 12 December 2013

[2] Stadelman, W.J. and O.J. Cotterill (eds). 1995 Egg Science and Technology, 4th Edition, Haworth Press, Inc., Binghamton NY.

Product Testing for Verification

Purpose: To verify the adequacy of process control (cooking) for the hazard of *Salmonella* and the adequacy of sanitation controls to prevent recontamination.

Sample identification: Whole omelets at the assembly table prior to packaging and freezing are sampled. Results from the omelets sampled represent one day of production because cleaning and sanitizing occurs daily.

Sampling procedure: Once per month, five (5) omelets are randomly selected throughout the day. Each omelet is from a different assembly station. Individual omelets are aseptically collected, placed in sterile, plastic sample bags, which are labeled with the date, time, product type, lot number and operator number. Samples are placed on a tray, which is run through the spiral freezer to mimic processing conditions. The frozen omelets are sent to our contract lab, identified below, in an insulated cooler with an ice pack using overnight express mail.

Product from the sampled lot is held until results are received and confirmed to be in compliance with acceptance criteria identified under "Results" below.

Laboratory: *Wee Beasties Laboratory* (987 Critter Drive, Yourtown, USA)

Test conducted: The contract lab samples a portion from each omelet and retains the remaining sample under refrigeration for further testing if results are not acceptable. Each portion is tested individually for *Enterobacteriaceae*. Of the 5 samples taken, 2 can have results between 10 and 100/g. No individual sample can have a count greater than 100/g.

Microorganism	Analytical Method	Sampling plan		Limits/g	
		n	c	m	M
Enterobacteriaceae	AOAC 2003.1	5	2	10	100

n = number of sample units
c = number of sample units that can have results between m and M
m = concentration separating good from marginally acceptable results
M = concentration separating marginally acceptable from unacceptable results

Interpretation of results:
Acceptable results – Release product if either of the following are observed
1. All results are ≤10/g
2. 1 or 2 results between 10 and 100/g; all others ≤10/g

Unacceptable results – Apply corrective action if either of the following are observed
1. More than 2 samples have results between 10 and 100
2. One or more results >100/g

Corrective action for unacceptable results:
1. Determine the disposition of the lot (day's production) by testing 25g from each of the five (5) retained omelets for *Salmonella* and *Listeria monocytogenes*. Product is on hold and release status until negative results are confirmed.
   a. If no pathogen is detected – Release the product and implement other corrective actions below
   b. If either pathogen is detected – Divert the product to rendering and implement other corrective actions

A3-15

2. Determine root cause
   a. Increase observation of cooking procedures and temperature verification at the Cook step to hourly.
      i. Observe assembly tables for signs of uncooked egg (e.g., liquid egg smears on the tables), which indicates undercooking and will remain and build throughout the day. Focus especially on tables that had the higher counts in the lab results.
      ii. Retrain cooking staff if issues are noted.
   b. Conduct stringent sanitation efforts in the Assemble/Wrap, Cook and hallway between these areas. Increase observation of cleaning procedures at the end of the day and before start up to identify issues. Also observe procedures in the Utensil and Small Equipment wash room and Mixing area.
      i. Make improvements if warranted in any of these areas.
   c. Review environmental monitoring results for *Listeria* spp. to identify potential issues, regardless of whether or not *Listeria* is found in the product.
      i. Direct cleaning and sanitation in areas of potential concern.
   d. If *Salmonella* is detected in sampled product, in addition to observation of cook procedures and temperature verification (see 2a), initiate environmental monitoring for *Salmonella,* focusing on the Assemble/Wrap area and transition hallway between Assemble/Wrap and Cook areas to identify potential environmental sources. Continue weekly until results are negative for 5 consecutive weeks, then reduce to monthly.
   e. Increase routine sampling for *Enterobacteriaceae* to at least weekly until 5 consecutive results are acceptable. Then return to the routine schedule.
3. Provide staff training
   a. Review the situation with staff to alert them to the issue. Seek input on potential areas of improvement that can help resolve the issue.
4. In the event of a persistent issue, engage experts (e.g., testing lab or consultant P.H. Books) for additional assistance.

A3-16

Process Preventive Control

Process Control	Hazard(s)	Critical Limits	Monitoring				Corrective Action	Verification	Records
			What	How	Frequency	Who			
Metal detection	Metal inclusion	Metal detector present and operating	All of the product passes through an operating metal detector	Visual examination that the detector is on and reject device is working	Beginning, middle and end of shift	Production employee	If the product is processed without metal detection, hold it for metal detection. Correct operating procedures to ensure that the product is not processed without metal detection	Pass X mm ferrous and Y mm non-ferrous and stainless standard wands through detector at start-up, middle and end of shift to assure equipment is functioning. Review of Metal Detector Log and Corrective Action and Verification within 7 working days	Metal Detector Log Manufacturer's Validation Study that determined detector settings and sensitivity standards Corrective action records
		No metal fragments that would cause injury or choking are in the product passing through the metal detector	Kick-out product for the presence of metal fragments	Examine product rejected by electronic metal detector to determine cause of kick-out	When product is rejected	Production employee	If metal is found in product, segregate product, inspect back to the last good check, rework or discard product depending on metal type and prevalence. Identify source of the metal found and fix damaged equipment if relevant		

A3-17

Allergen Preventive Control

Ingredient Allergen Identification

Raw Material Name	Supplier	Allergens in Ingredient Formulation								Allergens in Precautionary Labeling
		Egg	Milk	Soy	Wheat	Tree Nut (market name)	Peanut	Fish (market name)	Shellfish (market name)	
Whole, liquid pasteurized egg	Your Egg Co.	X								None
Grade A pasteurized milk	A Local Dairy		X							None
Pan release oil, ABC Brand	My distributor			X						None
Salt, XYZ Brand	My distributor									None
Buttermilk biscuit	Flaky Co.		X		X					None
Pasteurized process cheese	Cheesy Co.		X							None

NOTE:

The above format is an alternative for an allergen specific hazard analysis. If you choose to use a form like this, then there is no need to duplicate allergen considerations in your hazard analysis chart. Duplication of information in multiple forms can create extra work and may lead to inconsistencies.

Some organizations may even choose to do an ingredient hazard analysis that considers not only allergens, but also other hazards. This may be a useful option for you.

How to Use the Chart

List all ingredients received in the facility. Identify allergens contained in each ingredient by reviewing ingredient labels or contacting the manufacturer. Any allergens listed in "May contain" or other precautionary labeling on ingredients should be listed in the last column and reviewed to determine if allergen labeling is needed on the finished product.

Allergen Control	Hazard(s)	Criterion	Monitoring				Corrective Action	Verification	Records
			What	How	Frequency	Who			
Receiving packaging (labeled carton)	Undeclared allergens – egg, milk, soy (wheat in biscuit only)	All finished product labels must declare the allergens present in the formula per listing	Ingredient listing and allergen declaration matches product	Visual check of carton label to match product formula	Before release to production	Label coordinator	If label is incorrect, reject labels and return to supplier or destroy. Identify root cause and conduct training as needed to prevent recurrence	Review of Label verification, Corrective Action and Verification records within 7 working days	Allergen Label Verification listing; Allergen Label Verification log; Corrective Action records; Verification records
Fill, weigh, label	Undeclared allergens – egg, milk, soy (wheat in biscuit only)	All finished product must have correct labeled carton	Label number matches product	Visual check of carton label to match product number	Beginning and end of run and when label stock is changed	Fill line operator	If label is incorrect, segregate product, inspect back to the last good check, relabel product; identify root cause and conduct training as needed to prevent recurrence	Review of Label Check, Corrective Action and Verification records within 7 working days	Allergen Label Verification listing Allergen Label Check Log; Corrective Action records; Verification records

© 2016 IIT IFSH

A3-19

Allergen Label Declaration

Allergen Verification Listing

Product	Allergen Statement	Label Number
Plain Omelet	Contains: Egg, milk, and soy	P 082015
Cheese Omelet	Contains: Egg, milk, and soy	C 082015
Cheese Omelet Biscuit	Contains: Wheat, egg, milk and soy	B 082015

Allergen Scheduling and Cleaning Implications

Production Line Allergen Assessment

Product Name	Production Line	Intentional Allergens							
		Egg	Milk	Soy	Wheat	Tree Nut (market name)	Peanut	Fish (market name)	Shellfish (market name)
Plain Omelet	1	X	X	X					
Cheese Omelet	1	X	X	X					
Cheese Omelet Biscuit	1	X	X	X	X Unique allergen				

Scheduling Implications:
Standard practice is to run the Plain and/or Cheese Omelet in the beginning of the shift and the Cheese Omelet Biscuit at the end of the shift to reduce the potential for allergen cross-contact. [*Consider adding when alternate production practices may be permitted, including approval for this, if you wish.*]

Allergen Cleaning Implications: (Required)
A full allergen clean is **required** AFTER production of Cheese Omelet Biscuit because it contains a unique allergen – wheat.

How to Use This Form
Complete for each production line. Identify each allergen contained in each product produced on the line. Identify any allergens unique to a specific product, then indicate scheduling information (i.e., run unique allergens last) and allergen cleaning information (i.e., full allergen clean before running cheese or plain omelets after a biscuit run.

A3-20

Sanitation Preventive Control

Objective: To address 1) cleanliness of food contact surfaces and 2) prevention of allergen cross-contact and cross-contamination (recontamination)

Assemble/Wrap Table Sanitation

Purpose: Cleaning and sanitizing of the assembly and wrapping table is important to remove potential allergens and reduce microbial cross-contamination or recontamination with environmental pathogens that may impact product safety.

Frequency:

Cleaning: At lunch break, after Cheese Omelet Biscuit production, at the end of daily production.

Sanitizing: Before operations begin, at lunch break, after Cheese Omelet Biscuit production, and at the end of daily production.

Who: Sanitation team member

Procedure:

Note: Blue cleaning tools are to be used ONLY for cleaning after a cheese biscuit run to reduce the potential for unintentional allergen transfer.

Cleaning
1. Remove unused packaging material to an area at the end of the shift to prevent it from getting wet. Cover it during the lunch clean up.
2. Remove gross soil with a squeegee.
3. Wipe table surface with a clean cloth dipped in ABC cleaning solution (Y oz. per gallon).
4. Rinse table with clean water. Detergent remaining on the surface can inactivate the sanitizer.

Sanitizing
1. Spray table surface with 200 ppm quaternary ammonium compounds solution, ensuring that entire surface is covered.
2. Allow table to air dry, about 5 minutes. Contact time required per label – 1 minute.

Monitoring (at frequency indicated above):

Inspect table for residual soil and cleanliness. Record on Daily Sanitation sheet.
Use test strip to measure the quat concentration BEFORE application. Record on Daily Sanitation sheet

Corrections:

If residual soil is observed on the table, reclean and sanitize.
If quat is not at the proper concentration, make a new solution.

Records: Daily Sanitation Sheet

Verification: Supervisor reviews and signs Daily Sanitation Sheet within 7 working days

A3-21

Assemble/Wrap Environmental Sanitation

Purpose: Cleaning and sanitizing of the floor and the table support (legs) in the Assemble, Wrap area is important to prevent establishment of environmental pathogens.

Frequency: Daily, after production

Who: Sanitation team member

Procedure:

Cleaning and sanitizing the table support structure
Cleaning is done in conjunction with cleaning of the table, following the same procedure, including table legs, and edges at the end of the day.

Cleaning floors
NOTE: Separate tools are used for floors because of the potential for higher levels of contamination.
1. Remove gross soil with a squeegee.
2. Mop floor using a washable mop head, using a clean mop each day
3. Rinse floor with clean water. Detergent remaining on the floor can inactivate the sanitizer.

Sanitizing
1. Spray floors with a 400-600 ppm quat sanitizer. Spray may also contact non-food contact table legs.
2. Allow floor to air dry overnight.

Monitoring (at each cleaning time):

1. Inspect floor and surrounding area for residual soil and cleanliness. Record on Daily Sanitation sheet.
2. Use test strip to measure the quat concentration BEFORE application. Record on Daily Sanitation sheet

Corrections:

1. If residual soil is observed, reclean and sanitize.
2. If quat is not at the proper concentration, make a new solution.

Records: Daily Sanitation Sheet, Daily Hygienic Zoning Record, Environmental Monitoring Sampling record and lab results

Verification: Environmental monitoring (frequency per procedure) and supervisor records review within 7 working days

Assemble/Wrap Hygienic Zoning

Purpose: Hygienic zoning in the assembly and wrapping table area is important to minimize the potential of re-contamination with environmental pathogens.

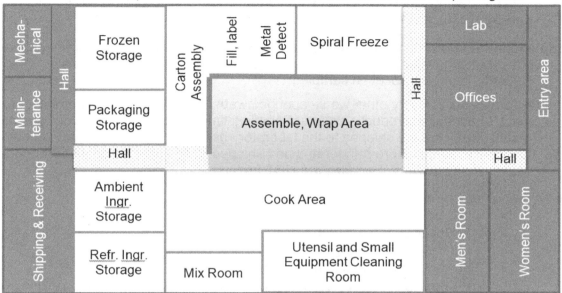

● Non-manufacturing, ⦂Transition, ○Basic GMP,◐ Primary pathogen control area – CONTROLLED ACCESS

Frequency: During production

Who: Employees and other individuals entering the Assemble, Wrap area

Procedure: Employees entering the Assemble Wrap area must (in the order listed):
1. Take a clean, blue smock from the rack outside the production area and put it on. Smocks must cover outer clothing that would be above the assembly table surface.
2. Take the correct size clean rubber boots from the shelves along the wall outside the Assembly Wrap area and put them on over shoes.
3. Take a blue hairnet from the box by the entry and put it on. Ensure that all loose hair is captured. Men with facial hair should also apply beard nets.
4. Wash hands just before entering the Assembly Wrap area following the procedures posted by the sink. Apply a clean pair of gloves.
5. When exiting the room deposit smocks and boots in the receptacles provided. DO NOT return them to the clean smock and shoe cover receptacle.

Maintenance workers and visitors must use foot covers and clean smocks when entering this area. Traffic in this area is minimized during production.

Monitoring: The sanitation supervisor visually observes the presence of the properly smocked employees, before start up and after lunch break, and every 2 hours.

Corrections: Employee is instructed to gown properly.

Records: Daily Hygienic Zoning Record, Environmental Monitoring Sampling Record and lab results

Verification: Environmental monitoring and records review within 7 working days

A3-23

Environmental Monitoring for Sanitation Preventive Control Verification

Purpose: Environmental monitoring is conducted to verify the effectiveness of sanitation and hygienic zoning procedures in the Assemble, Wrap area to control environmental pathogens such as *L. monocytogenes.*

Sample identification: Based on observation when sampling, "worst case" areas are sampled; e.g., standing water or product residue, around table legs, crevasses major traffic areas. Record the specific location sampled.

Sampling procedure: Every other week, sponge swabs are collected during production, at least 3 hours after production starts. Sampling time is not uniform to avoid bias of results. Samples are shipped to the laboratory using the sampling kit provided by the laboratory. Samples are refrigerated and shipped in an insulated cooler with a gel pack with next day delivery. Samples are NOT frozen.

The following number of samples collected each time.
- 4 in Assemble, Wrap area
- 2 in Hall between Assemble, Wrap and Cooking
- 1 at employee gowning area
- 3 other samples based on observed conditions

Laboratory: *Wee Beasties Laboratory* (987 Critter Drive, Yourtown, USA) conducts the analysis using FDA BAM procedures. Analysis is started within 48 hours of sampling.

Test conducted: For routine samples, the contract lab composites sponges from the same area following XYZ[1] recommended procedures to run as one test for *Listeria* species. *Investigation samples must be run individually.* The test result sheet identifies the specific method number used.

Interpretation of results:

Acton for a negative result – Continue routine operations

Corrective action for a positive result:

1. If a composite is positive, the positive areas are re-sampled within a day of notification and prior to implementing intensive sanitation procedures. Additional samples (number depends on size of area) are taken in other potential problem areas in an attempt to identify a site of contamination. All samples are run individually, without compositing.
2. Intensive sanitation procedures are implemented after sampling is complete.
3. Production can continue after sanitation is complete and product can be shipped.
4. If all re-samples are negative, resume the normal sampling frequency.
5. If one or more re-samples are positive, perform corrective action investigation to resolve the issue. Implement a hold and finished product testing procedure per the Product Testing for Verification corrective action protocol.

---

[1] XYZ would be a scientifically valid method, such as AOAC, ISO, FDA etc.

Supply-chain Preventive Controls Program

Approved Suppliers for Ingredients Requiring a Supply-chain-applied Control

Ingredient (requiring supply-chain-applied control)	Approved Supplier	Hazard(s) requiring supply-chain-applied control	Date of Approval	Verification method	Verification records
Pasteurized process cheese	Cheesy Co., Cowtown, USA	Vegetative and sporeforming pathogens such as *Salmonella*, pathogenic *E. coli*, *L. monocytogenes* and *C. botulinum*	10/08/2010	Copy of 3rd party audit by a qualified auditor obtained from supplier	Audit report kept in Supplier Verification file

Receiving Procedure for Ingredients Requiring a Supply-chain-applied Control

Purpose: Ensure that all ingredients requiring a supply-chain-applied preventive control are received from approved suppliers with appropriate preventive controls in place.

Frequency: Each delivery

Who: Receiving clerk

Procedure:

1. Verify that each load of Pasteurized Process Cheese was produced by Cheesy Co. located in Cowtown, USA by checking the bill of lading and manufacturer name on the cases received.
2. Document on receiving sheet

Corrections: If product is not from the approved supplier:

1. Receiving clerk places product on hold, notifies QA
2. QA reviews status and
   - Rejects load, or
   - Attaches to the receiving record documentation of verification activity applied for use of cheese from temporary supplier, allowing release for use
   - Marks the receiving record and sample "Food for research or evaluation use" and attaches a sticker stating "Food for research or evaluation use" and retains the shipping document (Bill of Lading) stating that the food is for research or evaluation purposes and cannot be sold or distributed to the public.

Records: Receiving Sheet, Food for Research or Evaluation Use sticker, Bill of Lading

Verification: Receiving records review within 7 working days

Determination of Verification Procedures

Ingredient: Pasteurized Process Cheese

Hazards requiring a supply-chain-applied control: Hazard analysis determined that vegetative pathogens, such as *Salmonella,* pathogenic *E. coli,* and *L. monocytogenes* and the sporeforming pathogen *C. botulinum* are hazards requiring supply-chain-applied controls in the production of pasteurized process cheese. We do not have a kill step for cheese.

Preventive controls applied by the supplier: The pasteurization process must kill the vegetative pathogens when the cheese is made. Cheese formulation must prevent growth of *C. botulinum.*

Conclusion: A 3rd party supplier audit by a qualified auditor is used to verify control of the identified hazards by the approved supplier Cheesy Company, located in Cowtown, USA.

Verification procedures: A copy of a 3rd party audit of their Cowtown location is requested from Cheesy Company on an annual basis and kept on file. The audit date, auditor qualifications, audit procedures and audit results are reviewed. If any requirements are deficient (including auditor qualifications) and follow up discussion with the Cheesy Company's Quality Manager in Cowtown takes place, as necessary, to determine what, if any, verification activities are needed for any deficiencies requiring corrective actions mentioned in the report.

Records: Copy of the audit report and, where necessary, verification of corrective actions taken by the supplier are maintained on file by the Food Safety Team Leader.

A3-26

Recall Plan

The Recall Plan is maintained by F.S. Leader, with a copy in the Plant Manager's Office.

Implementation Records

Implementation records and forms used for Preventive Controls include the following:

- Monitoring records for preventive controls
  - Cook Log
  - Metal Detection Log
  - Allergen Label Check Log
  - Allergen Run Order Log
  - Daily Sanitation Log

- Corrective actions records
- Verification records
- Supply-chain program records
- Training records for the qualified individuals (in personnel files)
- Food Safety Plan Reanalysis Report

Applicable records and examples of forms follow.

Monitoring Records Forms

Cook Log

Hazard: Vegetative pathogens such as *Salmonella*

Parameters, values or critical limits: Omelet surface temperature is ≥158°F (70°C) instantaneous before transfer to assembly table.

Who, How, Frequency: QA Technician, or designee, checks an omelet surface temperature each cook station 4 times/shift (every 2-3 hr) using an infrared thermometer.

Corrective Action: Hold product back to the last good check and evaluate - rework, discard, or release. Determine root cause – retrain or correct as appropriate.

Date:

Time	Cook Station	Cook name	Temperature (°F)	QA Tech (initials)
Verification Reviewer Signature:			**Date of Review:**	

A3-28

Metal Detection Log

Hazard: Metal inclusion
Parameters, values or critical limits:
1) All of the product passes through an operating metal detector and
2) No metal fragments that would cause injury or choking are in the product passing through the metal detector

Procedure: Pass X^2 mm ferrous and Y mm non-ferrous and stainless standard wands through detector at start-up, middle, end of shift and when any product change occurs to assure equipment is functioning.

Corrective action:
1) If the product is processed without metal detection, hold it for metal detection. Correct operating procedures to ensure that the product is not processed without metal detection
2) If metal is found in product, segregate product, inspect back to the last good check, rework or discard product depending on metal type and prevalence. Identify source of the metal found and fix damaged equipment if relevant

Date: _____

Time	Product	Lot Number	Detector present and on (Yes/No)	Detector rejects ferrous, non-ferrous, and stainless standards (Yes/No)	Line Operator (Initials)
Verification Reviewer Signature:				**Date of Review:**	

---

^{2} X and Y values are determined during equipment calibration.

Allergen Label Check Log

Hazard: Undeclared allergens

Parameters: All finished product labels must declare the allergens present in the formula as follows:
Plain Omelet: Egg, milk, soy
Cheese Omelet: Egg, milk, soy
Cheese Biscuit Omelet: Wheat, egg, milk, soy

Corrective Action: If label is incorrect, segregate product, inspect back to the last good check, relabel product; identify root cause and conduct training as needed to prevent recurrence

Date	Time	Product	Lot Number	Proper Label Applied (Yes/No)	Line Operator (Initials)
Verification Reviewer Signature:				Date of Review:	

Allergen Run Order Record

Hazard: Allergen cross-contact from other products handled at this step; e.g., Cheese Omelet Biscuit.

Parameter: Routinely, run the Plain and/or Cheese Omelet in the beginning of the shift and the Cheese Omelet Biscuit at the end of the shift to reduce the potential for allergen cross-contact. If necessary, Cheese Omelet Biscuit can be run before the Plain or Cheese Omelet **IF a full allergen clean** is performed AFTER production of Cheese Omelet Biscuit because it contains a unique allergen – wheat.

Corrective Action: If full allergen clean was not performed after running Omelet Biscuit, segregate product, hold all product produced after the Omelet Biscuit up to the next full allergen clean; evaluate product and determine appropriate disposition; identify root cause and conduct training as needed to prevent recurrence

Product Name	Date	Start Time	End Time	Allergen Clean After Run (Yes/No)	Initials for allergen clean
Verification Signature				**Date:**	

A3-31

Daily Sanitation Control Record – Omelet Line

Date: _____

Sanitation Area and Goal	Pre-Op Time:	Start Time:	Lunch Break Time:	Post-Op Time:	Comments and Corrections	Operator Initials

Condition & Cleanliness of Food Contact Surfaces
• Equipment cleaned and sanitized (S/U)*
• Sanitizer type and strength: _Quaternary ammonium compound, 200 ppm_
                   Omelet line (ppm)+
            Dish room dip tank (ppm)+						

Prevention of Allergen Cross-Contact • Cleaning after Cheese Omelet Biscuit (S/U/NA)&						

Condition & Cleanliness of Non-food Contact Surfaces
• Floors and wall splash zones cleaned and sanitized (S/U)
• Sanitizer Strength:
  Sanitizer Type: _Quaternary ammonium compound_
  Strength: _400-600 ppm_
       Floors and wall splash zones (ppm)+						

* S = Satisfactory, U = Unsatisfactory
+ Enter ppm measured per test strip
& NA = not applicable because Cheese Omelet Biscuit run after other products

Verification signature:	Date:

Corrective Action Records

Corrective action records are maintained by the Food Safety Team Leader. An example of the Corrective Action Form follows.

Corrective Action Form	
Date of Record:	Code or Lot Number:
Date and Time of Deviation:	
Description of Deviation:	
Actions Taken to Restore Order to the Process:	
Person (name and signature) of Person Taking Action:	
Amount of Product Involved in Deviation:	
Evaluation of Product Involved with Deviation:	
Final Disposition of Product:	
Reviewed by (Name and Signature):	Date of Review:

Verification Records

Verification records are maintained by the Food Safety Team Leader. Examples of verification forms are included as indicated below:

Verification Record	Location
Omelet cook step validation study	Study included in process control section of this plan
Verification of monitoring and corrective action	Documented on the relevant forms, examples of which are in the previous sections
Calibration of monitoring and verification instruments • Daily Thermometer Accuracy Check • Annual Thermometer Calibration Log	Example forms follow
Product Testing	Procedure included with Cook process control record. Results forms provided by testing lab
Environmental Monitoring	Procedure included with Sanitation Preventive Controls. Results forms provided by testing lab
Annual Food Safety Plan Reanalysis Report Form	Example form follows
Supply-chain Program	Procedures includes with Supply-chain Preventive Controls in the Food Safety Plan. Receiving Log maintained in receiving files. Bill of Lading maintained for research product received. Audit results are maintained in by the Food Safety Team Leader
Training	Maintained in personnel files

Daily Thermometer Accuracy Check

Verification: Check each thermometer daily for accuracy. Temperature must be ±2°F (1°C) from standard.

Date of Calibration	Instrument Number	Boiling Water Temp (212±2°F)*	Ice Bath Temp (32±2°F)	Temperature within Specification (Yes/No)	Line Operator (Initials)
Verification Reviewer Signature:				Date of Review:	

* Temperature adjustments may be needed for different altitudes

Annual Thermometer Calibration Log

Verification: Send each thermometer to Accurate Instrument Checker Lab for calibration twice a year. Temperature must be ±2°F (1°C) from standard. Keep records of results on file.

Date of Calibration	Instrument Number	Method of Calibration	Calibration Results	Temperature within Specification (Yes/No)	Line Operator (Initials)
Verification Reviewer Signature:				Date of Review:	

A3-36

Receiving Log

Verification: Pasteurized process cheese must be received from Cheesy Co., Cowtown, USA

> This teaching example is not realistic for many companies because there is only one ingredient requiring a supply-chain-applied control. Most companies have receiving procedures and many require approved suppliers for both quality and safety considerations. Your standard receiving records may be suitable as the record verifying that raw materials and other ingredients requiring a supply-chain-applied control come from an approved supplier if it is set up to do so. A check list, a bar code scan, a computer spread sheet and other methods could be used to verify receipt from approved supplier locations. Use a format that works for your organization, keeping in mind that the record must be created when the activity occurs and that the activity must be verified by or under the supervision of a preventive controls qualified individual.

Supplier Audit Verification

Purpose: Review of 3rd party audit for suppliers of supply-chain-applied control		
Supplier Name, location		
Date of Review		
Date audit conducted		
Audit procedures in the report (yes/no and comments)		
Audit performed by (e.g., certification body name)		
General audit conclusion		
Required corrective action(s) noted		
Supplier response to corrective action		
Trends noted from previous reports		
Conclusions of the review		
Reviewed by:		Date:

A3-37

Food Safety Plan Reanalysis Report

Checklist	Date reviewed and initials of reviewer	Update needed Yes/No	Date Updated Completed:	Person Completing the Update (initial or sign)
List of Food Safety Team				
List of products and processes in place at facility				
Product flow diagrams				
Hazard Analysis				
Sanitation Preventive Controls				
Food Allergen Preventive Controls				
Process Preventive Controls				
Supply-chain Preventive Control Program				
Recall Plan				

(Add rows as needed if different plans are used for different products)

A3-38

Appendix 4: Foodborne Pathogen Supplementary Information

Microbial growth can be limited when conditions are outside of an organism's growth parameters, and certain time-temperature combinations can inactivate foodborne pathogens in foods. This appendix presents several tables with information on parameters that can be used to inhibit growth or inactivate certain microorganisms.

- Table A4-1 summarizes conditions that limit or prevent foodborne pathogen growth or toxin formation, including temperature, pH, water activity and maximum percent of water phase salt.

- Table A4-2 provides information on time-temperature combinations that, under ordinary circumstances, will prevent growth of foodborne bacterial pathogens. This includes information on maximum cumulative time and internal temperature combinations for exposure of foods that, under ordinary circumstances, will be safe for the bacterial pathogens that are of greatest concern. The exposure times are derived from published scientific information. Because bacterial growth is logarithmic, linear interpolation using the time and temperature guidance may not be appropriate. Furthermore, the food matrix effects bacterial growth (e.g., presence of competing microorganisms, available nutrients, growth restrictive agents). Consideration of such attributes is needed when using the information in Tables A4-2.

- Table A4-3 provides information on time-temperature combinations for destruction of *L. monocytogenes.* Lethal rate, as used in this table, is the relative lethality of 1 minute at the reference internal product temperature of 158°F (70°C) (i.e., z=13.5°F (7.5°C)). For example, 1 minute at 145°F (63°C) is 0.117 times as lethal as 1 minute at 158°F (70°C). The times provided are the length of time at the designated internal product temperature necessary to deliver a six logarithm (6D) process for *L. monocytogenes.* The length of time at a particular internal product temperature needed to accomplish a six logarithm reduction in the number of *L. monocytogenes* (6D) is, in part, dependent upon the food in which it is being heated. The values in the table are generally conservative and apply to all foods. You may be able to establish a shorter process time for your food by conducting scientific thermal death time studies. Additionally, lower degrees of destruction may be acceptable in your food if supported by a scientific study of the normal initial levels in the food. It is also possible that higher levels of destruction may be necessary in some foods, if especially high initial levels are anticipated.

- Table A4-4 lists properties of common bacterial foodborne pathogens. Information such as pathogenicity, primary sources, types of foods involved in transmission, contributing factors, atmosphere required for growth, whether the organism is a sporeformer, and other properties are included.

The tables are followed by an alphabetical listing of the organisms (bacteria, viruses and parasites) identified by Painter et al. (2013) as being relevant for transmission through food. More information on foodborne pathogens is available in FDA's *Bad Bug Book* (see references).

Table A4-1 Limiting conditions for pathogen growth

Organism	Temperature °F (°C)			pH			Water Activity (aw)			Max. % water phase salt
	Minimum	Optimum	Maximum	Minimum	Optimum	Maximum	Minimum	Optimum	Maximum	
Bacillus cereus	39 (4)	86-104 (30-40)	131 (55)	4.3	6.0-7.0	9.3	0.92	-	-	10
Campylobacter	86 (32)	108-109 (42-43)	113 (45)	4.9	6.5-7.5	9.5	>0.987	0.997	-	1.7
Clostridium botulinum • Proteolytic ABF	50 (10)	95-104 (35-40)	-118 (48)	4.6	-	9	0.935	-	-	10
• Non-proteolytic BEF	38 (3.3)	82-86 (28-30)	113 (45)	5.0	-	9	0.970	-	-	5
Clostridium perfringens	50 (10)	109-117 (43-47)	126 (50)	5	7.2	9.0	0.93	0.95-0.96	>0.99	7
Enterohemorrhagic *Escherichia coli* (EHEC)	44 (6.5)	95-104 (35-40)	121 (49.4)	4	6-7	10	0.95	0.995	-	6.5
L. monocytogenes	31 (-0.4)	99 (37)	113 (45)	4.4	7.0	9.4	0.92	-	-	10
Salmonella	41 (5.2)	95-109 (35-43)	115 (46.2)	3.7	7-7.5	9.5	0.94	0.99	>0.99	8
Shigella	43 (6.1)	-	117 (47.1)	4.8	-	9.3	0.96	-	-	5.2
Staph. aureus • growth (anaerobic)	45 (7)	99 (37)	122 (50)	4	6-7	10	0.83 (0.90)	0.98	>0.99	20
• toxin (anaerobic)	50 (10)	104-113 (40-45)	118 (48)	4	7-8	9.8	0.85	0.98	>0.99	10
Streptococcus group A	50 (10)	99 (37)	<113 (<45)	4.8-5.3	7	>9.3	-	-	-	6.5
Vibrio spp.	41(5)	99 (37)	114 (45.3)	4.8	7.6-8.6	11	0.94	0.91-0.99	0.998	10
Yersinia enterocolitica	30 (-1.3)	77-99 (25-37)	108 (42)	4.2	7.2	10	0.945	-	-	7

From FDA 2011. *Fish and Fishery Products Hazards and Controls Guidance.* 4th Edition and International Commission on Microbiological Specifications for Foods. 1996. *Microorganisms in Foods 5: Microbiological Specifications of Food Pathogens.* Blackie Academic and Professional, New York.

Table A4-2. Cumulative time and temperature guidance for controlling pathogen growth and toxin formation in foods[1]

Potentially Hazardous Condition	Product Temperature	Maximum Cumulative Exposure Time
Bacillus cereus growth and toxin formation	39.2-43°F (4-6°C)	5 days
	44-59°F (7-15°C)	1 day
	60-70°F (16-21°C)	6 hours
	Above 70°F (21°C)	3 hours
Campylobacter jejuni growth	86-93°F (30-34°C)	48 hours
	Above 93°F (34°C)	12 hours
Clostridium botulinum germination, growth and toxin formation Type A and proteolytic Types B and F	50-70°F (10-21°C)	11 hours
	Above 70°F (21°C)	2 hours
- Type E and non-proteolytic Types B and F	37.9-41°F (3.3-5°C)	7 days
	42-50°F (6-10°C)	2 days
	51-70°F (11-21°C)	11 hours
	Above 70°F (21°C)	6 hours
Clostridium perfringens growth	50-54°F (10-12°C)	21 days
	55-57°F (13-14°C)	1 day
	58-70°F (15-21°C)	6 hours[2]
	Above 70°F (21°C)	2 hours
Escherichia coli pathogenic strains growth	43.7-50°F (6.6-10°C)	2 days
	51-70°F (11-21°C)	5 hours
	Above 70°F (21°C)	2 hours
Listeria monocytogenes growth	31.3-41°F (-0.4-5°C)	7 days
	42-50°F (6-10°C)	1 days
	51-70°F (11-21°C)	7 hours
	71-86°F (22-30°C)	3 hours
	Above 86°F (30°C)	1 hour
Salmonella species growth	41.4-50°F (5.2-10°C)	2 days
	51-70°F (11-21°C)	5 hours
	Above 70°F (21°C)	2 hours
Shigella species growth	43-50°F (6.1-10°C)	2 days
	51-70°F (11-21°C)	5 hours
	Above 70°F (21°C)	2 hours
Staphylococcus aureus growth and toxin formation	50°F (10°C)	14 days
	51-70°F (11-21°C)	12 hours[2]
	Above 70°F (21°C)	3 hours
Vibrio species growth	≤50°F (10°C)	21 days
	51-70°F (11-21°C)	6 hours
	71-80°F (22-27°C)	2 hours
	Above 80°F (27°C)	1 hour[3]
Yersinea enterocolitica growth	29.7-50°F (-1.3-10°C)	1 days
	51-70°F (11-21°C)	6 hours
	Above 70°F (27°C)	2.5 hours

[1] Adapted from FDA 2011. *Fish and Fishery Products Hazards and Controls Guidance.* 4th Edition and assumes high water activity food with pH near neutrality
[2] Additional data needed
[3] Applies to cooked, ready-to-eat foods only

Table A4-3 Inactivation of *Listeria monocytogenes*

Internal Product Temperature (°F)	Internal Product Temperature (°C)	Lethal Rate	Time for 6D Process (Minutes)
145	63	0.117	17.0
147	64	0.158	12.7
149	65	0.215	9.3
151	66	0.293	6.8
153	67	0.398	5.0
154	68	0.541	3.7
156	69	0.736	2.7
158	70	1.000	2.0
160	71	1.359	1.5
162	72	1.848	1.0
163	73	2.512	0.8
165	74	3.415	0.6
167	75	4.642	0.4
169	76	6.310	0.3
171	77	8.577	0.2
172	78	11.659	0.2
174	79	15.849	0.1
176	80	21.544	0.09
178	81	29.286	0.07
180	82	39.810	0.05
182	83	54.116	0.03
183	84	73.564	0.03
185	85	100.000	0.02

Note: z = 13.5°F (7.5°C)

From FDA 2011. *Fish and Fishery Products Hazards and Controls Guidance.* 4th Edition and assumes high water activity food with pH near neutrality

Table A4-4. Properties of common foodborne bacterial pathogens

Organism	Pathogenicity	Primary Sources	Transmitted by	Contributing Factors	Atmosphere	Spore/ non-spore	Other
Bacillus cereus	Produces two toxins – diarrheal and emetic (vomiting)	Soil	Rice, starchy foods, meats, vegetables, milk products, sauces	Temperature abuse	Facultative – grows with or without oxygen	Sporeformer	Extensive growth required for illness. Emetic toxin is heat stable
Brucella spp.	Infection causes fever, sweating, weakness, muscle aches, headache	Unpasteurized milk and undercooked meat	Uncooked/ unpasteurized milk and meat	Consumption of infected unpasteurized milk products	Aerobic	Non-sporeformer	Survives but proliferates poorly outside of the animal host
Campylobacter spp.	Infection causes diarrhea and potential nerve damage	Raw poultry, raw milk products, contaminated water	Raw poultry, raw milk products, contaminated water	Cross contamination and undercooking	3-5% oxygen optimum	Non-sporeformer	-
Clostridium botulinum	Toxin in food causes blurred or double vision, paralysis of respiratory muscles, death	Wide spread	Food with anaerobic environment	Temperature abuse	Anaerobic – requires absence of oxygen	Sporeformer	Mesophilic and psychotropic strains
Clostridium perfringens	Toxin causes diarrhea and abdominal pain	Soil and intestinal tract of healthy people and animals	Meats, stews or gravy, especially those containing spices	Inadequate hot holding and reheating	Anaerobic	Sporeformer	-
Shiga-toxin Producing *Escherichia coli* (STEC)	Infection causes bloody diarrhea and sometimes kidney failure and death	Intestinal tract of ruminant animals (e.g, cows, sheep)	Raw and undercooked beef, leafy greens, sprouts, and unpasteurized milk and juices	Poor GAP, inadequate heating, and person-to-person	Facultative - grows with or without oxygen	Non-sporeformer	-
Listeria monocytogenes	Infection causes severe illness in susceptible people – mortality 15-30%	Occurs widely in agriculture (soil, plants and water)	Refrigerated RTE foods that support growth	Environmental pathogen spread by environmental contamination, equipment, people, incoming raw ingredients	Facultative	Non-sporeformer	-

Table A4-4. Properties of common foodborne bacterial pathogens *(continued)*

Organism	Pathogenicity	Primary Sources	Transmitted by	Contributing Factors	Atmosphere	Spore/ non-spore	Other
Mycobacterium bovis	Infection causes respiratory symptoms and tuberculosis	Cattle and raw milk	Raw milk products	Lack of milk pasteurization and exposure to aerosols from infected animals	Grows very slowly and under reduced oxygen	Non-sporeformer	-
Salmonella spp.	Infection causes nausea, vomiting, diarrhea, fever, headache	Intestinal tract of people and animals	Meat, poultry, eggs, raw milk and many other foods (nuts, spices, produce, chocolate, flour)	Cross-contamination, undercooked food, poor agricultural practices, environmental contamination	Facultative	Non-sporeformer	-
Shigella spp.	Infection causes diarrhea, which may be watery to bloody. The infection is called dysentery	Human intestinal tract	Fecal contamination from contaminated water or infected food workers	-	Facultative	Non-sporeformer	-
Staphylococcus aureus	Produces heat stable toxins after extensive growth	Boils, nasal passages and skin	Recontaminated cooked foods, and foods with high salt or high sugar	Recontamination and temperature abuse	Facultative	Non-sporeformer	Poor competitor
Streptococcus spp. group A	Infection causes sore throat, tonsillitis and fever	Infected sites of humans and animals, raw milk	Infected workers handling food and consumption of raw milk or meat products	-	Facultative	Non-sporeformer	-
Vibrio spp.	Infection symptoms vary depending on strain, ranging from diarrhea to high fever	Salt water environment and seafood	Marine seafood products	-	Facultative	Non-sporeformer	Requires salt to reproduce
Yersinia enterocolitica	Infection causes abdominal pain, fever and diarrhea. May mimic appendicitis.	Raw pork, raw milk	Cross contamination between raw pork products and RTE foods	-	Facultative	Non-sporeformer	-

Descriptions of Common Foodborne Pathogens

Bacillus cereus causes either vomiting with short onset (30 minutes to 6 hours), or diarrhea and cramps in 6-15 hours. Different strains produce two different toxins – the one responsible for short-onset vomiting is heat resistant. The toxin that causes diarrhea is produced in the intestines. Symptoms mimic those of either *S. aureus* (vomiting type) or *C. perfringens* (diarrheal type). Many foods are associated with the diarrheal type of illness, while rice and other grains and starchy foods are associated with the vomiting type. Transmission of illness is caused by consumption of food containing preformed toxin for the vomiting type of illness, or high levels of vegetative cells produced during growth under temperature abuse for the diarrheal disease. *B. cereus* spores are resistant to normal cooking processes and the vegetative cells grow with or without oxygen ("facultative"). Refrigeration and freezing inhibit *B. cereus* growth but do not kill the bacteria.

Brucella spp. rarely cause illness in the United States because of pasteurized milk. It may be an issue with raw milk products if stringent controls are not in place.

Campylobacter causes diarrhea 2-7 days after eating contaminated food and may cause nerve damage 1-6 weeks after infection. The live bacteria invade the cells lining the intestine. The primary source is fecal contamination of raw poultry and meat and transmission is associated with cross contamination from raw meat or poultry drippings or consumption of undercooked animal products. *Campylobacter* is sensitive to heat and drying, grows in reduced oxygen environments, grows best above body temperature, and survives but does not grow during refrigeration and freezing.

Clostridium botulinum produces several types of toxins. Types A, B, E and F toxins are concerns in food and cause the severe disease called botulism. Blurred or double vision, dry mouth, difficulty swallowing, paralysis of respiratory muscles, vomiting and diarrhea may be present. Symptoms develop 18-36 hours (sometimes days) after eating contaminated food and death can occur unless treatment is received. Recovery may be slow (months, rarely years). *C. botulinum* spores may be present in soil and the intestinal tract of animals and are wide spread in nature. The spores are heat resistant and, under the right conditions in the absence of oxygen, can come out of dormancy and produce toxin.

Some *C. botulinum* strains (type E and some strains of B and F) can grow at refrigeration temperatures, but most cannot. The spores of strains that grow under refrigeration are not as heat resistant as other spores. The toxin is destroyed by high heat (boiling for 5 min); however, the disease is so severe that heating to destroy toxin is not an appropriate control method. *C. botulinum* can grow in many foods under strict anaerobic (low oxygen) conditions. A pH $\leq$4.6 prevents toxin production by *C. botulinum,* and toxin production for those strains that grow under refrigeration is inhibited at pH<5.0. Sodium nitrite used in cured foods slows toxin production.

Clostridium perfringens causes diarrhea and abdominal pain 6 -24 (typically 8-12) hours after eating food contaminated with large numbers of vegetative cells (>10^6/g), which requires growth in the food. When these viable cells are consumed, they form spores and release toxin in the intestines. *C. perfringens* is found in soil and the intestinal tract of healthy people and animals. Spores survive normal cooking processes, including boiling. Spices are a potential source for *C. perfringens* as the spores can persist on spices for long periods of time. Inadequate hot holding or cooling of cooked food, particularly meats, pot pies, stew or gravies, allows bacteria to multiply because the spores can survive the cooking process. *C. perfringens* has one of the most rapid growth rates for foodborne pathogens, and can double in less than 10 minutes at optimum temperature. This pathogen grows best without oxygen.

Cryptosporidium parvum is a rarely reported parasite but is notable for its resistance to chemical agents, including standard levels of chlorine. It is sensitive to drying and ultraviolet light. *Cryptosporidium* causes diarrhea, and infection can be fatal for immunocompromised people. Foodborne outbreaks have involved apple cider and unpasteurized milk, as well as contaminated water.

Cyclospora cayetanensis is a rarely reported parasite that causes prolonged diarrhea. Death rarely occurs. Outbreaks are frequently associated with fruits (berries), leafy green and other salads, and herbs like basil.

Escherichia coli is a bacterium that is normally present in the intestinal tract of humans and other animals and most strains of *E. coli* are not associated with disease. However, certain strains, like *E. coli* O157:H7, produce a toxin called Shiga-toxin in human intestines, causing severe disease. These disease-causing strains are called enterohemorrhagic, Shiga-toxin producing *E. coli* or STECs. They cause diarrhea, which may be bloody, and occasionally fever, generally 2-3 days after ingestion of food (range 1-5 days). Kidney failure and death, especially in children, may result. Very low numbers of some STECs can cause illness. The primary source of STECs is fecal contamination from ruminants, including sheep and deer. These animals typically show no sign of illness. Consumption of raw or undercooked hamburger, contaminated produce, sprouts, and unpasteurized milk and juices have been linked to illness. *E. coli* O157:H7 and other STECs are killed by mild heat treatments. They can grow with or without oxygen. The optimum temperature for growth is around human body temperature, and the organism grows in some moist foods with a pH as low as 4.4.

STECs, or Shiga-toxin producing *E. coli*, as a group includes some stains that cause illness and some that do not. Those that cause illness are sometimes called enterohemorrhagic *E. coli*, or EHEC. The O157:H7 strain currently predominates in the US, causing ~75% of the EHEC infections worldwide. Other non-O157 EHEC serotypes also cause of foodborne illnesses. In the United States O111, O26, O121, O103, O145, and O45 are the most common non-O157:H7 serotypes isolated from clinical infections. However, other EHEC serotypes, such as O113, O91, and others, also can cause severe illness. Thus, public health concerns related to EHEC can change rapidly.

***Giardia intestinalis* (or *lamblia*),** like other parasites, causes diarrhea and is the most common parasitic cause of diarrhea in the U.S. Contaminated water is the primary source for outbreaks, but food and people spread the disease, and only one cyst may be enough to cause illness. Illness occurs about 2 weeks after eating contaminated food, so tracing the source of illness can be very difficult. Foodborne outbreaks with identified vehicles include ice, lettuce-based salads, chicken salad and unspecified vegetables.

Hepatitis A virus is causes the severe disease hepatitis. The health department will be notified if a food worker contracts hepatitis A. Symptoms of hepatitis A include weakness, fever and abdominal pain. As the illness progresses, the individual usually becomes jaundiced (skin turns yellow). The severity of the illness ranges from very mild (young children often experience no symptoms) to severe, requiring hospitalization. The fatality rate is low and deaths primarily occur among the elderly and individuals with underlying diseases. Illness occurs about 2 weeks after eating contaminated food (but can be much longer), so tracing the source of illness can be very difficult. Hepatitis A transmission can be prevented by practicing good personal hygiene and exclusion of ill workers, vaccination of food handlers, thorough cooking of food and preventing cross-contamination. Hepatitis A appears to be more heat resistant than other viruses. A laboratory study showed that hepatitis A viruses in infected oysters were inactivated after heating at 140°F (60°C) for 19 minutes.

Listeria monocytogenes can cause meningitis, a severe infection with symptoms including sudden fever, intense headache, nausea, vomiting, delirium and coma in people with suppressed immune systems. Up to one third of those who are hospitalized die. In a healthy person, infection with *L. monocytogenes* may cause no symptoms or a flu-like illness and diarrhea. This organism is a particular problem for pregnant women (causing miscarriage) and the elderly. Illness occurs about 2 weeks after eating contaminated food (but can be much longer) so tracing the source of illness can be very difficult. Refrigerated ready-to-eat foods are associated with listeriosis and five key factors influence risk of contracting listeriosis from such foods: 1) the amount and frequency of consumption of the food, 2) the frequency and extent of contamination, 3) the ability of the food to support *L. monocytogenes* growth, 4) the temperature of refrigerated storage and 5) the duration of refrigerated storage. Ready-to-eat meat products, unpasteurized dairy products and other low-acid ready-to-eat foods have been associated with listeriosis outbreaks. *L. monocytogenes* is an environmental pathogen, thus post-heat-processing contamination from the plant environment, including plant personnel, equipment, floors, walls, drains and condensation from coolers is a primary source of contamination. This non-sporeforming bacterium is killed by pasteurization temperatures, grows with or without air, and can grow at refrigeration temperatures and in higher salt concentrations than some other pathogens. Acid conditions slow growth but may allow survival. *L. monocytogenes* is extremely hardy compared to most bacteria, withstands repeated freezing and thawing, and survives for prolonged periods in dry conditions.

Mycobacterium bovis is another foodborne bacterial pathogen that rarely causes foodborne illness in the U.S. because of implementation of milk pasteurization requirements and removal of infected cattle. The primary source is cattle and raw milk. The hazard can be easily avoided by using pasteurized milk. Consumption of raw or undercooked meat, such as venison, of infected animals can also be a source of illness.

Norovirus is highly infectious and can cause illness when as few as 10-100 virus particles are consumed. People are the primary source of norovirus and when someone is ill they can shed millions of viral particles through vomit and feces. Because of this, people with norovirus must be excluded from handling food. If a food worker is diagnosed with norovirus, it is important to clean and disinfect surfaces that they may have contaminated. This is likely to require higher concentrations of sanitizers than those used for food contact sanitizing. Norovirus causes nausea, vomiting, diarrhea, abdominal cramps and occasionally fever 24-48 hours after initial contact. Norovirus outbreaks can be prevented by excluding ill workers, by proper personal hygiene, by properly cooking food and by preventing cross-contamination and by cleaning and disinfecting surfaces that were contaminated by an infected individual.

Salmonella is among the most common causes of bacterial foodborne illness and can be an environmental pathogen. The infection causes diarrhea, fever, abdominal cramps and vomiting. Occasionally, *Salmonella* may cause bloodstream infections and death. Severe cases may also result in reactive arthritis. Foodborne illness symptoms generally appear 12 to 72 hours after eating contaminated food. The intestinal tract of animals is the primary source of *Salmonella*, thus raw animal products (meat, poultry, eggs, milk products) are frequently associated with outbreaks. Because *Salmonella* survives well in many environments, many other foods have been associated with outbreaks, such as yeast, coconut, sauces, cake mixes, cream-filled desserts, gelatin, peanut products, chocolate and cocoa, and soy ingredients. Fresh fruits, vegetables and nuts can be contaminated during growing if Good Agricultural Practices are not applied.

Salmonella is easily killed at traditional cooking temperatures, grows with or without air, grows best at human body temperature, grows very poorly at refrigeration temperatures and does not grow above 115°F (46°C). Unlike most other pathogens, *Salmonella* can grow at a pH as low as 3.7 under otherwise optimum conditions. It survives well in frozen and dry foods, as well as in dry processing environments. Attempts to wet-clean dry processing environments have been shown to spread contamination and increase the risk of product contamination because of growth in environmental niches like cracks and crevices that cannot be reached by sanitizers. It is best to keep dry environments dry when *Salmonella* is a potential concern.

Shigella causes diarrhea (often bloody), fever and stomach cramps 1-2 days after consuming contaminated food or beverages, with symptoms usually lasting 5-7 days. *Shigella* is transmitted primarily by people who are infected, thus it is essential for people with diarrhea to be restricted from handling food. *Shigella* is a relatively fragile bacterium that does not survive cooking or in dry environments. It can be transmitted by foods such as fresh fruits and vegetables, especially if washed in contaminated water.

Staphylococcus aureus causes a relatively mild illness with vomiting, nausea, abdominal cramps and diarrhea 1-6 hours after eating food contaminated with toxin. The toxin is produced after extensive growth in the product and is very heat stable, even withstanding processing times and temperatures used in canning foods. While the toxin is heat stable, the bacterium is killed by mild heat. Toxin production is favored by the presence of oxygen. The limits for toxin production are more restricted than those for growth. *S. aureus* is a poor competitor; thus, toxin formation may not occur in foods that have many competitive microorganisms, such as raw foods and foods that undergo a controlled fermentation.

From 25 – 50% of healthy people and animals can carry *S. aureus* on their skin and in their noses; thus food may be easily re-contaminated, especially if handled extensively. If this occurs along with temperature abuse, rapid growth and subsequent toxin formation is likely in foods with few competing organisms, such as cooked foods or foods with lower water activities that inhibit competing organisms but permit *S. aureus* growth.

Streptococcus group A infections are rare causes of foodborne illness. Transmission through food can be easily avoided by exclusion of ill workers and milk pasteurization.

Toxoplasma gondii is a parasite and a leading cause of death from foodborne illness in the United States, particularly for babies infected in the womb and people with suppressed immune systems. People infected with *Toxoplasma* may be asymptomatic, but it can spread to a variety of organs including the brain, eyes, heart and other muscles. Raw meat products and cat feces are the primary source of this parasite. Freezing food to ≤9°F (-13°C) for 24 hours or more usually prevents infectivity. Cooking meats to recommended temperatures also is an effective control measure.

Trichinella spp. is the parasite that causes trichinosis, which is associated with consumption of raw meat products. In the past, pork was the primary type of meat involved; however, transmission through commercially raised pork is now rare. Trichinellosis is more commonly associated with game meat. As with other parasites, *Trichinella* is susceptible to freezing and cooking.

Vibrio species of concern for food include *V. cholera*, *V. parahaemolyticus* and *V. vulnificus*. Because vibrios are a concern for seafood products and generally not other foods, they are not addressed in this training program. Refer to the *Fish and Fishery Products Hazards and Controls Guidance* or Seafood HACCP curriculum for more information on vibrios, as well as other regulatory requirements.

Yersinia enterocolitica foodborne illness is primarily associated with cross contamination from raw pork products. It is a relatively uncommon foodborne illness for other foods.

Additional Reading

FDA. 2012. The *Bad Bug Book Foodborne Pathogenic Microorganisms and Natural Toxins,* 2nd Edition.

FDA 2011. *Fish and Fishery Products Hazards and Controls Guidance.* 4th Edition.

.Painter, JA, RM Hoekstra, T Ayers et al. 2013. Attribution of foodborne illness, hospitalizations, and deaths to food commodities by using outbreak data, United States, 1998-2008. *Emerg. Infect. Dis.* 19(3):407-415.

International Commission on Microbiological Specifications for Foods. 1996. *Microorganisms in Foods 5: Microbiological Specifications of Food Pathogens.* Blackie Academic and Professional, New York.

NOTES:

APPENDIX 5: Sanitation Basics

Sanitation Basics Objectives

In this module, you will learn:

• General sanitation basics

• Basic cleaning and sanitizing principles

NOTE: This information is intended to supplement information in Chapter 11: Sanitation Preventive Controls but is not a comprehensive overview of Good Manufacturing Practices

---

Chapter 11: Sanitation Preventive Controls addresses the regulatory requirements for sanitation preventive controls. Sanitation processes are also a GMP requirement. This appendix provides more detail on the basic cleaning and sanitizing process. This appendix includes some text from Chapter 11 because sanitation preventive controls build on the sanitation fundamentals discussed here.

Cleaning and Sanitation Basics

• Why do you need to clean and sanitize?
  ▪ Risks from pathogens and spoilage organisms
  ▪ Pests
  ▪ Allergen concerns
  ▪ Quality concerns – e.g., flavor carryover

Definition:
Pest: Any objectionable animals or insects including birds, rodents, flies, and larvae.
- 21 CFR 117.3

The EPA definition of pest includes objectionable microorganisms. Sanitary practices help to keep all of the above under control.

A strong sanitation process is a fundamental prerequisite for a strong food safety program. Without an adequate sanitation process food may become contaminated with microorganisms that could endanger public health or cause spoilage. Major recalls have been caused by sanitation lapses that led to contamination or recontamination of food.

Sanitation removes the food residue that both attracts and supports the growth of pests within and outside of the facility environment. Pests need the same things that people do to live and reproduce – water, air, food and habitat. Through sanitation, food, habitat and sometimes water are removed so pests are less likely to be attracted.

In addition to pests, very small amounts of food allergens can cause adverse reactions in food allergen sensitive individuals. An adequate sanitation program is essential to prevent allergen cross-contact between foods that contain allergens and those that do not.

A strong sanitation program helps assure that the products produced are both safe and wholesome. Additionally, a robust sanitation program may also address quality concerns that are outside of the food safety program.

Sanitation Process

How to Clean

- Various methods depending on situation
- Wet cleaning
  - Removes food residue with water and chemicals
  - Match cleaning chemical and method to surface and soil
    - Manual, foam, CIP, COP
- Dry cleaning
  - Removes food residue with mechanical action
  - Ensure method is the best fit for surface or equipment
    - Vacuum, brush, blast (avoid spread of allergens)
- Combination

The cleaning method should take into account the equipment being cleaned, as well as the hazards that must be controlled. Wet cleaning is frequently the most effective way to remove food residue, especially when the cleaning solution is selected with the particular food residue in mind. Manual, foam/gel, Clean-In-Place (CIP) and Clean-Out of-Place (COP) methods can be effective in wet cleaning situations.

Many types of foods and raw materials are handled in a dry environment – e.g., cereal, baking products, dairy powders, packaging etc. Dry cleaning methods should be used and environments should be maintained in a dry condition to prevent establishment of environmental pathogens. Dry cleaning methods typically use mechanical action and are discussed after wet cleaning.

Risky Cleaning Procedures

- Methods that can move hazards to areas that are unexpected or where they cannot be captured or removed
- Examples:
  - Pressurized air
  - High pressure water or steam
  - Vigorous dry brushing

FSPCA

Allergens and microbial contamination can be carried as dust by compressed air or suspended in liquid where high pressure water or steam is used. The possibility that these hazards will re-enter the processing stream is very difficult to control. These methods should be avoided unless capture systems, such as vacuums, are available.

Wet Cleaning

Wet Cleaning Sanitation Process

Pre-clean

Pre-Rinse

Washing

Post-Rinse

Inspect

Sanitize

FSPCA

Before work areas and equipment can be sanitized, they must be cleaned. Using a sanitizer on a dirty surface can be ineffective because the food residue may bind the active ingredients. Therefore, sanitation is usually a two-step process – clean and then sanitize. In the food and beverage industry, cleaning consists of several distinct steps, including pre-cleaning, pre-rinsing, washing, post-rinsing, inspecting and sanitizing.

Pre-cleaning involves use of a broom, brush, squeegee or other appropriate tool to sweep up food particles and residue from surfaces prior to pre-rinsing. Pre-clean can decrease the time and chemical requirements for the full cleaning process. Pre-rinsing with potable water to remove any remaining small food particles and residue wets and prepares the surface for detergent application.

Washing involves using the appropriate detergent based on the nature of the soil, the type of surface to be cleaned and the type cleaning method used (e.g., manual, foam/gel, CIP, COP). Detergent not only helps to remove residues from surfaces, but also helps to suspend it so it can be removed during rinsing. The effectiveness of a cleaning process is influenced by four major factors – chemical concentration, mechanical action, time and temperature. Follow the manufacturer's instructions for detergent contact time and recommended temperatures to balance these four factors.

In the post-rinse phase, potable water removes detergent and remaining loose soil on the surfaces. This process prepares the surfaces for sanitizing. All detergents must be removed because they may inactivate certain sanitizers.

Inspecting the cleaned surfaces can provide immediate information about the effectiveness of the cleaning program. For example, if there is evidence of residues or water beading, the surfaces need to be re-cleaned. Tools such as flashlights, black-lights and spot lights can help to identify left over soil, which indicates ineffective cleaning. ATP, microbiological and protein swabs can also be helpful to verify the effectiveness of cleaning. If a surface is hard to reach or to see, it is also likely to be hard to clean. Dismantling equipment is sometimes necessary to ensure that the cleaning process accomplishes what you think it is doing.

Sanitize to inactivate pathogens after the surfaces are cleaned and rinsed. All sanitizers must be used in accordance with the EPA-registered (or similar registration in other countries) label use instructions, including approval for use in food establishments.

A reputable chemical company provider is a good resource for further information on all of these areas.

Wet Cleaning Methods

- Manual
  - Hand cleaning using the bucket and brush method
- Foam/Gels
  - Apply cleaners to soiled surfaces to increase contact time
- Mechanical:
  - Spray washers
  - CIP (Clean-In-Place)
  - COP (Clean-Out-of-Place)

There are different ways in which food residues can be removed:

Manual methods involve washing objects by hand using a bucket (or sink) to hold the cleaning solution and a brush or other tool to scrub. Items can be left in a soak tank to increase the contact time and reduce the amount of scrubbing needed to remove soils.

Foam/Gel methods involve more concentrated cleaners that can be applied to the surface of soiled equipment. The higher concentration can reduce the time it takes to remove soil. A water spray removes the cleaner and loosened soils.

Mechanical methods include spray washers, CIP systems and COP systems. Spray washers can be conveyor (similar to a car wash) or batch (cabinet washers). CIP systems clean internal surfaces of production equipment without disassembly. Cleaning solutions contact the surfaces by pumped circulation and automatic spraying. COP systems clean disassembled equipment parts that are placed in a tank where the cleaning solution circulates.

For any mechanical process, it is important to follow defined process parameters (e.g., concentration, velocity etc.) to assure adequacy of the process. This is discussed in the validation section below.

Sanitary Design and Environmental Niches

Hollow roller on conveyor looks clean.

Note organic matter in center when shaft is removed.

Photo: Robert L. Baker, ConAgra Refrigerated Foods, Inc.

Photo: John Butts, Land O' Frost

FSPCA

Sanitary design is an important consideration to prevent product contamination. An example of a potential source of environmental contamination is the hollow roller on a conveyor illustrated above. The equipment looks clean but when the shaft is removed, organic matter that can support microbial growth is evident in the center of the roller. This type of site may be impossible to clean and sanitize with a normal cleaning procedure.

Redesign of equipment to eliminate hollow rollers is the preferred solution to prevent this type of niche in ready-to-eat facilities that use wet cleaning methods. Cracks and crevices in equipment, floors and walls present similar cleaning and sanitizing challenges. The required elements for cleaning – time, temperature, mechanical force and chemical concentration – simply cannot be reliably applied in these tight areas. If such equipment is used, keeping it dry is important to prevent a potential source of contamination. Disassembling equipment for thorough cleaning may be necessary if the equipment cannot be redesigned. References on sanitary design are provided at the end of the chapter.

Dry Cleaning

Dry Cleaning Considerations

- Removal of food residue from dry processing environments without the use of water
  - Reduces the risk of establishing environmental niches for pathogen growth
- Tools include vacuums, scrapers, brushes, alcohol wipes
- Avoid redistribution of food particles to other equipment or other areas of the facility
- Inspection of dry cleaning results

Where wet cleaning increases the risk of environmental pathogens such as *Salmonella*, dry cleaning methods should be used. Tools used for dry cleaning can include vacuums, scrapers and brushes. The tools must be hygienically designed and in good repair without cracks etc. Hygienic zoning (see Appendix 6) should be present for effective application of dry cleaning. For example, it is recommended that the dry cleaning tools be dedicated to the area or room that is being cleaned.

During dry cleaning, food residue is removed using physical or mechanical action, such as vacuum systems, brushing and blasting with high pressure. As previously discussed, it is essential that cleaning does not spread hazards (e.g., pathogens or allergenic material) to other surfaces. Capture systems (e.g., vacuums) must be used for some of these techniques. Dry cleaning of enclosed processing lines may use push-through material; e.g., for allergen cleaning. Equipment should be as clean as possible using dry methods before push-through is used.

An area that has been dry cleaned should be inspected for effectiveness of the cleaning. The area may not be shiny and completely free of dust; however, there should be very little remaining residue on the equipment. Because some food residues may remain, the effectiveness of dry cleaning procedures to remove food allergens must be considered. Each facility application is different, therefore, this must be evaluated on a case-by-case basis (See Chapter 10: Food Allergen Preventive Controls).

Sanitation Basics Summary

- Cleaning and sanitizing are essential elements of a food safety system.
- Cleaning is required before sanitizing can be effective.
- Dry cleaning and wet cleaning should be applied as appropriate to the environment.

Cleaning and sanitizing are required under GMPs and certain elements of these practices may be a sanitation preventive control. Cleaning is required before sanitizing can be effective. Certain facilities are best cleaned using dry cleaning techniques to prevent formation of environmental niches that can harbor environmental pathogens. Other facilities or locations within facilities require wet cleaning and sanitizing to ensure sanitary operations.

Additional Reading

See the FSPCA website for updated information on GMP and sanitation training programs.

3-A Sanitary Design Standards

American Meat Institute. 2011. Safe Equipment Design Checklist –American Meat Institute. 2003. Sanitary Equipment Design Bakka, R.L. and T. Boufford (ed.). 2004. *Making the Right Choice – Cleaners.* Ecolab Inc., Food and Beverage Division. St. Paul, MN

Beuchat, L. et al. 2011. *Persistence and Survival of Pathogens in Dry Foods and Dry Food Processing Environments.* ILSI Europe Emerging Microbiological Issues Task Force. Boufford, T. (ed.). 2003. *Making the Right Choice – Sanitizers.* Ecolab Inc., Food and Beverage Division. St. Paul, MN

Cramer, M.M. 2006. *Food Plant Sanitation: Design, Maintenance, and Good Manufacturing Practices.* Taylor & Francis.

Fredell, D. and T. Boufford (ed.). 2007. *Making the Right Choice – Sanitation Process.* Ecolab Inc., Food and Beverage Division. St. Paul, MN

Environmental Protection Agency. Tolerance exemptions for active and inert ingredients for use in antimicrobial formulations (Food-contact surface sanitizing solutions). 40 CFR180.940.

Graham DJ. 2006. Snapshots in Sanitary Equipment: Developing an Eye for Hygiene. *Food Safety Magazine.*

Graham, D.J. 2004. Using Sanitary Design to Avoid HACCP Hazards and Allergen Contamination. *Food Safety Magazine.*

Graham, D.J. 2009. Equipment sanitary design considerations when purchasing. *Food Safety Magazine.*

Grocery Manufacturers Association. 2009. Control of *Salmonella* in low moisture foods. Available at Grocery Manufacturers Association. Equipment Design Checklist for Low Moisture Foods.

Imholte, T.J. and Imholte-Tauscher, T.K. 1999. *Engineering for Food Safety and Sanitation*. 2nd ed. Technical Institute of Food Safety.

Marriott, N.G. and Gravani, R.B. 2010. *Principles of Food Sanitation*. 2010. 5th ed. Aspen Publications.

National Seafood HACCP Alliance. 2000. *Sanitation Control Procedures for Processing Fish and Fishery Products*. 1st edition.

Pehanich, M. 2005. Designing food safety into your plant. Food Processing Sanitary Design. Web site.

United Fresh Produce Association. 2003. Sanitary Equipment Design Buying Guide & Checklist.

NOTES:

APPENDIX 6: Hygienic Zoning and Environmental Monitoring

Chapter 11: Sanitation Preventive Controls introduced hygienic zoning as a potential preventive control and environmental monitoring as a verification activity for sanitation and zoning practices. This appendix provides more information on hygienic zoning and environmental monitoring, which may be of interest to participants who have not attended courses on these topics. Some of the information in this appendix includes text from Chapter 11 because sanitation preventive controls build on the fundamentals discussed here in certain facilities.

Environmental monitoring is used to verify the control programs designed to significantly minimize or prevent environmental pathogen contamination of ready-to-eat foods are working effectively. Sanitation may not be the only control necessary to prevent recontamination of exposed ready-to-eat foods, especially when raw and ready-to-eat products are produced in the same facility. This section discusses different pathways for environmental pathogen contamination, the basic principles for dividing a facility into hygienic zones, the objectives of environmental monitoring, how to implement a program, as well as investigation and corrective actions appropriate when environmental pathogens are detected. Useful records for capturing environmental monitoring results are also discussed.

Types of Biological Contaminants

Transient Microorganisms

- Introduced via raw materials, personnel, packaging materials
- Removed through normal cleaning and sanitizing
- Typically do not become established in the environment

Resident Microorganisms

- Become established in the environment
- May persist for long periods
- Normal cleaning and sanitizing may control numbers but may not eliminate

The first step in understanding environmental pathogens is to understand how microorganisms behave in a food environment. Simplistically, there are two basic types of microbial contaminants – transient and resident microorganisms. Transient microorganisms can enter a food establishment on ingredients, raw materials, personnel and other incoming items. Essentially they hitchhike. Normal cleaning and sanitizing should remove transient strains so they do not persist or become established in a food facility. Even with good sanitation procedures, transient strains will appear from time to time in an establishment and may be detected occasionally thorough testing. This is to be expected.

Conversely, resident microorganisms become established in the food processing environment. They may find their way into nooks and crannies, referred to as environmental niches or harborages, and persist for long periods of time. These niches are difficult to clean, thus a resident strain may form a colony that periodically contaminates food. The objective of hygienic zoning is to reduce the potential for transient organisms to enter sensitive areas in the facility, such as packing areas where a ready-to-eat product is exposed to the environment. The objectives of an environmental monitoring program are:

1) to verify that hygienic zoning efforts are effective and
2) to detect environmental niches and thus target corrective action to remove resident strains.

This requires vigilant sanitation practices and an understanding of the importance of setting up a rigorous program to detect resident strains.

The need and extent of zoning and environmental monitoring depends on the product. Typically this technique is applied in facilities that make ready-to-eat products. For example, the needs for a flour mill versus a ready-to-eat refrigerated food facility versus a canning facility are very different.

Facility Hygienic Zoning and GMPs

- Documented assessment of the facility, considering:
  - Infrastructure
  - Personnel, materials and other traffic flow
  - Cross over areas
  - Room air
  - Compressed air, if used in direct product contact
  - Adjacent and support areas

Each facility must determine the need for and scope of a zoning program based on potential risk to their products. The assessment should take into account the structure itself, personnel, packaging and ingredient traffic flows, and any cross over areas. It should also consider potential contaminants from raw materials, air flow, support areas and activities taking place in the facility. Zoning may be implemented in a facility for food safety or for quality reasons (e.g., to control mold contamination); however, the sanitation preventive controls need only address environmental pathogens that are relevant to the product (typically ready-to-eat foods) being produced.

> ### Assessing the Need for Zoning and Environmental Monitoring
>
> 1. Does the product formulation have an intrinsic property that would kill the environmental pathogen of concern (e.g., a high acid level)?
> 2. Is the product or ingredient associated with pathogen contamination?
> 3. Does the product receive a validated process control designed to kill environmental pathogens?
> 4. Is the product exposed to the environment after the kill step and before packaging?
> 5. Are ready-to-eat ingredients used to produce a ready-to-eat product?
> 6. Does a refrigerated ready-to-eat product support the growth of *Listeria monocytogenes*?
>
>

Questions that may be considered in determining if zoning and environmental monitoring is useful in a facility include the following:

1. Does the product formulation have an intrinsic property that would kill the environmental pathogen of concern?

   If an intrinsic property kills environmental pathogens (e.g., very high levels of acid as in a vinegar-based sauce), environmental monitoring may not be warranted. Validation (see Chapter 13: Verification and Validation Procedures) of the effectiveness of such intrinsic properties would be needed to ensure that the pathogen is indeed controlled by the intrinsic property.

2. Is the product or ingredient associated with pathogen contamination?

   The potential for a pathogen to become established in the processing environment increases when an ingredient has a history of pathogen contamination. *Salmonella* has a history of environmental contamination in low moisture foods such as cereals, peanuts, nuts and nut butters, spices, dried herbs, milk power and chocolate. *L. monocytogenes* has a history of association with ready-to-eat food outbreaks, especially those that are refrigerated.

3. Does the product receive a validated process control designed to kill environmental pathogens?

   A validated process control, such as cooking, reduces the risk.

4. Is the product exposed to the environment after a kill step and before packaging?

   If the unpackaged product is exposed after cooking, there is an increased risk for recontamination. Exposed ready-to-eat food handling should take place in an environment that has stricter hygiene standards, with periodic environmental monitoring to verify that hygiene controls are adequate to minimize the potential for product recontamination with environmental pathogens.

5. Are ready-to-eat ingredients used to produce a ready-to-eat product?

    Sometimes there is no kill step in a process when ready-to-eat ingredients are combined to produce a ready-to-eat product. As with product exposed to the environment after a kill step, enhanced hygiene controls are warranted to reduce the risk of contamination with environmental pathogens.

6. Does a refrigerated ready-to-eat product support the growth of *Listeria monocytogenes*?

    L. monocytogenes outbreaks typically involve foods that support the growth of the organism. Sanitation practices that reduce the prevalence of *L. monocytogenes* in the environment are essential to avoid environmental contamination of these products. Environmental monitoring is used to verify that sanitation practices are adequate to maintain an environment that is unlikely to contribute to product contamination. Many facilities test for *Listeria* spp. as an indicator for *L. monocytogenes*.

Hygienic Zoning

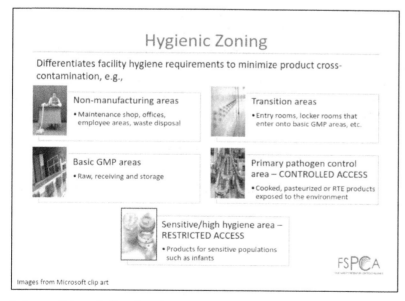

It is useful to define hygiene requirements for different areas based on the risk for contaminating product. Identification of the following may be useful:

- *Non-manufacturing areas* include maintenance areas, offices and employee areas such as cafeterias. These areas should meet basic sanitation requirements but are not required to meet GMPs. Individuals working in these areas, however, should understand that more strict requirements for sanitation apply in other areas of the facility, and that they must comply with those requirements when they enter other areas.

- *Transition areas* may include an entry room (or door), locker rooms, and similar areas that enter into basic GMP areas. Smocks, hairnets, footwear and other personal equipment required for entry into GMP areas should be available in transition areas. Requirements for entry should be listed and availability of equipment such as hand washing stations, foot foaming stations etc. as relevant to avoid contamination of the facility should be considered.

- *Basic GMP areas* include raw receiving and storage areas, as well as general food processing areas. These must be kept clean to meet basic GMP requirements. Separation of raw ingredient handling areas and tools from those used for cooked or pasteurized product is necessary to prevent cross-contamination. This includes using linear flow of product and traffic, whether by foot, cart, forklift or other means, to prevent cross-contamination. If a facility has cross over areas that cannot be engineered out, special attention must be paid to preventive controls in order to avoid accidental cross-contamination.

- *Primary pathogen control areas* are those where cooked, pasteurized or ready-to-eat products are exposed to the environment, e.g., packaging areas for such products. More stringent sanitation requirements should apply to these areas to minimize the potential for cross-contamination. Controlling personnel access (e.g., through color coded uniforms, special foot ware etc.) and dedicating equipment such as carts and fork lifts may also be useful to keep environmental contaminants from 'hitchhiking' into this more sensitive space.

- *Sensitive/high hygiene* areas include those areas producing food for sensitive populations such as infants, and foods dedicated to clinical settings.

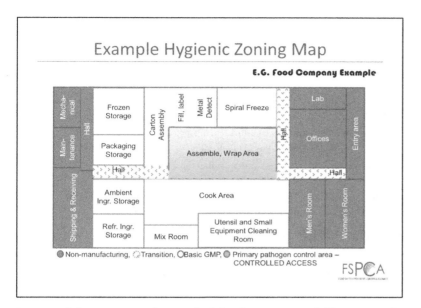

It is useful to post a color-coded facility map to differentiate hygienic zones and showing proper traffic flows to help reinforce zoning and compliance. Such a map can be used to orient new employees and visitors and to remind everyone about the need to minimize cross-contamination. Implement controls for access and entry into controlled hygiene processing areas. Define and enforce proper attire for each zone of the facility, determine who can go where and the entry requirements. For example, do they have to wear a mask to go into sensitive areas? What about captive footwear? Ideal transition areas have signs and physical barriers that force the proper requirements such as turnstiles, air showers and hand washing stations at entry that cannot be bypassed. Pictures on signs are most effective.

Environmental Monitoring

Environmental Monitoring

- Purpose –
  - Verify the effectiveness of sanitation programs
  - Verify that hygienic zoning is working to:
    - Protect product from cross-contamination or recontamination
    - Prevent microbial harborage
  - Understand "normal" environmental conditions vs. something has changed or something unusual is going on
- Must be tailored to each facility
- May include pathogens or indicator organisms
- A useful program diligently *tries to find* the organism!

The primary objectives of environmental monitoring are to verify or confirm the effectiveness of sanitation and zoning controls and to direct activities to improve control. Environmental monitoring is useful when the environment needs to be controlled to prevent microbial contamination and when testing will be beneficial to verify control of the pathogen of concern.

An effective environmental monitoring program *diligently tries to find the pathogen* or indicator of concern so that corrections can be made *before* product is compromised and the effectiveness of interventions can be evaluated. For example, a robust environmental monitoring program can assist with detection of the presence niche pathogens and differentiate them from transient strains. This can create a better understanding of how to react to findings. A relentless seek-and-destroy culture as it relates to environmental monitoring is essential.

Environmental Monitoring Development

- Biased targeted to the specific facility, equipment, history, products, ingredients and final product
- Low moisture foods – *Salmonella*
- RTE refrigerated foods - *Listeria monocytogenes* or *Listeria* spp.

An environmental monitoring program must be designed specifically for the facility and consider the products made, the ingredients used, any history with past environmental pathogens and other relevant factors. It is a biased sampling in that it looks for worst-case sampling sites and tries to find problem areas, rather than a random sampling program that tries to identify the "average" situation. This may seem risky at first and some may question "Why would I *try* to find an environmental pathogen in my facility?" The answer is – you have a better chance of finding a potential pathogen in the environment *before* you would find it in product and this may prevent a major recall or worse – an outbreak. Investigations of several outbreaks suggest that the facility environment was the source of the outbreak strains

Salmonella survives very well in a dry environment. When water is introduced and nutrients are available (e.g., food dust), *Salmonella* can multiply, which increases the chance of it being transported to another area either by the moisture movement itself or by contaminating a mobile object or person. *Salmonella* outbreaks thought to involve environmental contamination have been associated with a number of dry food products including bakery mixes, peanut butter, nuts and breakfast cereals. Therefore, environmental monitoring for *Salmonella* in many ready-to-eat, low moisture food processing environments is frequently needed.

Listeria monocytogenes outbreaks are associated with refrigerated, ready-to-eat products, thus environmental monitoring to detect the potential for recontamination is frequently needed. *Listeria* spp. monitoring is used as a more general test in some facilities because it is easier to detect a potential problem. However, testing the environment for *L. monocytogenes* may be appropriate in some facilities. The decision should be made in consultation with a qualified food microbiologist who understands the microbial ecology of the facility type.

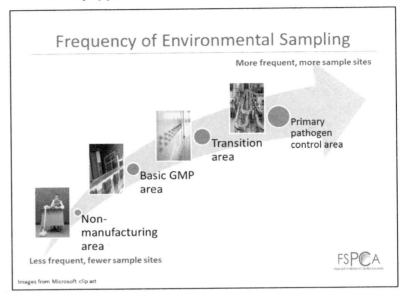

Since the objective of environmental monitoring is to detect potential sources of contamination, sampling typically focuses on the areas of greatest concern. More frequent sampling take place in primary pathogen control areas. Sampling of non-manufacturing areas is rare.

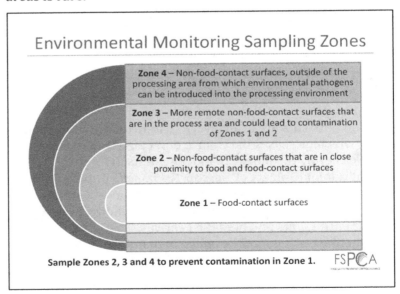

Within each area, the actual sampling location is described in terms of zones. **Zone 1** represents food contact surfaces, such as vessels, conveyors, utensils and even hands that come into direct contact with the food.

Zone 2 includes areas adjacent to food contact surfaces and are sometimes referred to as indirect product contact surfaces. Examples are bearings, equipment panels or aprons.

Zone 3 includes everything else within the production or processing area – floors, walls, ceilings, drains and other equipment.

Zone 4 encompasses all other non-production areas of a facility, such as hallways, maintenance shops and employee welfare areas.

Best practices focus monitoring in Zones 2, 3 and 4 locations. These zones tend to have a higher frequency of contamination, thus sampling these zones increases the likelihood that a potential contamination source is detected *before* it is found in product. Early detection and correction helps to prevent contamination of product contact surfaces/areas (Zone 1). Zone 1 sampling is infrequent, but when this is done, product should be held until results are found to be negative to prevent the potential for a recall situation.

Environmental Monitoring – People and Tools

- Requires training in technique
  - Identify likely sampling spots
- Tools vary by facility and product type
  - Swabs, sponges, gauze and other options
  - Contact plates
  - Floor sweeps
  - Dust accumulation
  - Air samplers
- Environmental monitoring courses are available for different product categories

---

Personnel must be trained to conduct environmental sampling and must have a sense for when to deviate from the plan based on observations or special events. The right tools allow sampling into cracks, crevices, high areas, large floor areas, drains as well as dry scrapings and air.

Where and When To Sample

- Clearly define where and when the samples to take samples
  - To evaluate cleaning and sanitizing effectiveness
    - After cleaning but before sanitizing
    - Prior to start of operations
    - After cleaning and sanitizing
  - During production operations
    - No less than 3 hours after the start of production
    - At end of run / end of operational shift
    - At shut-down before cleaning
  - During special events
    - During construction periods
    - New process area, equipment or line
    - Following major maintenance activity

Prepare a map of the facility with all drains demarcated. Determine a site list for the facility. Ensure more samples from Zones 2 and 3 are taken each time, with a few from Zone 4.

Take swabs during production, at least 3 hours in. Samples may be composited to reduce costs by taking individual samples from each site and combining them to form the composite sample. Do not use the same sponge for multiple sample sites as this could spread potential contamination.

Increase sampling when focusing on water, harborage and high traffic areas and sites that are more likely to be a source of contamination based on equipment and plant infrastructure conditions. It is good practice to sanitize the site after sampling.

Target and Action Limits

- Establish a baseline to monitor trends
  - Requires more sampling than needed for ongoing monitoring
  - Attempt to capture a snapshot of the stable/routine operation
  - Several sets of data may be collected to cover seasonal variability
- Detection of a pathogen in Zone 1 requires immediate action as product may be contaminate

---

Detection of a pathogen in a Zone 1 sample requires immediate action because the safety of the product produced on the line is in question. Expert consultation is advised when this occurs to evaluate data collected over time, sanitation practices and other factors relevant to determining the disposition of the lot.

For indicator monitoring, the target and action levels should be established after baselines have been established. It is difficult to interpret results if there is no basis for comparison. Facilities that make the same product can have very different profiles. Baseline data collection typically involves a higher level of sampling over a defined period of time and is an attempt to capture a snapshot of the stable/routine operation. Several sets of data may be collected to cover seasonal variability. If all sites are not sampled at each sampling time, a rotation system can be used. Because the objective of the program is to proactively identify potential sources of contamination, it is advisable to sample worst-case conditions if they are observed. These could include standing water, drip areas from roof leaks, accumulated product etc.

Sampling frequency during the initial months of the program may be increased to aid in establishing a norm for the facility, taking into account factors such as seasonality, weather, adjacent establishments and personnel changes.

A three-phased approach to sampling is a best practice: 1) routine samples (focus on high risk), 2) investigational samples and 3) follow up sampling to confirm the effectiveness of corrective actions. The frequency of sample collection may be increased or decreased based on a review of the facility's historical data, a determination of traffic patterns and product risk.

Investigation of a Positive Finding

- Review infrastructure and equipment in the area
- Targeted cleaning
- Review records
  - Cleaning
  - Environmental data
  - Maintenance and mechanical down time
- Test samples from composites individually
- Corrective action depends on:
  - Location (zone) of positive finding
  - Trends – single isolate or repeated finding

Finding a positive environmental sample is an opportunity to investigate to see if something has failed in the control program. Keep in mind that some positive results are transient microbes, thus no change may be necessary. Conversely, some positive results require action to prevent product contamination.

A good investigation is a combination of observation, inspection and intensified sampling. If the positive sample was a composite, then resample the entire area. These samples are tested individually to help identify and isolate the problem area. In addition to retesting, observe equipment (assessable and disassembled), process, personnel, and cleaning and sanitizing to discover factors that may have contributed to the contamination event. It is also important to look at the flow of materials to determine if cross flows are an issue. Based on the investigation, changes in procedures may be needed. Sometimes corrective action may focus on a niche in the facility or equipment that needs to be removed, corrected or cleaned. New procedures may be needed, and personnel may need to be trained on these changes. Once the necessary correction is made, a deep cleaning and sanitizing regimen should follow. It is then necessary to confirm effectiveness through repeated intensified sampling for an extended period of time. Re-sample extensively post cleaning and sanitizing, during operations, at change over, and shut downs over extended period.

If repeated positives occur after an event, the corrective action taken is not effective. This may be due to a harborage or niche area that was not addressed or discovered. Review facility, equipment and operational controls to ensure that all possible measures have been taken. Facilities have had to halt production in certain areas because of environmental niches that were not possible to eliminate.

Additional Monitoring for Adverse Events

- Adverse Event – a situation known to be associated with increased potential for environmental contamination
- Examples
  - Roof leak
  - Floor drain back-up
  - Construction or new line installation

Roof or water leaks, floor drain back-ups in exposed-product areas, construction or equipment installation, and transition between construction and production areas can increase the prevalence of environmental pathogens. Procedures should be in place to protect processing areas and product during such events.

For situations involving leaks and entry of water in dry environments, environmental monitoring for *Salmonella* is advisable. Taking these swabs immediately and before cleanup is useful because this likely represents the worst case situation – if no *Salmonella* is detected in these swabs, the environment may not be compromised. However, if the organism is detected, immediate action should be taken to sanitize the area without extensive use of water, which is likely to make the situation worse.

During construction events, traffic patterns should be evaluated to minimize a potential source of contamination. Dust and traffic should be controlled in in the event of construction. Upon completion of construction activities; the area should be cleaned and sanitized, and swabs should be taken before production begins again. Additional environmental monitoring following these events will help verify restoration of controls.

Environmental Monitoring Records

- Track and trend environmental data
- Collect and record data to provide actionable information, e.g.:
  - Use spreadsheets to identify trends
  - Show positive results on a facility map
- Ultimate goals:
  - Demonstration of a controlled environment
  - Demonstration of responding to positive findings

Tracking and trending of environmental monitoring data is a best practice. The reporting format for the results will influence the information provided. If you are going to the effort of collecting environmental monitoring data, make sure that you maximize the value of the information so that you can use it to protect your product and facility. Results in an actionable format maximize the value of the data. For example, spreadsheets help with identification of trends for routine and intensified monitoring. Facility mapping can also be used to show where positives occur and to determine if the positives are in the same location, which could indicate an environmental niche. Results reported on a map can be used to demonstrate the effectiveness of preventive controls for environmental pathogens.

Tracking Results Example

Week	Week 1	Week 2	Week 3	Week 4	Total
Area A	1/25*	0/25	1/25	1/25	3/100
Area B	0/25	1/25	1/25	0/25	2/100
Area C	0/25	0/25	0/25	1/25	1/100

* Number of samples positive / Number of samples taken

NOTE: Numbers represented are **hypothetical**. Some facilities will take many more samples a week, others will take fewer. This could represent samples taken to establish a baseline or to identify a potential source of an issue identified with less intensive routine sampling.

FSPCA

The above slide is an example of using a spreadsheet to report environmental monitoring results over time. The facility has three areas. Twenty-five swabs are taken in each area on a weekly basis to establish a baseline. Note that the number of samples taken and the frequency will vary considerably between facilities.

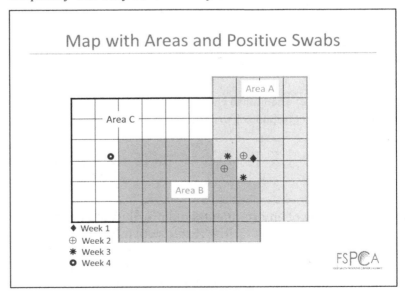

Map with Areas and Positive Swabs

- ◆ Week 1
- ⊕ Week 2
- ✳ Week 3
- ◉ Week 4

FSPCA

Results from environmental sampling are plotted on a grid, indicating different sampling areas. The circles indicate the location of positive swabs and the circle's color represents different weeks.

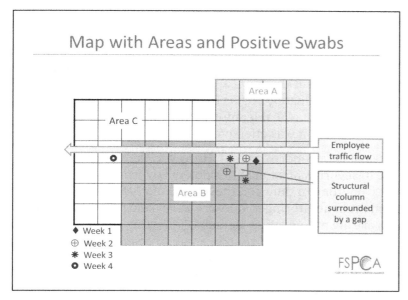

This enhanced map has the same plotting of the positive results, but also shows infrastructure (e.g., a structural column) and traffic flow. The facility determined there was a likely contamination source above the column and conducted additional investigation to identify and eliminate the source. It was discovered that moisture dripping down along the column transferred contamination through a gap between floors. The moisture splashed from the column to the floor or other structures in the different area and was then transferred by employee traffic to Area C.

Interpreting Environmental Results

- Assemble data from all sources
- Reconstruct what was happening with swabs were collected
- Develop potential interpretations from results
- Conduct additional testing to confirm conclusions
- Document root cause, take action to correct
- Take more samples to demonstrate effectiveness

Pull information together from all of data sources available, and then reconstruct what was happening when the swabs were collected. This may involve review of production schedules, sanitation schedules, visitor logs and other information sources to determine if

A6-17

something out of the ordinary occurred. Based on the information gathered, identify a potential source of contamination, then confirm what you believe was happening through additional observation or data gathering. It is important to document the conclusion of the investigation, document the root cause and take corrective action to fix the issue. Your ultimately goal is to identify a root cause that makes sense based on available information, then take action and demonstrate the action was effective.

Negative results are good, to a point. However, they can provide a false sense of security. Most facilities detect environmental pathogens from time to time and these are usually transient strains. If environmental monitoring results are always negative, ask why the results are always negative. Remember, testing is not a "control" – positive results may also be good to a point because you can act on them before a pathogen is detected in a product.

Environmental Monitoring Program Revisions

- Review the program at least annually and modify as necessary when:
  - Indicated by corrective actions
  - When ingredients and processing changes are made
  - Following adverse events
  - When equipment modification, repairs, replacements are made
  - When there are consistently no positive findings

The environmental monitoring program should be reviewed and refreshed at least annually. With a robust program, modifications take place as needed, such as when indicated by corrective actions and when there are ingredient, process or equipment changes. If there are consistently no positive findings and this is not what should be expected, this may indicate that the program is not being managed with an aggressive seek and destroy attitude. Most knowledgeable auditors are going to be skeptical of an environmental monitoring program that never has a positive result in the long term.

Hygienic Zoning and Environmental Monitoring
Summary

- Hygienic zoning can minimize sanitation issues in a facility.
  - Identify areas based on risk of contamination
  - Manage traffic flow between areas
- Environmental monitoring is a verification tool for sanitation.
  - Expect to periodically find the target organism.

Hygienic zoning can be used to minimize sanitation issues in a facility. Environmental monitoring is a useful technique to verify the effectiveness of sanitation programs and these are required in facilities that produce ready-to-eat products that are exposed to potential environmental contamination.

Additional Reading

Beuchat, L. et al. 2011. *Persistence and Survival of Pathogens in Dry Foods and Dry Food Processing Environments*. ILSI Europe Emerging Microbiological Issues Task Force. Grocery Manufacturers Association. 2009. Control of *Salmonella* in low moisture foods.

Innovation Center for US Dairy. 2012. Pathogen Control Program Tools.

International Commission on Microbiological Specifications for Foods. 2002. Sampling to assess control of the environment, in *Microorganisms in Foods 7: Microbiological Testing in Food Safety Management*. Kluwer Academic/Plenum

Kornacki, J.L. 2010. *Principles of Microbiological Troubleshooting in the Industrial Food Processing Environment*. Springer Science + Business Media.

Pehanich, M. 2005. Designing food safety into your plant. Food Processing March 7, 2005

A6-19

NOTES: